JAPANESE AND AMERICANS
A Century of Cultural Relations

Japanese and Americans

A century of cultural relations

By ROBERT S. SCHWANTES

Published for the
COUNCIL ON FOREIGN RELATIONS

GREENWOOD PRESS, PUBLISHERS
WESTPORT, CONNECTICUT

Library of Congress Cataloging in Publication Data

Schwantes, Robert S
    Japanese and Americans.

    Reprint of the 1st ed. published for Council on
Foreign Relations by Harper, New York.
    Bibliography: p.
    Includes index.
    1. United States--Relations (general) with
Japan. 2. Japan--Relations (general) with the
United States. I. Title.
E183.8.J3S35 1976   301.29'73'052   76-28326
ISBN 0-8371-9101-7

JAPANESE AND AMERICANS

Originally published in 1955 for the Council on Foreign Relations
by Harper & Brothers, New York

Reprinted with the permission of Council on Foreign Relations, Inc.

Reprinted in 1976 by Greenwood Press,
a division of Williamhouse-Regency Inc.

Library of Congress Catalog Card Number 76-28326

ISBN 0-8371-9101-7

Printed in the United States of America

To
Marion

FOREWORD

CULTURE, in its broadest sense, is a way of life. The culture of a people is much more than masterpieces of art, music and literature, important as these are. It is to be found in a people's beliefs, traditions, activities and the expression of all of these in their daily lives and thoughts.

The interchange of culture in this broad sense is a means of helping to bring people of different countries closer together in their appreciation and understanding of each other and each other's way of life. It makes possible an awareness of the problems of other peoples and it leads to a recognition of the existence of many common purposes, common interests, and common objectives. In this way cultural interchange can lay the groundwork for solution of mutual problems.

Just as it would be considered folly to let political and economic relations between countries drift, so it is wasteful and even dangerous to let the cultural aspects go unanalyzed and undirected. In any country the attitude of its citizens toward another nation is a powerful factor in the forming of international policies.

In the case of Japan and the United States the knowledge and appreciation that the people of each country hold of the other have had to bridge vast gulfs of distance, language and civilization. But despite the differences, I continue to be more and more impressed by the number of aspirations and hopes that we have in common. Perhaps we seek to achieve our goals and meet our problems by different means. But that very difference makes for a more rewarding opportunity for cultural interchange.

It is my firm conviction that we in this country can learn much from Japan. Her intellectual and artistic contributions can greatly enrich our own national life. In like manner there is much in our cultural development that can be rewarding for the people of Japan.

Mr. Schwantes' book can, I believe, be helpful in the achievement of this end. I was asked to write a foreword to it because I served as chairman of a Council on Foreign Relations study group on American cultural relations with Japan for which the author prepared working papers. While Mr. Schwantes is entirely responsible for the book, he has been able to make use of ideas and points of view expressed in the group's discussions.

The other members of the study group were:

Joseph W. Ballantine	William Henderson
Joseph Barber	Kenneth Holland
Percy W. Bidwell	William L. Holland
Hugh Borton	W. Phillips Davison
Henry Bovenkerk	Alpheus W. Jessup
Arthur H. Dean	Kenneth S. Latourette
William Diebold, Jr.	Donald H. McLean, Jr.
Frederick S. Dunn	J. Morden Murphy
Russell Durgin	Douglas W. Overton
Charles B. Fahs	Carleton Sprague Smith
George S. Franklin, Jr.	John Stegmaier
Harold G. Henderson	Shepard Stone

Mr. Schwantes' book is a workmanlike record of the first century of Japanese-American cultural relations. Its scholarship and sound historical perspective make an important contribution to our knowledge of how nations of different cultural backgrounds can learn to live on friendly and peaceful terms.

John D. Rockefeller, 3rd.

January 22, 1955

PREFACE

WRITING AN account of the cultural relations between two peoples has been an experiment that has involved special problems and more than the usual chances for error. I should say at the outset that my point of view has been that of an American sincerely interested in friendly relations with the Japanese. Japanese readers, if there are any, may see many of these questions and events in a different light. It would have been presumptuous for me to try to anticipate or state their views.

Of necessity this book contains many Japanese words and names. Except in a few well-known place names like Tokyo and Kobe, I have indicated the long vowels that are an essential part of their pronunciation and meaning. Personal names are written in the Japanese manner, surname followed by given name. Thus the recent Prime Minister appears as Yoshida Shigeru instead of Shigeru Yoshida.

Many obligations have accumulated during the seven years since I began this study. Professors Arthur M. Schlesinger and Edwin O. Reischauer directed my work on a doctoral thesis submitted at Harvard University in 1950. An appointment as Carnegie Research Fellow at the Council on Foreign Relations from 1952 to 1954 made it possible for me to finish the research and writing under optimum conditions. The Council also afforded me the opportunity to work with a study group headed by John D. Rockefeller, 3rd. Henry Bovenkerk, Frederick S. Dunn, John W. Gardner, Harold L. Hazen, Harold G. Henderson, Kenneth Holland, Harold Strauss, and Dorothy Ward were kind enough to serve the group as discussion leaders. Several other experts attended particular meetings of the group as guests. To the regular members of the group I am indebted for stimulation, expert knowledge and advice, and much critical attention to my manuscript. Responsibility for the opinions expressed, however, is entirely my own.

The book could not have been written without libraries and the help of librarians. I am especially indebted to the staffs of the Harvard-Yenching Institute, the East Asiatic Library of Columbia, and the Japanese Section of the Orientalia Division of the Library of Congress for help in using their fine collections of books in Japanese; to the Rutgers University Library, the Connecticut Historical Society, and the Missionary Research Library for the use of manuscripts and other special materials; and to Ruth Savord and her assistants for unfailing service from the special library on foreign affairs at the Council on Foreign Relations.

During my term at the Council George S. Franklin, Jr., William Diebold, Jr., and Joseph Barber gave me much encouragement and helpful advice. With the other Carnegie Fellows—Gale McGee, Henry L. Roberts, Wytze Gorter, and George Lipsky—I discussed subjects far afield that in the end proved to be relevant. Percy W. Bidwell and William Henderson were close to the project from the beginning, and both have labored over the manuscript as editors. Marguerite Hatcher's work in preparing successive drafts went far beyond the requirements of duty.

Hugh Borton, Shimizu Osamu, Marius B. Jansen, and Ardath W. Burks have given me the benefit of their broad knowledge and deep understanding of Japanese affairs. They have saved me from many errors. The shortcomings that remain are my fault, and in no sense the responsibility of the many people who have helped me.

ROBERT S. SCHWANTES

February 7, 1955

CONTENTS

PART I

CULTURAL RELATIONS:
THE THIRD DIMENSION

INTRODUCTION

ONLY IN the last two decades have Americans begun to recognize that cultural relations are an aspect of international
affairs fully as important as politics and economics. Cultural
influence itself is as old, of course, as the contact of peoples.
To take an example from our own history, the early settlers
at Jamestown and Plymouth both learned from and taught
the aboriginal Indians. Americans have continued to draw
from the great stream of Western civilization that flows
through Europe. But until modern nations began to use cultural media as instruments of foreign policy, these phenomena seemed too much a matter of course and too intangible
to deserve notice and analysis. The insidious activities of the
Auslandsorganisation of the Nazi Party, especially in Latin
America, first awakened our concern. Today the ideological
and cultural offensives of the Soviet Union make us keenly
aware of the struggle for men's minds.[1]

By cultural relations I mean all the ways in which peoples learn about each other. This definition follows the anthropologists' broad concept of culture as the whole pattern
of life. Literary and artistic productions—culture in the narrow sense—are only one means of communication. Cultural
relations include both direct personal contacts between individuals and groups of people from different countries and
more impersonal communications through the printed word,
the movies, and the radio. From knowledge gained in all
these ways, people form opinions and attitudes, favorable or
unfavorable, about a foreign nation and its way of life. In
combination with existing political and economic conditions, these opinions and attitudes enter into the determina-
tion of foreign policy. False propaganda merely perverts a

[1] Ruth Emily McMurry and Muna Lee, *The Cultural Approach: Another
Way in International Relations* (Chapel Hill: University of North Carolina
Press, 1947) discusses the official cultural programs of the leading nations.

healthy and normal process. Indeed, as control of policy becomes more democratic, what the peoples of the world know and think about each other becomes more and more important.

As a leader of the free world, the United States cannot be indifferent to the opinions of either allies or neutrals. We are, therefore, actively promoting cultural exchanges with many parts of the world. Public funds support information centers abroad and make possible interchange of personnel for study, work, and observation. The scientific knowledge and special skills that we supply through technical assistance programs help other countries to develop economically. International broadcasts attempt to carry a "campaign of truth" to the peoples behind the Iron Curtain. Private organizations like The Rockefeller Foundation and The Ford Foundation supplement government activities with projects of their own. Individual Americans and voluntary groups of all kinds are becoming increasingly aware of their international responsibilities.

So far, however, cultural activities are largely acts of faith rather than of certainty. The goals are usually stated in such vague terms as "mutual understanding" and "appreciation of other cultures." Cultural contacts with foreign peoples may have great psychological value for individuals, but their political implications are not clear. We are not really sure that increased communication will promote world peace. Just as in personal relations, better acquaintance may only accentuate antagonisms. We are not really sure what will be the total social effect of techniques and ideas transplanted from one culture to another. Our relations with crucial neutral areas like India and Indonesia are still very new. The problem is to get some evaluation of what we are doing without waiting for the verdict of time.

Two ways of proceeding are possible, and each can make an important contribution. One is on-the-spot evaluation by social scientists. Through interviews, questionnaires, and analyses of the content carried by mass media, sociologists and cultural anthropologists can get fairly precise answers to limited questions about the efficiency of communication among peoples. Statistical techniques can be applied to the measurement of changes in attitude.[2] Psychologists can explore in individual cases the combinations of enrichment and disturbance that result from exposure to more than one culture. By careful work and accumulation of results, the social scientists should eventually be able to make valuable predictive recommendations for cultural policy. But while they are studying parts of the problem, we must continue to deal with the whole of it.

The historian helps to fill the need for an immediate, broader type of guidance by bringing together what can be learned from past experience. What impact has the United States had abroad? How have foreigners learned about American life? What images or stereotypes have been dominant in their thinking? How have these affected political relations? Not that we can expect history to repeat itself in any simple cyclical fashion. But a study of history reveals the manifold possibilities and the complexities in human relations. Cultural interaction is seen as a rich and changing pattern instead of isolated threads. Though history may be unable to measure these phenomena precisely, it has the advantage of breadth and suggestiveness. At the same time, it provides a sense of continuity that is a powerful stimulus to thought and action. We can tell better where we want to go when we know where we have already been. For these reasons I have used an historical approach in this case study of cultural relations.

A study of American cultural relations with Japan is particularly apt for several reasons. The contrasts are sharp between the new forms of Western civilization unfolding on the broad American continent and the veritable museum of Oriental culture in the narrow islands of Japan. The time involved is short enough to allow fairly intensive study. Yet the century that has passed since Commodore Perry arrived in Japan in 1853 has been time enough to produce distinguishable results. In addition, relations between the two countries have been more than casual. For America Japan has been in turn protégé, competitor, enemy, occupation

---

[2] For one example see Hilda Taba, *Cultural Attitudes and International Understanding: An Evaluation of an International Study Tour* (Institute of International Education Research Program, Occasional Paper No. 5, 1953).

ward, and now a sovereign partner. The Japanese, on the other hand, have recognized from the outset that their neighbor across the Pacific was a political and cultural entity separate from Europe. In speaking of the West they often used the term *Ō-Bei*—Europe and America.

Another striking fact is that many of the cultural activities that we are now launching with high expectations and a sense of pioneering have been going on for a long time in connection with Japan. Japanese students, for example, have been coming to the United States since the late 1860's. We can study their attitudes toward America and the contributions they have been able to make to their own society. American teachers had an important part in creating a modern educational system for Japan. Missionaries brought new values and patterns of thought. Long before Point Four, many Americans were contributing their "know-how" to Japan's remarkable economic development. A start, at least, had been made at acquaintance with each other's art, literature, and history.

Today we hear much about the plans and problems of underdeveloped areas. Japan is the one Asiatic country that has successfully made the transition from static underdevelopment to fairly advanced industrialization. After the Meiji Restoration in 1868, the new leaders of the nation deliberately set out to acquire the material elements of Western strength: weapons, industry, and modern communications. Without much aid in the form of foreign capital, they were able to import advanced technology and evolve new economic institutions. Nations just beginning the sequence of development may find the experience of Japan more relevant than that of Britain or America. What gives us cause for concern, however, is the fact that in Japan economic progress was not accompanied by democracy; and substantial prosperity did not make her satisfied to be a peaceful member of the international community. Japanese borrowing from Western civilization was selective and unbalanced. By conscious attention to cultural relations, can we do more to affect the development of social and political institutions in other late-developing countries?

Nearly seven years of military occupation greatly intensified and accelerated cultural interaction between America and Japan. During that time we tried consciously to eradicate those elements of Japanese life which we thought had contributed to war. The reforms were meant to be in the interest of the Japanese people themselves, but again and again we substituted our "better" ways for their "inferior" or "dangerous" ways. We had ultimate, though indirect, control of public policies, of the economy, even of the minds of the people. What will be the permanent effects of our policies upon their institutions and psychology? It is too soon yet to know, but we can note the tendencies that are emerging. Action under such authoritarian conditions of control may have generated its own reaction.

Today the free world cannot afford to lose the industrial capacity and skilled labor of Japan. To the long-range task of strengthening tendencies toward democracy and respect for human values already existing in Japan is now added an urgent need to combat the propaganda and subversive influence of communism. Because of the legacy of the Occupation, however, we face the problem of striking a balance between initiative and restraint in our future cultural efforts there. What tools can we use without producing intolerable friction? What should the government do, and what should be left to private effort? How can we help the Japanese to work toward constructive goals without seeming to dominate or compel them?

The principle of the "two-way street" in cultural relations deserves more than lip service. Influence and appreciation should flow in both directions. Americans can learn from foreigners as well as teach them. A true exchange of the best elements of culture would enrich life throughout the world. But the predominant emphasis on American influence in Japan throughout this book shows how unbalanced our relations have been. Americans have played a much greater part in the changes that have occurred in Japan over the past century than Japanese have in the equally great changes here. Japanese have been, on the whole, more interested in America than Americans have been in them. Feelings of inferiority make the Japanese hypersensitive. We can better appreciate their position if we recall how Americans felt toward Britain in the nineteenth century. In this study we shall be searching for ways to redress the balance, to open up the other side of the street.

But will cultural relations ever be decisive, even if they are widely developed and conducted intelligently? One cannot escape the conclusion that, in the existing system of relations between national states, power—political and economic power—has primacy. Before 1900 the absence of serious conflicts of interest between the United States and Japan made cultural cooperation easy. Mutual understanding in the fullest sense became difficult as soon as Japanese expansion on the mainland of Asia clashed with our Open Door policy. The many genuine ties between the two peoples could not counterbalance political and economic factors enough to prevent war, although they certainly aided in reconciliation. Today the great bipolar power struggle overshadows all else. Will the Japanese decide that their interests coincide with ours? Everything we do, not just what we say, will influence that decision.

This case study of relations with Japan will produce no definite prescriptions for cultural policy in all parts of the world. Cultural interaction always occurs in a specific context. Details of policy must be based upon an intimate knowledge and understanding of the two or more cultures involved. But by penetrating a way into the complexities of one situation, we can get some insights and suggestions that will be applicable to others. Certain problems in cultural relations are general and persistent, however different the circumstances in which they appear.

CHAPTER ONE

EYES ACROSS THE PACIFIC

NEARLY ALL Americans, though they may not be able to distinguish Iran from Iraq, or Nigeria from Liberia, have a definite mind-picture of Japan. The Japanese respond with recognition to mention of *Beikoku*—America. Across thousands of miles of Pacific Ocean the two peoples see each other, often through distorting glasses, but with constant interest.

A large number of people in each country have had direct experience of the other through travel. In the period 1900 to 1919 the number of Americans visiting Japan ranged from two to five thousand per year. We have a definite figure of 55,364 entries in the decade 1920–29, with a peak of 8,527 in the last year. Despite the depression, American travel to the Far East during the thirties held close to the 1929 level.[1] Since 1945 occupation duty in Japan and military service in Korea have brought a vastly increased number of Americans from all social levels to Japan. International air travel also makes Japan accessible to vacationers who do not have the time for a Pacific cruise. In addition to Pan American World Airways' trans-Pacific service and Northwest Airlines' Alaskan route, Japan Air Lines has since February 1954 provided regular flights between Tokyo, Honolulu, and San Francisco. Facilities for travel promotion and entertainment of visitors are now rapidly being restored. During the first half of 1953, 6,881 American tourists visited Japan.[2]

[1] *Hompō Nyūkoku Gaijin-sū oyobi sono Shōhigaku Shirabe (An Investigation of the Number of Foreigners Entering Japan and of their Expenditures)* (Mimeographed; Tokyo: Kokusai Kankōkyoku, 1930), p. 12; August Maffry, *Oversea Travel and Travel Expenditures in the Balance of International Payments of the United States, 1919–38* (Washington: GPO, 1939), pp. 19-21.
[2] *Japan Travel News*, December 1, 1953.

Immigration complicates the statistics on the number of Japanese visitors here. Between 1868 and 1924 the Japanese government issued about 200,000 passports to persons bound for the continental United States. Until restrictions were imposed in 1907, many also entered by way of Mexico, Canada, or Hawaii. A majority of the total number can be classified as immigrants, but many of these returned to Japan after a few years and undoubtedly regaled their families and friends with vivid information about the United States. In the decade 1911 to 1920, 32,394 non-immigrant Japanese entered the country.[3] After immigration was stopped in 1924, Japanese could still be admitted as students, on government service, as temporary visitors for business or pleasure, for trade under existing treaties, or for transit through the country. From two to three thousand in these categories came each year.[4] For several years after World War II SCAP allowed Japanese to go abroad only on approved missions. Although exchange control still limits travel, in 1952–53, the first full year of independence, 5,458 Japanese came to the United States.[5] The large number of Japanese who over the years have had first-hand experience of America is one of our greatest potential assets in cultural relations.

The traveler abroad is cast in a double or even triple role. First of all he is an observer, absorbed in new sights and experiences. In addition, he may have more serious purposes: business, speech-making, or plans for writing. But whether he realizes it or not, he also stands as a conspicuous representative of his own country and culture. From actions that may seem to him unimportant his hosts may draw sweeping conclusions about national character. This point can be il-

[3] *International Migrations* (New York: National Bureau of Economic Research, 1929, 1931), V. 1, p. 934, V. 2, pp. 623-625; Ichihashi Yamato, *Japanese in the United States: A Critical Study of the Problems of the Japanese Immigrants and their Children* (Stanford: Stanford University Press, 1932), p. 62.

[4] *Annual Report of the Commissioner General of Immigration, 1925–1940* (Washington: GPO, annual).

[5] *Annual Report of the Immigration and Naturalization Service, United States Department of Justice . . . for the Fiscal Year Ended June 30, 1953* (Washington: Author, 1953), Table 16. To get this figure I have subtracted the number of "returning resident aliens" from the total number of nonimmigrant aliens admitted whose country of birth was Japan. Government officials, businessmen, and students are included.

lustrated by anecdotes about two prominent American visitors to Japan. Dr. J. C. Berry recalls when the Rev. Joseph Cook of Tremont Temple, Boston, came to Kyoto in the early 1880's. A ricksha man was pulling the portly divine from the railroad station to the lecture hall. "Hot and impatient with the slow moving runner, Dr. Cook prodded the poor man in the back with his big umbrella. Such lack of consideration and courtesy so inbred in every Japanese incensed the runner. Down went the shafts. And out pitched our pompous American, pith hat, frock coat and all!" [6] If this incident was widely known, it must have diminished the effect of Dr. Cook's Christian message. William Jennings Bryan, by contrast, won the hearts of the Japanese in 1905 by taking the trouble to go all the way to Kagoshima to visit the parents of a student whom he was helping through the University of Nebraska.[7]

When he returns home, the traveler becomes the center of a widening circle of information and influence. His judgments about customs and conditions abroad carry authority, often out of all proportion to the casual and unrepresentative character of his experience. If he chooses to write articles or a book, his audience is widened and the effect of his opinions prolonged. Even the most naive rehash of the guide books has the effect of calling attention to the area visited. But fortunately only those travel books survive that contribute something fresh or striking to the popular image of a foreign land.

The American Image of Japan

Of the thousands of American visitors few have been disappointed by Japan. The scenic and historical treasures of Kamakura and Nikkō, of Nara and Kyōto, lie only short distances from the ports. The Japan Travel Bureau and the Tourist Industry Division of the Ministry of Transportation helpfully provide information and guides. The shops are full of curios at prices hardly to be resisted. Tours through

[6] Katherine Fiske Berry, *A Pioneer Doctor in Old Japan: The Story of John C. Berry, M.D.* (New York: Revell, 1940), pp. 175-176.
[7] *Japan Weekly Chronicle*, November 23, 1905.

the Yoshiwara quarters for licensed prostitutes produce a delightful blend of fascination and moral condemnation. Japan is a perpetual discovery that invites and yet resists the effort to capture it in words.

One young naval officer caught in romantic language the almost magical impression that Japan first makes upon the casual visitor:

> Those ten short days gave me a glimpse of Japan I shall not soon forget—the old Japan of our childhood fancies, the country of toy houses and fairy gardens, of flowers and flower-like children, of black-eyed women as bright and dainty as nodding nasturtiums. Japan, the land where grave and courteous scholars go hand in hand with little girls among the cherry blossoms, where at dusk the lanterns shine like stars on the steep hillsides, and one seems to hear the violins crying out above the hushed harbors of Japan the longing of Madame Butterfly, who forever waits a foreign ship and a foreign lover. Japan at evening—it is a land of dreams.[8]

The visiting businessman saw another Japan, a Japan of smoking factories and busy shipyards, of humming spinning machines and looms tended night and day by shifts of plain country girls. This was the modern Japan of enterprise, our competitor in the export markets of the world. Few Americans penetrated far into the older, more static Japan of the villages, where patient effort produced the rice and the fish for a frugal nation.

Every visitor makes for himself some generalizations about the Japanese, what sort of a people they are and what makes them tick. The opinions that gain currency through popular books or magazines are influential in forming pictures of the Japanese in the minds of the untraveled millions. In recent years, the cultural anthropologists have claimed that they,

[8] Lt. Melvin F. Talbot, (S.C.), U.S.N., "Thoughts on Leaving the Orient," *Atlantic Monthly*, V. 167 (June 1931), p. 769. The theme of the exotic and self-sacrificing Japanese woman has recurred in American writing, most recently in James Michener's novel *Sayonara*. Madame Butterfly has become so identified with Puccini's music that we forget she was an American creation. John Luther Long first cast the observations of his missionary sister into a story filled with quaint "pidgin," then joined with David Belasco in creating a tearful piece for the American stage. Mrs. Irvin H. Correl, "Madame Butterfly: Her Long Secret Revealed," *Japan Magazine*, V. 21 (May 1931), pp. 341-345.

rather than the perceptive traveler or the literary man, are best qualified to study *national character*. By this concept they mean that all the people of a nation, despite individual differences, share the same social tradition to such a degree that their behavior shows certain regular patterns.[9] Perhaps this is only saying that the Japanese act like Japanese because they have lived in Japan. But what the anthropologist attempts to do is to translate this social experience into national psychology. The results depend, of course, upon the concepts available to describe the workings of the mind. An interpretation formed with the help of Freud may be very different from one inspired by Herbert Spencer. In addition, national character studies often have the weakness of explaining what they set out to explain, without giving a fully rounded picture of personality. Through a few examples of national character analysis, amateur and professional, we can follow some of the changes in the ideas that Americans have had about the Japanese.

In the early 1880's Benjamin S. Lyman, fresh from seven years of geological and mining work in Japan, made one of the first attempts to give a scientific account of "the character of the Japanese." [10] For Lyman all mental activity could be divided into the simple categories of intelligence, suffering (emotion), and will (action). The Japanese, he observed, seemed highly intelligent because they were quick in perception and strong in memory. But their imitativeness and credulity were evidence that they were "unreflective and not deep in reasoning and originality." In the artistic taste of the Japanese, which lay within the realm of emotion, Lyman found "the same remarkable readiness with its consequent grace and exuberance in the lighter details, the same love of outward observation, and the same lack of the profound that is essential to high art." In action they were quick and resolute, but they did not reflect carefully about motives or bother about details of execution. Lyman also

[9] See Margaret Mead, "National Character," in International Symposium on Anthropology, *Anthropology Today: An Encyclopedic Inventory* (Chicago: University of Chicago Press, 1953), p. 642.
[10] Benjamin Smith Lyman, "The Character of the Japanese: A Study of Human Nature," *Journal of Speculative Philosophy*, V. 19 (April 1885), pp. 133-172.

noticed what has been so often corroborated: that the actions of Japanese were determined more by the social situation than by any fixed values. This could lead to either lying for politeness' sake or calculated rudeness to display power.

Lyman's elaborate analysis, published in the *Journal of Speculative Philosophy*, reached only a limited circle of readers. But the most popular early book on Japan, William Elliot Griffis' *The Mikado's Empire*, gave much the same picture. "In moral character, the *average* Japanese is frank, honest, faithful, kind, gentle, courteous, confiding, affectionate, filial, loyal. Love of truth for its own sake, chastity, temperance, are not characteristic virtues." Neither Lyman nor Griffis seems to have questioned whether Japanese mentality could be described adequately in the terms appropriate for Western experience. They assumed the Japanese to be basically like Americans, and rapidly becoming more so as a result of modernization. As Griffis put it: "Japanese are simply human, no better, no worse, than mankind outside." [11]

Observers who dug more deeply in an effort to explain seeming paradoxes in Japanese behavior were inclined to go to the opposite extreme, to regard the Japanese as entirely different from Westerners. "The ideas of this people are not our ideas," wrote Lafcadio Hearn, "their sentiments are not our sentiments, their ethical life represents for us regions of thought and emotion yet unexplored or perhaps long forgotten." [12] Percival Lowell believed that he had found the secret of the soul of the Far East in "impersonality," or lack of individualism. Subordinated to his family, living and dead, a Japanese had little choice in occupation or marriage, and not even a personal birthday. Conventional politeness replaced personalities in his speech. His art showed great sympathy with the great flux of nature, but little for his fellow man. The highest ideal of his Buddhist faith was individual annihilation, to become "but an indistinguishable particle of the sunset clouds and vanish invisible as they into the starry stillness of all-embracing space." Lowell ex-

---

[11] William E. Griffis, *The Mikado's Empire* (8th ed.; New York: Harper, 1895), p. 569.
[12] Lafcadio Hearn, *Japan: An Attempt at Interpretation* (New York: Macmillan, 1904), pp. 13-14.

plained this pervading impersonality, in terms borrowed from Spencer, as a case of arrested evolutionary development. The Japanese had fallen behind in "the great march of mind." Their civilization might be more finished in some ways, but it was "distinctly more aboriginal fundamentally." [13]

Because of their stylistic excellence Lafcadio Hearn's writings have been perhaps the most influential single contributor to the American stereotype of romantic Japan. His rather precious sketches create an impression of Japan as tranquil, exotic, and ultimately unknowable. Hearn's own attitudes toward Japan were, to be sure, neither simple nor uncritical. Distressed by the imitative industrialization and petulant anti-foreignism of his own day, he found solace in rhapsodic appreciation of the folk culture that was rapidly passing away. When he came to make a serious analysis of national character, he found the strength of the nation, even the secret of her modern success, in the "Race Ghost," in the ancient ideals of duty and obedience. All his tales of ghosts and goblins, superstitions and Buddhist beliefs were efforts to capture the mystery and wisdom of ancestral experience.[14]

But even in a Japanese house with a Japanese name and wife, professing a Buddhist faith, Hearn was Westerner enough to feel that, on an absolute scale, Japan's civilization was inferior. "When one compares the utterances which East and West have given to their dreams, their aspirations, their sensations," he wrote, "a Gothic cathedral with a Shintō temple, an opera by Verdi or a trilogy by Wagner with a performance of geisha, a European epic with a Japanese poem—how incalculable the difference in emotional volume, in imaginative power, in artistic synthesis." [15]

The same tendency to explain the new by the old was found with variations in Nitobe Inazō's *Bushido: The Soul of Japan*, which was widely read in the United States in the enlarged edition of 1905. "What won the battles on the Yalu, in Corea and Manchuria, were the ghosts of our fathers,

[13] Percival Lowell, *The Soul of the Far East* (Boston: Houghton Mifflin, 1888), pp. 25, 195, 217-218 and *passim*.
[14] *Kokoro: Hints and Echoes of Japanese Inner Life* (Boston: Houghton Mifflin, 1896) contains his most penetrating early judgments. *Japan: An Attempt at Interpretation* was his final and most systematic evaluation.
[15] Hearn, *Kokoro,* cited, p. 13.

guiding our hands and beating in our hearts." Beneath the surface, Nitobe asserted, even the Japanese of most advanced ideas were motivated by *bushidō*, by the old samurai ideals of courage, honor, loyalty, sincerity, and benevolence. At the same time, he would admit, *bushidō* left less desirable marks in the national character in the form of conceit and an "exaggerated sensitiveness and touchiness." [16]

For twenty-five years after the Russo-Japanese War the Japanese played no role in world history that demanded serious analysis of their motives. Even yet it is difficult to assess the permanent imprint of this quarter-century of experience. The First World War brought rapid industrial growth and the competing intellectual currents of democracy and bolshevism. In the 1920's new personality types seemed to be emerging: "salarymen" commuting to office jobs from the suburbs, radical students, flappers and "modern boys" frequenting movie theaters and dance halls. Miriam Beard caught many of the paradoxes of this era of rapid change in her *Realism in Romantic Japan*. This incipient individualism was gradually repressed during the 1930's, as the militarists tried to force all Japanese into a standard mold of Shintoist ethics.

The shock of Pearl Harbor suddenly made character study no longer a matter of idle interest for Americans. What were the roots of Japanese aggressiveness? How could one explain their action, so fanatical and brutal as soldiers, so pliable as prisoners? Psychologists and cultural anthropologists came forward with explanations that we can now recognize as far too simple. Weston La Barre asserted that the Japanese exhibited all the traits of compulsive neurosis: hiding of emotion and attitudes, self-righteousness, precision and perfectionism, conformity to rule, hypochondria.[17] Geoffrey Gorer argued that the aggressive tendencies of the Japanese were

---

[16] Nitobe Inazō, *Bushido, The Soul of Japan: An Exposition of Japanese Thought* (New York: Putnam, 1905), pp. 176-177, 188-189.
[17] Weston La Barre, "Some Observations on Character Structure in the Orient: the Japanese," *Psychiatry*, V. 8 (August 1945), pp. 319-342. La Barre disregarded all behavior inconsistent with the pattern. It apparently did not occur to him that the experience of being torn away from home and occupation might be sufficient cause for these symptoms of neurosis among the Japanese in relocation camps whom he used as subjects.

the result of frustrations produced by strict toilet training and other restrictions during childhood.[18] John Embree punctured this theory by testifying from his field work in Suye-mura what travelers had often noted: that children were treated very indulgently in Japan and showed little evidence of frustration.[19] Another psychological analysis, published after World War II, proposed a dual consciousness—"feudal" and "modern"—that accounted for marked "instability of temperament" among the Japanese.[20]

Ruth Benedict's *The Chrysanthemum and the Sword* [21] was by far the best of the wartime character studies. Even without field experience in Japan, she was able to draw many sharp insights from interviews and printed materials. Instead of imposing rigid analytical concepts drawn from Western social science, she tried to expose the full content of some of the terms that the Japanese themselves use in speaking of their actions. For example, she showed how *on*, obligations incurred, must be repaid through performance of duties, either the limitless *gimu* owed to the Emperor and to parents or the more precisely measured *giri* that kept accounts square with others. The triumph of duty over human feelings (*ninjō*) is a favorite subject for Japanese tragedy. Miss Benedict recognized the pleasant permissive aspects of Japanese child rearing, but suggested that tension between this remembered freedom and the severe restraints of adult life might explain some of the extreme vacillations in behavior.

Although Japanese scholars have been impressed by the range and depth of Benedict's analysis, they have also subjected it to healthy criticism.[22] Minami Hiroshi points out that she too readily accepted the reactionary ideals of the thirties as descriptions of reality and ignored all the progres-

---

[18] Geoffrey Gorer, "Themes in Japanese Culture," *Transactions of the New York Academy of Sciences,* 2d series, V. 5 (March 1943), pp. 106-124.

[19] John F. Embree, "Standardized Error and Japanese Character: A Note on Political Interpretation," *World Politics,* V. 2 (April 1950), pp. 439-443.

[20] Francis J. Horner, *A Case History of Japan* (New York: Sheed and Ward, 1948), pp. 149-155.

[21] Boston: Houghton Mifflin, 1946.

[22] A translation entitled *Kiku to Katana* was published in 1948. *Minzokugaku Kenkyū (Studies in Anthropology),* V. 14 (1949), pp. 263-297, gives critiques by five Japanese social scientists.

sive tendencies between the First World War and 1941. Wat-suji Tetsurō observes that many traditional elements of culture to which lip service is still paid are no longer functional. Benedict's picture of the completely authoritarian family did not fit the experience of Watsuji's generation, when men in fact often chose their own occupations and wives. Kawashima Takeyoshi thinks that by failing to indicate differences between classes and occupational groups, Benedict exaggerated the homogeneity of the Japanese people and the stability of their value system.

The Japanese have made a few attempts to test Benedict's concepts by empirical research. Professor Kawashima found that in an agricultural village near Tokyo 70 percent of those questioned had no clear consciousness of *on* to the Emperor, only 50 percent to teachers, and that many people of all ages denied a feeling of *on* to their parents.[23] In a poll taken in March 1952 by the Japanese National Institute of Public Opinion Research, only 35 percent of the respondents agreed with Benedict in defining *giri* as repayment for a specific benefit received.[24] These are merely tests of how people put their views in language, of course; Japanese behavior in specific situations might still unconsciously follow the traditional patterns. But such studies, fragmentary as they are, suggest that values may be changing rapidly in postwar Japan.

The permanent effect of defeat and the American occupation upon patterns of Japanese personality and behavior can hardly be assessed so soon. Clearly some of the old sanctions have been removed and old loyalties loosened. Kawashima found, for example, that after the land reform few farmers admitted any feeling of *on* toward their former landlords. In the National Institute poll 72 percent thought that the number of people who did not "know *giri*" was rising. Many young people denied this only because they thought the question was a criticism of their own attitudes. Douglas G. Haring has emphasized recently a point that Hearn had

[23] Kawashima Takeyoshi, " 'On' no Ishiki no Jittai (A Field Study of Consciousness of 'On')," *Chūō Kōron*, V. 66 (March 1951), pp. 119-129.
[24] Jean Stoetzel, "The Contribution of Public Opinion Research Techniques to Social Anthropology," *International Social Science Bulletin*, V. 5 (1953), pp. 496-497.

recognized: that the restraint and social pliability of the Japanese can be explained as the result of centuries of police coercion. Unless the police state returns, we may expect growing manifestations of spontaneity and individualism.[25]

Theories of national character are merely tentative generalizations, of course, attempts at understanding. They are useful so far as they help to organize our own observations of the Japanese as individuals and as a people. But we must beware lest they become stereotypes limiting our vision. The life of a whole nation is too rich and varied to be summed up in any one formula. Certainly we would not accept one as applying to ourselves.

The Japanese Image of America

Since 1860, when they sent their first official mission to the United States, the Japanese have been eager observers of American life. No bibliography of Japanese books on America has ever been compiled, but there are certainly a hundred, and perhaps twice that many. Most of those that I have seen are personal narratives of travel and observation. As yet the Japanese have produced few analytical studies of our national character. This may be because social science has been so undeveloped in Japan that they have not had the theoretical concepts around which to organize their impressions.

The views of the more systematic European observers of American life have often been accepted as authoritative. As early as 1881 Kozuka Ryū published a translation of Tocqueville's *Democracy in America*. Hugo Münsterberg's *The Americans,* André Maurois' *The Miracle of America,* and André Siegfried's *America Comes of Age* have been widely read. A partial translation of James Bryce's *American Commonwealth* came out in 1944, at the height of the war.[26] Critical accounts by French intellectuals like Sartre and Jean Cocteau receive particularly respectful attention. Georges Duhamel's now outdated strictures on the America of the

---

[25] Douglas G. Haring, "Japanese National Character: Cultural Anthropology, Psychoanalysis, and History," *Yale Review,* V. 42 (Spring 1953), pp. 375-392; Hearn, *Japan,* cited, pp. 418-419.
[26] *Amerika Kokka Ron,* translated by Nabara Hirosaburō.

1920's in *Scènes de la vie future* have even been translated recently. But despite the derivative character of much of the opinion about America, it is possible to construct, out of casual remarks and the travel accounts, something resembling a generalized Japanese image of the United States.

The Japanese visitor usually enters or leaves the country —often both—by the Pacific coast. As he crosses the Rocky Mountains and the Middle West by train or plane, he gets a fuller and more accurate view of America than does the European whose travels may not take him farther beyond New York than Boston and Washington. He may come to the healthy conclusion that he cannot generalize, that there are many Americas. Tsurumi Yūsuke wrote that "the person who wants to observe American customs has not done enough when he has seen New York and Chicago. For the life of America is not in the big cities, but in the small towns and the country. . . . The true strength of America is in its local social customs." [27] The Japanese are also impressed by the diversity that has been the result of immigration. "For America to attempt to construct a single cultural form," observes Hosoiri Tōtarō, "would be more than a mistake; it would be almost a crime. That would mean the end of the American experiment." [28]

Size, power, and success are the ideas that dominate the Japanese view of the United States. "Everything reveals a huge scale of measurement," a fictional Japanese girl writes quaintly in her travel diary.[29] Compared to their own straitened circumstances, nothing seems more fortunate to the Japanese than the space and the abundant natural resources that Americans enjoy. Suma Yakichirō remarked that this was indeed the country of C.I.O.—enough coal, enough iron, enough oil.[30] The Japanese often accuse Americans of having, as a result, a "silver spoon" mentality. Americans have

[27] Tsurumi Yūsuke, *Hokubei Yūzeiki (Account of a Lecture Tour in North America)* (2d ed.; Tokyo: Dai Nihon Yūbenkai Kōdansha, 1928), p. 290.

[28] Tsuru Shigeto, ed., *Amerika Shisō Shi (History of American Thought)* (Tokyo: Nihon Hyōron-sha, 1950–1951), V. 4, pp. 185-186.

[29] Noguchi Yone[jirō], *The American Diary of a Japanese Girl* (Tokyo: Fuzambō, n.d.), p. 29.

[30] Suma Yakichirō, *Beikoku oyobi Beikokujin (America and Americans)* (Tokyo: Dai Nihon Yūbenkai Kōdansha, 1941), pp. 11-12.

always had enough, they have never had to struggle. "They are strangers to worldly cares and utterly ignorant as to how aggravating it is to be discriminated against, or how trying it is to be poor and have an empty stomach." [31] Critics complained that Americans could not, therefore, appreciate Japan's need to expand on the continent of Asia.

With a mixture of envy and revulsion the Japanese accuse Americans of materialism and money-madness. "Money-worship is the national religion of the American people, and realistic 'almighty-dollarism' is their motto. The American ideal is to become a millionaire. The famous person in America is a rich man. . . . The American view of life is shot through and through with this thoughtless materialistic optimism." [32] Even those who defend Americans do so within the framework of power and success. Thus Suzuki Hanzaburō argued that Americans wanted wealth not for its own sake, but as a symbol of power, personality, and ability. [33] One student who came here after World War II reached a more sophisticated conclusion about the American attitude toward money by making a distinction between being materialistic and being practical. "Materialism pretends there is no such thing as human feelings. Practicality simply deals with them sensibly—in such things as the Travelers Aid, the Point Four, CARE packages, compulsory education, and food and help to helpless lands." [34]

Americans may have *bummei* (civilization), Japanese intellectuals often say, but they lack *bunka* (culture). They know how to live comfortably, but their life is deficient in intellectual height, spiritual richness, and internal beauty. If culture exists anywhere in the West, it is in France, or even in the country that was able to produce Pushkin, Dostoievsky, and Tolstoy. But America is still much too young to have cultural distinction. At best she has a mass-produc-

---

[31] Nagata Hidejirō, *America, a Land that is Dear to Me.* (N.p., 1938), p. 5; see also Suma, cited, p. 25.
[32] Koyama Shōichi, *Amerika no Kaibō (A Dissection of America)* (Tokyo: Shinseisha, 1941), p. 149.
[33] Suzuki Hanzaburō, *Beikoku Kokuminsei no Shin Kenkyū (A New Study of American National Character)* (Tokyo: Rakuyōdō, 1916), pp. 32-45.
[34] Hisashi Ko and Laurence Critchell, "What You Americans Did to Me," *Saturday Evening Post*, December 20, 1952, p. 66.

tion culture, an *ero-bunka* of jazz, movies, and television.[35]
Not that the Japanese have many qualms about adopting
either our material comforts or our popular amusements. By
adding these things to their classic and artistic virtues, the
argument seems to go, the Japanese can create a higher synthesis of culture for the world. "The only thing for us to
do," said Nambara Shigeru, "is to create such cultural ideals
as will infuse life into modern civilization by recovering the
internal unity of the relations of mankind and the harmony
of spirit and nature." [36] Sometimes the goal is spoken of as
Wakon Beisai—Japanese spirit and American practical ability.

Americans could, it is true, learn much from the Japanese,
especially about the place of harmony, simplicity, and restraint in both artistic work and daily living. But the Japanese judgment on American culture often rests on certain
fallacies. First of all, the Japanese take too seriously and literally the strictures that American intellectuals level against
their own society. Sinclair Lewis and H. L. Mencken exaggerated in order to provoke response; so do the *Nation* and
the *New Republic,* in their own way. Then, too, the Japanese often indulge in unfair selective comparisons: between
a great painter like Sesshū and advertising posters, between
Nō plays and dance marathons. Our cultural programs should
strive to acquaint them with our best creative work. Tsurumi
Yūsuke's criticism of the American home illustrates still
another fallacy.

Enter the house of any American and look around. There is
no harmony between the chairs and tables and the size of the
rooms. No harmony between the color of the wallpaper, the color
of the chairs, and the color of the carpet. The host comes in and
sits in a convenient chair. He does not even have the taste or the
training to think about the harmony between the place where
he is seated and all the furniture in the room. Then he speaks
in a shockingly loud voice, and makes extravagant statements.

[35] Itō Michio, *Amerika* (Tokyo: Hata Shoten, 1940), pp. 122-124; Fukuda
Sadayoshi, "Han-Bei Shisō (Anti-American Thought)," *Bungei Shunjū*, V. 31
(September 1953), p. 76.
[36] Nambara Shigeru, "The Ideals of Educational Reforms in Japan," *Educational Record,* V. 31 (January 1950), p. 9.

Everything is taken on the basis of its own individuality, without any study of the balance between the part and the whole.[37]

The criticism of American taste may be to some extent just. But it is also clear that Tsurumi is being ethnocentric, applying standards appropriate to his own society but not to another.

Japanese admiration for the American past is not entirely consistent with their argument that our faults are the results of newness. They tend to idealize the first settlers of America and the pioneers who conquered the West. Ōkuma Shigenobu, for example, thought that the founders of New England displayed the same noble spirit as the samurai. "The Puritans came to America with high ideals. They did not come for money and they drew no profit from the aborigines. Their life was one of privation and constant physical danger and in all their dealings they were guided by noble standards of duty." [38] To explain discrepancies between the historical America they admire and distasteful features of contemporary life, the Japanese resort to theories of cultural decadence. Sometimes capitalism is the culprit, the displacement of Emerson and Longfellow by J. P. Morgan.[39] Despite their own complaints about racial discrimination, Japanese have blamed the deterioration in American culture upon new immigrants from southern and eastern Europe.[40] One critic, who in the late 1930's may have been echoing Nazi propaganda, blamed the Jews in America for the prevalent Mammonism.[41]

The Japanese picture of Americans as a people, however, assigns fully as important a role to environment as to heredity. The opportunities provided by rich resources account for the energy, the ambition, the optimism of the typical American. Kanzaki Kiichi draws from Münsterberg the judgment that Americans are primarily a people of will rather

---

[37] Tsurumi, cited, p. 13.

[38] Poultney Bigelow, *Japan and Her Colonies* (New York: Longmans Green, 1923), p. 228.

[39] Tsurumi, cited, p. 20.

[40] Kanzaki Kiichi, "Beikoku Kokuminsei Kanken (A Personal View of American National Character)," *Gaikō Jihō* (*Diplomatic Review*), no. 539 (May 15, 1927), pp. 37-40.

[41] Koyama, cited, p. 149.

than of intellect. They think that anything is possible if only they work hard enough for it.[42] Tsuru Shigeto tells how puzzled he was because Americans kept asking whether he was happy. He finally concluded that for them happiness meant primarily the freedom and the means to do what they wanted to do. For the Japanese accustomed to find satisfaction in adequate performance of socially defined roles, the idea of setting one's own goal is difficult to grasp.[43] One young visitor noted how the contrast between the positive spirit of the American and the cautious negativism of the Japanese appeared even in little things. American school children raised their hands even when they didn't know the answer; for fear of being humiliated by a mistake, Japanese students would not push themselves forward even when they were quite sure. In reply to the greeting "How are you?" the optimistic American would reply "Fine!" A Japanese would begin to depreciate his health and feelings.[44]

Japanese visitors are usually enthusiastic about the open friendliness of Americans. In this country they feel a welcome sense of relief from the restrictive conventions of their own society. "The people are outspoken and without affectation, so that you can talk to anyone like a friend without reservation. It makes no difference whether it is someone you have known for a long time or someone you have just met." [45] One Japanese social psychologist has pointed out, however, that tensions and stratifications exist in America that the outsider is not likely to detect. Social differences are expressed not by symbolical clothing or honorific language, but by nuances of speech and action. The American who is intent upon divining the psychological processes of others and responding in an appropriate role may be anything but ingenuous and sincere.[46]

American family relationships are also difficult for Japa-

42 Kanzaki, cited, p. 40-41.
43 Tsuru Shigeto, Amerika Yūgakki (Record of Studies in America) (Tokyo: Iwanami Shoten, 1950), pp. 146-153.
44 Nakamura Kaju, Gakusei no Mitaru Amerika (America as seen by Students) (5th ed.; Tokyo: Gakusei Kaigai Kengakudan, 1927), pp. 255-258.
45 Yanagi Sōetsu, "Amerika Inshōki (Impressions of America)," Kaizō, V. 12 (November 1930), p. 66.
46 Minami Hiroshi, Amerika no Shisō to Seikatsu (American Thought and Life) (Tokyo: Shinzenbisha, 1949), pp. 118-119.

nese to understand and approve. The deference of husband to wife, and of men to women in general, is entirely contrary to their own customs. "In the presence of a woman," wrote one journalist, "the American male acts like a second-class private before the regimental commander." [47] The breezy familiarity of children, calling parents "pop" and "mom," is interpreted as rudeness. "You do not believe that children 'belong' to their parents. They belong to themselves." [48] Japanese think that so much of American life occurs outside that the home becomes little more than a mailing address, or a temporary parking place for the automobile. Even when Japanese realize that loose family organization forces Americans to develop habits of independence and self-reliance, they are not sure that the gain is worth the cost. To them the conflict between individualistic democracy and family obligations may be very real.

In such limited sources it is hard to find a clearcut Japanese image of America. But the imprecision may be inherent. Except in denying that we have much spiritual culture, the Japanese have not been particularly doctrinaire about America. They have recognized that variety and complexity is the essence of American life. Our effort in the years ahead should be not to simplify their ideas but to enrich their vision. Certainly we should not try to hide the faults and contradictions in our way of life. We should be well satisfied when someone like Professor Natori Junichi of Waseda University is able to see them in such balanced proportion as this:

Of course America is not heaven. Even in a country of equality there are classes, in a country of freedom there is lack of freedom, in a progressive country there are conservatives. In a religious country the power of material things is strong. In a country of peace there are disputes. In a country of individualism there are nationalists, and in a country of highly-developed scientific reason sentimentalism is widespread. [49]

[47] Kiyozawa Kiyoshi, *Amerika o Hadaka ni su* (*Exposing America*) (Tokyo: Chigura Shobō, 1930), p. 18.
[48] Ko and Critchell, cited, p. 66.
[49] Natori Junichi, *Amerika no Seishin Bunka: Amerika Tamashii no Kenkyū* (*The Spiritual Culture of America: A Study of the American Spirit*) (Nagano: Shinyūsha, 1948), p. 93.

Representative Men

The Japanese, for all their alleged impersonality, like to think of relations between countries in terms of individuals. For this reason the Americans who have commanded their respect and affection are of particular interest. Many persons who are remembered for their cultural contributions will be discussed in the chapters that follow. But in popular esteem two Americans tower above all the rest: Commodore Matthew C. Perry and Townsend Harris.

The Japanese are thankful to Commodore Perry for "opening the door" of their country to intercourse with the Western world. That he succeeded in his mission without the use of actual violence is further to his credit. Only a few realists have pointed out that Perry had truly imperial ambitions for American trade in the Pacific.[50] When Marquis Ōkuma tried to curry support for a treaty with Russia in 1916 by claiming for Nikolai Rezanov the honor of opening Japan, the *Asahi Shimbun* gave him a sharp rebuke. The occasional visits of foreigners during Tokugawa times were remembered only by scholars, it said, but the name of Commodore Perry was a household word known and admired by everyone in Japan.[51]

As a symbol of Japanese-American friendship, Perry has been the subject of much official oratory. The monument erected at Kurihama, his landing place, in 1901 by the Friends of America Association has been the backdrop for many of these ceremonial occasions. William H. Hardy, one of the last survivors of the expedition, was welcomed there when he visited Japan in 1917. In 1933 James De Wolf Perry, presiding bishop of the Protestant Episcopal Church, stood before the monument and shook hands with the great-grand-daughter of the Japanese official who first received his ancestor. Parties of Japanese sailors used to pay it visits. In

[50] See statement by Tokutomi Iichirō, *Japan Weekly Chronicle*, September 16, 1920: "He came, of course, not in our interests, but for the development of America on the Pacific. If no trouble then arose between the two countries that was thanks to our kowtowing diplomacy rather than to the generosity of the other party."

[51] *Japan Magazine*, V. 7 (October 1916), p. 366.

1928 the American Ambassador solemnly presented a button and piece of braid from the Commodore's uniform, his wedding ring, and a lock of his hair as gifts to the Japanese people. Such rituals have value, of course, only if they symbolize real interests in common and are not used to obscure or ignore serious friction.

During 1953 great publicity accompanied a series of Perry centennial celebrations in various parts of Japan. The Japanese Chamber of Commerce and the Federation of Industrial Organizations joined with the America-Japan Society in coördinating the plans of local groups. A historical pageant was staged at Kurihama; Niigata had an industrial exhibition and a baseball game between Japanese and Americans; the City of Tokyo presented old stone lanterns to Washington, Newport, and Providence. Yokohama, Nagasaki, and Hakodate celebrated the centennial of the opening of their ports during 1954. For the Japanese these festivals not only commemorated the past, but marked their second emergence into the community of nations after the San Francisco peace treaty. By contrast the reciprocal observances held in the United States were subdued. Perry is more of a hero in Japan than in America.[52]

Townsend Harris, the first American consul and minister to Japan, shared the limelight with Perry. On May 23, 1953 an elaborate "Monument in Commemoration of the Opening of Japan" was unveiled at Shimoda, where Harris spent lonely months waiting for a chance to negotiate a treaty of commerce. The Japanese have always believed that Harris gave much more consideration to their interests than they would have received if the first trade treaty had been with a European power. His courage in risking assassination by staying at the capital, Edo (modern Tokyo), in 1861 when the other ministers sought refuge from attacks by *rōnin* (lawless adventurers) has also caught the Japanese imagination.[53] Okamoto Kido's play about Harris' career, entitled *Amerika no Tsukai* (*The American Envoy*), enjoyed considerable

[52] Hori Toshikazu, "Perry Centennial Celebrations in Japan," *Contemporary Japan*, V. 22 (1953), pp. 178-192; Glenn W. Shaw, "The Perry Centennial in America," same, pp. 3-19; *Nippon Times*, special issue of July 5, 1953.
[53] See remarks by Shibusawa Eiichi, "A Radical Solution of the Japan-American Question," *Japan Magazine*, V. 11 (October 1920), p. 258.

popularity in 1919 and 1920. Yamada Kōsaku made his supposed romance with the servant girl Okichi the subject of an opera called "Black Ships," first performed in 1940 and revived in 1954. Even though Harris was included in the Perry celebrations, the centennial of his treaty in 1958 should not go without notice.

General Douglas MacArthur may well become the third in a trinity of American heroes. The Japanese speak of him as having completed the work of opening the country to modern civilization that Perry and Harris began. They admired the grand style in which he played the role of military Shōgun wielding the real power behind the Imperial throne. Reverence rather than idle curiosity marked the crowds that watched his daily trips between living quarters and office building in Tokyo. But MacArthur's lack of political success at home and his peremptory relief from command have been sobering lessons on the role of a military man in a democracy. The General's remark before a U.S. Senate committee that "measured by the standard of modern civilization, they (the Japanese) would be like a boy of twelve as compared with our development of forty-five years" hurt Japanese pride. MacArthur's ultimate reputation in Japan will probably depend upon the extent to which the results of the Occupation are accepted or rejected.

Henry Willard Denison is still another American in the field of diplomacy whose career should be revived in memory. From 1880 until his death in 1914, Denison was legal adviser at the Japanese Foreign Office and confidant of successive foreign ministers. His quiet technical work did not bring him often to public attention, but nomination as one of Japan's two representatives on the Hague Court was merely one indication of the esteem in which he was held. Denison advised Itō Hirobumi at Shimoneseki in 1895; and ten years later he was responsible, on the Japanese side, for drafting the final text of the Portsmouth Treaty with Russia. By serving as a channel for frank informal communication, he often smoothed the course of Japanese-American relations. In memory Denison can serve as a symbol of trust and cooperation between the two countries in the field of diplomacy.

The Japanese also share some of our American national heroes. Through the Dutch they got considerable information about the United States long before the time of Perry, and they felt a vague admiration for the "good and valiant general" named Washington who dared defy the British. Mitsukuri Shōgo's *Kon-yo Zushiki* (*World Atlas*), published in 1847, gave a fairly accurate short biography.[54] The Japanese mention with pride the fact that a block of stone taken from Shimoda by Commodore Perry forms a part of the Washington Monument.[55] The myth about little George's hatchet has had a natural appeal in a country where cherry trees are special objects of affection. In 1932, at the time of the bicentennial celebrations, the *Yomiuri Shimbun* published a special section for children, cherry trees were planted in Kobe and Osaka, and pupils in schools in the Kansai area competed in writing essays on the life of Washington.[56]

"Washington was a great American, but Lincoln is a hero of all countries and a divine man," writes Professor Natori. "I even think that American history is an extension of his acts, and that the true world culture is an image of his spirit." [57] Lincoln has certainly been revered in Japan. The Emperor is said to keep a bust of the Great Emancipator in his private study beside those of Napoleon and Darwin. Prince Tokugawa Iesato, Count Soejima Michimasa, and the well-known Christian leader Ebina Danjō spoke proudly of the inspiration of Lincoln in their own lives. Union leader Suzuki Bunji drew strength from Lincoln's statement that "Labor is the superior of capital, and deserves much the higher consideration." Above all, the Japanese have admired Lincoln's sincerity, his plainness, and his brooding sense of tragedy—traits which give him in their eyes an almost Oriental character.[58]

[54] Sakamaki Shunzō, *Japan and the United States, 1790–1853* . . . (Tokyo: Asiatic Society of Japan, 1939), pp. 121-142.
[55] *Japan News-Week*, April 20, 1940.
[56] United States, George Washington Bicentennial Commission, *History of the George Washington Bicentennial Celebration* (Washington: George Washington Bicentennial Commission, 1932-33), V. 4, pp. 166-176.
[57] Natori, cited, p. 137.
[58] *Japan Times and Mail Weekly*, June 18, 1925; Watase Tsunekichi, *Ebina Danjō Sensei* (*Professor Ebina Danjō*) (Tokyo: Ryūginsha, 1938), p. 93; Suma, cited, pp. 192-193.

The young people of Japan, especially, have made Lincoln their hero. Stories about his life have been included in their schoolbooks. Uchigasaki Sakusaburō tells how reading the biography that Matsumura Kaiseki published in 1889 gave him a new sense of idealism. Later Uchigasaki himself published a life of Lincoln that went through several editions. When the America-Japan Society began in 1926 to hold annual Lincoln essay contests, both middle school and university students responded enthusiastically. Most of them stressed Lincoln's lowly birth and his struggle for education. One young man wrote that in the personality of Lincoln "we have clearly seen the symbols of the spirit of America—self-reliance, truthfulness and faithfulness." [59]

Woodrow Wilson was the one American political leader who had a host of Japanese admirers during his own lifetime. At first he was respected primarily for winning high office "by virtue of moral and intellectual merit." Several Japanese had studied under Wilson at Johns Hopkins and Princeton, and his writings on *The State* and *Congressional Government* were fairly well known among intellectuals. [60] As the First World War drew to an end, many Japanese, like people elsewhere in the world, looked to Wilson as their leader in a great crusade for democracy and international peace. One of several biographies published at this time stated that he was "not the Wilson of the United States, but the Wilson of the world. His every frown and smile affects the peace or war of the world." [61] Led by Tsurumi Yūsuke, then a young lawyer for the Imperial Government Railways, over two hundred university graduates organized a Wilson Club. They shared the disappointment over the Treaty of Versailles; and when Wilson died in 1924, Tsurumi wrote, "It was as desolate as when the winter sun sinks away." [62]

The lacunae in the list of famous Americans known to the

[59] America-Japan Society, *Special Bulletin* No. 4 (1927).
[60] *Japan Weekly Mail,* April 12, 1913; "President Wilson in Japanese Eyes," *Japan Magazine,* V. 8 (May 1917), pp. 15-16.
[61] Tanaka Tatsu, *Daitōryō Uiruson (President Wilson)* (Tokyo: Jitsugyō no Nihon-sha, 1918), p. 1.
[62] Tsurumi's personal recollections of Wilson and his associates are collected in *Danjō Shijō Kaijō no Hito (Men on Platforms, in the News, and on the Streets)* (Tokyo: Dai Nihon Yūbenkai Kōdansha, 1928), pp. 2-185.

average Japanese are perhaps as significant as the inclusions. His understanding of American democracy has been limited by lack of information about Jefferson and Jackson. Kaneko Kentarō seems to have been almost alone in his admiration for the practical genius of Alexander Hamilton.[63] International tensions during the 1930's kept the Japanese from appreciating Franklin D. Roosevelt's leadership in the New Deal. The low opinion that the Japanese have traditionally had of businessmen may explain their lack of interest in American captains of industry. Edison and Ford have been written about quite extensively, but primarily as inventors. In the case of Edison, the fact that the bamboo filaments for his early incandescent lamps came from a grove near Kyoto adds local interest and pride.[64]

Americans have been much less aware of the Japanese as individuals. Except for Itō Hirobumi and Ōkuma Shigenobu, the leading statesmen of the past century were not widely known to the public outside Japan. The war made the name of Tōjō Hideki familiar to all Americans, but only as the stereotype of a ruthless militarist. During the seven years that Yoshida Shigeru was premier, Americans gradually got a picture of him as stubborn and irascible in public affairs, quiet and artistic in private life.[65] But his associates and his rivals remained faceless names.

Best known over the years were a small handful of Japanese who acted as unofficial spokesmen for their country on fairly frequent visits to America. Some of these have already been mentioned. Kaneko Kentarō was a graduate of Harvard Law School, Itō's assistant in drafting the Constitution of 1889, a friend of Theodore Roosevelt, and promoter of the America-Japan Society. Shibusawa Eiichi became known as the elder statesman of the Japanese business world after he toured America in 1909 at the head of a delegation from chambers of commerce in Japan. In later years Count Kaba-

---

[63] Viscount Kaneko, "The Japanese Student: An Address before the Students of the First National College," *Japan Magazine*, V. 4 (November 1913), p. 373.
[64] In 1934 a monument to Edison was erected on the spot, in the grounds of the Iwashimizu Hachiman shrine. *America-Japan Society Bulletin*, V. 2 (2d quarter, 1938), pp. 4-5.
[65] See Lindesay Parrott, "Yoshida—'Deep Bows and a Temper'," *New York Times Magazine*, September 6, 1953; *Newsweek*, January 22, 1951.

yama Aisuke was well known for both his business and his cultural activities. Nitobe Inazō, the first Japanese exchange lecturer, was a classmate of Woodrow Wilson's at Johns Hopkins; his marriage to the daughter of a prominent Philadelphia Quaker family attracted attention. Americans were grieved to hear that after seven years as Under-Secretary General of the League of Nations he was forced by army leaders to retract publicly his criticisms of militarism and to come to the United States to defend the aggression in Manchuria. During the 1920's the young liberal politician Tsurumi Yūsuke was a frequent speaker on university platforms and at public affairs forums. But he, too, forfeited confidence during the next decade when he insisted that Japan wanted only stability in China and that public opinion would bar any imperialistic moves.[66] Americans preferred the breezy frankness of Ambassador Saitō Hiroshi, who told reporters in 1934 that he came "to drink good American whiskey with good American friends." Later Saitō admitted that his forthright apology for the bombing of the *Panay* had "put him in the dog house" at home. The return of his body to Japan in the cruiser *Astoria* in 1939 was practically the last friendly gesture in prewar relations.

Americans need much more information about Japanese personalities and life patterns. Journalists should give us vignettes of contemporary figures. Scholars should project the biographies of great men of the past against a rich background of their times. Translations of representative novels can give an understanding of the life of the many types of "common men." When Americans know more about the Japanese as individuals, they may have greater respect for them as a group. For the false, stereotyped "Jap" of race prejudice—spectacled, bucktoothed, obsequiously polite but sinister and arrogant—they can then substitute a more accurate and sophisticated concept of Japanese national character.

Contact and Friction

The Japanese have a saying "*tōki wa hana no nioi* (at a distance the fragrance of flowers)," which they sometimes

[66] *New York Times*, February 17, 1932.

couple with another: *"chikaki wa ibari no nioi* (close up the stench of urine)." This cynical comment applies rather well to relations between peoples. They may admire each other from afar, but have trouble getting along when they are brought into close and constant relations. Contact produces friction, in direct proportion to the mass involved. The real tests of cultural relations between America and Japan have come when large groups of their peoples were brought together, in one case by immigration, in the other by the circumstances of military occupation.

Since about 1900 prejudice and discrimination against Japanese immigrants in the western United States have been constant irritants to relations between the two countries. The damage done would seem less senseless if the conflict of cultures had been really serious. But the somewhat smoother course of race relations in Hawaii suggests that even a much higher percentage of Orientals is no threat to social stability. Most people on the West Coast were willing to admit that as individuals the Japanese were clean, hard-working, and law-abiding. Charges that they were by nature completely unassimilable were belied by the rapid Americanization of the second generation, so rapid as to create serious tensions with their parents. By the 1920's the *nisei* (second generation Japanese-Americans) were attending universities and rising into professional occupations. To all appearances, the Japanese were following the familiar pattern of the American melting pot.[67]

Why, then, the recurrent campaigns of hate and prejudice that so embroiled bilateral relations? Some Caucasian farmers and laborers did feel genuine economic competition from the efficient and industrious Japanese. But the California laws of 1913 and 1920 denying aliens ineligible to citizenship the right to own or to lease land were never really effective. The Japanese continued to hold a dominant position in market gardening. In many places the laws were evaded with full community approval, and legal leases could always be arranged in the name of American-born children

[67] Ichihashi, *Japanese in the United States*, cited, pp. 207-227, 348-363; Carey McWilliams, *Prejudice; Japanese-Americans: Symbol of Racial Intolerance* (Boston: Little, Brown, 1945), pp. 73-105.

or shadow partners.[68] Carey McWilliams suggests that the prime movers of the agitation had more devious purposes. Large landholders used the Japanese as scapegoats to divert attention from their own monopoly advantages and oppressive labor policies. Politicians of both parties used anti-Japanese harangues to confuse elections and to distract attention from corruption. William Randolph Hearst was always ready to make sensational charges in order to build up newspaper circulation and his own reputation.[69]

Were the Japanese also playing a double game? McWilliams offers some circumstantial evidence of timing in support of the theory that the Japanese government avoided a settlement of immigration issues in order to keep a sore open in relations with America. Japanese consuls, according to this argument, planted rumors and magnified grievances, actually victimizing their own countrymen. The truth on this point could only be established by careful study of Japanese archives. If Japanese policy in other fields is any guide, I suspect that official action until at least 1931 was shifting and inconsistent rather than persistently diabolical. Our refusal to allow Japanese to become American citizens strengthened their policy of exercising paternalistic supervision over their emigrants. At all times, however, the immigration question did play into the hands of anti-American elements in Japan. Militarists demanding money for armaments could always claim that they were defending the national honor against the Californians.

When the United States Congress barred all immigration from Japan in 1924, the whole question clearly entered a new phase of resentment on grounds of race. Previously, the Japanese had been inclined to believe that California's action did not represent American opinion. They understood that the peculiarities of the federal system and implications for the Negro question kept the national government from upholding their rights under treaties. The Japanese government had met specific complaints by stopping the flow, first

[68] Leonard Bloom and Ruth Riemer, *Removal and Return: The Socio-Economic Effects of the War on Japanese Americans* (Berkeley: University of California Press, 1949), pp. 69-86.
[69] McWilliams, cited, pp. 14-66.

of laborers, then of picture brides. But now an act of the national Congress seemed to stigmatize them as an inferior
Asiatic people, not even entitled to a small quota. Their
pride was deeply wounded.

Friendships and loyalties built up by seventy years of cultural contacts were severely shaken. Kaneko resigned as
president of the America-Japan Society. Nitobe vowed never
to set foot in the United States again. Aged Viscount Shibusawa said that he could not die in peace unless the injustice
to his people were rectified.[70] The shock ran deep among the
people. Matsumoto Tōru tells how his mother wept for
shame because everything she had been saying in defense of
America had been proven false.[71] After 1924, exclusion was
the fact that stopped all argument. Resentment only deep-
ened when even American friends thought the principle too
unimportant to keep up an effective campaign for revision.

The McCarran-Walter Act of 1952 has removed the most
blatant legal discriminations, although the "Asia-Pacific tri-
angle" provision still makes an invidious distinction on
grounds of race. Japan now has an annual quota of 185,
which is more important in principle than as a contribution
to her population problem. Spouses and children of American citizens are coming in considerable numbers as non-
quota immigrants. Japanese who have lived here for decades
are finally able to qualify for citizenship, and are doing so
enthusiastically.[72]

We can hardly expect, however, that this law will dissolve
all the stubborn problems of prejudice and race relations.
The man in Japan who would like to come to the United
States, but cannot, is all the more ready to believe that even
nisei have a hard time here. Accounts of the wartime evacuation and relocation of West Coast Japanese that exaggerate
the very real injustices have been widely told in Japan by
the minority who chose repatriation. Popular magazines
print tales of the adjustment problems of unhappy war
brides in America. The Japanese-Americans have probably

---

[70] Nitobe Inazō, *Editorial Jottings* (Tokyo: Hokuseido, 1938), V. 1, p. 4.
[71] Matsumoto Toru and Marion O. Lerrigo, *A Brother is a Stranger* (New York: John Day, 1946), pp. 25-26.
[72] *Christian Science Monitor*, May 27, 1953.

gained in acceptance by being dispersed more widely, but prejudice is slow to die. Envy, suspicion, and conflict are part of being human. But we can at least keep such problems away from the distorting searchlight of national honor.

Since the peace treaty came into effect in April 1952, Americans in Japan have had the disturbing experience of finding that their very presence is a source of friction. Their intentions are good, they protest. After all, American military forces are protecting Japan from possible invasion. Good friends among the Japanese assure them that no reflection upon them as individuals is intended. Yet the security forces as a whole are subjected to constant public criticism and demands that "Yanks—go home!" Part of this can be dismissed as the machinations of Communist agitators. But the obvious response by the Japanese public suggests that anti-Americanism must have some basis in fact.

For one thing, resentments and tensions that accumulated during the years of occupation are now being discharged. The outwardly tranquil and cooperative attitudes that the Japanese displayed may even have increased the internal voltage. Initially, they felt great relief because the American troops did not come in and rape and loot and kill. But relief is an emotion that quickly dies. Replacement troops were younger, less restrained, more arrogant than the original veterans of combat. Along with the many conscientious and hard-working occupation officials came a few outright carpetbaggers who bullied and exploited. Even with the best of intentions on both sides, the difference in role was unbridgeable—the sharp boundary, as Mrs. Mishima has put it, "between abundance and hunger, rainbow-colored cleanliness and gray sordidness, privileged victors and a nation in bondage." [73]

Unfortunately, the military situation in the Far East made it impossible to dramatize the return of sovereignty in 1952 by any wholesale withdrawal of troops. With little perceptible change, American occupation forces became security forces. As many uniforms and military vehicles crowded the streets as before. Headquarters units continued to use desir-

[73] Mishima Sumie, *The Broader Way: A Woman's Life in the New Japan* (New York: John Day, 1953), p. 229.

able office buildings. Around the country the expansion of
bases nibbled away some of the limited rice land. Fishermen
complained that naval maneuvers and gunnery practice in-
terfered with their catches. In a popular book entitled *Kichi
no Ko* (The Children of the Bases) young children told how
they were unable to sleep or study because of the constant
roar of plane motors, how explosions shook objects from
shelves in their homes, how their morals were being threatened in the dissolute atmosphere surrounding military
camps.[74]

Touchiness about morals is symptomatic of the new state
of public sensitivity. Originally the Japanese showed little
reluctance to adapt their system of prostitution to the entertainment of American soldiers. Grim economic necessity and
the lure of excitement gave rise to much competition by
amateurs. Beer halls and brothels have been profitable businesses. Troops on rest and recreation orders from Korea have
provided a changing clientele. But now the cry of "Protect
Japan's chastity!" has been raised. To balance international
accounts with dollars earned by sale of Japanese bodies is
declared a disgrace. The problem of mixed-blood children
born out of wedlock has been exaggerated out of all proportion to the facts.[75]

The incident that has become a popular symbol of anti-
Americanism came, however, where it could least have been
expected. Instead of a naval base like Yokosuka or a busy
airfield like Tachikawa, the scene was the little village of
Uchinada in Ishikawa prefecture. There a very small party
of Americans had been using a strip of beach for test-firing
of Japanese-made ammunition. In June 1953 the people of
the village carried their protests against continued use of the
firing range to officials in Tokyo, clashed with the police in
demonstrations against both the government and the Amer-

[74] See dispatches by William J. Jorden, *New York Times*, September 7, 8, 1953.
[75] Popular tales about hundreds of thousands of occupation illegitimates were
deflated when the Ministry of Welfare found that, as of February 1, 1953, the
total number of mixed-blood children abandoned by their fathers was 3,289.
Most were living with mothers or other relatives; over 200 were in homes run
by missionaries. Only 482 were being cared for in Japanese child-welfare institutions. Lloyd B. Graham, "Those G. I.'s in Japan," *Christian Century*, V. 71
(March 17, 1954), p. 330.

ican forces, and engaged in sit-down strikes on the beach.
Labor unions and university students rallied to their support. That they lost out ultimately does not matter. Uchinada now stands beside Hiroshima, according to one com-
mentator, as a symbol of grievance against Americans.[76]
So long as our forces remain in Japan, such incidents and
grievances will continue. Exemplary conduct on the part of
Americans can reduce the friction, but not remove it entirely. Similar problems arise, after all, when American
forces are stationed in Britain and France. What we must
recognize is that these unavoidable cultural frictions are
part of the environment in which our more directed efforts
to promote mutual understanding must operate. The irrita-
tions close at hand may keep some Japanese from seeing the
beauties far away across the Pacific.

Images as Reflection and Projection

The connection between these images of national character and the concrete acts that make up official relations
between two countries is as difficult to define as it is to deny.
Certainly the opinions that one people have of another are
more significant now that international issues are subjected
to public discussion than they were in the days when diplomacy was handled almost privately. But are the images
causes or effects of policy? Perhaps they are both.

Images are, first of all, reflections of experience. They
mirror, however imperfectly, the collective experience of a
people. For the Japanese the primary picture of America has
been that of a progressive nation which has helped them to
enter the modern world. A trinity of heroes—Commodore
Perry, Townsend Harris, and Douglas MacArthur—symbolize this relationship. Upon this favorable image shadows
were cast from a heedless America that did less than justice
to Japanese immigrants. Americans, on the other hand, have
seen Japan as an apt and talented learner, able to combine

[76] Usui Hoshimi, "Uchinada," Kaizō, V. 34 (August 1953), pp. 116-122; Fukuda, cited, p. 79. Contamination of the fishing boat Fukuryū Maru by fall-
out from an American hydrogen bomb experiment in the summer of 1954,
resulting in the death of Kuboyama Aikichi, has become another symbolic
focus for anti-Americanism.

the efficiency of the new with the beauty of the old. Differences in social etiquette have contributed to a minor caricature of the "Honorable Jap" as ludicrous and ineffective; but, on the whole, even in the unfriendly stereotypes of the "Yellow Peril" and the fanatical wartime enemy Americans have given the Japanese people credit for ability and character.

Images of national character are, at the same time, projections into the future. They provide a pattern of expectation for future events and issues. Americans and Japanese expect each other to act in certain ways; and unless the facts of new policy are too incongruous, they will be fit to the projected image. Despite the manifestations of anti-Americanism, indications are that the images of America now current in Japan are still generally favorable. The traits that a scientific sample of young people polled by the Japanese National Commission for UNESCO chose most often as descriptive of Americans were "progressive," "practical," and "intelligent."[77]

For the American image of the Japanese we have no measure so precise, but the distortions of wartime enmity seem now to be giving way to favorable preconceptions. The problem is to focus this diffuse public opinion on both sides of the ocean more effectively than in the past, in order to get constructive action on specific problems of policy. In this the greatest asset may be the fact that these images are no longer stereotypes based on ignorance or indifference: they are constantly renewed by the eager play of eyes across the Pacific.

[77] *Sei-shōnen no Kokusai Ishiki ni kansuru Chōsa (Research on the International Consciousness of Youth)* (N.p.: Nihon Yunesuko Kokunai Iinkai, 1954), pp. 21-22. Next in order the terms "selfish" and "generous" were chosen with almost equal frequency.

PART II

PROBLEMS AND GOALS

INTRODUCTION

VITAL CULTURAL relations must, above all, be relevant—relevant to the main concerns of national life. Too often the word "cultural" connotes things that are aesthetic, polite, decorative, but too peripheral to be basically important. In the much broader sense in which I use the term here, cultural relations mean the total impact of one people upon another.

We cannot separate our cultural relations with Japan, therefore, from general goals of foreign policy. As one of the leaders of the free world, the United States needs the co-operation and friendly support of a prosperous democratic Japan. But Japan has not yet been able, since World War II, to find a new position of stable equilibrium. Her economy is precariously dependent upon spending for American and other United Nations military forces in the Far East. Signs of serious dissatisfaction with the political and social order imposed by the Occupation are appearing. These are the questions to which we must make cultural relations relevant. Americans must try to understand the problems that face the Japanese, and do what they can to help solve them.

Doubts are often expressed whether Americans can help the Japanese (or other Asian peoples) to solve their basic problems. Are the situations so different that our experience is not applicable? Do different cultural inheritances, different patterns of thought, impose a barrier? As with most such questions, the answers lie somewhere in the broad middle ground of more or less, rather than at the categorical poles of yes or no. Fortunately, we already have a century of experience upon which to draw.

Japan's history over the past century is marked by striking continuity amid change. The keynote has been rapid development. Emerging from the cocoon of self-imposed isolation into the competitive industrial and imperialistic world of the mid-nineteenth century, Japan's problem has been to catch up, to become modern. To do so she consciously accepted the role of the learner, of the imitator. America was one, though not her only, teacher. Japan's early achievements in production and trade were striking; victory in wars against China and Russia won her recognition as an important factor in world politics. She adopted the form, at least, of Western political and legal institutions. But World War II seemed to render a verdict of ultimate failure. Most Japanese thought that they had learned the wrong lessons. Faced with much the same problems in new forms, they must again look abroad for help and guidance.

In the chapters that follow we shall see what contributions Americans have been able to make to three of Japan's persistent problems. The basic economic dilemmas have the advantage of being most concrete and tangible. Experience here reveals most clearly the difficulties and the opportunities. Attempts by the military occupation to remake Japanese political and social life had no such backing of continuity. Here the problem for the historian is to explain the limited character of American influence before 1945. The third problem area, that of education, is in a sense subsidiary to the other two. Through education a nation creates and transmits both the skills needed for economic development and the attitudes requisite for citizenship. But in Japan, as in America, education has attained such institutional autonomy that we shall treat it as a separate problem.

CHAPTER TWO

ECONOMIC COOPERATION

TODAY JAPAN's most urgent problems lie paradoxically in the very area of her past success—in the field of economic development. Japan alone among Asian nations has attained an advanced state of industrial technology, an efficient agriculture, and a literate skilled labor force. By 1936 she was the sixth industrial country of the world, ranking behind the United States, France, the United Kingdom, Germany, and Italy. To the older handicraft and textile industries she was rapidly adding large-scale production of metals, machinery, and chemicals. Despite wartime deterioration, destruction, and defeat, Japan has retained an impressive industrial plant. From Japan's achievements her more backward Asian neighbors may draw hope and guidance as they embark on ambitious development programs of their own.

Yet Japan's success has been in some respects precarious. Only moderately endowed with natural resources, she has been forced to rely heavily upon processing imported raw materials for resale in world markets. To insulate herself from growing trade restrictions, Japan began during the 1930's to create by force of arms an assured market and source of supply in a "Great East Asia Co-prosperity Sphere." Stripped of her conquests, she now again has to trade in competitive markets in order to prosper. For a population of over eighty-eight million, Japan had to import food worth over $650,000,000 during 1954. At the end of 1953, industrial production was 173 per cent of the 1934–36 level, and the volume of imports 101, but the volume of exports came to only 44 per cent of the prewar level. Exports increased slightly during 1954 but industrial production dropped

45

somewhat and imports fell sharply to 56 per cent of the pre-war level in September.[1] International accounts have been balanced temporarily only by special procurement contracts for UN forces in Korea and by expenditures of American personnel in Japan. The Japanese government has estimated that without this help even the meagre level of imports of recent years could be sustained only if annual exports were raised from the 1953 level of $1.3 billion to over $2.1 billion.[2] The immediate adjustment may be cushioned by expenditures for Korean reconstruction and by mutual security aid in support of Japanese defense. But eventually Japan must have a self-sustaining economy expanding at least rapidly enough to take care of her growing population. It will be hard for democracy to grow if there are no prospects for a rising standard of living.

Americans should not assume that Japan's difficulties arise merely from blindness to economic facts, and that they could be solved quite readily if advice were only accepted from some of our experts. It is a serious mistake to overestimate the economic naïveté of the Japanese. They have been assiduous students of Western economics since the days early in Meiji when a great debate developed as to whether classical free trade doctrine or the American theory of protectionism better applied to their country during the early stages of industrialization.[3] Today Japanese economists do their thinking in a thoroughly post-Keynesian world. Tsuru Shigeto, Ohara Keiji, and Nakayama Ichirō, to name a few outstanding examples, are fully informed on the whole range of recent thinking in the United States and in Europe.[4] Recently a few Japanese have begun to apply the methods of econometrics to their problems. On the whole, however,

[1] Bank of Japan, *Economic Statistics Monthly,* December 1954, pp. 83, 97.

[2] *Economic Survey of Japan, 1952–1953* (Tokyo: Economic Counsel Board, 1953), p. 21. Under the deflationary financial policy adopted by the Japanese government in 1954, exports increased to 1.6 billion.

[3] Okada Shumpei, "Amerika Keizaigaku no Nihon e no Yunyū (The Introduction of American Economics into Japan)," *Amerika Kenkyū (American Studies),* V. 3 (January–February 1948), pp. 16-20.

[4] See Ohara Keiji, *Amerika Keizai Shisō no Chōryū (Main Currents in American Economic Thought)* (Tokyo: Keisō Shobō, 1951) and Nakayama Ichirō, *Kindai Keizaigaku no Tenkai: Kanzen Koyō no Riron (The Development of Recent Economics: The Theory of Full Employment)* (Tokyo: Yuhikaku, 1940).

Japanese economists tend to stress theory and to be disdainful of the hard work of empirical analysis. Many are strongly oriented toward Marxism. For that reason, it is true, visits to Japan by leading American economists could be of great benefit, especially so if they were prepared to apply their analytical skill to Japanese experience.

But Japan's economic problems are too fundamental and too complex to yield quickly to any simple manipulative solution. They must be tackled by the sustained effort of businessmen, workers, and farmers, with the support and guidance of the government. First of all, Japanese industries must be made efficient enough to compete actively in world markets, in order to earn the things that Japan must buy. At the same time domestic food production must be increased by every reasonable means to lighten the import burden. To these processes Americans can make what are in the broadest sense cultural contributions. Ways in which we can help, as well as some of the inherent difficulties, may be indicated by the record of past technical relations with the Japanese in the fields of agriculture and industry.

Technical Assistance in Agriculture

With industrialization the relative importance of agriculture in Japan has declined, but it still occupies about 45 percent of the people. From narrow islands in which at most only 17 percent of the land is suited for cultivation, the Japanese have since 1870 wrested a striking increase in the production of food and raw materials. This expansion of output, together with annexation of the food-surplus areas of Formosa and Korea, made it possible for a population that doubled between 1875 and 1935 to enjoy a rising standard of living. Siphoned off through heavy land taxes and voluntary savings, part of the wealth created in agriculture formed the basis for much of Japan's capital equipment and industrial progress. Unfortunately, the process can hardly be repeated in order to give Japan a new spurt of development; the hard-pressed land is already too close to the economic limit of output.[5]

[5] Bruce F. Johnston, "Agricultural Productivity and Economic Development in Japan," *Journal of Political Economy*, V. 59 (December 1951), pp. 498-503.

Agricultural advance since the Meiji Restoration has been due more to improved methods of production than to increased acreage. One analyst estimated that between 1880 and 1920 the output of rice, wheat, barley, and potatoes increased 77 percent on an acreage which had expanded by only 21 percent. By our standards Japanese agriculture remains very labor-intensive, but during this period the productivity of farm workers seems to have doubled.[5a] Better seeds and tools and liberal use of fertilizers were the factors primarily responsible for increased output. For knowledge of these things Japan turned to the West and, in the early years of the Meiji period, particularly to the United States.[6]

At first Japanese officials optimistically assumed that the pattern of agriculture which they admired in the United States could easily be reproduced at home. Even before the Restoration, Inoue Kaoru called together the rich peasants in the Osaka area and, on the basis of Tsuge Zengo's reports of a trip to America, lectured them on the advantages of extensive farming. When Itō Hirobumi visited the United States on financial business in 1870, he spent $700 for agricultural tools. The next year Hosokawa Junjirō made the rounds of the agricultural fairs to collect new fruit and vegetable seeds. In 1871 the Ministry of Education employed an American named George A. H. Hall to put these acquisitions to use in new experimental gardens. Among the foreign books on agriculture chosen for translation were two of the manuals published by Orange Judd, *Harris on the Pig* and *Parsons on the Rose*.[7]

In 1874 and 1875 the government began to distribute the imported plants to the prefectures for trial under field conditions. A high rate of failure because of poor adaptation to soils and climate punctured the balloon of uncritical en-

[5a] Same, p. 499.
[6] Pertinent documents are collected in Nōrinshō Nōmu-kyoku, *Meiji Zenki Kannō Jiseki Shūroku (Archives Concerning the Promotion of Agriculture during the Early Meiji Period)* (2 v.; Tokyo: Dai Nihon Nōkai, 1939).
[7] Tsuge Tsuyoshi, *Kindai Nihon Nōshi Kenkyū (Studies in the Agricultural History of Modern Japan)* (Tokyo: Hikari Shobō, 1943), pp. 145-156, 238-240; Koike Motoyuki, "Meiji Shoki ni okeru Nōgyō Gijutsu no Hattatsu (The Development of Agricultural Techniques in Early Meiji)," in Keiō Gijuku Keizai-shi Gakkai, *Meiji Shoki Keizai-shi Kenkyū (Studies in the Economic History of the Early Meiji Period)* (Tokyo: Ganshōdō, 1937), V. 1, pp. 29-77.

thusiasm. Some permanent additions were made to the Japanese flora, however. A fairly extensive apple-growing industry was developed in northern Honshū, with the Ralls Genet and the Jonathan the most popular varieties. Since the native cherry trees are famed for their flowers rather than their fruit, most of the edible varieties grown in Japan came from the United States. The Oregon, Fultz, and California strains of wheat were widely planted until about 1920, when the Ministry of Agriculture and Forestry began to make new crosses. Tobacco from Maryland, Connecticut, and Kentucky was tried in Okayama, Kagoshima, and Tochigi prefectures, where native varieties had long been grown.[8]

Japanese experiments with imported tools and machinery also had mixed results. The government collected over 30,000 specimens from all parts of the world, and in 1879 set up a shop for manufacture and repair of tools in connection with the Mita Nursery. Although the foreign implements usually proved to be more efficient than those traditionally used in Japan, they were also much more expensive to manufacture and maintain. The most lasting gains in efficiency came through slight modifications of Japanese hoes, picks, forks, and broadcast sowers based on comparisons with foreign models.[9]

After a decade of rather indiscriminate trial of foreign methods, the Japanese government began to realize that substantial advances in agriculture would have to be along more traditional lines. Under the so-called "old farmer (rōnō)" policy, it began to make a careful study of the methods used by men who had been successful in practical farming. One of the men revealed by this process, Funatsu Denjihei, was put in charge of the Bureau for Encouragement of Agriculture.[10]

[8] Murakoshi Michio, *Naigai Shokubutsu Genshoku Dai-zukan* (*General Botanical Dictionary Illustrated in Color*) (12 v.; Tokyo: Shokubutsu Genshoku Dai-zukan Kankōkai, 1933–1935), V. 6, pp. 67-78; V. 10, pp. 82-83; *Japan News-Week*, May 6, 1939; Tsuge, cited, pp. 275-277. For American botanical borrowing from Japan, see Henry F. Graff, "The Early Impact of Japan upon American Agriculture," *Agricultural History*, V. 23 (April 1949), pp. 110-116.

[9] Tsuge, cited, pp. 242-265.

[10] Okutani Shōji, *Kindai Nihon Nōsei Shiron* (*Essays on the History of Agricultural Policy in Modern Japan*) (Tokyo: Ikuseisha 1938), pp. 30-31.

The *rōnō* policy did not, however, mean rejection of all modern methods for improvement of agriculture. In time an extensive network of experiment stations and test farms was dispersed throughout the country. Development of varieties of rice responsive to fertilization and suited to special climatic conditions received special emphasis. In 1945 an estimated 69 percent of the rice acreage was planted to varieties introduced by the stations.[11] Kuwana Inokichi, who received his training in entomology at Cornell and Stanford, developed a Plant Quarantine Service. The agricultural school set up at Komaba, near Tokyo, in 1876 developed into the College of Agriculture of Tokyo University. Except for Charles C. Georgeson, who taught there from 1885 to 1889, the foreign professors were Britishers and Germans rather than Americans. But many of the Japanese professors in Tokyo and in the prefectural agricultural schools had received part of their training in the United States. Tamari Kizō, for example, who studied at Michigan State and the University of Illinois in the eighties, became head of the first Higher Agricultural School at Morioka in 1903. Six years later he started a similar institution at Kagoshima. Tamari was a thoroughgoing empiricist who urged upon his students the importance of verifying the accuracy of what they read in books by actual observation and experiment.[12]

Japan also makes intensive use of fertilizers to build up and maintain high agricultural productivity. Compost from grass and leaves, fish products, and oil cake are used to the limit of supply. The carts carrying buckets of human excreta out from the cities strike the eye, and nose, of every visitor. Not so obvious is the extent to which Japan depends upon chemical fertilizers. In 1936 consumption amounted to about 3,500,000 tons. As a result of the loss since the war of Manchurian sources of soy bean cake, chemical supplements have further replaced organic fertilizers. The Ministry of Agri-

[11] *The Agricultural Experiment Stations of Japan* (Tokyo: Natural Resources Section, SCAP, 1946), p. 8.
[12] *Shinsen Dai Jimmei Jiten (New Biographical Dictionary)* (Tokyo: Heibonsha, 1939–1941), V. 4, p. 216.

culture and Forestry estimated the demand in 1952 at 3,900-000 tons.[13]

Although the government had made a few earlier experiments, the practical introduction of chemical fertilizer was the direct result of Japan's participation in the New Orleans Industrial and Cotton Exposition in 1884. One of the Japanese commissioners, Takamine Jōkichi, was impressed by an exhibit of superphosphate produced in South Carolina. He investigated the process of mining and manufacture and purchased several tons to send back to Japan. After tests by the Ministry of Agriculture had shown its value, Takamine appealed to Shibusawa Eiichi for capital to begin manufacture. The Tokyo Artificial Fertilizer Co. began production in 1888, using machinery and phosphate ore imported from the United States.[14] Because of its novelty and high price, superphosphate gained acceptance slowly; production did not exceed a few thousand tons per year until about 1900. At that time the manufacture of ammonium sulphate for use as nitrogen fertilizer was also begun on a small scale.[15] Artificial fertilizer, then, was a case in which a technique borrowed from the United States required a considerable investment of Japanese capital before it could contribute significantly to agricultural productivity.

Before World War II the raising of silkworms was an important supplementary activity and source of income for many Japanese farmers. The mulberry trees whose leaves were used as food for the worms could be grown on upland areas unsuitable for irrigated crops. The way in which the requirements of the American market influenced technological development in this industry is an interesting example of technical relations. In 1874 Tomita Tetsunosuke, vice-consul in New York, collected samples of raw silk from various places in Japan and presented them to the Silk Associa-

[13] E. B. Schumpeter, ed., *The Industrialization of Japan and Manchukuo, 1930–1940: Population, Raw Materials and Industry* (New York: Macmillan, 1940), pp. 225-228, 248-252; *Nihon Keizai Nenkan, 1953 (Economic Yearbook of Japan)* (Tokyo: Nihon Keizai Shimbun-sha, 1953), p. 282.

[14] *Takamine Hakushi (Doctor Takamine)* (Tokyo: Shiobara Matasaku, 1926), pp. 29-30; Shibusawa Eiichi, *Seien Kaiko Roku (Recollections of Seien)* (Tokyo: Seien Kaiko Roku Kankōkai, 1927), V. 1, pp. 505-514.

[15] *Meiji Taishō Shi (History of the Meiji and Taishō Periods)* (Tokyo: Jitsugyō no Sekai-sha, 1929-30), V. 8, pp. 138-171.

tion of America, asking for suggestions for improvement in quality. American manufacturers found the hand-reeled fibers too thin and uneven for satisfactory use on their high-speed machinery. Tomita and Arai Ryōichirō, a pioneer Japanese merchant in New York, urged improvements in reeling techniques and sent to Japan some of the machinery that had been used in the United States during the abortive silk-worm boom of the 1830's. Further technical developments in reeling were borrowed from the established industries of France and Italy, but the end in view was largely the production of what came to be known as the Standard American Skein. In 1895 the government established silk conditioning houses in Yokohama and Kobe to control the quality of exports. The United States became Japan's best customer for raw silk and Japan the principal source of supply for American mills. The displacement of silk by synthetic fibers in recent years has meant financial loss for Japanese farmers and a serious loss of dollar exchange for the nation.[16]

Although Japanese experts have been aware of technical developments in the United States, American examples have been of only limited and tangential value in the improvement of agricultural production in most of Japan. There rice has been the principal crop, and a heavy continuing production has been obtained only by applying a vast amount of human labor to the work of irrigation, fertilization, and hand culture. The basic problems were entirely different: in the United States a small population had to bring into production a huge continent; in Japan a relatively large number of people had to live off a limited amount of arable land. The one part of Japan that resembled the United States in climatic conditions and undeveloped land was the northern island of Hokkaidō. There Americans did help in the 1870's and 1880's with basic development work that has some resemblance to projects now being carried out elsewhere in the world under the Point Four program.

At the time of the Meiji Restoration Japanese leaders were aware of the way in which Russia had wrested the Mari-

[16] Matsui Shichirō, The History of the Silk Industry in the United States (New York: Howes, 1930), pp. 10-11, 62, 66; United States Tariff Commission, Broad-silk Manufacture and the Tariff (Washington: GPO, 1926), pp. 35-36.

time Provinces from China, and were afraid that Hokkaidō, too, might be absorbed if it were not more fully settled.[17] Explorations by two American geologists, Raphael Pumpelly and W. P. Blake, whom the Shogunate had sent into the area in 1862 and 1863, already indicated the presence of needed minerals. To hold and develop the area a Colonization Commission (Kaitakushi) was established in 1869, and a number of new garrison-villages were set up. In 1871 the vigorous young Vice-Governor of Hokkaidō, Kuroda Kiyotaka, went to the United States to observe at first-hand the process of frontier settlement. When he inquired about hiring an American adviser, President Grant recommended that the position be offered to General Horace Capron, who since 1867 had been United States Commissioner of Agriculture. Capron accepted on condition that he could choose his own staff and be responsible directly to the Emperor. Before sailing for Japan, he took Kuroda on a tour of the United States, directing his attention to methods of agriculture, stock raising, and manufacture of farm machinery, and to the educational facilities for improvement in those arts.[18]

The American mission that worked in Japan for four years under Capron's direction was at best a qualified success. Part of the difficulty seems to have been the General's own personality; one of his subordinates described him as "a fussy old man with extravagant notions as to his own importance." [19] The American staff was rent by quarrels over salaries, which ranged from Capron's $10,000 per year in gold, plus transportation, subsistence, and furnished quarters, to a mere $125 per month in silver for the practical agriculturists. The Japanese officials consulted Capron about everything from the organization of the United States gov-

[17] John A. Harrison, *Japan's Northern Frontier: A Preliminary Study in Colonization and Expansion with Special Reference to the Relations of Japan and Russia* (Gainesville, Fla.: University of Florida Press, 1953) is based on a wide variety of Japanese sources.
[18] Merritt Starr, "General Horace Capron, 1804–1885," *Journal of the Illinois State Historical Society*, V. 18 (July 1925), pp. 276, 290-295; *Shinsen Hokkaidō Shi (New History of Hokkaidō)* (Tokyo: Hokkaidō Chō, 1937), V. 3, p. 240.
[19] Statement by Edward M. Shelton, who was in charge of the Kaitakushi experimental farm near Tokyo. Herbert H. Gowen, "An American Pioneer in Japan," *Washington Historical Quarterly*, V. 20 (January 1929), p. 15.

ernment to the care of a sick animal, but did not inform him about their own plans. The Kaitakushi quickly developed a cumbersome bureaucracy, and these officials were often at cross-purposes with the American experts.

Some concrete results could be seen, however. Thomas Antisell, Benjamin S. Lyman, and Henry S. Munroe made topographical and mineralogical surveys of Hokkaidō. Civil engineer A. G. Warfield built a road from the coast to the new capital city of Sapporo, which was laid out on the American rectangular plan. Edward M. Shelton, Louis Boehmer, and Edwin Dun made a start at introducing new methods of agriculture. But even when generous subsidies were offered, it proved difficult to get Japanese to go to cold Hokkaidō to do such unfamiliar work as clearing and breaking land. Those who did go tended to drift off to the coast villages to engage in fishing. At one point Capron proposed that thirty pioneer families be brought from America and settled in the northern island so that the Japanese could learn new methods through direct association with them. The expense involved and the legal difficulties of providing some form of self-government prevented the execution of this interesting plan.[20]

The achievement of greatest long-run consequence was the establishment of an agricultural school. Preparatory instruction was begun in Tokyo in 1872, and in the summer of 1875 the school moved to permanent quarters at Sapporo. Leading Japanese officials who visited the United States in 1872 with the Iwakura embassy had been impressed by the combination of technical education and military drill at the state universities set up under the Morrill Act. So the Kaitakushi obtained the services of William Smith Clark, president of Massachusetts Agricultural College, for one year in order to launch their new school.[21]

[20] *Shinsen Hokkaidō Shi,* cited, V. 3, pp. 386-387; Makino Shinnosuke, "Hokkaidō Kaitaku no Shoki ni okeru Gaijin no Kōsaku (The Work of Foreigners in the Early Development of Hokkaidō," *Shirin,* V. 20 (January 1935), pp. 37-66; (April 1935), pp. 313-339.
[21] *The Semi-centennial of the Hokkaidō Imperial University, Japan, 1876–1926* (Sapporo: Hokkaidō Imperial University, 1927), pp. 3-12; William S. Clark, "The Agriculture of Japan," *Twenty-sixth Annual Report of the Secretary of the Massachusetts Board of Agriculture* (Boston, 1879), p. 112.

Clark's energetic and enthusiastic personality made an imprint upon Sapporo Agricultural College that persists even in the present Hokkaidō University. Besides directing the college, the preparatory school, and the experimental farm, Clark taught botany, agriculture, ethics, psychology, and English. He made the students choke down tomatoes and other unfamiliar foods and report their impressions—Westernization by the shock treatment. He introduced field sports and organized military drill. A fervent Christian himself, he converted nearly all the students and laid the basis for a non-denominational church in Sapporo out of which came Uchimura Kanzō and other religious leaders. In his parting words he gave the school a characteristic motto: "Boys, be ambitious!" [22]

For fifteen years Clark's work was continued by eight other American teachers, several of them graduates of Massachusetts Agricultural College. The college farm imported American horses and cattle and began the sale of milk and butter. Wheat and corn were introduced, and oats were found to do exceptionally well in the cool, moist climate. William Penn Brooks and Edwin Dun made the first experiments in growing sugar beets, which have since become a crop of considerable importance in Hokkaidō. By 1882 over 1,350,000 fruit trees and bushes had been distributed, although many of these were lost through winter-killing. From the wide variety of American vegetables introduced at this time, cabbage and onions have become fairly important commercial crops. The College also demonstrated the use of American horse-drawn farm machinery and taught methods of maintenance and repair. The new techniques were brought to the people through a farm paper and through agricultural fairs. With the departure of Arthur A. Brigham in 1893, however, the technical work was all left in the hands of a Japanese faculty headed by a Johns Hopkins graduate, Satō Shōsuke.[23]

[22] Ōshima Masatake, Kurāku Sensei to Sono Deshitachi (Professor Clark and his Pupils) (Rev. ed.; Tokyo: Shinkyō Shuppansha, 1948) is a reminiscent account by a student who became a leader in agricultural education.
[23] Details of the work of the American teachers are given in Fifth Annual Report of Sapporo Agricultural College, Japan, 1881; Sixth Report of the Sapporo Agricultural College, covering the years 1881–1886 inclusive; and

Lasting American influences upon the rural life of Hokkaidō are apparent to even a casual visitor to the Ishikari
plain area. White frame houses and red dairy barns, often
flanked by silos, look out over large fields divided by barbed-
wire fences. Teams of horses pull mowers and hay-rakes and
haul loads of wheat and oats to American-type threshing
machines. Even the plants and animals are familiar: Per-
cheron horses, Holstein cows, red clover, McIntosh apples,
and Concord grapes.[24]

The depth of American influence should not be overesti-
mated, however. The customs of the people remain distinctively Japanese. The College and government officials have
had to make constant efforts to maintain the methods and
attitudes of extensive farming. The farmers prefer rice as a
food and will plant it even at the sacrifice of higher production of some other crop. Hokkaidō experiment stations have
worked to develop hardy early-maturing strains; when the
variety known as Nōrin #11 was released to farmers in 1937,
it became possible to grow irrigated rice in practically all
parts of the island. In 1951 Hokkaidō farmers planted 358,-
000 acres in rice as compared to 183,000 acres in oats and
73,000 in wheat.[25]

Point Four enthusiasts expect that by working with American technicians other peoples will learn our economic philosophy, democratic principles, and way of life.[26] Has American guidance changed the outlook on life of the people of
Hokkaidō? Observers have often noted a distinctive spirit.
"The people have a certain kind of energy, a briskness of

Tōhoku Imperial University, College of Agriculture, *American Influence
upon the Agriculture of Hokkaidō, Japan* (Sapporo: Tōhoku Imperial University, 1915).
[24] For a view by the practiced eye of a geographer, see D. H. Davis, "Agricultural Occupation of Hokkaidō," *Economic Geography*, V. 10 (October 1934),
pp. 348-367.
[25] *Nōrinshō Tōkei-hyō 1951 (Statistical Tables of the Ministry of Agriculture
and Forestry, 1951)* (Tokyo: Nōrinshō Nōrin Keizai-kyoku Tōkei Chōsa-bu,
1952), pp. 47, 48, 81.
[26] See *Point Four: Cooperative Program for Aid in the Development of Economically Underdeveloped Areas*, Department of State Publication 3719
(Washington: GPO, 1950), pp. 8-14. I have discussed this point at length in
"Perspective on Point IV: The Case of Japan," *Far Eastern Survey*, V. 23
(September 1953), pp. 126-130.

manner, and an upstanding independence of spirit that are much less noticeable in the inhabitants of the older and more highly organized communities of the southern islands," wrote W. D. Jones in 1921.[27] The people of Hokkaidō have been aptly compared to the expansive Westerners in the United States. To some degree this spirit may be the result of contact with Americans. More likely it comes from the frontier conditions themselves: fewer traditions, richer resources, more room. The Hokkaidō frontier, however, has never produced the volatile spirit of free enterprise that characterized our westward movement. From the beginning settlement there has been promoted and supported by a paternal government.

The graduates of Hokkaidō University have followed Dr. Clark's advice to "be ambitious," in a country where open confession of ambition is regarded as bad taste. But one of the best outlets for men with drive and capacity for innovation was in Japan's colonial ventures. In 1924 an American visitor noted that over a hundred Sapporo men were at work improving Formosan agriculture.[28] Later many graduates played a part in the development—and exploitation—of Korea and Manchuria. Technology knows no politics; it can serve one cause as well as another.

The average Japanese does not think of Hokkaidō as a pilot project in economic development that deserves emulation. To him it is a cold, forbidding place to which he would rather not emigrate. This is unfortunate, for about 34 percent of all the land in Japan available for reclamation is located in Hokkaidō.[29] An ambitious postwar program of settlement and land clearance is far behind schedule. Since this area has such great potentialities for increased food production, the Japanese might benefit, in publicity as well as in practical aid, by renewing American ties with Hokkaidō University. This might be done through a faculty exchange and technical assistance arrangement with one of our major agricultural colleges.

[27] *Geographical Review,* V. 11 (January 1921), p. 30.
[28] Harold and Alice Foght, *Unfathomed Japan: A Travel Tale in the Highways and Byways of Japan and Formosa* (New York: Macmillan, 1928), p. 339.
[29] Edward A. Ackerman, *Japan's Natural Resources and their Relation to Japan's Economic Future* (Chicago: University of Chicago Press, 1953), p. 21.

Japan's later colonial acquisitions presented new problems of agricultural development. After a thorough investigation of the resources of Formosa, the Japanese government decided to concentrate on improving its sugar industry. Nitobe Inazō was brought from his teaching post at Sapporo to take charge of a special Sugar Bureau. Cuttings of Rose Bamboo cane were imported from Hawaii and distributed to plantations. Although this cane had a high sugar content, it proved to be so vulnerable to wind damage that after 1911 it was gradually replaced by new varieties brought from Java. Recovery of a maximum percentage of sugar was made possible by use of modern crushers which the government purchased in the United States and loaned to manufacturers.[30] In Korea, agriculture displayed the familiar pattern of rice growing and sericulture. In an effort to get a controlled source of supply for her textile mills, Japan encouraged the growth of American-type upland cotton. Large undeveloped areas in Manchuria gave the Japanese a chance to try the kind of extensive mechanized farming characteristic of the American West. Before World War II the South Manchurian Railway and the experiment stations were encouraging the use of Caterpillar tractors and International Harvester reapers.[31]

Loss of colonial areas as a result of World War II and the repatriation of Japanese formerly resident abroad, along with regular population increases of over a million a year, have created a serious food deficit. In the calendar year 1952 Japan imported over 1,660,000 metric tons of wheat, over 975,000 tons of rice, and 945,000 tons of barley.[32] Normal increases in population and predictable losses in production through deterioration of land or its conversion to other uses are estimated to increase the deficit by an average of 366,000

[30] Shinobu Seizaburō, *Kindai Nihon Sangyō Shi Jōsetsu* (*Introduction to the Industrial History of Modern Japan*) (Tokyo: Nihon Hyōron-sha, 1946), pp. 334-342; *Japan Times and Mail Weekly*, May 12, 1923; *Far Eastern Review*, V. 3 (April 1907), p. 342.

[31] "Mechanical Farming in Manchuria," *Contemporary Manchuria*, V. 3 (October 1939), pp. 42-62.

[32] Economic Counsel Board, *Japanese Economic Statistics, II: Foreign and Domestic Commerce*, March 1953, pp. 11, 31.

MT of rice each year.[33] To meet this situation the Ministry of Agriculture and Forestry has projected a five-year program for increasing food production that would cost the government about 300 billion yen outright, plus 125 billion yen in capital loans. By the end of fiscal 1957 reclamation and improvement of land and improvement of seeds are expected to increase food production by the equivalent of about 2,-250,000 tons of unpolished rice. At best the net reduction in grain imports would be only about 750,000 tons.[34] A poor rice crop in 1953 on account of floods and bad weather already suggests that these goals may be chimerical.

The long-run effect of the land reforms carried out under Occupation guidance upon agricultural productivity is still uncertain. The transfer of over 4,800,000 acres of farm land and a million acres of pasture from landlords to owner-operators is a fact of great social significance. Since the land was bought by the government at prices that inflation had made unrealistically low and resold to farmers on low-interest loans, a considerable redistribution of wealth resulted. The chances of Communist influence in rural areas have been correspondingly reduced.

From a strictly economic point of view, however, the results may not be entirely advantageous. It can be hoped that ownership will give farmers incentive for maximum production by use of more efficient techniques. Farmers may refuse, however, to make the marginal effort and may take part of their gain in leisure or time for other activities. The multiplication of vested interests by the reform diminishes the chances of changing the system of scattered piece-meal plots. Although fragmentation is in some places dictated by topography and in others provides a sort of insurance against complete crop failure, experience has shown that consolidation of homogeneous lowland fields can appreciably increase output.[35] At the time of the reform many landlords became amateur operators in order to avoid losing their holdings. Fixed prices and rents will impede transfers that would bring land

[33] Bank of Tokyo, *Weekly Review of Economic Affairs in Japan*, December 27, 1952, pp. 8-10.
[34] *Mainichi Shimbun*, July 14, 1953.
[35] Mark B. Williamson, *Agricultural Programs in Japan, 1945-1951* (SCAP, Natural Resources Section Report No. 148, October 1951), pp. 65-68.

into the most productive use. A greater proportion of the land is now held in very small lots by those who will not make the best use of it, because farming is for them only a subsidiary occupation.[36]

It is significant that the five-year plan is stated in rice units. Rice is the preferred food in Japan, but it is also the item in which increased production will be most difficult. Aside from introducing the use of DDT and other new insecticides to control rice leaf hoppers, SCAP was able to make few technical contributions in this field. Japan may gain something from the program of seed selection and hybridization sponsored by the Food and Agriculture Organization at the Central Rice Research Institute in Cuttack, India, but she probably can contribute more from her own long experience.

Of the 3,800,000 acres that the Japanese government designated in 1947 for reclamation, 94 percent is upland suitable only for non-irrigated crops.[37] As the Japanese strive to increase production of wheat, barley, corn, and legumes American experts could be of great assistance. More work could profitably be done in food processing and nutrition, in an effort to discover forms in which these foods will be more palatable to the Japanese. One recent development of this kind on a commercial scale is a mixture of starch, wheat flour, and broken rice, which is shaped into kernels of "artificial rice." [38]

Keeping more livestock and wiser use of animal products might be another promising attack upon the food problem. In 1950 the annual per capita consumption of meat and fowl in Japan was 6.6 pounds, of milk and its products 5.2 pounds, compared to 271 pounds of rice, 61 pounds of sweet potatoes,

[36] In 1951 35.6 percent was held in lots smaller than 1.2 acres, compared to 16.7 percent in 1941; 4.5 acres is considered a minimum for full-time farming under Japanese conditions. "Japan's Land Reform," *Fuji Bank Bulletin*, V. 4 (May 1953), pp. 22-34; Colin D. Campbell, "Weak Points in the Japanese Land Reform Program," *Journal of Farm Economics*, V. 34 (August 1952), pp. 361-368.

[37] Ackerman, cited, pp. 378, 381.

[38] Bank of Tokyo, *Weekly Review*, October 3, 1953, p. 1; J. C. Dodson, "Synthetic Rice Developed in Japan," *Foreign Agriculture*, V. 17 (November–December 1953), pp. 206-207.

55 pounds of wheat, and 49 pounds of fish and shellfish.[39] Small dairy and meat industries have developed to supply the larger cities, but in most of the country these foods are not in demand. Fewer than 30 percent of Japanese farm families own any cattle, and 80 percent of these have only one head, used principally as a draft animal.

Government interest in livestock raising has in the past centered on purposes other than food production. In the 1870's Ōkubo Toshimichi put a California grazier, D. W. Ap Jones, in charge of a Government Sheep Farm at Shimōsa, in the hope of producing a domestic supply of raw material for the pilot-plant woolen mill at Senju. Diseases and poor pasturage cut down the flocks so badly that the experiment was soon abandoned.[40] The shortage of foreign wool during World War I caused another flurry of interest in sheep breeding; since 1945 there has been a similar pressure to reduce the necessity for imports. The 482,000 sheep in Japan in 1951 could, however, at best supply only about 4 percent of Japan's demand for wool.[41] During the 1930's government efforts were concentrated on raising horses for the army. In recent years, however, "more livestock" has become a popular cry. On November 26, 1951, the Diet passed unanimously a resolution that it was urgent "to increase food production through an enlarged livestock industry." Representative Ogasawara Yasomi declared that "As a nation which is expected to play in the future an active international role, we must get rid of the outlook on the world based on rice and pickled radish." [42]

Serious physical and economic difficulties will be encountered, however. The coarse and unnutritious wild grasses are so persistent that it is hard to create artificial pasturage. Concentrates for winterfeeding are scarce and expensive, now that Japan does not have Manchuria as a source of sup-

---

[39] Nōrinshō Tōkei Chōsa-bu (Ministry of Agriculture and Forestry, Statistics and Survey Division), *Nihon Nōgyō no Genkyō* (*The Current Status of Japanese Agriculture*) (Tokyo: Nōrin Tōkei Kyōkai, 1951), p. 99.
[40] Okutani, cited, p. 15; *Tokio Times*, February 3, 1877.
[41] U. S. Department of Agriculture, Office of Foreign Agricultural Relations, *The Livestock Industry in Japan* (Foreign Agriculture Circular FLM 1-52), p. 10.
[42] *Mainichi Shimbun*, November 27, 1951.

ply. It has been estimated that the number of calories obtainable if an acre of grain is consumed directly by humans is six to seven times the number of meat or milk calories that results from feeding the same grain to animals. Considerable capital outlays would be necessary to provide shelter for livestock, and Japan does not now have fences to protect crops from damage. Since it would be uneconomical for the small farmer to keep breeding stock, SCAP experts urged the use of artificial insemination. Through LARA (Licensed Agencies for Relief in Asia) the Heifer Project Committee supported by American churches donated twenty-five high-quality young Holstein bulls to Japanese breeding stations, but many more will be needed if every farmer is to have a cow.

As Japanese farmers try to increase and diversify food supplies by cultivating uplands and raising more livestock Americans should give them every possible support. The Japanese will be leaving the area of familiar experience and will need to learn new techniques. Unfortunately, since Natural Resources Section of SCAP disbanded in 1952, American technical assistance in the field of agriculture has been quite limited. The Kiyosato Educational Experiment Project supported by the Episcopal Brotherhood of St. Andrew has a model dairy plant and a tractor lending facility; and the Brotherhood intends to establish similar demonstration projects in Hokkaidō, Shikoku, and Kyūshū.[43] Since 1952 groups of young Japanese farmers, drawn from all prefectures, have come each year to California to work on American farms and absorb new techniques at the grass-roots level.[44] More extensive programs could now be developed in connection with mutual defense aid.

Luckily, a Japanese agricultural extension service is being developed through which new ideas can be quickly disseminated. The prewar agricultural associations were dissolved by the Occupation because they had become repressive organizations for policing crop quotas, grain collections, and rationing critical materials. A new extension system was established in 1948 on the American system of maximum serv-

43 *Nippon Times*, September 28, 1953.
44 *The Mainichi*, January 17, 1953.

ice to the individual farmer. Now 9,100 farm advisers, 860 home advisers, and 375 specialists are working in the villages. Through 30,000 Agricultural Study Clubs and 4-H Clubs (that name is used) over a million rural youths have become a receptive audience.[45]

This review of past experience suggests strongly that, because of basic economic limitations, American technical assistance in the field of agriculture is not likely to produce spectacular results. We have seen how marginal American technical influence has been, except in the special case of Hokkaidō. The Japanese have already reached a high standard in intensive land use and soil conservation. Only further opening of the land reserve in Hokkaidō and raising of livestock on the uplands hold promise of substantial increases in the output of food. As in the past, the greatest American contribution can be help in the application of scientific experimentation to specific problems. Piecemeal gains from application of new techniques may in many cases involve costs and effort that can be justified only in the light of the chronic underemployment that characterizes Japanese agriculture. Unless science can make radical innovations in converting natural resources into human food, Japan must be reconciled to a permanent food deficit, a deficit that can be filled only by trading her industrial products abroad.

Technical Assistance for Japanese Industry

When SCAP sent an industrial survey group to the United States as part of its program for reorientation of Japanese leaders, American businessmen gave only grudging cooperation. One executive rejected what he called a "sob-sister request." Others talked with the party, but refused to let the Japanese inspect their plants. Most were willing to do business with individual firms, but in view of the Japanese record of product imitation and patent infringement, they did not want to run the risk of losing trade secrets.[46] In such

---

[45] Garritt E. Roelofs, "An Extension Service in Japan," *Extension Service Review*, V. 22 (December 1951), pp. 200-201; *Foreign Agriculture*, V. 16 (October 1952), p. 178.

[46] Emily C. Keeffe and Elizabeth Converse, *The Japanese Leaders Program of the Department of the Army: An Evaluative Report on the Program and Its*

fields as agriculture and forestry, advanced techniques are in the public domain and can easily be transmitted from one country to another by government missions or individual experts. In industry, however, new processes and products are developed at great expense in private laboratories, and rights to their use or manufacture may be obtained only by payment of patent royalties or license fees. An American company owning such rights will probably want an agreement with the foreign firm about spheres of competition; it may want a stock interest and a voice in management. On a strictly business basis, however, the sharing of industrial knowhow is a common thing.

Although Japanese manufacturing was never heavily dependent upon foreign capital (8 percent of total paid-up capital in 1937), before World War II technical and investment tie-ups had developed between a number of Japanese and American businesses. The Goodrich Rubber Co., after helping the Furukawa interests to start the manufacture of tires, withdrew in 1935. Most of the elevators in use in Japan were built and installed by the Tōyō Otis Co., which used Otis patents and was partially financed by Americans. The manufacture of cash registers was dominated by the Japan National Cash Register Co. The Japan Plate Glass Company was a joint enterprise of Sumitomo (one of Japan's principal industrial and financial combines) and Libby-Owens-Ford.[47]

The electrical industries of Japan are the best case, however, for detailed examination of the way in which American firms gave technical assistance under mutually profitable business arrangements. The use of electricity was a technological revolution in which Japan followed the industrial countries of the West with very little time lag. A shortage of coal combined with the favorable location of mountain streams has led to unusual reliance upon hydro-generation: 85 percent of total output in 1950.[48] Electricity is widely

Conduct by the Institute of International Education, 1950–1951 (Institute of International Education Research Program, Occasional Paper No. 1, October 1952), pp. 75-76.
[47] Akiyama Hachirō, "Foreign Capital Contributed Greatly to Industrial Progress," Contemporary Opinions on Current Topics, November 28, 1940.
[48] Ackerman, cited, p. 201.

used for power in both large factories and small workshops; and over 90 percent of all buildings, rural as well as urban, are lighted at least meagerly.

From about 1895 until 1930 Japan bought large quantities of electrical equipment from the United States. The volume reached over $10,000,000 per year during the middle twenties, on account of rapid expansion of facilities and reconstruction after the earthquake. Part of this trade was sustained by the $114,150,000 of loans floated in the United States by the Daidō, Nihon, Tōhō, Tokyo, Ujigawa, and Shinetsu utilities systems between 1924 and 1928. By importing foreign capital and techniques, Japan early began to manufacture part of her own equipment; by 1930 she could satisfy her needs for all but the most specialized items and also export in quantity. In 1937 the electrical machinery industry accounted for 64 percent of all the foreign capital invested in Japanese manufacturing.[49]

Since electricity was first used in Japan, as in other parts of the world, for communications rather than for lighting or power, the first technical connections came in that field. British engineers built the first telegraph lines during the early seventies. The magneto telephone was introduced from America in 1877, the year after Bell exhibited it at the Philadelphia Exposition, and was used experimentally by the Ōsaka police and for direct connections between government offices. In 1888 the Japanese government sent Ōi Saitarō abroad to study the technical aspects of wire communications. With four switchboards that Ōi purchased from the Western Electric Co., public telephone service was begun in Tokyo and Yokohama in 1890.[50]

In 1898 Western Electric's agent in Japan, Iwadare Kunihiko, started a native company to manufacture telegraph and telephone equipment. When Japanese laws were changed the next year to allow direct foreign investments, Western Electric took stock in his Nihon Denki Kabushiki Kaisha (Japan Electric Co., Ltd.) in exchange for patents and tech-

[49] *Japanese Industry Today: Foreign Investment Possibilities* (Tokyo: Foreign Capital Research Society, 1952), p. 67.
[50] *Meiji Kōgyō Shi (Industrial History of the Meiji Period)* (2d ed.; Tokyo: Kōgakkai Meiji Kōgyō Shi Hakkōsho, 1925–1931,), V. 5, pp. 160-168.

nical aid. In 1920 it also made an arrangement for technical cooperation with Sumitomo in the manufacture of electric wire and cable. Even after Western Electric sold its foreign interests to the International Telephone and Telegraph Corporation in 1925, technical relations apparently continued. Nihon Denki engineers were regularly trained in American plants. The president of this company also contributed to the general progress of electrical knowledge in Japan by establishing the Iwadare Foundation, which invited American experts to lecture in Japan and each year sent a number of Japanese graduates in electrical engineering to the United States for advanced study.[51]

The initial steps in electric lighting in Japan were largely the work of Fujioka Ichisuke. He had received his theoretical training under British professors at the Kōbu Daigakkō, where carbon arc lamps had been built experimentally as early as 1878. After attending the International Electrical Exhibition held at Philadelphia in 1884, Fujioka built a small generator and lighted the Bankers' Association building in Tokyo with incandescent lamps. After further study of the then very new lighting systems of America and Europe, he designed a power plant for the Tokyo Electric Light Co. (Tōkyō Dentō Kaisha), which began to supply current to the public in 1887.[52]

Fujioka's next venture was the manufacture of light bulbs, by a company which eventually took the name of Tōkyō Denki Kabushiki Kaisha (Tokyo Electric Co., Ltd.). After about a decade of independent operation, Fujioka sought financial and technical assistance from John R. Geary, the General Electric representative in Japan. In January 1905 GE invested 100,000 yen in one-fourth of the capital stock. For twenty years the rights to the tungsten filament, which GE introduced in 1907, gave Tōkyō Denki a great advantage over its competitors in lamp manufacture. GE made further investments as the company extended its operations to the manufacture of electrical appliances, and for a number of years Geary was president of Tōkyō Denki. In 1939 the In-

[51] D. F. G. Eliot, "Twenty-five Years of Successful Coöperation in Japan," *Far Eastern Review*, V. 20 (February 1924), pp. 83-87.
[52] *Meiji Taishō Shi*, cited, V. 7, pp. 547-548.

ternational General Electric Co. was reported to hold 33 percent of the capital stock, on which it had been receiving annual dividends of 12 percent.[53]

The extension of generating facilities created a growing market for heavy electrical machinery. In 1892, after studying the few examples then existing in the United States, Takagi Bumpei and Tanabe Sakurō built Japan's first hydroelectric plant on the Lake Biwa-Kyōto canal, using two Edison 550-volt DC generators. The beginning of high tension, long-distance transmission in 1899 called for large step-up and step-down transformers. The first electric street railway was built in Kyōto in 1895, and electrification of the regular railroad lines began in 1904.[54]

In 1909 the General Electric Co., which had been supplying a good deal of this equipment from its American plants, entered into a manufacturing arrangement with the Shibaura Seisakusho, a well-established engineering works in which the Mitsui combine held the major interest. In return for patents and a cash investment, GE received one-fourth of the capital stock. The next year Kishi Keijirō, head of the Electrical Section, took ten young Shibaura engineers to Schenectady to study GE operations. Under this arrangement Shibaura was able to take advantage of the stimulus of World War I to expand production greatly and even to enter the export trade. After almost total loss in the earthquake and fire of September 1923, it rebuilt its plant at Tsurumi according to advanced American principles of factory layout.[55] During the 1930's the company's earnings on paid-up capital ranged from 20 to 29 percent, out of which it regularly paid dividends of 10 percent.[56] In 1939 Shibaura and Tōkyō Denki merged under the name of Tōkyō Shibaura Denki Kabushiki Kaisha. With this company GE cooperated actively until the outbreak of war in 1941.

53 *Oriental Economist*, V. 6 (April 1939), p. 254.

54 *Meiji Taishō Shi*, cited, V. 7, pp. 555-561, 577.

55 *Meiji Taishō Shi*, cited, V. 11, pp. 137-138; *Tōyō Keizai Zasshi*, no. 506 (November 25, 1909), p. 38; no. 900 (June 12, 1920), p. 31; "Linked with America in Big Industry: Success of the Shibaura Engineering Works," *Far Eastern Review*, V. 18 (November 1922), pp. 665-669; *The Digest* (International General Electric Co.), V. 4 (August 1924), p. 11.

56 *Oriental Economist*, V. 6 (April 1939), p. 255. In 1939 IGE held 14.3 percent of the stock.

Other American electrical manufacturers had similar Japanese tie-ups. Beginning in the 1890's the Westinghouse Electric Co. sold large numbers of motors, turbines, transformers, electric locomotives, and other equipment in Japan. When Guy E. Tripp, chairman of the board of directors, went to Japan in 1923 to advise on reconstruction after the earthquake, he signed a contract to furnish patents and technical services to the Mitsubishi Electric Co. (Mitsubishi Denki K. K.). According to a company officer, Westinghouse profited "by receiving a continuous revenue for services, and royalties in lieu of exports that it was certain to lose within a comparatively few years." It also had a small stock interest. Mitsubishi Denki engineers, including Katō Takeo, the present head of the research and production technique divisions, have been trained in the United States in Westinghouse plants.[57] Before the war Fuji Electric had close relations with the Siemens Schuckert and Siemens Halske interests, Tokyo Electric Manufacturing with the English Electric Co. Of the major concerns, only Hitachi was free of foreign capital participation.

Without these tie-ups with foreign firms the rapid advance of the Japanese electrical industries would have been impossible. The flow of technology has not been entirely in one direction, however. The Japanese made some original contributions, especially in metallurgical work, of great importance to electrical manufacturing. In 1917 Honda Kōtarō developed a magnetic cobalt steel three times as effective as the permanent magnets then in use. Mishima Tokushichi of Tokyo University produced a series of aluminum-nickel-iron alloys which have become the basis for the GE Alnico magnets used in nearly all loudspeakers and in many small motors and generators. Mitsuda Ryōtarō made important innovations in transformer design. By the 1930's Japanese electrical engineers were becoming keen competitors of their American teachers.[58]

Resumption of technical and business relations between

[57] Denki Zasshi Ohm, V. 14 (July 1927), pp. 287, 307; New York Times, November 27, 1923.
[58] R. A. Chegwidden, "A Review of Magnetic Materials especially for Communications Systems," Bell Telephone System Technical Publications, Monograph No. B-1605 (New York: Bell Telephone Laboratories, 1948), p. 8.

Japanese and American firms after World War II was delayed by uncertainty about reparations policy and by SCAP restrictions on trade and use of foreign currencies. Until the attack on Korea Americans were not certain what degree of prosperity Japan should be allowed. Then it became clear that she must become economically strong if she was to stay out of the Communist orbit. Although Japan's immediate industrial recovery has been stimulated and supported by large special procurement orders for the United Nations forces, she faces great obstacles in regaining a secure position in world trade. No longer does she have the advantage of overwhelmingly cheaper labor costs.[59] Her technology is in many cases a dozen years behind American practice, her machine tools and industrial plant outmoded. Only 30 percent of her metal-working tools are under 10 years old. The high cost of coal is a severe handicap to large segments of the economy. Most coking coal has to be imported, and, calorie for calorie, boiler coal costs twice as much in Japan as it does in the United States. Working in narrow seams without much mechanical equipment, the Japanese miner produced an average of 0.8 ton per day in October 1951, compared to an output of 6.75 tons by the average worker in American pits. Mining costs have been so high that in the postwar years Japan has been able to import coal from the United States more cheaply than she could produce it at home.[60]

Since late 1950 the Japanese have been in active search of technical assistance. Each quarter the Foreign Investment Commission has published a list of fields in which technical tie-ups and investment are particularly desired. The original list of forty items included manufacture of synthetic fibers, coke, and antibiotics; catalytic cracking of petroleum; and welded ship construction.[61] The United States Department of Commerce and the business press have publicized this

[59] Available statistics indicate that, except in coal production, Japan's advantage in labor costs still exists but is declining. In cotton spinning the labor cost per pound of thread was 1.8¢, compared to 8.6¢ in the United States and 7.5¢ in the United Kingdom. *Economic Survey of Japan (1952–1953)*, cited pp. 143-147.
[60] Same, pp. 112-113, 176; Tsūsanshō Kigyōkyoku, *Kigyō Gōrika no Sho Mondai (Questions Involved in the Rationalization of Enterprises)* (Tokyo: Sangyō Kagaku Kyōkai, 1952), p. 51.
[61] *Foreign Commerce Weekly*, May 21, 1951, p. 15.

information and periodic revisions of the list. In April 1954, following the conclusion of the Mutual Defense Assistance Pact, the Foreign Operations Administration extended the operation of its Contact Clearing House Service to Japan. Through a network of business organizations in both America and Japan, this Service disseminates information about companies, especially smaller companies, desiring to enter into technical assistance contracts.

By the end of 1953, 344 contracts involving royalties extending over more than one year had been concluded under the Japanese Foreign Investments Law of 1950; 245 of these were with American firms. Cases where payments did not extend over more than a year were handled separately under the Exchange Control Ordinance. In this category Americans were parties to 109 of 220 contracts concluded by March 31, 1953. By the end of that year $18,600,000 had already been remitted as payment for technical assistance.[62]

Both old and new enterprises are involved.[63] Standard Vacuum, California Texas, and Tidewater Associated oil companies have taken interests in leading Japanese refining and distributing companies. The Japanese government has set aside $35,000,000 in foreign exchange for purchase of steel-making and finishing equipment in the United States, and the Fuji and Yawata companies are already building new facilities under contracts with Armco International Corporation. Japan is also trying to make a major saving on imports by expanding greatly its production of synthetic fibers. Technology in this field has advanced by leaps and bounds since the day when Japan was the world's leading producer of rayon. Asahi Kasei Kōgyō K. K. now has a tie-up with Dow Chemical for production of saran, Tōyō Rayon with Dupont for nylon processes. Among the new plastics, polyvinyl chloride is being produced in rapidly growing quantities. The B. F. Goodrich Chemical Corporation helped the Furukawa interests to build a plant, and Mitsubishi has an alliance with Dow. With the coming of commercial televi-

---

[62] Same, April 12, 1954, p. 7; *Sangyo Keizai Overseas Edition*, June 1, 1953, p. 18.
[63] For further details see Jerome B. Cohen, "Private Point Four in Japan," *Fortune*, April 1953, pp. 148-149, 184-188.

sion, several Japanese companies have made contracts with RCA for manufacture of receivers.[64]

Japanese rearmament is being directly facilitated by a number of contracts for use of technical data and rights. In the summer of 1953 the manufacturers of the Willys automobile made an agreement with New Mitsubishi Heavy Industry for manufacture of jeeps and other vehicles. With assistance from Pratt and Whitney and North American Aircraft Co., the same firm arranged to make T-33 and T-28 jet trainers. From Lockheed the Kawasaki Aircraft Co. has obtained rights to manufacture a trainer and the F-49C fighter plane.[65]

These arrangements for American technical assistance, and more like them, are essential first aid measures to help Japanese industries improve their efficiency and competitive position. But in a Japan which is sensitive about its sovereignty and independence, voices are already being raised against American domination of economic life. Over the long term it is highly desirable that Japan should grow out of her position of dependence, and through improved scientific education and industrial research develop a creative technology of her own. The goal should be not isolated independence but a world-wide exchange of skills and knowledge in which Japan can participate as an equal partner. To do this she must have an adequate number of well-trained, alert, and creative engineers.

An Engineering Education Mission that SCAP brought to Japan in the summer of 1951 found serious shortcomings in the existing system of professional training. Teaching was done almost entirely through lectures, to the neglect of the individual work with textbooks and problems that forces the student to develop mental discipline and analytical powers. After a decade of isolation, libraries and laboratory facilities were outdated and inadequate. Because of poor cooperation with industry the engineering schools were not adjusting their curricula to current needs. The Japanese

[64] *Foreign Commerce Weekly,* October 20, 1952; *Japanese Industry Today,* p. 26; N. T. Takagaki, "Prospects of the Polyvinyl Chloride Industry in Japan," *Far Eastern Economic Review,* V. 15 (August 27, 1953), pp. 280-282; *Mainichi Shimbun,* August 13, September 2, 1953.
[65] *The Mainichi Overseas Edition,* April 15, 1954, p. 3.

engineer produced by this system was more interested in theoretical science than in practical application. He often lacked the imagination and daring needed to tackle problems of development and production involving factors that cannot be measured precisely. Inclined to consider himself a finished expert upon graduation from the university, he was resistant to on-the-job training. Although his intellectual ability was high, the Japanese engineer was too often the prisoner of his training and the traditions of his profession.[66]

Avoiding direct recommendation as much as possible, the fifteen members of the American engineering mission tried to stimulate the Japanese to analyze their own procedures and problems by presenting in panel discussions and group meetings detailed explanations of American practice. Only time will tell whether this stimulus will gather momentum or die away. Exchanges of views between Japanese universities, and between education and industry, have continued; and a Japanese Society for Engineering Education has been organized. The chairman of the mission, Harold L. Hazen of Massachusetts Institute of Technology, has suggested that a few young engineering professors should be brought to the United States to observe the teaching work of their American counterparts. In a few years a follow-up mission, perhaps smaller in size, might go to Japan to renew contacts and to assess progress.

Japanese industry need not wait, however, for the gradual cumulative effect of improved training of engineers. Shindō Buzaemon of the Natural Resources Board has urged that Japan adopt the American system of consulting engineers in order to get maximum benefit from the best of her older experienced men.[67] A system of Japan Industrial Standards has been established. The Japan Federation for Scientific Technology (Nihon Kagaku Gijutsu Remmei) has been pushing the adoption of quality control methods. The feeling that rejection of any product, such as a part of a ma-

[66] "Report of the Engineering Education Mission to Japan, 5 July to 26 August, 1951." This unpublished report has been summarized by the chairman in H. L. Hazen, "The 1951 ASEE Engineering Education Mission to Japan," *Journal of Engineering Education*, V. 42 (June 1952), pp. 481-488.
[67] *Daiyamondo*, January 1, 1952, pp. 38-39.

chine, was a personal disgrace to the workmen who had made it has heretofore limited the effective use of such controls.[68]

In their attitude toward Japanese business men, Americans have been inconsistently patronizing about their abilities but fearful of their competition. Only a few of Japan's business leaders have seemed to display the true spirit of free enterprise. Fukuzawa Momosuke, the adopted son of educator Fukuzawa Yukichi, was a daring entrepreneur, first in railroads, then in public utilities. Perhaps his early training in the employment of the Pennsylvania Railroad was reflected in his later career.[69] Mutō Sanji, who also went through a school of hard knocks in America, was responsible in the 1920's for organizing the Jitsugyō Dōshikai, Japan's closest approach to a political party in support of *laissez-faire* principles. But most Japanese business men have seemed unduly subservient to government leadership, and, on the other hand, not sufficiently cost- and profit-conscious.

The explanation lies in the historical development of modern Japan. Factory industries of the Western type have been developed under forced draft. In the 1870's the government itself built the first railroad and telegraph lines, set up a model woolen mill, a cement factory, cotton mills, and shipyards, and operated some of the principal mines. These properties were then gradually turned over to private entrepreneurs at nominal prices.[70] The periods of great industrial expansion have coincided with wars or preparation for war when national rather than personal interests were paramount. Through an elaborate system of subsidies and tax exemptions, the government has shifted the risks in industries of "national importance" to the country at large. When the government stood so ready to bail out failures or to give compensating advantages, it should be no surprise that business men phrased their goals in terms of national interest rather than private profit. Even Shibusawa Eiichi, who usually preached independence of the capitalist, had

[68] Same, May 1, 1952, pp. 26-27; August 11, 1952, pp. 36-37.
[69] *Far Eastern Review*, V. 16 (December 1920), p. 641; V. 21 (June-July 1925), p. 496.
[70] Horie Yasuzō, "Government Industries in the Early Years of the Meiji Era," *Kyoto University Economic Review*, V. 14 (January 1939), pp. 67-87.

this to say about the enterprise for manufacture of artificial fertilizer mentioned earlier:

I did not begin this work with the object of profit alone. The principal consideration was the benefit of the state, and I also thought it necessary for the encouragement of the agricultural villages. Moreover, because it was an enterprise planned in the faith that in the future it would be a promising business, I decided that I must finish it no matter what difficulties were encountered. So when my partners said that there was nothing to do but abandon it, I immediately gave my own opinion that I alone would take over the company and carry it through even if it did run into debt.[71]

The existence of the great *zaibatsu* combinations of financial and industrial power strengthened these tendencies. The distinction between what was good for Mitsui and Mitsubishi and what was good for the country often became very faint. Through their power to give or withhold contributions, the *zaibatsu* had great influence in the political parties. On the highest level of the bureaucracy, Inoue Kaoru was considered to be a Mitsui man, and at a later date both Katō Takaakira and Shidehara had close connections with Mitsubishi. Day-by-day interests in policy execution were taken care of by company men who had offices in the various ministries as *shokutaku* (non-official staff).[72] On the economic level, the operations of each combine were so extensive that the costs or profit of any single operation were not important. For the smaller company, security lay in an alliance with one of the giants, whereby it could secure loans from the *zaibatsu* bank, preferential access to raw materials, and the services of an efficient marketing organization at home and abroad. One of the effects of SCAP's policy of liquidating the big holding companies has been to weaken Japan's ability to sell abroad. But now that the 1953 revisions of the Anti-Monopoly Law permit cartels whenever they are deemed necessary for combating depression, for rationalization of enterprises, or promotion of international trade,

[71] Shibusawa, cited, V. 1, pp. 517-518.
[72] Justin Williams, "Party Politics in the New Japanese Diet," *American Political Science Review*, V. 42 (December 1948), p. 1172. The *shokutaku* system was abolished in 1948.

something like the prewar patterns of integration may be expected to reappear. Whether or not the long run results are good from the American point of view, the Japanese believe they will achieve immediate gains.

Recent books and articles testify to a lively interest in Japan in various management techniques used in America: controllership, cost accounting, time-motion standards, and public relations, for example.[73] In 1951 a first group of Japanese came to the United States to learn the Training Within Industry program of job instruction, job methods, and job analysis that was developed by our War Manpower Commission. Perhaps more could be done in the field of specialized education for business. Japan has had, of course, an extensive system of "commercial education" which dates back to 1875, when an American named William C. Whitney was brought to Japan as teacher in the Shōhō Kōshūjo, an institution which developed into the Tokyo University of Commerce, now known as Hitotsubashi University. But much of this commercial training has been limited to the physical operations of bookkeeping and foreign trade correspondence. On the higher levels, emphasis has been placed on commercial law. The Japanese have shown interest in the Harvard Business School system by which potential executives learn by examining all the variables in concrete business situations. Japanese educators would probably need help, however, in the difficult and costly task of preparing usable case materials.

"Rationalization of industry" is now a popular cry in Japan, and the government has allocated considerable funds for its encouragement. Once before, during the first half of the 1930's, the Japanese did succeed in making striking gains in productive efficiency.[74] But this occurred during a general increase in production and employment, and at a time when depreciation of the yen had encouraged an expansion of exports. Today the general conditions may not be so favorable. When there is already excess capacity for manufacture of

[73] See two surveys published by Daiyamondo-sha, Tokyo: *Amerika no Keiei Gijutsu* (*American Management Techniques*) (1950), and Awaji Enjirō, *Amerika no Rōmu Kanri* (*American Labor Management*) (1952).
[74] See analysis by G. C. Allen in Schumpeter, cited, pp. 647-679.

machinery and chemicals, entrepreneurs will hesitate to build new efficient plants merely in anticipation of possible exports to, let us say, Southeast Asia. The most obvious means of rationalization, by getting rid of some of the surplus labor that characterizes Japanese industry, will be difficult for social reasons. The right of workers to a job during periods of slack production or after they are too old to be efficient is a recognized part of the paternalistic social pattern. The same reasoning explains the large allowances given on the termination of employment. These conditions add to the dilemmas faced by Japanese entrepreneurs and government planners in trying to reduce costs.

Technical assistance from American sources can unquestionably contribute a great deal to the efficiency of large-scale enterprises in Japan that are oriented toward the vital export trade. But we should not expect too much in the way of accompanying political results. Diffusion of technology is a worldwide phenomenon rather than any distinctively American contribution. In the past the Japanese drew from the United States in fields where we held a lead, as in electrical manufacturing; but they borrowed equally from Great Britain, for example, in textile manufacturing and from the German chemical industries. Now that the United States is an industrial leader in so many fields, the Japanese will be looking to us for a greater range of technical processes and knowledge. But it is extremely doubtful whether borrowing of technology creates any special ties of loyalty or friendship. On the contrary, sharing of technical knowhow may only intensify competitive rivalry for markets. Both parties to a technical tieup enter it primarily from expectation of financial gain. From the standpoint of public policy, the most that we can hope is that our technical assistance will help to make the Japanese economy healthy enough, viable enough to permit constructive social and political development.

American Influence upon the Japanese Labor Movement

The removal of traditional restraints long enough to allow Japanese working classes to establish a position of economic and political power was undoubtedly one of the most significant actions of the American occupation. Police controls over labor were revoked, radical leaders were released from jail, and General MacArthur himself informed Premier Shidehara that labor should be encouraged to form unions "that it may be clothed with such dignity as will permit it an influential voice in safeguarding the working man from exploitation and abuse and raising his living standard to a higher level." Like our Wagner Act, the Trade Union Law passed by the Diet in December 1945 gave unions a firm legal status, but it did not go as far in forbidding unfair practices by employers. The Labor Disputes Adjustment Law of 1946 set up prefectural Labor Relations Boards and a Central Board—on each of which labor, management, and the public had equal representation—to conciliate, mediate, and arbitrate in disputes. The Labor Standards Law of 1947 did not come up to the American level, but it made an attempt to give the minimum protections recommended by the International Labor Organization.[75]

The Japanese people used their new privileges enthusiastically, if somewhat naively. Labor organization was usually local and spontaneous, sometimes encouraged by employers, and often with no clear purpose in mind. Unions were part of the exciting new democracy; even patients in hospitals formed "unions" to bargain with the administration over service and rations. Union membership was close to 5,000,000 by the end of 1947, and it went on climbing to a peak of 6,900,000 in March 1949.[76] The small Labor Division of SCAP tried to direct this chaotic energy into patterns familiar in American experience: strong autonomous unions federated on lines of logical economic interest, collective bargaining, and recourse to strikes only when procedures for peaceful settlement of disputes had been exhausted. Japanese unionists were eager to learn how things were done in America; and men like Professor Matsui Shichirō of Dōshi-

[75] Ayusawa Iwao, "Developments in Organized Labor," *Contemporary Japan*, V. 21 (1952–1953), pp. 225-245, 410-424, 541-554; Miriam S. Farley, *Aspects of Japan's Labor Problems* (New York: John Day, 1950), pp. 26-65.
[76] Ayusawa, cited, pp. 416, 419; Muramatsu Tsuneo, "Japan," in George W. Kisker, ed., *World Tension: The Psychopathology of International Relations* (New York: Prentice-Hall, 1951), p. 203.

sha University, who had studied labor economics under John R. Commons at the University of Wisconsin, were suddenly listened to like oracles.

Luckily, prewar experience had given the Japanese some idea of the form and function of unions. Twice before attempts had been made to follow the American example. In 1897 Jō Tsunetarō and Sawada Hannosuke had returned to Japan after taking part in the hurly-burly labor struggles of San Francisco. With a group of young Christians at Kingsley Hall, a settlement house just opened in Tokyo by the American Board Mission, they organized a labor body called Shokkō Giyūkai (Workers' Volunteer Society). From this nucleus they began to organize craft locals of the AF of L type in the iron and printing industries. After staging a few strikes, the infant labor movement succumbed to the impact of depression and the government's Public Peace Police Regulations. Strictly economic action was then suspended for a decade, and many of the leaders turned to Socialist political agitation.[77]

A second start was made in 1912 by Suzuki Bunji, who was associated with the Rev. Clay MacCauley in the management of Unitarian Hall in Tokyo. Stimulated by the visit of Sidney and Beatrice Webb to Japan, Suzuki named his new organization the Yūaikai after the Friendly Societies of Great Britain. It remained primarily a mutual benefit and educational society until 1915, when Suzuki went to the United States to attend the conventions of the AF of L and the California Federation of Labor. "My last visit to America has not only given me great educational advantages," Suzuki reported, "but it was truly an epoch-making event in the labor movement of Japan." During the eight months after his return Suzuki traveled nearly ten thousand miles within Japan, made over one hundred formal speeches, and participated in the settlement of many labor disputes. Yūaikai membership quickly increased from 10,000 to 30,000.[78]

[77] Hosotani Matsuta, *Nihon Rōdō Undōshi (History of the Japanese Labor Movement)* (Tokyo: Dōyūsha, 1948), V. 1, pp. 24-25; Harada Shuichi, *Labor Conditions in Japan* (New York: Columbia University Press, 1928), p. 181.
[78] *Report of Proceedings of the Thirty-sixth Annual Convention of the American Federation of Labor, held at Baltimore, Maryland, November 13 to 25 inclusive, 1916,* p. 189.

When Suzuki returned to the United States in 1916, he urged Samuel Gompers to come to Japan the next spring for the fifth anniversary meeting of the Yūaikai. He hoped that such a visit would convince conservative Japanese that labor leaders were not necessarily dangerous fanatics. Gompers declined, however, on the ground that he could not get away at a time when America was facing the possibility of war. Privately he explained that such a trip would be inconsistent with American labor's stand in favor of exclusion of all Japanese immigrants.[79] Suzuki renewed his invitation in 1921 in vain. Embarrassment over the immigration question stifled all effective cooperation between the labor movements in Japan and America.

Boom conditions in Japan during World War I that drove prices upward much faster than wages created growing labor unrest. After this found open expression in the rice riots of August 1918, the Home Minister in the new Hara cabinet announced that the Police Regulations would not be used to prevent "a wholesome development of labor unions." The Yūaikai then began to organize workers openly, and at its 1919 convention took the name of Japan Federation of Labor (Dai Nihon Rōdō Sōdōmei). By the end of 1921 the unions had about 100,000 members. The progress and limitations of the Japanese labor movement were dramatically brought to the attention of the world at the first conference of the International Labor Organization, held at Washington in 1919, where charges were made that the Japanese government had chosen the labor delegate without consulting the wishes of the unions.[80]

Japanese management responded to the new conditions by trying to extend the old patterns of paternalism. In December 1919 Shibusawa Eiichi took the lead in forming the Harmonization Society (Kyōchōkai), which was financed by private subscriptions and a subsidy from the government. On a trip abroad in 1911, Shibusawa had been much im-

[79] Report of Proceedings of the . . . Annual Convention of the American Federation of Labor . . . 1917, pp. 65-67; Report of Harvey H. Guy to Japanese consul, San Francisco, March 27, 1917, Japanese Foreign Office Archives, Library of Congress, MT 3. 8.2.287-2, pp. 185-190.
[80] The Socialist and Labour Movement in Japan. By an American Sociologist (Kobe: Japan Chronicle, 1921), pp. 38-40, 52-61.

pressed by the social and cultural facilities that the Waltham Watch Co. provided for its workers.[81] He feared that labor legislation "would tend to lead both parties to a cold and perfunctory relationship destroying the beautiful relations of affection and loyalty being inculcated in the labour life of Japan." [82] But in the Kyōchōkai labor was not even allowed the degree of participation that it enjoyed in its American counterpart, the National Civic Federation. As a result, the Kyōchōkai proved to be singularly unsuccessful in settling strikes. Its greatest contributions were the academic studies of labor questions that appeared in its journal, *Shakai Seisaku Jihō*.[83]

From the beginnings made during World War I a small labor movement survived until in 1940 all workers were forced into the fascistic Industrial Patriotic Association. A peak of 420,000 members was reached in 1936. Internecine quarrels and shifting alignments with competing proletarian parties were so constant that, as one observer commented, "like certain of the lesser organisms," organized labor "would seem to perpetuate itself by fission." [84] The legal position of labor remained vague and anomalous. Technically, inciting others to strike was a criminal offense; yet strikes were organized and carried out without incurring the full brunt of the law. Paternalistic employers often continued to pay wages during a work-stoppage and sometimes even donated a lump sum to pay strike expenses. Although considerable legislation regulating conditions of factory work stood on the books, its application was subject to so many exceptions that it gave no real protection.[85]

[81] These were made possible by a temporary competitive advantage based upon early adoption of machine methods. In the 1920's outside competition brought pressure upon wages and produced labor troubles for Waltham. Charles W. Moore, *Timing a Century: History of the Waltham Watch Company* (Cambridge: Harvard University Press, 1945), pp. 175-177.
[82] Obata Kyūgorō, *An Interpretation of the Life of Viscount Shibusawa* (Tokyo: Daiyamondo Jigyō K.K., 1937), pp. 167-168.
[83] *Saikin no Shakai Undō (Recent Social Movements)* (Tokyo: Kyōchōkai, 1929), pp. 991-999.
[84] E. H. Anstice in *Japan Weekly Chronicle*, July 17, 1930.
[85] *Japan Weekly Chronicle*, July 31, 1930; Ayusawa Iwao, *Japan and the International Labour Organisation* (London: League of Nations Union, n.d.), pp. 8-9.

The postwar labor movement of Japan, although greatly expanded in size and vigor, has a closer resemblance to prewar conditions than to the American pattern of unionism that SCAP tried to foster. Of the 5,700,000 union members in June 1952, about a third were in 24,330 small "enterprise" unions that did not extend beyond a single plant or a single company. Although outright company unionism is forbidden by the Trade Union Law, many of these small bodies are unduly influenced by the prestige or financial situation of the employer, who views them with paternalistic indulgence. Wages are generally determined not by the work done, but under a complicated system of allowances and bonuses by the age, sex, seniority, and family burdens of each employee. In outright violation of the law, much of the casual labor for building construction and shipbuilding is still recruited through bosses known as *oyabun* (the parent of the parent-child relation). During the years of headlong inflation workers did not want to have their pay frozen in firm collective agreements, but by July 1953 over 70 percent of those eligible were covered by such contracts. The terms of the collective agreements are often vague and general, however, and definite grievance machinery is not provided for handling disputes.[86]

Instead of carping at imperfections in the Japanese labor movement, however, Americans should look for ways in which they can contribute to progress. Japan's inexperienced labor leaders on the local level need concrete information about the function of shop stewards, about union finances, about credit unions, about the many details of practical unionism. Fortunately, American labor is now awake to its international responsibilities. The Congress of Industrial Organizations (CIO) contributes to the Regional Activities Fund of the International Confederation of Free Trade Unions, which is conducting training courses and publishing a union weekly in Japan. The Free Trade Union Committee of the AF of L has sent out Richard Deverall as its own rep-

[86] Ayusawa, "Developments," cited, pp. 543-550; *Monthly Labor Review,* V. 68 (January 1949), pp. 47-49; Solomon B. Levine, "Prospects of Japanese Labor," *Far Eastern Survey,* V. 23 (July 1954), pp. 107-110.

resentative in Asia. In addition to giving help on practical matters, he has endeavored to alert Asian workers to the dangers of communism.[87]

At the other extreme from the many small one-company locals in Japan, the larger industrial unions and the labor federations devote much of their energy to militant political activity. At this Americans should not be surprised or disappointed. In the whole picture of world labor, the Gompers ideal of rewarding friends and punishing enemies without making definite alliances is exceptional; even in the United States the principle seems to be breaking down. In Japan the government manages directly nearly all communications and several monopoly industries, and it exercises strong controls over the rest of the economy. In many instances, therefore, labor can protect its interests only through exercising effective influence on public policy. In addition, MacArthur's 1948 about-face in denying government employees the right to bargain collectively, as well as to strike, left this important group with no recourse but the polls.

The danger of direct control of unions by Communist minorities has been diminished by the internal "democratization" drives begun in 1948. But the General Council of Trade Unions (Sōhyō) formed in 1950 has failed in its original purpose of separating unionism and politics, and instead has become directly connected with the Left-wing Socialists. Its last three annual conventions have been devoted to oratory about American imperialism and the dangers of rearmament, with very little attention to concrete economic questions. Sōhyō has refused to affiliate with the International Confederation of Free Trade Unions, although several of its components are members. It often seems to fall uncritically into line with the Communist "peace offensive." National unions of textile workers, seamen, radio and theater workers which seceded from Sōhyō in the fall of 1953, in protest against these political tendencies, have become the nucleus for

[87] Lewis L. Lorwin, *The International Labor Movement: History, Policies, Outlook* (New York: Harper, 1953), pp. 236, 301, 307. In "Helping Asia's Workers," *American Federationist*, September 1951, pp. 16-17, Deverall complains that the American information centers in Japan have been timid and ineffective in supplying materials on labor problems.

a competing federation, the All-Japan Labor Union Congress (Zenrōren).[88]

By provoking legislation that may in the future be used against legitimate objectives of labor, Sōhyō's militancy has accelerated rather than halted the "reverse course" toward authoritarian controls. The coal miners and electrical power workers crippled the economy so badly during the long work stoppages in the fall of 1952 that the Diet substantially deprived them of any right to strike. The Anti-Subversives Act of 1952 is worded so loosely that it could easily be turned against the unions. The criticisms of domestic consumption levels so often voiced in Japan also conceal the assumption that economic problems would be solved if only the working people would accept a permanent sacrifice in standard of living.

Demands for differential sacrifice will lead only to crippling strife. What is needed in Japan is the creative cooperation of all classes in efficient and expanding production. The farmer must produce every possible ounce of food. The entrepreneur must cut unit costs low enough to be able to compete in export trade. The worker must recognize that his job and his wage depend upon his productivity. The government must maintain incentives by keeping rewards reasonably equal. The great example and hope that America offers the rest of the world today is her ability to produce cheaply and yet maintain a high standard of living. Instead of apologizing for our materialism, Americans should stand ready to use our material skills for solution of the world's problems. "Greater production is the key to greater prosperity and peace," President Truman said in enunciating his famous Point Four, "and the key to greater production is a wider and more vigorous application of modern scientific and technical knowledge." On this point we should not merely exhort the Japanese, but help them with all the concrete forms of technical assistance at our command.

[88] Nakayama Ichirō, "Japan's Labor Movement," *Nippon Times,* September 20, 1953; Yakabe Katsumi, "Sōhyō no Tatte iru Chiten (The Point Where Sōhyō Stands)," *Chūō Kōron,* V. 68 (September 1953), pp. 67-73.

CHAPTER THREE

INSTITUTIONS AND IDEOLOGY

JAPAN'S SECOND great problem over the past century, second only to economic development, has been to develop modern political and social institutions to match her technology. This, too, she set about consciously and deliberately, partly out of sincere admiration for the ways of the West, partly to escape any imputations of inferiority or backwardness. But the machinery of representative government, the formal grant of civil liberties, the substantial degree of social mobility, all remained a façade. The men who succeeded to power at the time of the Restoration were afraid to entrust the destiny of their nation to the free operation of these forces. Real power flowed in such informal channels that it could be exercised without corresponding responsibility. Small groups were able to sanctify their selfish purposes by mystical appeals to patriotism. In the end these self-appointed guardians of the national interest betrayed the Japanese people into a disastrous war.[1]

Accompanying the historical disaster in Japan was a corresponding failure on the part of Americans during the years before World War II. It was not so much a failure in participation, for only under the unusual conditions of military occupation can one nation even hope to shape decisively the institutional growth of another. Rather it was a failure of understanding, an inability to assess correctly the course of events in Japan and to make an adequate response. Americans thought Japan to be more stable than she was, more

[1] For a general picture of the modern political development of Japan, I am greatly indebted to Nobutaka Ike, *The Beginnings of Political Democracy in Japan* (Baltimore: Johns Hopkins Press, 1950) and to Robert A. Scalapino, *Democracy and the Party Movement in Prewar Japan: The Failure of the First Attempt* (Berkeley: University of California Press, 1953).

like Western nations than she was. They made the error of viewing politics and society, abroad as well as at home, too exclusively in terms of constitutional and legal provisions, without plumbing the realities of power and interest that lay beneath.

From 1945 to 1952 American military authority—exercised with restraint, but coercive nonetheless—directed a thoroughgoing reformation of Japanese public life. Legal obstacles to free and equal development of individuals were replaced by secure guarantees of civil rights. The Japanese Constitution was revised to give the people effective means of exercising their sovereignty. Women were given a status of complete legal equality with men. General MacArthur himself has admitted that "in reshaping the lives of others we have been guided by the same pattern from which is taken the design of our own lives." [2] The great questions for the future are whether the Japanese, despite differences in cultural heritage, will desire or will be able to assimilate permanently these American influences upon ideals and institutions and to make them contribute to a free and creative national life.

Relevance and Understanding: Prewar Experience

We must recognize at the outset that American guidance in political development is a new departure for Japan. The prewar experiments with a parliamentary system followed, for the most part, other models and traditions.

Early in 1868 the young Emperor Mutsuhito was induced to issue a Charter Oath which set forth in five articles a series of broad progressive principles. The first stated that "A broadly-based assembly shall be convened, and all issues shall be decided by discussion." The hope expressed in the second article that "those above and below shall be of one mind" indicated, however, what was to be a persistent preference for concert rather than conflict of opinion. Shortly after the promulgation of the Oath, Fukuoka Kotei and

[2] Statement for *Life* magazine, "On Significance of 4th July," in Supreme Commander for the Allied Powers, Government Section, *Political Reorientation of Japan, September 1945 to September 1948* (Washington: GPO, 1949), V. 2, p. 773.

Soejima Taneomi were commissioned to draw up a modern frame of government to replace the ancient seventh-century administrative structure that had been pressed into service immediately after the Restoration.

Largely by coincidence the drafters found themselves at this early date more familiar with American institutions than with those of Europe. Fukuzawa Yukichi's *Seiyō Jijō,* then the most complete book on "Conditions in the West," devoted more space to the government of the United States than to that of any other country and gave translations of the Constitution and the Declaration of Independence. A few years before Soejima had studied the American Constitution under Guido Verbeck, a Reformed Church missionary living at Nagasaki. A history of the United States originally prepared by Elijah C. Bridgman for use in the Chinese mission field was also at hand as a reference.[3]

The constitution promulgated on June 11, 1868 under the name of *Seitaisho* drew directly upon American experience at two points. The provision that officials were to be changed after four years was probably an imitation of the American presidential term. More significant was the incorporation of the concept of separation of powers. Article Two stated that the power and authority of the government, the Dajōkan, was threefold: legislative, executive, and judicial. "Thus the balance of authority is preserved amongst the different branches of the Government." The next article elaborated by affirming that "the legislative branch cannot possess executive functions, nor can the executive branch possess legislative functions." [4]

The specific provisions that followed suggest strongly, however, that the drafters of the *Seitaisho* did not understand the full implications of the principle of separation. The supreme judicial power was given to the upper house of the bicameral legislature. This body also chose officials for the highest executive posts. The most powerful of these, the two *hoshō,* had to hold seats in the upper chamber, where

[3] William Elliot Griffis, *Verbeck of Japan* . . . (New York: Revell, 1900), pp. 174-175; Osatake Takeshi, *Nihon Kensei Shi Taikō (Outline of Japanese Constitutional History)* (Tokyo: Nihon Hyōron-sha, 1938–1939), V. 1, pp. 16-17, 25.
[4] Walter W. McLaren, *Japanese Government Documents, 1867–1889* (Tokyo: Asiatic Society of Japan, 1914), pp. 7-15.

they helped to determine the policies which they executed. The lower house was presided over by officials drawn from the executive side. Even in the American system the separation of powers is not complete, of course, but during its short life of a little over a year the *Seitaisho* structure showed no evidence of working checks and balances. Power remained concentrated in the hands of the same small group of samurai and court officials who had engineered the Restoration.[5]

As the leaders of the Meiji government continued a cautious adjustment to Western concepts and institutions, they were able to draw upon a growing library of books on political subjects. Eager students of foreign languages were translating or compiling accounts of Dutch, French, and British institutions. The British system of government, particularly, required extended exposition, for it was not embodied in definite constitutional documents. In 1869, for example, Fukuzawa Yukichi published *Talks on the British Parliament (Eikoku Giji-in Dan)*. Another outstanding teacher and publicist, Nakamura Masanao, initiated the more theoretical study of political problems by translating John Stuart Mill's famous essay *On Liberty*.

American political institutions continued to receive their share of attention. In 1871 Ga Noriyuki of the Department of Foreign Affairs quarried two books on government and law out of school texts by Andrew W. Young. Two years later Nakamura Masanao published *Kyōwa Seiji (Republican Government)*, an adaptation of Ransom H. Gillet's *The Federal Government: Its Officers and their Duties*. While they were studying in the United States, Nabeshima Naoyoshi, former head of Kashima *han* (territorial clan) in Hizen, and two of his retainers prepared a book entitled *Beisei Satsuyō (Epitome of American Government)*. Mori Arinori, the Japanese minister in Washington, also prepared a report on *Life and Resources in America*. Although he was during these early years one of the more liberal members of the bureaucracy, Mori deplored the abuse of freedom in America. "It has been so profitable with designing and selfish

[5] For a full discussion see Robert A. Wilson, "The Seitaisho: A Constitutional Experiment," *Far Eastern Quarterly*, V. 11 (May 1952), pp. 297-304.

men, to increase the number of voters, that they have se-
cured the passage of laws which allow all men to vote in
view of the single idea of personal freedom. This is undoubtedly all wrong, and the evil effects of this state of things are
being manifested every day." [6]

As members of the high-level Japanese mission that toured
the world during 1872 and 1873, Iwakura Tomomi, Kido
Takayoshi, Ōkubo Toshimichi, and Itō Hirobumi, along
with many lesser officials in the government, had an opportunity for first-hand observation of Western institutions.
During the six months spent in the United States, visits to
state legislatures, sessions of Congress, and government departments in Washington gave the Iwakura Embassy a view
of the exterior aspects of American government. Since Ōkubo
and Itō were absent most of the time on a trip back to Japan
to get credentials for treaty revision, responsibility for study
of political questions fell primarily upon Kido. He ordered
Hatakeyama Yoshinari, who had studied in America for several years, and Kume Kunitake, the chronicler of the expedition, to prepare for him notes on the United States Constitution. Whereas most members of the Embassy came back
convinced that material development was needed if Japan
was to survive in the ruthless world of power politics that
Bismarck had described to them, Kido urged that national
strength depended upon evolution of the constitution and
the laws.[7]

Creation of a Council of Elder Statesmen (Genrō-in) in
1875 was a concession to Kido's gradualist—but still essentially conservative—views. The next year the Emperor directed
the Genrō-in to draft a constitution, giving the president a
copy of Alpheus Todd's *On Parliamentary Government in
England* as a guide. Guido Verbeck served as an official adviser in this work. He directed the translation of a great
variety of legal and political documents, including the *Code
Napoléon,* Bluntschli's *Allgemeines Staatsrecht,* and the constitutions of American states. As an immigrant to the United

---

[6] Mori Arinori, *Life and Resources in America* (Washington: Author, 1871),
p. 14.
[7] Ōtsu Junichirō, *Dai Nihon Kensei Shi* (*Constitutional History of Japan*)
(Tokyo: Hōbunkan, 1927–1928), V. 1, pp. 827-832.

States from the Netherlands, Verbeck was self-consciously proud of his Americanism, but he tended to be cautious about the transferability of institutions. "Passing out of feudalism into republicanism," he once warned, "is like trying to make a yard-fowl give birth at once to a living chicken." The drafts of a constitution presented in 1878 and 1880 actually owed more to Belgian and Prussian models than to the British system. Even so, they were rejected because they gave too much power to an elected legislature.[8]

Ex-president Ulysses S. Grant made a visit to Japan in 1879, just when constitutional questions were under lively discussion. During a long interview with the Emperor, his advice on politics was listened to with great respect. Grant stated that elective assemblies were "very good for all countries in due time." "But you must always remember that privileges like this can never be recalled. . . . It is exceedingly dangerous to launch out too suddenly." While the Japanese people were being educated gradually for political responsibility, there should be an advisory council of the leading men, with power to debate, but not to legislate—a prescription that fitted almost exactly the existing Genrō-in. Thus Grant's advice, which bore great weight because of his reputation as a military leader, reinforced the conservative preferences of the government leaders.[9]

If the Satsuma-Chōshū oligarchy that held control of the Meiji government was little attracted by an American system based on broad suffrage, neither were the dissident samurai who led the opposition. Neither Itagaki Taisuke nor Gotō Shōjirō, leaders of the Jiyūtō (Liberal Party), had any direct acquaintance with American institutions until they went abroad in 1882 and 1883. Furusawa Shigeru, who penned the memorial for a popular assembly presented in 1874, was an ardent admirer of British parliamentary institutions, which had a natural appeal in view of the self-consciousness

[8] Osatake, cited, V. 2, pp. 460-482; Griffis, *Verbeck of Japan*, cited, pp. 277-283; Guido F. Verbeck, "The First Visit to a Daimyo: A Reminiscence," *Far East*, V. 3 (March 20, 1898), p. 238.
[9] *Guranto Shōgun to no Go-taiwa Hikki (Memorandum of the Conversation between His Majesty and General Grant)* (Tokyo: Kokumin Seishin Bunka Kenkyūjo, 1937), pp. 16-18; John Russell Young, *Around the World with General Grant* (New York: American News Co., 1879), V. 2, pp. 540-547.

of the samurai as an elite group. Some of the younger hot-heads mouthed the liberty-or-death sentiments attributed to Patrick Henry, but intellectually the nascent party movement rested upon the utilitarian ideas of John Stuart Mill and Herbert Spencer rather than upon the Lockean concepts of natural rights that prefaced the Declaration of Independence. Both Itagaki and Ōkuma Shigenobu, the leader of the Kaishintō (Progressive Party), stressed the potential contributions of an elective assembly to national strength and stability, rather than protection and opportunity for individuals.[10]

When the government yielded to popular demand in 1881 to the extent of promising a national assembly for nine years later, the task of drafting a constitution was entrusted to Itō Hirobumi. According to one of his assistants, Kaneko Kentarō, during these years Itō kept *The Federalist* with him as a reference. Kaneko, too, admired the career of Alexander Hamilton; and both he and Itō seem to have recognized that the formation of the American Constitution was essentially a conservative action, designed to strengthen the nation through increased centralization of power. As they set out to devise a frame of government that would fit the special needs of the Japanese state, they were consciously emulating the work of the "founding fathers" at Philadelphia.[11]

For more detailed guidance, however, Itō turned to German legal scholars. During a trip to Europe in 1882 and 1883, he and his assistants listened to lectures by Rudolf von Gneist of the University of Berlin and by Lorenz von Stein at Vienna. Stein was invited to come to Japan as a consultant, but declined on account of advanced age. In the actual work of drafting the constitution, Itō had the help of two German advisers, Herman Roessler and Albert Mosse. Roessler particularly urged a strong position for the throne and

[10] Scalapino, cited, pp. 40-91.
[11] Kaneko Kentarō, *Kempō Seitei to Ō-Beijin no Hyōron* (*The Establishment of the Constitution and the Opinions of Europeans and Americans*) (Tokyo: Nihon Aonenkan, 1937), pp. 71-72; Osatake Takeshi, *Nihon Kensei Shi no Kenkyū* (*Studies in Japanese Constitutional History*) (Tokyo: Ichigensha, 1943), pp. 318-321; Kaneko Kentarō, "Ō-Bei Kembutsu Iken (Thoughts from Travel in Europe and America)," *Kokka Gakkai Zasshi*, V. 4 (July 1890), pp. 383-386.

a clear limitation of the power of the legislature.[12] The Japanese "founding fathers" were perfectly willing to be eclectic, however. By analogy to the "fundamental political principle of England" mentioned in the works of Edmund Burke that he had translated in 1881, Kaneko found a modern context for the ancient concept of an enduring and unchangeable "national polity (*kokutai*)." In the hands of ultra-nationalists the *kokutai* was in later years to become a veritable fetish.[13]

Before the Emperor Meiji promulgated the new constitution on February 11, 1889, it received some consideration from the new Privy Council, which was made up of elder statesmen and headed by Itō. Although Kaneko compared these closed sessions to the deliberations of the Philadelphia Constitutional Convention, nothing like the state constitutional conventions and accompanying newspaper debates followed. The Japanese people received their constitution as a gift from the throne, without any chance to discuss the wisdom of its provisions.

Instead, as the time drew near for opening of the Diet in 1890, attention focused on the practical details of parliamentary government. Among the books that the government translated for guidance were Thomas Jefferson's *A Manual of Parliamentary Practice* and L. S. Cushing's *Elements of the Law and Practice of Legislative Assemblies in the United States of America*. The rules of procedure actually adopted, however, left much more to the discretion of the presiding officer than in American practice. Kaneko was sent abroad in the summer of 1889 to study the working of Western legislatures. He considered a detailed investigation of the procedures of the United States Congress unnecessary because they were derived largely from English precedents, so he spent most of his time in Europe. Indicative of his emphasis upon externals was his choice, upon his return, of "The Architec-

---

[12] Yoshino Sakuzō, "Sutain, Gunaisuto, to Itō Hirobumi (Stein, Gneist, and Itō Hirobumi)," *Kaizō*, V. 15 (February 1933), pp. 60-77; Suzuki Yasuzō, "Nihon Kempō Seitei ni taisuru Heruman Resureru no Kiyo (The Contribution of Herman Roessler to the Establishment of the Japanese Constitution)," *Meiji Bunka Kenkyū (Studies in Meiji Culture)*, no. 5 (1935), pp. 46-71.
[13] Kaneko, *Kempō Seitei*, cited, pp. 94-107.

ture of Legislative Buildings" for a speech before the new Political Science Society.[14]

Kaneko had also carried with him copies of Itō's explanatory *Commentaries on the Constitution,* which he presented to Western leaders and scholars with a request for critical comments. The American critics were so impressed by the formal grant of a constitution that they failed to discern its weaknesses. Secretary of State James G. Blaine had not had time to read the *Commentaries* and could offer only very general advice. He approved of making the ministers of state responsible to the Emperor, a system which had some resemblance to the American executive cabinet. Address to the throne would be, he thought, a better way of removing delinquent officers than the American system of legislative impeachment, which had fallen into disuse. Professor James Bradley Thayer of Harvard Law School urged a broad interpretation of Article 67 to put all the regular expenses of government outside the control of the Diet. He also recommended that the new government should include all the surviving Restoration leaders, just as Washington's cabinet had brought together such diverse spirits as Hamilton and Jefferson.[15]

Kaneko also sent a copy of the *Commentaries* to his old friend, Oliver Wendell Holmes, Jr., then an associate justice on the Massachusetts Supreme Court. The Justice offered his congratulations on the conservative tone of the constitution; he had been afraid that rapid changes might destroy the ancient virtues of the Japanese government and people. "The thing that I like about this Constitution is that its basis is in ancient history and customs; yet to adorn these it has adopted the ideals of European and American constitutionalism." Justice Holmes did raise certain questions which may have been intended to reveal politely his mental reservations, but to judge by Kaneko's record they were largely rhetorical. He rejected the idea that the constitution satisfied the form but not the substance of the Charter Oath.

[14] Inada Masatsugu, "Kempō Kisō no Sankō Shiryō ni tsuite (Reference Materials for Drafting the Constitution)," *Kokka Gakkai Zasshi,* V. 55 (November 1941), p. 1352; Kaneko, *Kempō Seitei,* cited, pp. 198-199; *Kokka Gakkai Zasshi,* V. 5 (April 1891), pp. 907-930; (May 1891), pp. 975-994.
[15] Kaneko, *Kempō Seitei,* cited, pp. 200-204, 381-385.

In promulgating this constitution, he said, the Emperor did not limit himself to form only; he also granted real power. "His object was not to quiet temporarily the feelings of the people, but to establish the basis of the Japanese state for hundreds of years to come." Holmes warned that the operation of political parties would divide the people into factions, and that there would be struggles to control the premier. The secret of successful application of the constitution would lie, he said, in the political education and ability of the people.[16]

In retrospect we can see what Holmes did not: that the Meiji Constitution contained the seeds of Japan's future political difficulties. The provision making cabinet ministers responsible directly to the Emperor, rather than to the legislature, paved the way for a continued monopoly of power by the oligarchy. The elected House of Representatives could initiate measures, but concurrence of the House of Peers and ministerial signature were necessary before they became law. The power of the purse was severely limited by the provision that when the Diet did not pass the budget the government could carry out the one of the preceding year. Initiative for any amendment of the Constitution had to come from the Emperor. Certain civil liberties of the subjects were specified, but these were to be enjoyed only "within the limits of law." The relation between representative institutions and absolute Imperial sovereignty was not fully worked out; it was not specified how national leaders would obtain and pass on the crucial power of speaking and acting in the name of the Emperor. Certainly it would not be by any decision of the people.

For the moment the people at large were out of the picture; property qualifications limited the suffrage to a mere 450,000. The more immediate question was the role of the political parties. By vigorous campaigning the popular parties together obtained a majority in the first House of Representatives. But they faced the "transcendental" cabinet of General Yamagata, chosen by the inner clique without reference to party strength. When the party men tried to cut

16 Same, pp. 373-381. Kaneko does not make clear whether this was an oral or written statement.

the government budget, they were met with what became a familiar pattern of resistance: corruption of the weaker members, intimidation of the stronger by hired thugs. When the Second Diet was dissolved for recalcitrance on finances, the government used the police and the army, as well as bribery, in an unsuccessful attempt to get a favorable majority. As John H. Wigmore, who from his vantage point as professor of law at Keiō was sending keenly realistic reports to the *Nation,* observed: "Until parliamentary government by party arrives . . . there cannot but be more or less indecision on current questions, more or less fluidity and lack of cohesion in the party materials. Until then there will be only one real party—the Opposition." [17]

For the first five years there was at least a vital opposition. But with the onset of the Sino-Japanese War the parties yielded all too quickly to appeals of patriotism and accepted the government program without a murmur. After the war they began to seek a share in power and patronage through alliances with the oligarchy. In 1895 the Jiyūtō came to the support of Itō's cabinet, and in repayment Itagaki was made Home Minister. The Satsuma cabinet headed by Matsukata that took office in 1896 courted a new Progressive Party (Shimpotō) grouping led by Ōkuma. These alliances were always unstable, however, and in 1898 the two factions joined in a new Constitutional Party (Kenseitō). To their own great surprise, Ōkuma and Itagaki were directed to form a cabinet. Unfortunately, the parties muffed their first chance to show that responsible government could be a success. Quarrels over the spoils of office split apart the two wings of the Shimpotō before it had a chance to carry out any constructive program. The Liberals joined in the public outcry against Minister of Education Ozaki Yukio for his hypothetical statement that if Japan were a republic like America, she would elect one of the *zaibatsu* president. After only four months the Cabinet was forced to resign, and control reverted to the oligarchy.[18]

17 *Nation,* V. 51 (August 21, 1890), p. 146.
18 Garrett Droppers' dispatches to the *Nation,* e. g., V. 64 (June 3, 1897), pp. 411-412; V. 65 (December 23, 1897), pp. 494-496; V. 67 (August 4, 1898), pp. 91-92; (October 6, 1898), pp. 256-257; (December 1, 1898), pp. 407-408, stand up very well in comparison with recent historical studies. The Westerner

During the next fifteen years the parties found themselves completely hamstrung. In 1900 General Yamagata Aritomo engineered an Imperial Ordinance which required that the Navy and Army Ministries be held by senior officers on the active list, thus making it possible for either service to wreck any cabinet. Civil service regulations were used to keep positions in the bureaucracy out of party hands. The Imperial University graduates admitted by examination were amenable to oligarchic control, and they could always exert pressure upward through the ranks upon any minister. In order to obtain leadership by Itō, the old Liberal group, now renamed the Seiyūkai, had to promise obedience, even to the extent of cooperating with Yamagata's protégé, Katsura Tarō. Bureaucrats like Hara Takashi began to infiltrate the Seiyūkai leadership, blurring the lines between government and party. The party might rebel, as it did in 1913 against Katsura's use of Imperial rescripts as bludgeons, but it could not exercise power without working arrangements with the oligarchy and the armed forces.[19]

These experiments in representative government proceeded with little reference to American experience, even by party leaders. Japanese attention focused on the material progress of the United States and its increasingly active role in the diplomacy of the Pacific area. Only after the beginning of World War I, after a time lag, did the revitalization of American public life by the various reform movements that we lump together as progressivism have an impact upon Japan.

From the standpoint of the Japanese government, some ideas filtering in from America were a positive menace. In 1887 a group of the more radical members of the Jiyūtō had gone to San Francisco. From this haven of the free press they sent back to Japan newspapers and magazines filled with political criticism that would never have been allowed under the Peace Preservation Ordinance. As fast as these journals

wishing to follow Japanese political life during those years also had the advantage of very full and informed reporting in the *Japan Weekly Mail* of Yokohama.
[19] Yanaga Chitoshi, *Japan Since Perry* (New York: McGraw-Hill, 1949), pp. 316-324; Scalapino, cited, pp. 179-199.

were banned, they reappeared under different titles and through new channels of surreptitious distribution.[20]

Socialist thought was also appearing as an offshoot of American Protestant mission work. In 1887 Tokutomi Iichirō, one of the young men Niishima Jō trained at Dōshisha, started a journal called *Kokumin no Tomo* (*The People's Friend*), which advocated a threefold program of political freedom, economic equality, and Christian morality. The missionary Charles E. Garst was such an earnest advocate of the theories of Henry George that he was popularly known as "Single-tax Tarō." Among the members of the Association for the Study of Socialism which began meeting in 1898 at Unitarian Hall, Tokyo, were Abe Iso-o, Katayama Sen, and Murai Tomoyoshi, all of whom had imbibed a Christian Socialist utopianism while studying at American theological seminaries.[21] For Abe the experience of first reading Edward Bellamy's *Looking Backward* had "some resemblance to that of St. Paul on the road to Damascus. At that time I became an avowed socialist." [22] It was Richard T. Ely's articles on social questions in the *Christian Union* that started Katayama on a career that led through socialism to communism and a long exile to Russia.[23] As long as these socialist intellectuals limited themselves to discussion and propaganda, they were tolerated by the government, but an attempt to establish a Social Democratic Party in 1901 was promptly suppressed. Likewise, a new Socialist Party established in 1906 was wrecked by the exposure four years later of Kōtoku Denjiro's direct action plot against the Emperor. The fact that Kōtoku and several of his associates had spent some time in the United States did not escape notice.[24]

[20] Ebihara Hachirō, "Sōkō Nihonjin Aikoku Dōmei Shimatsu (An Account of the Japanese Patriotic League in San Francisco)," *Meiji Bunka Kenkyū*, No. 2 (1934), pp. 98-117.

[21] Abe Kōzō, "Meiji Kōki ni okeru Kirisutokyō to Shakai-shugi (Christianity and Socialism in the Latter Part of Meiji)," *Riron*, V. 4 (January 1950), pp. 1-13; Matsumiya Kazuya, *Nihon Kirisutokyō Shakai Bunka Shi* (*History of Christian Society and Culture in Japan*) (Tokyo: Shin Kigen-sha, 1948), pp. 184-186, 189-192.

[22] *Japan Mission Year Book, 1934,* pp. 247-248.

[23] Katayama Sen, *Jiden* (*Autobiography*) (Tokyo: Kaizō-sha, 1931), p. 194.

[24] Hyman Kublin, "The Origins of Japanese Socialist Tradition," *Journal of Politics*, V. 14 (May 1952), pp. 257-280, gives an excellent account of the early socialist movement.

Japan's participation in World War I on the side of the Allied powers raised new questions of political philosophy. The slogan of democracy used in opposition to German absolutism and militarism obviously had implications at home. The issue was posed for public discussion early in 1916 by a long article on "The True Meaning of Constitutional Government and the Means of Attaining its Perfection," written for the New Year's number of *Chūō Kōron* by Professor Yoshino Sakuzō of Tokyo Imperial University. From the student Y.M.C.A. and Ebina Danjō's Hongo Congregational Church, Yoshino had gained a liberal Christian point of view. During study in England he had observed the movement for limitation of the power of the House of Lords. In America he had been impressed by the fact that a system of broad suffrage could bring to the top leaders of the stature of Theodore Roosevelt and Woodrow Wilson.[25]

To avoid offense to the sacred position of the Emperor, Yoshino made a careful distinction in terms. He was not discussing, he said, *minshu shugi,* the doctrine that the sovereignty of the state resides in the people. Instead, he was proposing *mimpon shugi,* which meant that sovereignty should be employed according to the will of the people for the general welfare. In practice this would mean universal suffrage and responsible party cabinets. "Since the people are the best judges of their own interest, constitutional government based on democracy is the form of government which best satisfies the deep psychological needs of men." [26]

Yoshino's article precipitated a great debate in the popular journals. Conservatives argued for the "personal rule of the Emperor;" socialists attacked his program as much too limited. Yoshino continued to elaborate his position in other articles for *Chūō Kōron,* and in the *Ōsaka Asahi* Ōyama Ikuo argued that democracy would finally be the realization of the Charter Oath. In December 1918 a group of sympathetic scholars organized the Reimeikai (Dawn Society) to sponsor monthly lectures. Yoshino's followers among the

25 *Yoshino Sakuzō Hakushi Minshu Shugi Ronshū; Dai Ikkan: Mimpon Shugi Ron (Dr. Yoshino Sakuzō's Collected Essays on Democracy; Vol. I: Essays on "Mimpon Shugi")* (Tokyo: Shin Kigen-sha, 1946), pp. 6, 322-323.
26 Same, pp. 30-31, 329.

students of the College of Law, Tokyo Imperial University
—the very training-ground of the bureaucracy—organized the
New Man Society (Shinjinkai). In February 1919 Waseda
University students formed the People's League (Minjin
Dōmei). But aside from the students and a portion of the
small labor movement, the democratic crusade enlisted little
organized support. Most serious was the failure of either of
the political parties to make its ideology the basis for a
strong practical movement toward universal suffrage and
responsible government.[27]

If this democratic movement had attracted more sympathy
and support abroad, it might have been able to gain in
strength and respectability at home. But the attention and
hopes of Americans were centered instead upon the ministries of Ōkuma Shigenobu (1914–1916) and of Hara Takashi (1918–1921). Ōkuma was hailed as the "Jeffersonian
Premier" and "Japan's first democrat." [28] But in office he
proved to be a great disappointment to the liberal cause. He
pushed through the Diet provision for two new divisions for
which the Army had long been asking without success. His
foreign policy was characterized by the aggressive Twenty-
one Demands upon China. Hara had the glamour of being
the first commoner, that is, the first person without a title of
nobility, to hold the office of premier. He did allow the labor unions a rather ambiguous status of neither illegality
nor official recognition. But his government was also responsible for jailing Professor Morito Tatsuo for writing a scholarly article on Kropotkin. And strangest spectacle of all,
Hara dissolved the Diet in 1920 because it insisted on too
rapid an advance toward universal suffrage.[29]

With the parties indifferent to ideals, the intellectual enthusiasm for democracy was slowly crushed to bits between
the twin millstones of communism and militant nationalism.
On the one hand, the success of the Bolshevist revolution

[27] Sugiyama Kenji, "Social Thinking in Japanese Universities and Colleges,"
Japan Mission Year Book, 1930, pp. 195-196; Kikukawa Tadao, *Gakusei
Shakai Undō Shi (History of Student Social Movements)* (Rev. ed.; Tokyo:
Unokuchi Shoten, 1947), pp. 18-54.
[28] *Literary Digest*, May 2, 1914; Carl Crow, "Japan's First Democrat," *World's
Work*, V. 30 (June 1915), pp. 150-155.
[29] Scalapino, cited, pp. 204-221, discusses this period with great insight.

made a deep impression in Japan. Just when economic and social tensions had been heightened by rapid wartime industrialization, the Communists appeared upon the scene with a practical program. To the intellectuals they offered the seductive doctrine of Marxism. Student groups like the Shinjinkai and the Minjin Dōmei were soon captured by the Communists. In reaction the government arrested radical students and prohibited all societies for the study of "social science." The true liberals were hardest hit, for they were not disposed to resort to clandestine activity. Professor Yoshino, for example, gave up pamphleteering for democracy and devoted the rest of his life to historical studies.

At the same time, ominous fascistic groups were appearing on the right. From the first the democrats had been attacked, often physically, by the Rōninkai, a branch of the notorious Black Dragon Society. Some of these nationalist groups were, in their own way, revolutionary in intent. Kita Ikki's Yūzonsha demanded a strong industrial state under the absolute control of the military; the Nōmin Jichi Kyōkai, in contrast, wanted to return to a decentralized agrarian society. The most respectable was the National Foundation Society (Kokuhonsha), organized in 1924 by vice-president of the Privy Council Hiranuma Kiichirō. Its emphasis on revival of the spiritual values of the indigenous Japanese culture was to become the official ideology.[30]

But before the ultra-nationalists gained sway in the 1930's, Japan was to reach its prewar peak in political evolution. From 1925 to 1932 Japan had, on the surface, a working system of responsible cabinet government. Legislation providing for universal adult male suffrage went into effect in the local contests of 1927 and the general election of 1928. A number of competing proletarian and agrarian parties appeared upon the scene.

During this period some interest was shown, in academic circles and in popular magazines, in the practical working of the American party system. Sasa Hiroo discussed in *Kaizō* the political role of labor in the United States, and Yoshi-

[30] Yanaga, cited, pp. 490-495; Kinoshita Hanji, *Nihon Fashizumu Shi* (*History of Japanese Fascism*) (Tokyo: Iwasaki Shoten, 1950–1951), V. 1, pp. 10-11, 41-45.

kawa Kijirō adapted for the Japanese audience some of
Charles E. Merriam's findings on the social makeup of American parties.[31] In 1922 Ōishi Kumakichi translated E. S.
Corwin's article-by-article commentary on *The Constitution
and What It Means Today* under the title *Beikoku Kempō
Yōron.* Nitobe Inazō and Minobe Tatsukichi lectured on
American history and public law at Tokyo University under
the terms of the endowment created by A. Barton Hepburn.[32] Another active student and publicist was Professor
Fujii Shinichi of Waseda University. To complement a
rather legalistic study of the federal and state constitutions
(*Beikoku Kempō Ron,* 1926), he published in 1927 "A Survey of American Party Government." Here Fujii explored
the relations between parties and democracy, with the conclusion that the Japanese "should wait to see whether the
Americans become the slaves of this system of democratic
government and fail to have wise rule, or whether they will
succeed in awakening public opinion and educating the people and thus really show the value of the system." [33]

Americans were inclined to take the new political developments in Japan at face value. A Far Eastern expert of the
War Department's Military Intelligence Division wrote that
the suffrage act marked "a turning-point in Japanese history
as great as was Magna Charta's in England." [34] In *Harper's*
Stanley High answered the question "Is Japan Going Democratic?" in the affirmative:

---

[31] Sasa Hiroo, "Amerika Rōdō Kaikyū no Seiji Kōdō (Political Activity of the
American Laboring Classes)," *Kaizō,* V. 10 (September 1928), pp. 64-81;
Yoshikawa Kijirō, "Beikoku Seitō no Shakaiteki Kōsei (The Social Structure
of American Political Parties)," *Gaikō Jihō,* no. 528 (December 1, 1926), pp.
76-96.

[32] In 1918 Hepburn, then just retiring as Chairman of the Board of the Chase
National Bank, endowed a professorship in American Constitution, History,
and Diplomacy. Joseph Bucklin Bishop, *A. Barton Hepburn: His Life and
Service to His Time* (New York: Scribner's, 1923), pp. 295-316. After several
years of study in the United States, Takagi Yasaka became the first holder
of this chair. His first major work, published in 1931, was an *Introduction
to American Political History (Beikoku Seiji Shi Jōsetsu).* It is devoted almost entirely to the period before 1800.

[33] Fujii Shinichi, *Beikoku Seitō Seiji no Kansoku* (Tokyo: Waseda Daigaku
Shuppanbu, 1927), p. 472.

[34] Margaret de Forest Hicks, "New Forces in Old Japan," *Century Magazine,*
V. 111 (April 1926), p. 729.

The Jingoes have not, by any means, been silenced. But their voices are no longer the voice of Japan. Their ultra-nationalism is being tempered by contact with a new Japan that feels itself a part of a world-wide movement to end war, to remedy economic injustice, to establish for the good of the common man the institutions of democracy.[35]

Indeed, the future might have lain in that direction if Japan had not become involved in a world depression. Under the pressure of economic distress the parties had neither the support from without nor the cohesion within to resist those who wanted to find a solution through aggressive expansion.

The consequences of our inadequate understanding of political complexities in Japan became apparent in the Manchurian crisis of 1931. It is difficult and dangerous, of course, to pull one thread out of that involved tangle. Public opinion in America strongly opposed any strong action in coöperation with the League of Nations. But in the early stages of the crisis the ruling consideration in Secretary of State Stimson's mind was the belief that the military action in Manchuria was a simple case of disobedience that the Wakatsuki-Shidehara ministry could quite easily bring under control. In order to avoid embarrassing the civilians, he opposed the use of an on-the-spot investigating commission.[36] An impartial report on the facts of the case was essential for any prompt action by the League. By the time the more pretentious Lytton Commission was constituted, visited the area, and made its report, the Japanese aggression was consolidated beyond repair.

Actually, without firm pressure from the outside, Wakatsuki and Shidehara had little chance of controlling the situation. If treaty violation could have been proved quickly, the Army might have been forced to place the responsibility on local commanders. The War Minister, General Minami, admitted that they were acting without orders, but he kept

---

[35] *Harper's Magazine*, V. 158 (January 1929), pp. 218-225.
[36] Stimson's position was most clearly stated in his telephone conversations with Norman Davis and Hugh Wilson on September 23, 1931. *Foreign Relations of the United States, 1931*, V. 3, pp. 43-47, 49-52. Until the United States raised a strong objection, the League was apparently determined to carry out the investigation, "if necessary under the authorization of China alone." Same, p. 37.

giving excuses that occupation of more territory was necessary in self-defense. To withdraw voluntarily from what were
considered legal positions would have been too great a strain
on the national honor. Many of the younger men in the Foreign Office were sympathetic to expansion. Playing a devious
political game of his own, Home Minister Adachi Kenzō
brought down the Minseitō Cabinet in December by insist-
ing on coalition with the Seiyūkai. Weak and divided, the
government did not want to make war, but it could not
make peace unless it was pushed hard by world opinion.[37]

In the 1930's Japan was feeling the full effect of the failure
of the Meiji Constitution to make a definite assignment of
ultimate authority. The surprising thing about the Japanese
totalitarian state was that power remained so diffuse and uncertain. Until his death in 1940, Saionji, the last of the
genrō (elder statesmen), usually threw his weight on the side
of moderation. The officials of the Imperial Household with
direct access to the Emperor avoided positive leadership but
could exercise restraint upon any situation. The political
parties were so rent with dissension that even amalgamation
into the Imperial Rule Assistance Association in 1940 could
not submerge factional differences. The Navy did not fully
share the enthusiasm for expansion on the Continent, and
even within the Army the young officer extremists and the
older administrators had quite different goals. The mass of
the people were anesthetized into rather fearful acceptance
of whatever action was declared to be necessary for the good
of the state.

Surface appearances of harmony and efficiency kept Americans from appreciating the full extent of this basic political
instability. Japanese institutions looked deceptively like our
own. When Professor Samuel McCune Lindsay of Columbia
University visited Japan in 1930 he reported that:

Here we found a country divided into prefectures like our own
states. In public life there were governors, politicians, and legis-
lators of these prefectures; mayors, councilmen, park and recrea-

[37] *Wakatsuki Reijirō Jiden: Kofūan Kaikoroku (Autobiography of Wakatsuki
Reijirō: Memoirs of Kofūan)* (Tokyo: Yomiuri Shimbun-sha 1950), pp. 375-
380, 383-387; Shidehara Kijūrō, *Gaikō Gojūnen (Fifty Years of Diplomacy)*
(Tokyo: Yomiuri Shimbun-sha, 1951), pp. 166-183.

tion commissions, local government officials without number, and traffic officers in the streets. All the way along the line, in fact, up to the imperial Ministers of State, we found almost exact duplicates of the corresponding officials in our own country. . . . The Japanese people in every walk of life are, at heart, exceptionally akin to the people of the United States.[38]

Furthermore, the Japanese seemed to be still learning from us. The trip to America and Europe for observation of matters relating to his specialty had become part of the training and perquisites of a higher bureaucrat. Kaneko Takemaro, who was private secretary to Japan's prime ministers in 1923 and 1924 and again from 1927 to 1934, made two such trips. The head of the Ministry of Justice secretariat, Sakano Chisato, was sent abroad in 1927. During the thirties many technical specialists went abroad to study new developments. The sight of frequent Japanese visitors, industriously using notebook and camera, gave an exaggerated notion of the influence that our system was exerting upon institutional development in Japan.

The truly distinctive features of American political life actually seemed either irrelevant or downright distasteful to Japanese before the war. Our federal system had no application to Japan's problems of centralized control. American diplomats had the unpleasant task of explaining repeatedly that because of dual sovereignty national officials could deal with state legislation discriminating against Orientals only through moral suasion. "If our Home Minister were to beg a prefectural governor to make a certain political decision, we would think it very strange," commented one Japanese observer, "yet in America . . . this is a common occurrence." [39] The interplay of sectional interests in the Congress made it impossible to repeal the immigration exclusion law to which the majority of the American people professed to be opposed. In comparison to the position of the Emperor, the necessity for the head of the American state to run the gauntlet of popular election seemed vulgar. In general, Japanese

[38] Samuel McCune Lindsay, "Japan as Seen in 1930," *Review of Reviews,* November 1930, p. 71.
[39] Suzuki Hanzaburō, *Beikoku Kokuminsei no Shin Kenkyū (A New Study of American National Character)* (Tokyo: Rakuyōdō, 1916), p. 113.

paid more attention to corruption in American politics than to its democratic base.

Through the printed page and personal observation the Japanese had in the years before 1941 obtained fairly adequate information about political institutions in the United States. Why, then, did the American example exert so little influence, excite so little interest in emulation? Fundamentally the answer may lie in differences in the conception of the function of government. At the risk of oversimplification, one might say that the American tradition has been an individualistic one, which has regarded the state with suspicion and limited its functions to protection of men's rights, leaving them free to pursue wealth and happiness. Even the expansion of government action under the New Deal had as its goal service and security for the individual. In modern Japan, by contrast, the national peril seemed so great, the need for national development so urgent, that attention was focused on the fate of the whole nation rather than on the welfare of its members. Coupled with a long historical experience of authoritarian rule, this led to concentration of ultimate authority in the hands of a few self-appointed leaders rather than in the people at large. It produced a government of men rather than of laws. Nor did the Japanese take much from the United States on the lower level of practical technique. The American system allowed too much local variation, too much uncertainty, too much room for experimentation. In their desire for firm control and ritual regularity, the Japanese preferred a uniform pattern of administration, a codified system of law. Other examples of Western-type institutions, particularly those drawn from Germany, seemed more congenial and adaptable.

Revolution by Directive: Occupation Reforms

Past relations, then, provided only a very limited basis for reform of Japanese political institutions under American guidance during the military occupation. There were, however, certain advantageous general conditions. The high degree of literacy of the Japanese people, unequaled elsewhere in Asia, provided a good basis for political progress.

Despite its many faults, the party system had given considerable familiarity with the processes and problems of popular government. The family and hierarchical relations that had always been such an obstacle to democracy had been weakened by the war and the postwar chaos; the grim problem of individual survival put nearly everyone on an equal basis.[40] The very shock of defeat gave rise to a widespread demand for fundamental change.

It was unfortunate that changes in the Japanese constitution could not have come about at the initiative of the government of the country and as the freely expressed will of the people. But the conservative Shidehara cabinet responded very slowly to SCAP requests for revision. The draft submitted early in February 1946 by the Constitutional Problem Investigation Committee headed by Matsumoto Jōji made little more than verbal changes in the Meiji Constitution. Severely disappointed, General MacArthur directed the Government Section of his headquarters to prepare a draft constitution for the guidance of the Japanese. In seven days of intensive work, officers of the Section prepared a basic law for the defeated nation. This draft underwent some changes in detail during discussions with the Cabinet and consideration by the two houses of the Diet, but its basic principles and general outline were retained in the Constitution promulgated on November 3, 1946, to go into effect six months later. The origin of the document behind closed doors in GHQ has given rise to bitter Japanese jibes about being unable to understand the Constitution because unable to read English. But the majority of the Japanese people seem to have understood that in no other way could a reform so thoroughgoing and so satisfactory have been obtained.[41]

The end result might be called a redefinition of Japanese institutions according to American principles.[42] The Emperor was retained, but only as "the symbol of the state and

[40] On this point see the remarks in Mishima Sumie, *The Broader Way: A Woman's Life in the New Japan* (New York: John Day, 1953), pp. 11, 17-18, 29, 133-134.
[41] *Political Reorientation of Japan,* cited, V. 1, pp. 98-111.
[42] The text of the new Japanese Constitution can be found in *Political Reorientation of Japan,* cited, V. 2, pp. 671-677.

of the unity of the people." All authority was explicitly stated to be derived from the sovereign people. The power of the people was to be exercised through elected representatives in the two houses of the Diet. Despite MacArthur's expressed preference for a unicameral legislature, a House of Councilors was provided to give somewhat the same kind of maturity and continuity that is provided by the House of Lords in Great Britain. The House of Representatives can, however, enact into law a measure rejected by the Councilors by repassing it by a two-thirds vote. The power of the Councilors to interfere with the budget or with ratification of treaties was also severely limited. The Supreme Court was empowered to review the constitutionality of laws, but no provision was made for executive veto.

The American type of elected executive was never even seriously considered; the Constitution followed Japanese prewar experience by providing for a cabinet form of government. Every precaution, however, was taken to make the cabinet responsible. The Prime Minister must be chosen by the Diet from among its own members, and a majority of the other ministers must also be drawn from the legislature. The ministers must appear before the Houses to give explanations and answer questions. If the House of Representatives passes a vote of no-confidence, the cabinet must either resign or dissolve the House and call new elections.

In operation Japan's cabinet system has shown some of the same weaknesses that afflicted the prewar parties. Except in 1947, when a series of elections close together exhausted some of the enthusiasm, about three-fourths of all those eligible have cast ballots for members of the House of Representatives. But in rural areas, particularly, firm semi-feudal loyalties to local bosses have made possible outright vote brokerage.[43] Cliques control the parties with little deference even to the wishes of the limited number of formal members. Factionalism has been rampant: the Socialists have split into left and right wings, and competition for leadership between Yoshida Shigeru and Hatoyama Ichirō divided the

43 See Robert E. Ward, "Patterns of Stability and Change in Rural Japanese Politics," University of Michigan, Center for Japanese Studies, *Occasional Papers*, no. 1, pp. 1-6.

Liberals. Yoshida's tenure as Premier continuously from 1948 to 1954 produced fairly consistent policies of conservatism in economic matters and cooperation with the United States, but much of the time he had to rely upon an unstable coalition in the Diet.

Gains by the Left-wing Socialists in the elections of April 1953 and February 1955 suggest that they may be the pole around which the opposition will coalesce. The Socialist cabinet of Katayama Tetsu, however, was unable to carry its program into effect in 1947–48, partly because it too had to depend on a coalition. Its attempts to govern by administrative orders without authorization from the Diet brought a severe rebuke from MacArthur.[44] The tendency for much radical opinion to stand outside the parties is also disturbing. Although the Communists have become a negligible factor at the polls, they are still strong in the labor unions.[45]

The Japanese press and people are becoming increasingly aware of the dangers and inefficiency of party splintering, and are hoping for something like a two-party system. Americans should not be disappointed if the result does not resemble our own system, where the Democratic and Republican parties are both fairly conservative and not far apart on major issues. Now that many depurged leaders have returned to public life, the Japanese Liberal and Democratic parties are coming to look more and more like the old Seiyūkai and Minseitō. It would be unfortunate if they merely jockeyed for power without facing up to the great problems that beset Japan. The people might again become disillusioned with the party system and turn to either militarism or communism. Japan would be better served by a clear-cut Labor or Socialist party that would offer a definite alternative in both economic and foreign policy. Americans should not be blind to this point because of the present opposition of the Socialists to rearmament.

[44] *New York Times*, September 6, 1947.
[45] For detailed accounts of the postwar Japanese politics see *American Political Science Review*, V. 42 (October 1948), pp. 927-969, (December 1948), pp. 1149-1180; Robert A. Scalapino, "Politics and Public Opinion in Japan," *Foreign Policy Reports*, V. 27 (March 15, 1951); and Scalapino, "Japan and the General Elections," *Far Eastern Survey*, V. 21 (October 29, 1952), pp. 149-154.

Few questions arouse greater interest in Japan at present than the interpretation of Article IX of the new constitution, which renounces "war as a sovereign right of the nation and the threat or use of force as a means of settling international disputes." This point was specified for inclusion by MacArthur himself, at a time when a permanently neutralized Japan seemed the best contribution to world peace. Under changed conditions it now seems that Japan ought to contribute to her own defense against Communist aggression. Ashida Hitoshi argues that by inserting the words "in order to accomplish the aim of the preceding paragraph" between the above statement of renunciation and the provision that "land, sea, and air forces, as well as other war potential, will never be maintained," he left the way open for armament in self-defense.[46] But read in conjunction with the statement in the preamble that "we have determined to preserve our security and existence, trusting in the justice and faith of the peace-loving peoples of the world," Ashida's point seems at least debatable. At present the majority of the Japanese people would probably be unwilling to amend the constitution with a positive statement of the right of self-defense. Another procedure would be to use a legal case to bring into play the Supreme Court's power of constitutional interpretation. The danger is that by urging the Japanese to circumvent what they believe to be the intent of their fundamental law Americans will be destroying Japanese faith in constitutionalism itself, in the supremacy of laws over men.

In order to reduce the possibility that the new political principles would be subverted in practice, SCAP put great emphasis on reform of the higher bureaucracy. Luckily, it was possible to take advantage of a request by the Minister of Finance for an expert American commission to study the civil service. The work was begun in November 1946 by a four-man Personnel Advisory Mission headed by Blaine Hoover, President of the Civil Service Assembly of the United States and Canada. Hoover then stayed on as chief of a new Civil Service Division in Government Section. In

[46] Ashida Hitoshi, "Japan: Communists' Temptation," *Contemporary Japan*, V. 20 (January-March 1951), pp. 21-23; *New York Times*, October 5, 1953.

January 1950 all senior administrators from vice-ministers down to section chiefs had to compete for their positions against outsiders. The press reported that as a result of these examinations 40 percent of the posts changed hands and 27 percent of the incumbents lost their jobs because of failure to qualify.[47] The Civil Service Division of SCAP also made a scientific classification of positions and trained over 1,200 persons in modern methods of personnel administration. A National Personnel Authority resembling our Civil Service Commission was given a position of substantial independence.[48]

The process of formal adjustment of the administrative system has been continued in accordance with the report of a Japanese "Hoover Commission" in 1951. But it is doubtful whether Japanese bureaucrats have yet thoroughly accepted the concept of service to the public. Japanese administration has traditionally paid more attention to codes of regulations than to the actual conditions to which they were intended to apply. If possible, a case was disposed of under existing rules; if not, a legally consistent revision was made. For this reason top posts were monopolized by men who had received a strictly legal training at Tokyo or Kyōto Imperial University. Technical details were disposed of by low-paid subordinates, and most of the contact with the people was handled by the police. Only by dint of great persistence did the Natural Resources Section of SCAP succeed in getting a professional forester appointed as head of the Forestry Bureau. Real change in administrative practice will depend upon a younger generation of civil servants trained to have respect for the pragmatic situations with which they deal.[49]

---

[47] *Mainichi Shimbun,* January 26, 1951.

[48] *Political Reorientation of Japan,* cited, V. 1, pp. 246-259; Foster Roser, "Establishing a Modern Merit System in Japan," *Public Personnel Review,* V. 11 (October 1950), pp. 199-206. There are some indications that the National Personnel Authority has now become a stronghold of bureaucratic obstruction. A bill to bring it under control of the Office of the Prime Minister failed to pass in 1952. Ardath W. Burks, "A Note on the Emerging Administrative Structure of the Post-Treaty Japanese National Government," University of Michigan, Center for Japanese Studies, *Occasional Papers,* No. 3, pp. 51-53.

[49] Milton J. Esman, "Japanese Administration—A Comparative View," *Public Administration Review,* V. 7 (Spring 1947), pp. 100-112.

Local Government. Occupation reforms in local government had the dual purpose of further reducing the power of the national bureaucracy and giving the people an opportunity for training in democracy. Before the war Japan had a highly centralized system in which all authority emanated from the Home Ministry in Tokyo down through the prefectural governors to a multitude of local officials. The elected assemblies of the prefectures, cities, towns and villages were used to secure compliance with policy sent down from on high rather than to take account of local needs and desires.

Japan had drawn upon the experience of the world in order to bring this system to what was, in its own way, a high peak of efficiency. As early as 1872 Yuri Kimmasa, the governor of Tokyo-fu, was sent to America to investigate municipal problems. He was most concerned with the physical services of cities—streets, waterworks, hospitals, etc.—but he also noted the functions of the city council. Yuri did not have a chance to apply directly what he had learned, however, for while he was gone he was jockeyed out of office.[50] In their concern for efficiency and uniformity of legal provisions, the Japanese turned primarily to German experience in local government. The basic Law of Municipalities and Towns adopted in 1888 was largely the work of adviser Albert Mosse, who was a protégé of Rudolf Gneist.

We must remember, however, that during the period of "civic renaissance" from 1895 to 1914 Americans, too, were turning to Germany for scientific methods of city planning and administration. To German ideas of efficient organization Americans added a characteristic respect for fact-finding and practical solutions. In 1920, when Germany was discredited and disorganized by defeat, the New York Bureau of Municipal Research caught the attention of the Japanese. When Gotō Shimpei took over as reform mayor of Tokyo, he asked his son-in-law, Tsurumi Yūsuke, to make some studies of urban problems in the United States. Tsurumi consulted Charles A. Beard, and Beard referred him to the Bureau of Municipal Research. Gotō was so impressed by its

---

[50] Yuri Masamichi, *Shishaku Yuri Kimmasa Den (Biography of Viscount Yuri Kimmasa)* (Tokyo: Yuri Masamichi, 1940), pp. 406-436.

work that he got money from Yasuda Zenjirō to establish a similar institute in Tokyo. Beard accepted an invitation to come to Japan to launch its work. The first step was a scientific survey of the problems of the capital city.[51] On the basis of this survey, Beard concluded that the basic difficulty was not any lack of knowledge about needs or modern methods of meeting them, but rather "in the absence of an adequate public spirit to support intelligent and enthusiastic municipal leaders." So he set out on a lecture tour of Japan, trying to interest the people in better cities. The essential reform, he urged, was the establishment of local autonomy by transferring all prefectural functions within the city to the municipal government. The people would have interest in their local affairs only if they had real responsibility.[52]

After Beard left Japan in 1923 the material problems of local government were greatly intensified by the wholesale destruction of Tokyo and Yokohama in the great earthquake and fire. As soon as he heard the news Beard cabled Gotō: "Lay out new streets, forbid building within street lines, unify railroad stations." He then returned to Japan for two months to help with plans for reconstruction of the capital as a truly modern city.[53]

The Tokyo Institute for Municipal Research was the one non-bureaucratic source of expert knowledge about local government upon which the Occupation could build. Through its journal *Toshi Mondai (Municipal Problems)* it kept Japan informed of progress in foreign countries. The Institute also maintained a specialized library and served as secretariat for the biennial National Conference on Municipal Affairs. Its representatives attended professional meetings abroad, including the city planning conference held in Washington, D.C., in 1927. In 1930 it was commissioned to

[51] Charles A. Beard, *The Administration and Politics of Tokyo: A Survey and Opinions* (New York: Macmillan, 1923).
[52] Beard's opinion as reported by Nakai Mitsuji, in *Report on Japan-American Pacific Coast Mayors' Conference, Tokyo Metropolis, October 30th-November 10th, 1951* (Tokyo: Liaison Office, Tokyo Metropolitan Government, 1952), p. 112.
[53] Tsurumi Yūsuke, "Gotō Haku to Biādo Hakushi (Count Gotō and Dr. Beard)," *Toshi Mondai (Municipal Problems)*, V. 8 (June 1929), pp. 1267-1280; Charles A. Beard, "The Awakening of Japanese Cities," *Review of Reviews*, V. 69 (May 1924), pp. 523-527.

make a survey of the organization and administration of public utilities in Japan's six largest cities. But since it stood for maximum local control, during the thirties the Institute was bypassed more and more by the Home Ministry.[54] On the subject of local government there were considerable differences of opinion within Occupation headquarters. Those concerned with Japan's pressing economic problems inclined toward retaining fairly extensive central controls. Others emphasized the need for local autonomy in order to give the people grass-roots training in democracy. The latter view was embodied in the new Constitution, which provided that all chief executives, officers, and members of local assemblies were to be chosen by direct popular vote. The Diet then abolished the once-powerful Home Ministry and passed a Local Autonomy Law which set out in detail the procedures by which local public bodies were "to manage their property, affairs, and administration." In April 1947, the Japanese people for the first time chose their own prefectural governors, mayors, and village headmen. To help some of these officials in their unfamiliar duties, SCAP arranged trips of observation for them in the United States under the National Leader Program.[55] Unfortunately, many suffered defeat in the elections of 1951 on the ground that they had brought back ideas that would require expenditures on an American scale.

The local seedbeds of democracy seem to have produced a vigorous growth. In the towns and villages, especially, the people have shown great interest in the conduct of local affairs. High standards of performance have been demanded of public officials; about 300 recall actions have been brought against mayors and assembly members, and many others have resigned to escape public censure. Local officials have found themselves in an uncomfortable middle position between the demands of constituents and their duty to execute a bewildering range of national legislation. The problem of raising by local taxation enough money to supply the necessary services has been almost insuperable. Professor George

[54] *Tōkyō Shisei Chōsakai to Sono Jigyō* (*The Tokyo Institute for Municipal Research and its Work*) (Tokyo: Tōkyō Shisei Chōsakai, 1948), pp. 13-21.
[55] Okuno Seiryō, *Amerika no Tabi* (*Travels in America*) (Tokyo: Chihō Zaimu Kyōkai, 1951), describes one such trip.

A. Warp of the University of Minnesota, who was in Japan in 1951–52 in connection with establishment of the Japan Local Self-government Institute, reports that some of the Occupation-inspired reforms may have to be abandoned. The many administrative boards and commissions that were set up, at a time when their efficiency in the United States was being questioned by political scientists, have proved to be both cumbersome and expensive. The Constitution will have to be amended if Japan is to use expert city managers.[56]

Rather then being merely correctives for the sake of efficiency, the changes now in the wind portend a return to central authoritarian controls. A bill passed in the last hectic days of the 1954 spring Diet session abolished autonomous local police forces, except in the six largest cities. Other recommendations made by the government's Local Institutions Investigation Council in 1953 are still under discussion. The prefectures may again become districts for national administration, with appointed governors. The proposed cabinet organ for local affairs sounds very much like the old Home Ministry. The Council also recommended that school boards be dispensed with except in the prefectures and in the big cities, where the members would be appointed instead of elected. The whole concept of local government as a training-ground for political democracy now seems to be in jeopardy.[57]

Civil liberties. For the first time in Japanese history, the new Constitution of 1947 gave the people secure protection in their personal rights against the actions of their own government. These rights were spelled out in considerably greater detail than in the American Constitution. In addition to freedom of speech, press, assembly, association, and residence, certain other rights that were conspicuously absent in prewar Japan were specified: marriage by mutual

---

[56] George A. Warp, "Nihon no Chihō Gyōsei ni Kansuru Jakkan no Kōsatsu (Some Observations on Local Administration in Japan)," *Toshi Mondai*, V. 43 (October 1952), pp. 1-33; and speeches by Warp printed in *National Municipal Review*, V. 41 (October 1952), pp. 443-448; V. 42 (April 1953), pp. 175-178, 188.

[57] *New York Times*, May 6, June 8, 1954; *Asahi Shimbun* and *The Mainichi*, August 22, 1953; Kurt Steiner, "Local Government in Japan: Reform and Reaction," *Far Eastern Survey*, V. 23 (July 1954), pp. 97-102.

consent, "the right to receive an equal education correspondent to their ability," and academic freedom. The economic
guarantees are not so property-centered as in our own fundamental law. The right of workers to organize and to bargain collectively was mentioned, and all people were to have
"the right and the obligation to work."

Legal system. Actual protection of these rights depends
upon the courts. In undertaking reform of the legal system,
the Occupation made no effort to overturn completely the
codes of law drafted during the late 19th century phase of
modernization on the basis of French and German precedents and Japanese custom. Instead SCAP sought to graft
upon the existing jurisprudence Anglo-American standards
of protection for human rights. The courts were reorganized
and made independent of executive control by the Ministry
of Justice. The many changes made in substantive law since
1945 are too complicated and technical for discussion here.
The matter of criminal procedure is so vital to security of
the individual, however, that Occupation authorities felt
justified in interfering more directly in its formulation than
in other fields of law.[58]

In prewar Japan anyone brought before a criminal court
suffered a strong presumption of guilt and received little
consideration for his rights of defense. In the absence of any
habeas corpus procedure he could be detained in jail for
long periods during investigation and preliminary examination of the case by the procurator. Third-degree methods were
used to obtain admissions of guilt, and a confession alone
was sufficient for conviction. At the public trial the judge
examined both defendant and witnesses. The accused had no
right to refuse to give incriminating testimony. The counsel
for the defendant could cross-examine witnesses only through
the judge. Hearsay evidence was freely admitted and could
serve as basis for conviction. Trials of "dangerous thinkers"
and other offenders against the Public Peace Preservation
Law followed a special procedure that gave them even less

[58] See Alfred C. Oppler, "The Reform of Japan's Legal and Judicial System
under Allied Occupation," *Washington Law Review,* V. 24 (August 1949), pp.
290-324.

protection.[59] Under such conditions it is not surprising that fewer than 1 per cent of all cases tried ended in acquittal.[60]

A limited form of jury trial was adopted in 1923, after thorough investigation and discussion of the working of the jury system in America and Europe.[61] With a few exceptions, a jury verdict on the facts was made mandatory for all offences punishable by death or life imprisonment. If the penalty could be more than three years imprisonment the defendant could demand a jury. But after the jury law went into effect in 1928, this right was seldom invoked.[62] The judge could refuse to accept the jury's verdict and submit the case to a second, or even a third jury. Never popular, the use of the jury was suspended in 1943 and it has not been restored since. As part of the democratic enthusiasm of the early twenties, the emphasis had been primarily on participation of the people in the administration of justice rather than on protection for the accused.

Articles 31 to 40 of the new Japanese constitution establish important safeguards based on Anglo-American practice: arrest only on warrant, no detention without adequate cause, right to counsel, right to obtain and examine witnesses, and protection against double jeopardy. In 1948 a high-level committee of Japanese and Americans revised the Code of Criminal Procedure to accord with these principles. Representatives of the bar associations were given a voice, as was the new Japanese Civil Liberties Union formed in 1947 under the guidance of Roger N. Baldwin.[63] A Habeas

[59] Harold S. Quigley, *Japanese Government and Politics* (New York: Century, 1933), p. 283; Tanaka Kazuo, "Law of Criminal Evidence in Japan," *Annals of the Hitosubashi Academy*, V. 2 (April 1952), p. 193.
[60] *Recent Developments in the Field of Criminal Justice in Japan* (Tokyo: Criminal Affairs Bureau, General Secretariat, Supreme Court of Japan, 1950), pp. 34-35.
[61] A party of officials headed by Ōi Daijirō spent several months in the United States in 1923. Some of their concerns were purely technical; the jury system made necessary physical rearrangement of Japanese courtrooms. *Japan Times and Mail Weekly*, August 25, 1923.
[62] Miyake Masatarō, *An Outline of the Japanese Judiciary* (2d ed.; Tokyo: Japan Times and Mail, 1935), pp. 5-6.
[63] Oppler, cited, pp. 303-304; Richard B. Appleton, "Reforms in Japanese Criminal Procedure under Allied Occupation," *Washington Law Review*, V. 25 (November 1949), pp. 401-430.

Corpus Act passed in 1948 gives additional protection against illegal detention.

The test of all these innovations will be in their application. For this reason SCAP sent more than sixty Japanese jurists to the United States to observe our courts in action. There are several indications, however, that old patterns are resistant to change. In nearly 60,000 cases tried in District Courts in 1949 the right of the accused to remain silent was invoked in only 0.23 percent. Confessions were obtained in 78.3 percent of these cases, although the confession must now be substantiated by other evidence. Judges complain that examination and cross-examination of all witnesses in open court increases the burden on dockets already overloaded by the postwar crime wave. Under stricter rules of evidence, the rate of acquittal has risen to between 1 and 2 percent, although this is still very low compared to British and American courts. The attitude of many Japanese jurists to the attempt of the new Code to both maintain the public welfare and secure the fundamental rights of individuals is indicated by the approving citation in an official report of the old proverb: "He who runs after two hares will catch neither." [64]

The Spirit of Democracy

Institutional forms can be changed quite rapidly; psychological reorientation of the Japanese people will take a much longer time. If their life is to be truly democratic, the Japanese must develop a heightened sense of individual independence and responsibility. In prewar days the typical Japanese was subservient in personal relations to the wishes of his family, in his public capacity to the dictates of the state. In government and in business, responsibility for individual initiative and decision was avoided by elaborate consultation and group approval.

The submergence of the Japanese personality should not be overstated, however, especially so far as concerns the urban classes. In the Meiji era Japan did offer varied careers for talent, and many found real satisfaction of achievement

[64] *Recent Development in Criminal Justice*, cited, pp. 35, 48-52.

in a new business firm or in a responsible government position. During and after the First World War, intellectuals began to discharge their growing sense of frustration by a self-conscious assertion of personality. In literature the potentialities of the liberated individual were expressed by the Shirakaba (White Birch) school of writers. Arishima Takeo, for example, found the gospel for the new day in the poems of Walt Whitman. Lecturing to the Shinjinkai in 1920, he recited lines which, in a Japanese context, were truly revolutionary:

> From this hour, freedom!
> From this hour I ordain myself loos'd
>   of limits and imaginary lines.
> Going where I list, my own master,
>   total and absolute,
> Listening to others, and considering well
>   what they say,
> Pausing, searching, receiving, contemplating,
> Gently, but with undeniable will,
>   divesting myself of the holds that would
>   hold me.
>   (From "Song of the Open Road") [65]

The conspicuous dress and amusements of the "modern boys" and "modern girls" of the 1920's was another way of asserting individuality. The militaristic control of the 1930's may have closed mouths but it did not wash brains. A great deal of private reading and speculation continued which since World War II has flowered into all shades of vigorous radicalism.

Postwar revision of the Civil Code has removed the principal legal obstacles to the development of individualism. Despite the arguments of conservatives that the existing family system was the basis of all peace and order, the institution of the "house" or large patriarchal unit, was abolished. Husband, wife, and minor children now form the family unit in law. Provision for inheritance in equal shares breaks the economic power of the larger family, although it does create the danger of excessive fragmentation of agricultural hold-

[65] *Arishima Takeo Zenshū* (*Collected Works of Arishima Takeo*) (Tokyo: Shinchō-sha, 1929-1930), V. 6, p. 435.

ings. The right of women to manage their own property and to share in their husband's estate is fully guaranteed. In case of divorce, a woman may demand a division of property.[66]

The women of Japan are perhaps the strongest source of potential support for the new political order. They realize that they owe their social and political rights to the American Occupation, and they are determined to fight any encroachments of returning feudalism. The bitter experience of defeat brought them a liberation for which they could otherwise hardly have hoped. In the Meiji era only a few unusual women like Kishida Toshiko and Fukuda Hideko participated in the struggle for popular government. From 1900 to 1923 women were forbidden by law to belong to political parties or to attend public meetings. A small women's suffrage movement did develop during the twenties, but it devoted most of its efforts to the preliminary step of getting the vote for all adult males. In 1928 one of the leaders, Ichikawa Fusae, visited the United States to study the part that women had played in the presidential campaign. Under the Hamaguchi cabinet there was some hope of getting the franchise in local elections. But after the Mukden incident women's suffrage, like other liberal movements, yielded to the relentless pressure of public opinion and patriotic demands.[67]

Despite their lack of preparation, Japanese women have played an active and mature role in postwar politics. Early in November 1945 Miss Ichikawa organized a Japanese League of Women Voters on the American model. Its efforts, together with those of SCAP, brought 67 percent of the females eligible to vote to the polls in April 1946. At that time thirty-nine women were elected to the House of Representatives. The reduction of this number to fewer than ten in recent elections probably indicates not apathy but a more sophisticated realization that voting for candidates of their own sex may not be the best way for women to make their votes count. Thousands have served on local assemblies, school boards, and administrative commissions. The women's

[66] Kurt Steiner, "The Revision of the Civil Code of Japan: Provisions Affecting the Family," *Far Eastern Quarterly*, V. 9 (February 1950), pp. 169-184.
[67] See Ide Kikuo, "History and Problems of the Women's Suffrage Movement in Japan," *Mid-Pacific Magazine*, V. 36 (September 1928), pp. 217-222.

organizations pushed hard for revision of the Civil Code provisions affecting the family. In the last two years they have set themselves firmly against the "reverse course" in Japanese life, including the movement for rearmament.[68]

What ideology, what basic values, underlie the many institutional changes that have occurred in Japan in recent years? With the help of the occupying forces, the Japanese for seven years were officially dedicated to the promotion of democracy. Americans high and low freely offered their private definitions of that elusive quality. In 1948 the Ministry of Education even published an ambitious *Primer of Democracy* for use by adult education groups and upper secondary schools. American publicists could very well draw upon this work for thoughtful restatements of our principles. Democracy is defined as "rooted in the minds and hearts of individuals. It is essentially a spiritual thing. It is a disposition and a willingness to deal with all human beings as individuals having worth and dignity of their own." The *Primer* then discusses in detail the political manifestations of democracy in Britain, Switzerland, and America. Social democracy is related to individualism, and the concept of self-abnegating service to the state so prevalent in Japan is definitely rejected. In personal relations the "vertical morality" of feudalism should be replaced by the "horizontal morality" of democracy. The question of economic democracy is handled in a way that might not satisfy the most strident American advocates of free enterprise. "Where democratic government prevails, we can, in accordance with the principle of majority rule, avail ourselves of the merits of capitalism, carry out more or less socialistic policies, or do both." But specific warnings are given against the insidious dangers of the new dictatorship of Communism.[69]

But we must remember that in Japan democracy is still an "ism." *Minshu-shugi* (democracy) is ranged semantically beside *shakai-shugi* (socialism) and *kyōsan-shugi* (communism) and must compete with them for practical results. "The unshaken optimism with which the Communists point

[68] Japan, Ministry of Labor, Women's and Minors' Bureau, *Statistical Materials Relating to Japanese Women* (1951); *Jiji Nenkan, 1953*, p. 283.
[69] Japan, Ministry of Education, *Primer of Democracy* (1948). No pagination in the English translation.

to the social progress of humanity," one Japanese woman has written, "is to them (the youth of postwar Japan) attractive and satisfactory in contrast to Western democratic liberalism; which is subtle in thought and often melancholy in temperament." [70]

Democracy as we know it in America is a condition more than a theory. That is why we have so much difficulty in defining it abstractly. The G.I.'s who tried to describe democracy to their Japanese friends in terms of electric refrigerators and a car in every garage were not entirely foolish; these material possessions do much to give Americans the self-respect and spirit of independence that lie at the root of democracy. Democracy is a quality manifested in varying degree in all parts of our way of life. We do not conclude that democracy is a failure because we still have discrimination against negroes, as our foreign critics are likely to do. Instead we try to make race relations more democratic. Democracy is not something we can give the Japanese all at once in a neat ideological package; it is a spirit and a method which we must help them to use in dealing with all their problems. For the Japanese there must be a continuing process of education. For Americans there is a challenge to make the best use of all the resources of cultural relations to strengthen democratic tendencies in Japan.

[70] Mishima, cited, p. 213.

CHAPTER FOUR

NEW EDUCATION FOR JAPAN?

IN THEIR efforts to encourage democracy in Japan, the Americans of the Occupation characteristically placed strong emphasis on education. Re-orientation and re-education of the Japanese people were made the special responsibility of a Civil Information and Education (CI & E) staff section in General Headquarters. The United States Education Mission that visited Japan during March 1946 was the first large group of outside advisers requested by SCAP. In their report the twenty-seven prominent educators of the Mission stated that the greatest hope for democracy lay in the children of Japan. "Sustaining, as they do, the weight of the future, they must not be pressed down by the heritage of a heavy past. We would, therefore, not only stop wrong teaching but also, as far as possible, equalize their opportunities, providing teachers and schools to inform their minds without hardening their hearts." [1]

For this stress on education there were at least two reasons. For one thing, Americans have, on the whole, an almost naive faith in the power of formal training to change people and to preserve the health of society. Perhaps it comes from watching immigrants from all parts of the world turn into fairly homogeneous Americans by the second generation. We rely upon education to maintain the high technical skills, the social mobility, and the attitudes of responsible citizenship that characterize our way of life. As a result, we tend to regard schooling alone as a sufficient guarantee of democracy. Prewar Japan itself is a warning that the social results of

[1] *Report of the United States Education Mission to Japan, submitted to the Supreme Commander for the Allied Powers, Tokyo, March 30, 1946* (Washington: GPO, 1946), p. 3.

education depend upon the political and intellectual milieu in which it operates. In school attendance and money spent for educational facilities, prewar Japan was among the leading countries of the world. Not basic ignorance, but susceptibility to indoctrination betrayed her people into a disastrous war.

Strong convictions that the Japanese people had suffered from badly warped values and ideology gave Americans additional reason for emphasis on re-education. We traced the fanaticism of the *banzai* charges, the *kamikaze* pilots, and the suicide boats back to the lessons that the Japanese had learned in the public schools. For this opinion there was some justification. Japanese militarists had used the schools, along with the press, the radio, and other means of communication to mobilize the people behind the war effort. A highly centralized system in which all curricula, textbooks, and teaching methods were controlled by the Ministry of Education (Mombushō) made this easy. The *Kokutai no Hongi (Cardinal Principles of the National Entity)* published in 1937 set a definite ideological line for the schools. Japan was a Divine Nation created by Amaterasu Ōmikami, the Sun Goddess, ruled by her descendants in an unbroken line of Divine Emperors, and endowed with a Divine Mission to bring the eight corners of the earth under the one roof of the Imperial Way.[2] History textbooks glorified martial virtues. In many schools the military officer responsible for drill and physical education dominated the other teachers and set the tone. In courses on ethics (*shūshin*) children learned how to be "good Japanese." Although most of the stories and homilies used for moral training were, as one analyst put it, "saccharine, bromidic, or insufferably dull— but hardly . . . dangerous," in an atmosphere of tension they helped to create nationalistic fervor.[3]

Fortunately, the wheels of bureaucracy turned so slowly that this system of indoctrination had never reached its ultimate efficiency. After years of deliberation, a thoroughgoing

---

[2] Robert K. Hall, ed., *Kokutai no Hongi: Cardinal Principles of the National Entity of Japan* (Cambridge, Mass.: Harvard University Press, 1949).

[3] Robert K. Hall, *Shūshin: The Ethics of a Defeated Nation* (New York: Teachers College, Columbia University, 1949), pp. 13-21.

reform intended to purge Japanese education of all individualism and foreign influences was announced in 1940, but it had little effect beyond the substitution of the name "national schools" for "elementary schools." Time and paper were lacking for a complete revision of textbooks. As the war became more critical, school courses were shortened, students spent more and more time on war production and civil defense, and finally evacuation, following the heavy air raids on Japanese cities, brought the educational system almost to a standstill.

The Occupation authorities first set out to destroy the old poisons. They banned military sports like *jūdō* and fencing and prohibited teaching of Shintō doctrines. They ordered the Ministry of Education to remove every one "known to be militaristic, ultranationalistic, or antagonistic to the objectives and policies of the Occupation" from administrative or teaching positions. After some embarrassment when the relatively innocuous character of the texts became apparent, CI & E suspended all teaching of ethics, Japanese history, and geography until new books could be compiled. Other textbooks were continued in use after deletions. The Japanese were exceedingly compliant, even anticipating some of the desired reforms. In June 1948 the Diet explicitly rescinded the once-sacred Imperial Rescript on Education.[4]

It is hard to separate the initiative of the Japanese in the slow work of creating a new educational system from the authoritative "suggestions" of SCAP. Although Americans paid ample lip service to the principle of indigenous institutions to fit Japanese needs, inevitably they recommended what was familiar and satisfactory at home. The professional books cleared for translation gave an idealized version of American experience. In matters of practical detail the preferences—or even the prejudices—of the lone Education Officer working with a prefectural military government team were often decisive. But the Japanese people themselves, who essentially share our faith in education, also displayed a great deal of zeal for change. We can hope that their wills were so deeply involved that they will maintain the reforms, in spirit

4 *Education in the New Japan* (Tokyo: Education Division, CI&E Section, SCAP, 1948), V. 1, pp. 137-139, 155-158.

if not in detail, rather than rejecting them as impositions by a conqueror.

Broad lines of policy laid down by an Education Reform Council made up of forty-nine prominent Japanese were embodied in a Fundamental Law of Education passed by the Diet on March 31, 1947. Compulsory schooling under conditions of equal opportunity and co-education was to extend over nine years. In defining the aim of education, the law stressed first full development of the personality of individuals, but noted also that the people should have "a deep sense of responsibility . . . as builders of the peaceful state and society." Schools were to create the attitudes of "intelligent citizenship" and "religious tolerance," without propagandizing for any party or sect. To avoid improper control or use of education, the "whole people" were made directly responsible for it.[5]

Whether structural reorganization was necessary in order to achieve these excellent aims, or whether the substance of reform was sacrificed for formal changes, is still a debatable question. The School Education Law of 1947 substituted a new 6-3-3-4 pattern for the existing system of six years of elementary school, five of middle school, three of higher school, and three of university. Mere imitation of the American sequence of elementary school, junior high, senior high, and college would not be sufficient justification for a reorganization that has imposed such a heavy financial and administrative burden. But according to an American educator deeply involved in these reforms, the Japanese themselves regarded a great expansion of facilities at the secondary level as fundamental.[6]

Opportunities for schooling have expanded. Four times as many students are attending the new lower secondary schools as were able to get into prewar middle schools; seven times as many the upper secondary schools as in the old higher schools, *semmon gakkō,* and university preparatory departments.[7] But in the process the quality of instruction often

[5] Text of law in *Education in the New Japan,* cited, V. 2, pp. 109-111.

[6] Robert K. Hall, *Education for a New Japan* (New Haven: Yale University Press, 1949), p. 264.

[7] *Asahi Nenkan, 1953 (Asahi Yearbook, 1953)* (Tokyo: Asahi Shimbun-sha, 1953), p. 436.

deteriorated because teachers were working within an un-familiar or uncertain frame of reference. Upgrading to uni-versity status vitiated the special role of some of Japan's ex-cellent technical schools.[8] Most serious of all, the Occupation withdrew leaving the educational system in confusion rather than in smooth working order. Changes will have to be made. Some may be for the worse.

.   The future of the popularly elected school boards, for ex-ample, is now very uncertain. The Japanese adopted this American device for local democratic control of education in 1948, on the recommendation of the Education Mission. At first boards were set up only for the prefectures and the larger cities. Then in October 1952 each of the 10,000 odd towns and villages in Japan elected its own board. Most of these control only one school. Lacking power to levy taxes for school purposes, they are dependent upon prefectural and city assemblies, which constantly interfere in educa-tional questions. Demand for some reform of this unwieldy system is widespread. The Yoshida government wished to abolish the boards except in prefectures and large cities, also to make the members appointive. Some liberals suggest that if there were a board for each *gun* (roughly equivalent to an American county) each of the 500 units would be large enough to offer a full twelve-year program, and local demo-cratic control could still be maintained.[9]

Decentralization also made necessary a new pattern of professional administration. The responsibility for curricula and teaching methods now fell upon local superintendents of education and principals. Officials from the Ministry of Education became consultants instead of inspectors; they could advise but not prescribe. To help prepare personnel for these unfamiliar functions, SCAP provided an Institute for Educational Leadership staffed by a changing group of specialists from the United States. Workshop methods gave practical experience in cooperation, as well as imparting in-formation about American practices. The thousands of edu-

[8] I am reserving discussion of universities for the next chapter, in connection with the many Americans who have taught in Japan.
[9] *Postwar Developments in Japanese Education* (Tokyo: Education Division, CI&E Section, SCAP, 1952), V. 1, pp. 157-158.

cators who had six- or twelve-week courses at IFEL have become seminal influences in their local communities.[10] "Curriculum" and "guidance" now occupy important places in the vocabulary of Japanese educators. The work of the California Curriculum Commission and the "Virginia Plan" of integrated studies designed to develop democratic attitudes have been widely discussed. Although the advisory courses of study drawn up by the Ministry of Education still enjoy great prestige, many localities are experimenting with original curricula. The integrated course in social studies usually forms the core. Pupils apply many different learning activities to local problems and local materials. Teachers are beginning to use textbooks as references and aids to learning rather than as unimpeachable sources of truth. Now anyone can prepare a textbook and present it to the Mombushō for approval. In 1953–54, for example, teachers of fifth year elementary social studies had a choice of eleven books.[11] Through home rooms and varied extracurricular activities the schools strive to develop the full potentialities of each individual and to guide him toward a suitable vocation. John Dewey's ideal of "education in life for life" is widely accepted in elementary and lower secondary schools, although practice falls short of his ideals. In the upper secondary years cramming for university entrance examinations is still considered more important than making knowledge meaningful through experience.[12]

The time that Japanese students must spend learning language arts has been substantially reduced by combining grammar, literature, calligraphy, and oral expression into a single course in "national language." No subject has generated more heat in postwar Japan than the question of

[10] Same, pp. 387-391; *Dai Rokkai Kyōiku Shidōsha Koshūjo Kenkyū Shūroku* (*Study Reports of the Institute for Educational Leadership, Sixth Session*) (Mimeographed; Tokyo: Institute, 1950–1951), *passim*.
[11] SCAP helped the Japanese to develop new textbooks by setting up twenty centers for display of American teaching materials.
[12] *Progress of Educational Reform in Japan* (Mimeographed; Tokyo: Ministry of Education, 1950), pp. 14-15; *Nihon Kyōiku Nenkan, 1950* (*Japanese Yearbook of Education, 1950*) (Tokyo: Meiji Shoin, 1950), pp. 349-353, 624-630; Harold E. Snyder and Margretta S. Austin, eds., *Educational Progress in Japan and the Ryukyus* (Washington: American Council on Education, 1950), p. 11.

language reform. In the early days of the Occupation, Robert K. Hall led a group within SCAP which believed that Chinese characters were a major obstacle to the development of democracy.[13] The American Education Mission recognized that basic language reforms could "come only from within," but made a strong recommendation for adoption of the Roman alphabet. Some officers in SCAP with extensive prewar experience in Japan, including Lt. Col. Donald R. Nugent, who became head of CI & E, were either satisfied with the existing system or dubious about the practicability of drastic change. The Japanese themselves, who had been discussing the merits and disadvantages of romanization or exclusive use of the *kana* syllabary since early Meiji, stand divided. The National Language Council has pondered the whole question in a leisurely fashion, and the National Language Research Institute has made some specific studies, but as yet no long-range policy has been announced. Abandonment of characters now seems unlikely.

Piecemeal progress toward simplifying the Japanese language, with occasional relapses, is a more likely prospect. Phonetic *kana* spelling is replacing the more complicated combinations based on ancient pronunciation. In 1946 the National Language Council issued a standard list of 1,850 characters to be taught during compulsory education. Except for proper names, newspapers and government documents try to limit themselves to this list. But since literary writers and many magazines refuse to accept this limitation, the problem of practical literacy will remain. In 1950 almost 85 percent of the elementary schools and half the lower secondary schools were voluntarily devoting some time to teaching Japanese in Roman letters. So far, however, the National Language Council has been unable to agree on a standard transliteration.[14]

[13] See his survey of the whole question in *Education for a New Japan*, cited, pp. 293-401.

[14] *Progress of Educational Reform in Japan*, cited, pp. 131-147; *The Development and Present Status of Romaji in Japan* (Mimeographed; Tokyo: CI & E, SCAP, 1950), pp. 7-17; Chiba Tsutomu, "Kokugo Shingikai no Rōmaji Chōsa Bunka Shingikai Ketsuretsu no Riyū (The Reasons for the Decisions of the Romaji Investigation Subcommittee of the National Language Council)," *Onsei Gakkai Kaihō (Reports of the Phonetics Society)*, no. 81 (May 1953), pp. 13-14.

Learning should not stop with graduation from school, of course. What we usually speak of as adult education the Japanese call "social education." A law passed in 1949 made it an additional responsibility of local boards of education. Although public libraries and museums are still a rarity outside the big cities, by May 1952 nearly 7,000 communities had citizens' public halls (*kōminkan*) that served as centers for public discussion, education, and social life. SCAP began in 1947 to sponsor two- to four-day adult education institutes in about a hundred communities each year. There discussion leaders were trained in techniques that would bring out free expressions of opinion. The Occupation also gave particular attention to youth organizations. Only a small minority of urban young people are in groups with Western affiliations like the Boy Scouts, Girl Scouts, YMCA, and YWCA. Over four million men and women between sixteen and thirty, especially those in rural areas, are members of the *Nihon Seinen Dan* (Japan Youth Corps). American youth leaders tried to re-orient this organization, once a strong support for the militarists, toward community service along democratic lines.[15]

Constant talk about the "new education," the "new schools," the "new curriculum," may in the long run only increase the chances of rejection as the pendulum swings away from SCAP reforms. The Occupation might have been wiser if it had emphasized continuity in educational development. Japan's modern history has been so variegated that it offers a choice of traditions upon which to build. Behind the bizarre wartime indoctrination in national mythology lay more normal and hopeful tendencies that could have been picked up again and strengthened. Japan's contact with Western educational experience and theory did not begin in 1945; it goes back over eighty years. Before examining some recent reactionary tendencies in Japanese education, we shall look at two previous occasions when the Japanese drew heavily from America. In this perspective the Japanese may find the postwar period of intensive tutelage more acceptable.

15 *Postwar Developments*, cited, V. 1, pp. 286-292, 305-316; *Jiji Nenkan, 1953*, p. 316.

Creating a Modern Educational System for Japan

The first important infusion of American influence came during the 1870's, following the Meiji Restoration. The Meiji leaders decided that a modern system of education based on Western models was an essential tool for building up the strength and prosperity of their nation. In 1871 they sent Tanaka Fujimaro, First Senior Secretary of the new Ministry of Education (Mombushō), abroad with the Iwakura Embassy to study the school systems of America and Europe. Even before he returned, however, organization was effected on the basis of information at hand. The educational code promulgated in September 1872 resembled closely in form the uniform centralized system established in France by the law of 1854. It divided Japan into 8 university districts, each made up of 32 middle-school districts. Each of these was divided into 210 primary school districts, so that there would be one school for each 600 persons. The hope was expressed that in the future there would be "no community with an illiterate family, nor a family with an illiterate person."

The Dajōkan proclamation introducing the new code stressed advancement for individuals rather than benefit for the state. In this it mirrored the utilitarian spirit so strong among the modernists of the early Meiji period.

It is only by building up his character, developing his mind, and cultivating his talents that man may make his way in the world, employ his wealth wisely, make his business to prosper, and thus attain the goal of life. But man cannot build up his character, develop his mind, or cultivate his talents without education—that is the reason for the establishment of schools. Language, writing, and arithmetic, to begin with, are daily necessities in military affairs, government, agriculture, trade arts, law, politics, astronomy, and medicine; there is not, in short, a single phase of human activity which is not based on learning. Only by striving in the line of his natural aptitude can man prosper in his undertakings, accumulate wealth, and succeed in life.[16]

16 Proclamation of September 4, 1872, translated in Hugh L. Keenleyside and A. F. Thomas, *History of Japanese Education and Present Educational System* (Tokyo: Hokuseido, 1937), pp. 87-88.

The aristocratic tradition of Tokugawa education, emphasizing "poetry, empty reasoning, and idle discussions," was explicitly rejected. Although there have been constant complaints about the narrowness of the upper rungs, modern Japan has had a single educational ladder extending from the primary school to the university. Considerable social mobility has resulted. In this respect the Japanese system resembled the situation in America more closely than that in Europe, where there were special preparatory schools for those intending to enter the *lycée*, the *gymnasium*, or the English "public school."

Since the Minister of Education was usually occupied with general affairs of state, the administration of this new educational system fell upon Tanaka Fujimaro, who was promoted to vice-minister upon his return from abroad. Tanaka had been much impressed by the system of common schools in several American states, especially in Massachusetts and Connecticut. United States Commissioner of Education John Eaton had loaded him down with school laws and official reports and with books by Horace Mann, Henry Barnard, and other American educators.[17] In higher education, on the other hand, Tanaka found the German universities to be much superior to those of America.

Tanaka also engaged an American adviser to come to Japan to help organize the school system. In preparation for the Iwakura Embassy, Mori Arinori, then Minister in Washington, had sent an identical letter to several prominent educators, asking for their opinions on "the elevation of the condition of Japan, intellectually, morally, and physically." One of the most careful replies came from David Murray, professor of mathematics at Rutgers College. Murray stressed the adaptation of the educational system to the national culture. "There are traditional customs which it would be unwise to undertake to subvert. There are institutions already founded which are revered for their local and national associations, which without material changes may be made the best elements of a new system." After interviews with mem-

---

[17] Letter from Eaton to Tanaka, May 8, 1872, Commissioner of Education Letter Books, V. 5 (National Archives). Much of this material was translated in the first two volumes of *Riji kōtei* (Tokyo, 1873).

bers of the Embassy, Murray was offered the position of
Superintendent of Educational Affairs. He arrived in Japan
in May 1873, about the time that Tanaka returned from
Europe.[18]

Murray's work during the next five and a half years covered a wide range: planning courses of study, inspecting
progress in the prefectures, recommendations on the construction and furnishing of school buildings.[19] In 1876 he
accompanied Tanaka to the Philadelphia Exposition and
helped him to make an intensive, comparative study of education. By purchase or donation they obtained many of the
Philadelphia exhibits for a new educational museum in
Tokyo. After a lengthy visit to Boston's outstanding schools,
Tanaka and Murray also bought a full set of the teaching
materials used there.

If Murray had wanted to make the Japanese schools exact
copies of American ones, he would have encountered little
resistance from Tanaka or from the Minister, Ōki Takato.
But he was so firm a believer in cultural relativism that instead he tried to apply a brake to indiscriminate borrowing.
He opposed Mori Arinori's plan for Japan to adopt the English language, and he urged that foreign textbooks should
be replaced by new ones compiled in Japanese.

Murray's emphasis on the training of Japanese teachers
also had as its goal what he called the "naturalization of education." Instruction in classroom teaching, as distinct from
the methods of individual recitation used by Japan's old
scholar-teachers, had been begun at a normal school opened
in Tokyo in 1872. There M. M. Scott, formerly a grammar
school principal in San Francisco, taught an advanced class
through an interpreter, and they imitated him in teaching
children in a primary training school. Most of the first gradu-

[18] The position was first offered to Birdsey G. Northrop, who was unwilling
to leave his work as Secretary of the Connecticut State Board of Education.
[19] The David Murray papers in the Library of Congress contain copies of
some, but not all, of the reports that he prepared for the Department of
Education. A Japanese version of his first general report, December 31, 1873,
is reprinted in *Meiji Ikō Kyōiku Seido Hattatsu Shi* (*History of the Development of the Educational System since the Beginning of Meiji*) (Tokyo: Mombushō Uchi Kyōiku Shi Hensankai, 1938–1939), V. 2, pp. 66-74. *Mombushō
Dai Ni Nempō, Meiji Shichinen* (*Second Annual Report of the Department of
Education, 1874*), pp. 24-32 gives a report of an inspection trip.

ates became teachers in prefectural normal schools and thus passed on their knowledge to other young teachers. In order to bring the new methods to those already in service, Murray used a distinctly American device, the short-term teachers' institute.[20] He also spoke so enthusiastically about the role of "schoolmarms" in America that a normal school for women was opened in Tokyo in 1874.

Despite the efforts of Tanaka and Murray, the educational system nowhere approximated the grandiose plan of 1872. Rioting peasants complained about the financial burden of the public elementary schools. In general the people preferred private schools that gave a more traditional type of instruction. In 1878 Murray found that even in Tokyo almost 70 percent of the primary pupils were attending private schools.[21] Since no standard curriculum would meet the needs of all classes and areas, each prefecture was allowed to draw up its own course of studies, subject to approval by the Ministry of Education. The whole concept of intermediate education was new, and most of the clan schools converted into middle schools retained a strong feudal flavor. A welter of private schools of varying degrees of competence offered instruction in foreign languages and science. The best was probably Fukuzawa Yukichi's Keiōgijuku in Tokyo, which had branches in Ōsaka, Kyōto, and Tokushima and supplied teachers for many other schools. By using English and American textbooks, Keiō set a high standard for "Western learning." Only in Tokyo was there anything resembling a university.

Tanaka's solution was to change the law to fit the reality. He had long admired the American system of local control over education, but not until the Satsuma Rebellion of 1877 put the central government under great financial strain did he have a chance to put it into effect. Under the new Educational Regulations of 1879, which Murray helped to draft, a popularly elected school committee in each town and vil-

[20] Aizawa Hiroshi, *Nihon Kyōiku Hyakunen Shidan* (*Historical Talks on One Hundred Years of Japanese Education*) (Tokyo: Gakugei Tosho Shuppan-sha, 1952), pp. 44-45; W. E. Griffis, "The Tokei Normal School," *College Courant*, V. 14 (January 3, 1874), pp. 3-4.
[21] "Public Schools of Tokio, A Report by David Murray . . . July 1878," Murray papers, Library of Congress.

lage was responsible for the establishment and maintenance of schools. To supplement local taxes, grants-in-aid from the central government were distributed to public schools and such private schools as were considered beneficial. The period of compulsory education was reduced from eight years to sixteen months. Public normal schools were provided for, but employment of competent teachers without diplomas was also permitted.[22]

The Japanese people had so little experience with the responsibilities of local government that the reform did not have the desired effect. They misinterpreted the loosening of central control as a decreased emphasis on education itself and either closed the elementary schools, or combined several into one in order to save expense. The percentage of children in school actually declined, and the education of girls, especially, was neglected.[23] To check these tendencies, a revised law issued in December 1880 extended compulsory education to three years, made the election of school committees indirect rather than direct, and gave more power of regulation to the prefectural governors. Vice Minister Tanaka assumed the responsibility for the failure of his reforms by resigning.

Tanaka's resignation, along with the departure of David Murray in 1879, marked the end of this first period of predominant American influence. Several other Americans had helped to develop special subjects. Between 1878 and 1881 Dr. George A. Leland introduced the Amherst College system of class calisthenics and marching and trained the first Japanese teachers of physical education. Under the direction of Tsuboi Gendō, Leland's system was widely used in the schools until 1913, when Swedish gymnastics were made standard. Luther Whiting Mason, Director of Music in the primary schools of Boston, spent two years in Japan (1880–1882) preparing materials for teaching music. The Japanese

[22] Murray's "Report upon a Draft Revision of the Code of Education in Japan" is in the Library of Congress. The Regulations are translated in the *Tokio Times,* October 25, 1879.
[23] Takahashi Shunjō, "Meiji Shōnen no Kyōiku Seido to sono Seishin (The Educational System of the First Years of Meiji and its Spirit)," *Shirin,* V. 16 (October 1931), pp. 618-619.

words that he set to Western tunes were for many years appreciatively called "Mason song." [24]

American influence was most obvious in the physical pattern of teaching and learning. The typical primary school was an impressive wooden building furnished with seats and desks, blackboards, and wall maps. The students sat in classes, and studied Japanese translations of Marcius Willson's *Readers,* H. N. Robinson's *Arithmetic,* and Monteith's or McNally's geographies instead of memorizing the *Thousand-character Classic* and the *Analects* of Confucius. An American clock timed regular recitation hours. And chances were that the student did his home work by the light of American kerosene, burned in a tin lamp made from the shipping can by some Japanese craftsman.[25]

Only when the schools were actually in operation did the Japanese find time for more theoretical study of education. First of all they translated the school laws of Western countries; then in 1874 the Ministry of Education published as a guide to school management a translation of *School Economy* by J. P. Wickersham, the Pennsylvania Superintendent of Education. Attention next shifted to the procedures of teaching and learning; the year 1876 saw Japanese versions of John S. Hart's *In the School-room,* David Perkins Page's *Theory and Practice of Teaching,* and Charles Northend's *The Teacher's Assistant.* A year before this the Mombushō sent three men to study at leading normal schools in America. All encountered in one form or another the prevalent theories of Pestalozzi, the Swiss educator who insisted that instruction follow the natural development of the child and that learning come through sense experience of actual objects rather than by memorizing verbal abstractions. Put in charge of the Tokyo Normal School upon their return to Japan, Isawa Shūji and Takamine Hideo introduced the in-

---

[24] Paul C. Phillips, "George A. Leland," *Amherst Graduates' Quarterly,* V. 14 (November 1924), pp. 29-33; Nihon Kyōiku Ongaku Kyōkai (Japan Educational Music Society), *Hompō Ongaku Kyōiku Shi (History of Music Education in Japan)* (Tokyo: Ongaku Kyōikusho Shuppan Kyōkai, 1938), pp. 62-105.

[25] David Murray, Address on "Education and Religion in Japan," Murray papers; John M. Birch to James D. Porter, Asst. Secy. of State, May 10, 1886, Nagasaki Consular Dispatches, National Archives.

ductive method of object teaching that they had learned at
normal schools in Bridgewater, Massachusetts, and Oswego,
New York. Through Takamine's translation, James Johon-
not's *Principles and Practice of Teaching* probably had a
greater influence in Japan than it did in America. Isawa's
more original *Kyōikugaku (Pedagogy)* was very important in
making Japanese teachers aware of educational theory.
Along with the theories of Herbert Spencer and Alexander
Bain, this American strain of Pestalozzianism dominated educational thought in Japan until the late eighties.[26]

The Meiji drive toward modernization gave Japanese education a Western orientation that survived even the reaction
of the 1930's. Postwar re-orientation would have been much
harder if SCAP had had to start with institutions that were
thoroughly Oriental and feudal. Today Japanese educators
look back to the early years of the Meiji period as a golden
age of freedom. "In this free atmosphere," Professor Kaigo
Tokiomi has said, "each *fu* and *ken* encouraged the schools
under its jurisdiction, and each school, each teacher, tried to
give the best education possible." [27] We have seen that the
freedom was as much the result of incomplete organization
as of design. But it is true that during these years education
served primarily to satisfy the intellectual curiosity and ambition of individuals. Benefit to the state was indirect and
secondary. In the years that followed, growing Japanese nationalism and a shift to German models reversed these priorities.

Of the two factors, the German influence is less important.
We are prone to explain all of Japan's failings by contamination from Germany, forgetting that Americans have learned
a great deal from the Germans without suffering serious
ideological corruption. The Japanese borrowed the things
that fitted their own predilections and needs.

For one thing Germany, and especially Prussia, offered
an example of successful state control of education. During

26 The fullest account is Inatomi Eijirō, *Meiji Shoki Kyōiku Shisō no Kenkyū*
(*A Study of the Educational Thought of the Early Meiji Period*) (Tokyo:
Sōgensha, 1944). Some of the translations are reprinted in volume 10 of *Meiji
Bunka Zenshū* (*Collection of Works on Meiji Culture*) (Tokyo: Nihon Hyōron-
sha, 1927–1930).
27 *Mainichi Shimbun*, May 13, 1953.

the depression of the 1880's local responsibility worked badly in Japan; by 1887 the percentage of children in school was lower than in 1871.[28] When Mori Arinori became Minister of Education in 1885, he prepared legislation that created a uniform system under the close control of the Ministry of Education. Each prefecture was to have one middle school and one normal school. The primary consideration was to train the personnel needed by the state. At the Higher Normal School in Tokyo, students were given public support, housed in dormitories under semi-military discipline, and required to teach for a definite period after graduation. The Ministry issued the first standard text on ethics in 1888, although the content was still basically utilitarian. In the formulation and administration of their bureaucratic system, the Japanese drew often upon German experience, but the guiding ideology was their own.[29]

German theories of education also began to receive attention in Japan. In 1889 Dr. Emil Hausknecht presented the ideas of Johann Friedrich Herbart to a special group of education students at Tokyo Imperial University. Books by Hermann Kern, Gustav Lindner, Wilhelm Rein, and other German educators were translated during the next decade.[30] This shift in theoretical orientation coincided with strong German influence upon the formation of the Japanese constitution and the legal codes. But it is somewhat of an oversimplification to interpret this shift to German theories merely as a turning-point in a battle between free thought and authoritarianism. The Japanese were catching up with Western educational thinking. They had borrowed Pestalozzianism, which had come to America only after a long lag, when it was already losing favor in Europe. The very year of Hausknecht's lectures, Charles De Garmo first systematically presented Herbart's theories to American educators. Soon Americans and Germans were sitting together in the pedagogical seminars of German universities. For both the greatest attraction was new and more concrete teaching

[28] Takahashi, cited, p. 622.
[29] Fujihara Kiyozō, *Meiji Kyōiku Shisō Shi* (*History of Meiji Educational Thought*) (Tokyo: 1909), pp. 291-300.
[30] Tsuji Kōzaburō, *Dai Nihon Kyōiku Tsūshi* (*General History of Japanese Education*) (Tokyo: Meguro Shoten, 1933), pp. 406-409, 435-437.

methods. By overemphasis on definitions and strictly logical analysis, object-teaching had become as sterile as the memorization it had supplanted. The Herbartians offered the five formal steps by which the learner's mind was prepared, new material presented, associations made with previous knowledge, generalizations drawn, and applications made to practical situations. Tuiskon Ziller and Wilhelm Rein had worked out elaborate lesson plans. Rein's "principle of historical culture"—that the best materials for character training came from the national history and literature—also appealed to a Japan just regaining interest and pride in its past.[31]

The nationalist trend in education, already evidenced in the revived study of Japanese and Chinese classics, received the stamp of highest official approval in the Imperial Rescript on Education issued on October 30, 1890. The tone of awed reverence for "the teaching bequeathed by Our Imperial Ancestors, to be observed by their descendants and the subjects, infallible for all ages, and true in all places," contrasted sharply with the iconoclastic words of the earlier Meiji Charter Oath: "All the absurd usages of old shall be broken through, and equity and justice to be found in the workings of nature shall serve as the basis of action." The body of the 1890 Rescript was a series of broad ethical injunctions essentially Confucian in inspiration: "Ye, our subjects, be filial to your parents, affectionate to your brothers and sisters; as husbands and wives be harmonious, as friends true. . . ." The duty of subject to ruler was elaborated to include obligations to respect the Constitution and obey the laws and to offer himself to the state in times of emergency.

In later years this Imperial Rescript came to be regarded as so sacred that it was a veritable fetish. A mispronounced syllable in a ceremonial reading was cause for disgrace, and principals in schools where copies were lost by fire often committed suicide. But until it received the additional exegesis of the *Kokutai no Hongi* (*Cardinal Principles of the National Entity*), the Rescript did not act as a straitjacket

---

[31] Charles De Garmo, *Herbart and the Herbartians* (New York: Scribner, 1895) is a good survey of the whole movement.

around Japanese education. Its pronouncements were too
general to be accurate guides to policy. Official emphases
changed with each successive ministry, and educators continued to espouse new theories and to experiment with
methods.

The Second Phase of American Influence: Progressive Education

Many of the revelations of educational gospel that postwar
American consultants made before sessions of the Institute
for Educational Leadership were not really new. For the
Japanese they revived memories of the 1920's, when they had
for the second time looked to America for significant models.
Then younger educators enthusiastic about individualism,
democracy, and social reform were attracted by the experiments in progressive education going on in the United
States. They tried out child-centered curricula and free
teaching methods in both private and public schools. In 1930
Japanese progressive educators formed a New Education Society (Shin Kyōiku Kyōkai) which affiliated with the World
New Education Fellowship. Just as in America, conservatives in Japan complained that the new educators stressed
method at the expense of intellectual content and achievement. At the time no one foresaw a more serious weakness:
that a social emphasis was no guarantee that the doctrines
taught would be democratic.[32]

Progressive education has its theoretical basis in the findings of psychologists about how a child develops. Instead of
regarding children as imperfect adults who need discipline
and mental calisthenics in order to develop latent powers of
reason, the modern educator recognizes that the interests and
behavior traits of each stage of growth have their own value.
School years are not just preparation for life, but a part of
life with distinctive experiences, problems, and satisfactions.

---

[32] Umene Satoru, "Nihon no Shin-kyōiku Undō: Taishōki Shingakkō ni
tsuite no Jakkan no Nōto (The New Education Movement in Japan: Some
Notes on the New Schools of the Taishō Period)," in Tōkyō Kyōiku Daigaku
Kyōikugaku Kenkyūshitsu, *Nihon Kyōiku Shi* (*History of Japanese Education*) (Tokyo: Kaneko Shobō, 1951), pp. 161-291, gives a general account of
the movement.

In child study the Japanese drew upon the experimental work of Americans as well as the earlier observations by such German scholars as Dietrich Tiedemann and Wilhelm Preyer. Motora Yujirō, who studied under G. Stanley Hall at Johns Hopkins in the 1880's, headed the Japan Child Study Society established in 1902. Another disciple of Hall's, Shinoda Toshihide, introduced child psychology in the Tokyo Higher Normal School for Women. Higuchi Kanjirō adopted Colonel Francis Parker's idea that children must take an active inquiring role in the process of learning. As early as 1899 he argued that the secret of activity teaching was to combine all the traditional subjects into one thematic curriculum.[33]

During the First World War Japanese educators began to read and translate books like Irving King's *Social Aspects of Education* and J. K. Hart's *Democracy in Education*. The most important stimuli came, however, from direct contacts with leading Americans. John Dewey, whose *Democracy and Education* and *The School and Society* were already well known in Japan, went to Tokyo in 1919 to give the lucid lectures on the instrumentalist point of view that were subsequently published as *Reconstruction in Philosophy*. On a trip to America in 1922, Sawayanagi Masatarō and Konishi Shigenao were so impressed by the Dalton High School, in which students worked at their own rate in various "laboratory" rooms, that they asked Miss Helen Parkhurst, the originator of the Dalton Plan, to come to Japan to lecture. Professor William H. Kilpatrick of Teachers College, Columbia University, made a speaking tour of Japan in 1927 under the auspices of the *Ōsaka Asahi*. In 1930 Carleton Washburne, famous for his management of the Winnetka system of individual instruction, came to observe the results of a decade's trial of progressive methods.

A few experimental private schools were in the vanguard. The Seijō Gakuen that Sawayanagi and Konishi started in

33 *Tetsugaku Daijisho (Encyclopedia of Philosophy)* (Tokyo: Dōbunkan, 1927), V. 2, pp. 1214-1216; *Kyōiku Daijisho (Encyclopedia of Education)* (Tokyo: Dōbunkan, 1918), V. 1, pp. 310-311; Fujihara Kiyozō, *Meiji Taishō Shōwa Kyōiku Shisō Gakusetsu Jimbutsu Shi (History of Educational Thought, Systems, and Personalities during the Meiji, Taishō, and Shōwa Periods)* (Tokyo: Tōa Seikeisha, 1942-1944), V. 1, pp. 724-725, 734.

Tokyo in 1917 was the most ambitious. To the original primary school they gradually added a middle school, high schools for both boys and girls, and a kindergarten. Seijō used a modified form of the Dalton Plan to put the children upon their own responsibility, and it brought them close to nature in a "woodland classroom." One visitor remarked how different the humming spontaneous activity there was from the usual Japanese school, where the children would be lined up with military precision.[34] Former teachers at Seijō founded Tamagawa Gakuen and Myōjō Gakuen. The Jiyū Gakuen (Garden of Freedom) run by Hani Yoshikazu and his wife Motoko was more in a Christian tradition. In a ranch-house building designed by Frank Lloyd Wright they taught upper middle-class girls "to think, to live and to pray." [35]

The new methods also began to penetrate the public schools. Kinoshita Takeji, principal of the model elementary school at Nara Higher Normal for Women, impressed his ideas about development of individuality and creative expression upon many teachers in western Japan. The work-study methods taught by Kitazawa Taneichi at Tokyo Higher Normal for Women had considerable influence in the east. Many public school teachers used modern study plans from the magazines that Okuno Shotarō and Satō Takeshi of Seijō elementary school published for each grade.[36] Without running afoul of Mombushō regulations and inspection, a progressive teacher could go quite far in the use of advanced methods. The work of Kawasaki Riichi, for example, was mentioned at the 1932 World Conference of the New Education Fellowship. In a primary school in Ochigun of Ehime prefecture, this man had for thirteen years required each student to draw up his own plan of study. As teacher he suggested methods of work and tested progress. Certainly this instance was not unique.[37]

Carleton Washburne found, however, that by 1930 serious

[34] *School and Society*, V. 34, (October 3, 1931), p. 466; Fujihara, *Meiji Taishō Shōwa Kyōiku*, cited, V. 3, pp. 579-582.
[35] Matsuoka Yoko, *Daughter of the Pacific* (New York: Harper, 1952), pp. 51-59.
[36] Fujihara, *Meiji Taishō Shōwa Kyōiku*, cited, V. 3, pp. 576-594.
[37] Wyatt Rawson, ed., *A New World in the Making: An International Survey of the New Education* (London: New Education Fellowship, 1933), pp. 238-239.

tensions were developing between the aims of progressive education and the dogmas of Japanese nationalism. Individuality was good so long as it did not make a person dissatisfied to live in the existing society. Intellectual curiosity and independent judgment should not go so far as to question decisions already taken by the government. Konishi Shigenao now said: "The students should be guided by the teacher to appreciate the present system." The progressives still professed an international outlook, but they made it clear that Japan's international actions were always righteous.[38] Five years later the forces of nationalism had won the tug-of-war even within the minds of the minority of educators with progressive tendencies. At the Pan-Pacific New Education Conference held in Tokyo in 1935, "unity, labor, loyalty, respect, the spirit of Shinto and the continuity of Japan with the traditions of her heroic past" were the themes stressed by the Japanese speakers.[39]

Some progressive methods fitted in easily and harmoniously with the goals of the new order. Tamagawa Gakuen, for example, sought to add "the essence of modern education" to the character training and the teacher-disciple nexus of the Tokugawa *juku* (private school). Emphasis was placed on the family relationship; three to ten students lived in a teacher's home, even taking his name.[40] New agricultural training centers used work-study methods to prepare settlers for Manchuria.[41] One must not forget that schools are more likely to mirror the prevailing ideology than to exert an independent influence.

Present Problems and Prospects

Today the big question is: how far will Japanese education be affected by the "reverse course" that has been apparent in public policy since the peace treaty came into effect? Already in the fall of 1951 it was clear that the Yoshida cabinet favored extensive changes, including increased at-

[38] Carleton Washburne, *Remakers of Mankind* (New York: John Day, 1932), pp. 12-40.
[39] *School and Society*, V. 42 (November 9, 1935), p. 653.
[40] Rawson, cited, pp. 235-236.
[41] Fujihara, *Meiji Taishō Shōwa Kyōiku*, cited, V. 4, pp. 359-362.

tention to vocational training, limitation of the power of boards of education, and greater "responsibility" for the central Ministry. The Liberal Party at one point proposed that the lower secondary course be reduced to two years and perhaps amalgamated with the primary school. The willingness of both educators and the public to resist these changes and to support the occupation reforms has been encouraging. Now that the sharp reaction that followed immediately the restoration of sovereignty has moderated somewhat, the greatest peril may be past. But constant vigilance will be necessary to separate desirable readjustments in the system from wrecking efforts.

Financial weakness makes Japanese education highly vulnerable. Buildings and equipment destroyed during the war have had to be replaced. In addition, adoption of the 6-3 system required a whole new set of facilities for the new three-year lower secondary schools. The ideal of completely tax-supported compulsory education has not been realized. The PTA's, of which the Occupation was so proud, have been used primarily to bring social pressure to force supplementary private contributions. In 1950 the funds provided by PTA's and parents amounted to 166 billion yen, about 10 percent of the total cost of compulsory education.[42] On the ground that local governments were diverting to other purposes some of the school funds received through tax equalization procedures, the Yoshida cabinet pushed through the 1952 Diet a law making the national government directly responsible for half the expenses of compulsory education. An attempt in 1953 to get full financial control failed because it was tied up with a provision making teachers employees of the central government, subject to appointment and dismissal by the Ministry of Education. Since Minister Ōdachi Shigeo had announced his intention to "clear the political world of intervention by school teachers," this was interpreted, probably correctly, as a move to break the power of the aggressive leftist Japan Teachers' Union.[43]

[42] Irie Michio, "Ao-jashin no Roku-san Sei (The 6-3 System of the Blueprint)," *Kaizō*, V. 23 (April 1952), p. 147; Tamaki Hajime, "PTA no Jittai (The Status of the PTA's)," *Chūō Kōron*, V. 68 (July 1953), pp. 218-227.

[43] Rōyama Masamichi, "Whither Educational System?" *Oriental Economist* V. 21 (April 1953), pp. 193-195; *The Mainichi*, December 20, 1953. In 1954

Although this attempt at recentralization was balked, the local communities of Japan seem all too ready to forget the principle of democratic control when they see a chance to shift some of their financial burdens to the central government.

Restoration of specific instruction in ethics has also been debated vigorously. The assumption in the postwar curriculum is that a self-imposed, democratic sense of morality can best arise out of the whole school experience, and that work in social studies will ensure adequate consideration for the rights of others. But those who are concerned about rising juvenile delinquency and licentious uses of freedom argue that since Japan's religions are essentially amoral, it is up to the schools to make a definite formulation of ethical principles. In November 1951 a draft "Outline of Ethical Practice for the Japanese People" prepared by Minister of Education Amano Teiyu leaked to the press. Although this document made some mention of the dignity of human personality, it also asserted that "the State is the parent body of the individual; without the State there would be no individuals." It described the position of the Emperor as a "moral focus." Brother-sister relationships, with connotations of family exclusiveness and hierarchical ranking, were set up as "the basic pattern for just human relations in a just society." The press attacked this restatement of Confucian principles so savagely that Amano was forced to abandon his plan of promulgating the "Outline" along with the peace treaty.[44] But similar opinions are still held in high places. On February 9, 1953, Amano's successor, Okano Kiyohide, told the Budget Committee of the House of Representatives that "the Imperial Rescript on Education was abolished after the war, but its spirit and contents have eternal truth." [45] Ōdachi announced that his policy would be to encourage morality and patriotism.[46]

Changes in curriculum have been demanded for the sake

---

the Diet passed two laws which severely restricted the political activities of teachers.

[44] The *Kokumin Jissen Yōryō* is translated and analyzed in R. P. Dore, "The Ethics of the New Japan," *Pacific Affairs*, V. 25 (June 1952), pp. 147-159.

[45] *Mainichi Shimbun*, February 9, 1953.

[46] Same, June 25, 1953.

of restoring to the Japanese people the national pride that they lost as a result of defeat. Although educators have expressed general satisfaction with the integrated social science course, the Ministry is encouraging separate teaching of Japanese history and geography.[47] Fencing with bamboo sticks and *jūdō* are again part of physical education. The government also wants to make Chinese classics (*kambun*) a required subject in the upper secondary schools.[48] Except for their former association with militaristic indoctrination, these subjects are not necessarily undesirable, of course. But Japanese liberals see them as straws in the gathering winds of reaction.

It would be a mistake, of course, to regard any and every change in the Occupation-imposed pattern as disastrous. The Japanese are beginning to have serious doubts whether their economy can support nine years of compulsory schooling devoted almost entirely to general cultural education. Ideally, under the present system, the student in lower secondary school has the opportunity to explore several vocational paths before he need make a choice. The upper secondary schools are supposed to offer a comprehensive practical curriculum as well as academic subjects. But their equipment for vocational training has been so inadequate that the results have been disappointing.[49] The Japan Economic Federation is now demanding that the schools turn out "people who will be immediately useful." [50] Miyahara Seiichi and Kaigo Tokiomi of Tokyo University have presented a new educational theory called "productionism (*seisan-shugi*)." Since 75 percent of the students will have no education beyond the ninth year, they argue, the lower secondary school should be used for outright job training.[51]

For her own economic health, Japan may need to adopt

[47] *Mainichi Shimbun*, February 11, 1953, May 29, 1953; *The Mainichi*, December 20, 1953.

[48] *Jiji Nenkan, 1953* (Tokyo: Jiji Tsūshinsha, 1952), p. 313.

[49] *Education Reform in Japan: The Present Status and the Problems Involved, 1950,* (Tokyo: Education Reform Council, 1950), p. 53.

[50] *Mainichi Shimbun*, Feb. 10, 1953.

[51] *Nihon Kyōiku Nenkan, 1950,* cited, pp. 629-630; Mombushō, Chōsa fukyū kyoku, *Kyōiku Yōran, 1950 (Outline of Education, 1950),* p. 137; Miyahara Seiichi, "Seisan-shugi Kyōiku Ron (The Production Theory of Education)," *Chūō Kōron*, V. 64 (October 1949), pp. 45-52.

some such solution. The Japanese may have to reconcile themselves to fewer but better schools and universities. But they will make these decisions reluctantly and bitterly, especially so since American pressure for rearmament will seem to be forcing them to sacrifice schools for guns.

Our best hope that Japan's educational system will survive the perils of reaction and continue to develop in the direction of democracy lies in the fact that the recent reforms were not, as many American officials and advisers believed, really new. We were not, as in Germany, imposing neo-modern ideas upon a nation with an older firmly established tradition of educational philosophy.[52] Instead we were dealing with a people who had already elected to follow our own progression from Pestalozzi to Herbart to Dewey. We were picking up the threads of development at the point where they had been abruptly cut in the 1930's. If Americans in the Occupation had been better aware of the advantages that two earlier phases of American influence had given them, they could have spent less time on forms and techniques and more on the vital spirit in which these were applied.

[52] American re-education of Germany, which offers many interesting parallels and contrasts, has been discussed in prospect in Werner Richter, *Re-educating Germany* (Chicago: University of Chicago Press, 1945); in progress in William F. Russell, "Teaching Germans to Teach Themselves," *Foreign Affairs*, V. 27 (October 1948), pp. 68-77; and in critical retrospect in William Ernest Hocking, *Experiment in Education: What We Can Learn from Teaching Germany* (Chicago: Regnery, 1954).

PART III

CHANNELS OF COMMUNICATION

INTRODUCTION

WE SPEAK at times of cultural relations between Japan and America as if countries themselves had eyes and ears and mouths. Communication actually occurs only between individuals. Even the mass communications that receive so much emphasis today depend upon the aggregate action of a multitude of living persons. To have any effect radio broadcasts must be listened to, newspapers and books must be read, motion pictures and art exhibits must be seen.

An active minority of individuals are responsible for most communications between countries and cultures. The travelers, businessmen, missionaries, students, and teachers who go from one country are the channels through which knowledge flows. Abroad they are representatives, consciously or unconsciously, of their own culture. When they return they share their experiences and attitudes. Even the more impersonal exchanges of cultural materials depend in most cases on the active efforts of a few interested persons.

Precisely because communication occurs between individuals, its efficiency and effect are complex matters that are hard to predict. The persons involved are never *tabula rasa;* both their perception and their attitudes are conditioned by previous experience, by their particular share in a cultural heritage. The meaning received may not be the meaning intended. Memories will shift and attitudes change in the light of later experience.

The chapters that follow describe and evaluate some of the principal types of cultural communication between Japan and the United States. The very continuity of experience suggests that these are natural deep-cut channels. Japanese students have been coming to the United States since the 1860's. Fulbright professors are the modern successors of the early foreign teachers of English and science. Exchange of cultural materials began on the decks of Commodore Perry's "black ships." Missionary work has been a characteristic part of the impact of West upon East. Statistical generalizations about these aspects of cultural relations are so few that we shall be talking most of the time about individual contributions and experiences. Finally, we shall examine the role of both the Japan Societies and the government in stimulating and directing the flow of cultural relations.

CHAPTER FIVE

INTERCHANGE OF TEACHERS

TRANSPLANTING TEACHERS is one of the most efficient ways
to make the way of life and point of view of one people
known to another. The teacher is the active party in the
educational process, intent on communicating his knowledge
and opinions to others. In a foreign country he faces a
new audience, whose receptivity may actually be heightened
by his strangeness. The foreign student must fit himself to
a system of education tailored for domestic needs; but the
perceptive teacher working abroad can, in contrast, adjust
his message to the understanding and curiosity of his listeners. The teacher is also one of the best channels for a
two-way flow of cultural understanding. He is usually a
careful observer of his new environment, and his ability to
analyze and communicate his experiences makes him one
of the most effective interpreters of its culture to his own
people.

Exchange of teachers between the United States and Japan
has been markedly unbalanced. Many Americans have
taught in Japan, but Japanese have usually come here as
students rather than as lecturers or visiting professors. Only
after 1910 were a few Japanese given opportunities to teach
us about their own culture. Even then they faced the problem of hurdling the language barrier, and some of the men
who would have been most competent were disqualified by
inability to communicate in English. Repeated series of general lectures on Japanese life were likely to show diminish-
ing returns; while interest in Japan was so limited before
1941 that specialized subjects were likely to attract only very
small audiences. But now Japanese teachers could help in
many ways to strengthen and extend the interest aroused

by World War II and the Occupation. We need to know more about Japanese literature, not just the classics, but also modern novels and poetry. The fine arts as practiced in Japan could be demonstrated in much greater detail. Japanese historians have much to teach us, not only about their own past but about all of Asia. We should also be alert to recognize the special contributions that Japanese scholars can make to many fields of knowledge, scientific as well as cultural. Only when we look upon them as scholars first, and Japanese only incidentally, will there be real equality.

The exact number of Americans who have taught in Japan during the past century is difficult to determine. The Ministry of Education prepared for William Elliot Griffis a list of 119 Americans employed full-time in public education institutions between 1860 and 1906.[1] My own list for the period 1860 to 1912 includes 234 names.[2] One can safely say that as many Americans have taught in Japan since the end of the Meiji era. The total number, then, would be near five hundred. This does not include, however, the many missionaries who established private schools and colleges as part of their evangelistic efforts. In recent decades some of these institutions have been truly professional in stature. But the Christian contribution of supplementary facilities and leadership in some branches of education can better be considered in connection with the general subject of missions. The part that American teachers at Sapporo Agricultural College played in the economic development of Hokkaidō has already been told in Chapter Two.

The influence of Americans teaching in Japan has depended in part upon their own ability and personality. Some were professionally competent; some were not. Some were impelled by a burning desire both to teach and to learn; others were merely looking for a soft berth in pleasant surroundings. We shall be concerned, therefore, with their motives and their rewards. Equally important in determining

---

[1] Griffis papers, Rutgers University Library.
[2] This is a revision of the list of 227 in my "American Influence in the Education of Meiji Japan, 1868–1912" (Unpublished dissertation, Harvard University, 1950), pp. 287-308.

influence, however, are the conditions under which they have worked. The foreign teacher played a much more important role in the revolutionary atmosphere of early Meiji than he did under the constrictive militarism of the thirties. The analysis of past experience will, therefore, be organized by periods.

Decentralized Power and Naïve Curiosity about the West, 1853–1870

The Japanese responded to overtures from Western powers with a curious mixture of rejection and curiosity. For fifteen years after Commodore Perry had breached Japan's wall of seclusion the hope of ultimately "driving out the barbarians" was never abandoned. But even the advocates of this policy of *jōi* saw the necessity for fighting fire with fire and eagerly sought to learn the secrets of Western military power. Rivalry between the Shogunate and the feudal lords (*daimyō*), and among the *daimyō* themselves, put a further premium upon Western knowledge. Since very few Japanese were yet able to go abroad, this curiosity could only be satisfied by using foreigners in Japan as teachers.

The first American teacher in Japan, Ranald MacDonald, preceded even the coming of Commodore Perry. The son of a Hudson's Bay Company factor and a Chinook Indian woman, MacDonald was a citizen of the United States only by virtue of the Oregon treaty of 1846. Motivated by love of adventure and a desire to become a "teacher as to things external" to a people with whom he imagined a vague racial kinship, he had a whaler set him adrift off the coast of Japan in 1848. Although the Japanese imprisoned him at Nagasaki until he was rescued by the *Preble* in 1849, they took advantage of his presence to train fourteen official interpreters in the English language. Two of them, Moriyama Einosuke and Hori Tatsunosuke, later took part in the negotiations with Perry.[3]

[3] William S. Lewis and Murakami Naojirō, eds., *Ranald MacDonald: The Narrative of his Early Life on the Columbia Under the Hudson's Bay Company's Regime; of his Experiences in the Pacific Whale Fishery; and of his Great Adventure to Japan; with a Sketch of His Later Life on the Western Frontier, 1824–1894* (Spokane: Eastern Washington State Historical Society,

154 JAPANESE AND AMERICANS

The opening of a few ports to trade increased the need for knowledge of foreign languages. When the American naval vessel *Powhatan* came to Nagasaki in September 1858, the governor asked the chaplain, the Rev. Henry Wood, to teach English to six young men of his suite. Several missionaries from China who came to Nagasaki for their health were also pressed into service as instructors.[4] In 1861 the Shogunate sent nine young men to Yokohama to study English under Dr. J. C. Hepburn, American medical missionary. Among them were such men of later prominence as Prime Minister Takahashi Korekiyo, diplomat Hayashi Tadasu, and entrepreneur Masuda Takashi. The next year a formal school for interpreters was established in Yokohama in connection with the customhouse, with Samuel Robbins Brown and other missionaries as teachers.[5]

Guido F. Verbeck was the American teacher who had the greatest impact upon the Japanese in their period of awakening. Verbeck came to Nagasaki in 1859 as a missionary of the Reformed Church in America, particularly qualified for the Japan field by the fact that his native tongue was Dutch, the Western language then most widely known. Since propagation of Christianity was still officially proscribed, he welcomed an invitation from the Governor of Nagasaki to become head teacher of a language school opened in 1863. There he used as his principal texts the United States Constitution and the New Testament, which he extolled as the basic foundations of American civilization. Part of his time was devoted to another school which the Saga *han* had opened in Nagasaki. Although he received invitations from the Lords of Kaga, Satsuma, and Tosa to come and open schools in their domains, Verbeck preferred to remain in Nagasaki until, after the Restoration, two of his former students,

1923) pp. 23-249; Shigehisa Tokutarō, *Nihon Kinsei Eigaku Shi (History of Modern English Studies in Japan)* (Kyoto: Kyōiku Tosho Kabushiki Kaisha, 1941), p. 246.
[4] Shigehisa, cited, pp. 277-286.
[5] William Elliot Griffis, *Hepburn of Japan and his Wife and Helpmates* (Philadelphia: Westminster, 1913), pp. 91-117; Fujimoto Jitsuya, *Kaikō to Kiito Bōeki (The Opening of Yokohama and the Silk Trade)* (Yokohama: Kaikō to Kiito Bōeki Kankōkai, 1939), V. 1, pp. 695-698; Griffis, *A Maker of the New Orient: Samuel Robbins Brown* (New York: Revell, 1902), pp. 185-190.

Ōkuma Shigenobu and Soejima Taneomi, called him to Tokyo to assume greater responsibilities in connection with the new University.[6]

Around the time of the Restoration, the various *han* tried to gain advantage in the struggle for power by establishing schools to teach Western languages and science. In 1867 Jonathan Goble, a marine on Perry's expedition who returned to Japan as a Baptist missionary, was teaching English for the *daimyō* of Tosa.[7] Through Verbeck, Matsudaira Shungaku of Fukui *han* obtained the services of a recent graduate of Rutgers, William Elliot Griffis, as teacher of the physical sciences. After persuading the defense-conscious Japanese that he could not immediately teach them how to blow up warships with submarine mines, Griffis began a systematic presentation of physics, chemistry, geography, geology, and physiology.[8] The deposed Shōgun opened a school for his retainers at Shizuoka in which another Rutgers man, Edward Warren Clark, taught in both English and French.[9]

Not all the teachers were of the caliber of Verbeck and Griffis, nor did all deserve the respect and confidence so generously accorded. In their inexperience the Japanese often accepted a foreign name as sufficient qualification for teaching, and some of the "professors" had graduated directly from the saloon or the waterfront. As Griffis said: "When [they were] teaching with pipe in mouth, and punctuating their instructions with oaths, or appearing in the classroom top-heavy, the Japanese concluded that such eccentricities were merely national peculiarities." [10] Some left behind a liberal number of Eurasian offspring. As late as 1890 the impulse to economize sometimes led a Japanese school to engage a beached sailor as an English teacher.

6 William Elliot Griffis, *Verbeck of Japan* . . . (New York: Revell, 1900), pp. 62-68, 123-132; Guido F. Verbeck, "Japan of Thirty Years Ago," *Japan Evangelist*, V. 5 (March 1898), pp. 93-96; (April 1898), pp. 110-113; *Meiji Ikō Kyōiku Seido Hattatsu Shi*, cited, V. 1, p. 81.

7 Otis Cary, *A History of Christianity in Japan* (New York: Revell, 1909), V. 2, p. 65.

8 William Elliot Griffis, *The Mikado's Empire* (8th ed.; New York: Harper, 1895), pp. 8-9, 431, 518-523.

9 See Clark's entertaining *Life and Adventure in Japan* (New York: American Tract Society, 1878).

10 Griffis, *The Mikado's Empire*, cited, p. 371.

In this first period both the teachers and the taught were well satisfied. The curiosity of the Japanese about the West was comparatively naive, and was easily satisfied by a smattering of English or a demonstration of shocks from a Leyden jar. Every action of the teacher, every strange object in his house, provided informal education. The missionaries were glad to be self-supporting at a time when the most that they could do was to learn Japanese and make useful contacts. Griffis' contract with the Fukui authorities shows that service in exciting new Japan paid well a young man just out of college. He received $300 a month, plus a Western-style house and a horse. The expenses of the voyage to Japan, and of travel to Fukui and back to Yokohama at the end of the engagement, were paid by the *han*. The only restrictions upon his conduct were stipulations that he must not get drunk and must not "enter into any trading operations with native merchants." Sunday holidays and the provision that he might "speak, teach, and do" as he pleased in his own house left the way open for religious teaching. To the superstitious peasantry the foreigner might be suspect, but students and most of their elders accorded him the respect that traditionally in the Confucian system of values adhered to the teacher.[11]

Centralization of Power and the Creation of New Institutions, 1870–1890

Abolition of the *han* in 1871 and the order that former *daimyō* must move to the capital destroyed both the local leadership and the economic support for these promising educational developments in the provinces. Verbeck, Griffis, and E. W. Clark were all called to Tokyo to teach. Many of their best students came with them, attracted by the opportunities for positions in the new government. Besides being the center of authority from which educational policy has emanated, Tokyo from that time on held a position of undue dominance in higher education. In 1935, for example, 57 percent of the students above middle-school level were attending the 102 institutions in the metropolitan area.[12]

11 Same, p. 402.
12 *Education in Tokyo* (Tokyo: Municipal Office [1937]), p. 167.

From the beginning of the Meiji era the institution that after several metamorphoses has become present Tokyo University led in prestige and popularity. Under the name of Nankō from 1870 to 1873 it was essentially a replica of an American grammar school. Verbeck was the principal, most of the teachers were Americans, and the students used such textbooks as Quackenbos' *English Grammar* and Willson's *Outlines of History*. A change of name to Kaisei Gakkō in April 1873 marked the addition of college-level courses in law, chemistry, engineering, and mining. Amalgamation with Tokyo Medical School in 1876 produced Tokyo University, and ten years later this institution merged with Kōbu Daigakkō, an engineering college founded by the Department of Public Works, to form Tokyo Imperial University. The literary and scientific departments were strongly American in tone until about 1890. Thirty-odd Americans were among the pioneer professors, and a considerable portion of the Japanese faculty had studied in the United States.

Science. Verbeck and other teachers in the Nankō had taught that form of general science known as natural philosophy, but real work in the specialized branches did not begin until the late seventies. When Edward S. Morse, marine zoologist of Salem, Massachusetts, came to Japan in 1877 in search of rare brachiopods, he was asked to stay and start a department of zoology at the university. At a marine laboratory at Enoshima he introduced to Japanese assistants and students Professor Louis Agassiz' techniques of study of living specimens. His discovery and description of the shell mounds at Ōmori marked the beginning of scientific archaeology in Japan. Through public lectures he also popularized the Darwinian theory of evolution, much to the alarm of the missionaries.[13]

On Morse's recommendation, Thomas C. Mendenhall was brought out in 1878 to begin advanced work in physics. Serious work in chemistry was begun by Frank F. Jewett, formerly private assistant to Dr. Wolcott Gibbs of Harvard, and in astronomy by Henry M. Paul of the U. S. Naval Ob-

[13] Dorothy G. Wayman, *Edward Sylvester Morse: A Biography* (Cambridge: Harvard University Press, 1942), pp. 234-270; Robert S. Schwantes, "Christianity *versus* Science: A Conflict of Ideas in Meiji Japan," *Far Eastern Quarterly*, V. 12 (February 1953), pp. 125-127.

servatory. Morse's successor in the chair of zoology, Charles O. Whitman, found, however, that the Japanese had only limited interest in pure research. "Any science that offers small opportunities for pilfering 'squeezers,' makes no promise to improve the rice crop or the flavor of the sake, serves none of the wants of sensual pleasure, jingles no bells, and refuses to make use of the sop of flattery," he wrote, "may be suffered to exist for the sake of appearance, but is certain to be stigmatized as unprofitable." [14] Both Whitman and Paul were glad to leave Tokyo when their contracts expired, and by 1885 the scientific courses were left in the hands of Japanese professors.

Engineering. As an outgrowth of his topographic and mineralogical surveys in Hokkaido for the Colonization Commission, Henry S. Munroe started in 1874–75 a course in geology and mining engineering at Kaisei Gakkō. Before he could make use of the $8,000 worth of teaching models, mineral specimens, and mining tools that he was authorized to order from abroad, however, he had to leave Japan; and his work was taken over by a German professor.[15] Shortly after this a course in civil engineering along American lines was begun by James R. Wasson and Winfield S. Chaplin. Their successor from 1882 to 1886, James A. L. Waddell, made a determined critical assault upon the prevailing British designs for railroad bridges.[16] With the incorporation of the Kōbu Daigakkō into the enlarged University in 1886, however, British teachers won control of all subsequent engineering instruction.

English and American literature. After the organization of the Kaisei Gakkō, James Summers attempted to lead the students on from elementary reading and composition to real study of literature. Although he was an Englishman, Summers used an American text, Underwood's *Hand-book,*

[14] C. O. Whitman, *Zoology in the University of Tokio* (Yokohama: Author, 1881), p. 29.

[15] Course plans and records are preserved in the Munroe papers, Connecticut Historical Society, Hartford.

[16] Waddell continued to give young Japanese engineers practical training in his office in Kansas City. "For twenty-five years I had at all times from two to five Japanese in my employ. They stayed generally from two to three years, but some remained four or five years." Waddell to W. E. Griffis, September 30, 1918, Griffis papers, Rutgers.

which devoted equal space to British and American authors. On one of the examination papers students were asked to write a description of Governor Van Twiller in Washington Irving's style and to paraphrase stanzas from Longfellow's "Psalm of Life." The teacher who really developed the literature course, however, was William Addison Houghton, a Yale graduate who came to the university in 1877. His teaching of Shakespeare was largely responsible for turning Tsubouchi Shōyō and a whole generation away from the old literary norm of "punishment for vice and reward for virtue" to an objective but aesthetic description of observed human life in all its complexity.[17] After Houghton left in 1882 the courses in English literature passed out of the hands of Americans for a decade. An American Ph.D. from Heidelberg, Augustus Wood, was employed from 1892 to 1896, but his reputation was quickly eclipsed by that of his successor, Lafcadio Hearn, probably the greatest of the American teachers—if any one nation can claim such a cosmopolite.

Hearn enjoys so high a reputation in both Japan and America that one suspects exaggeration of his influence. For one thing, his knowledge of the Japanese language was not remarkable; he never learned to read *kanji* (characters), and he communicated with his wife and children in a private "Hearn-language." Poor eyesight confirmed his natural tendency to be a recluse. He was overly-sensitive and irascible, and eventually quarreled with nearly all his friends and associates. Yet we have the testimony of his students at Matsue Middle School, at the Fifth Higher School in Kumamoto, and at Tokyo Imperial University that he was an inspiring teacher. He taught the way they wanted, in lectures dictated so slowly that volume after volume has been printed from their verbatim notes. His world-view, the evolutionary philosophy of Herbert Spencer tinged with a kind of cosmic mysticism, was congenial to them. Perhaps most important was his appreciation of the deep substratum of emotion in the Japanese personality. "I taught literature," he wrote, "as the expression of emotion and sentiment—as

[17] Kawatake Shigetoshi and Yanagida Izumi, *Tsubouchi Shōyō* (Tokyo: Fuzambō, 1939), p. 103; Oda Masanobu, "Remarks on the Study of Meiji Literature," *Monumenta Nipponica*, V. 5 (January 1942), pp. 203-204.

the representation of life. In considering a poet I tried to
explain the quality and the powers of the emotion he produces. In short, I based my teaching altogether upon appeals
to the imagination and the emotions of my pupils. . . ." [18]

But it is the Hearn who wrote *Kokoro* and *Kwaidan,*
rather than Hearn on Shakespeare, who has permanently
captured the admiration and loyalty of the Japanese. As
Koizumi Yakumo he has become the saint of a cult; he is an
emotion, no longer a fact. In an effort to understand, Hearn
became almost more Japanese than the Japanese. He dis-
tilled out the mystery and beauty in their lives and gave
them an elixir of escape from the realities of industrialization. He took their folk tales and romanticized and embellished them. He gave back a past to a people who in haste
had thrown it away. For this the Japanese have been grateful. No modern teacher is likely to be a second Hearn, but
all might learn from him that aesthetic sensitivity is a better
approach to the Japanese than ruthless logic.

Philosophy. The rapid social changes of the Restoration
period made the Japanese lose temporarily all confidence in
traditional ideas and authorities. The teachings of Confu-
cianism and Buddhism were dropped from the curricula
of the new schools, and a variety of Western books was
used as logical guides to morality. The most popular was
probably *Saikoku Risshihen,* Nakamura Masanao's translation of Samuel Smiles' *Self-Help. Elements of Moral Science* by Francis Wayland, former president of Brown University, was also widely read. Fukuzawa Yukichi used Wayland in the Keiō-gijuku, and it was also taught in the Nankō
until educational officials discovered its essentially Christian
tone.[19]

Specialized university instruction in philosophy was begun
in 1878 by Ernest F. Fenollosa, who came from Harvard on
the recommendation of E. S. Morse and Charles Eliot Norton. Fenollosa began with a course in "Political Philosophy"
based largely on Hegel and Spencer, a course in "Political

[18] Elizabeth Bisland, ed., *The Life and Letters of Lafcadio Hearn* (Boston:
Houghton Mifflin, 1906), V. 2, p. 481; "Lafcadio Hearn in the Class Room,"
New East, V. 1 (June 1917), p. 38.
[19] William Elliot Griffis, "Education in Japan," *College Courant,* V. 14 (May
16, 1874), p. 232.

Economy" which presented both the free trade views of
the British classical school and the protectionist theories of
Henry Carey, and a survey of the "History of Modern Philosophy." In subsequent years his lectures and reading as-
signments became more and more elaborate as he explored
the connections of politics with sociology, ethics, and meta-
physics. When Fenollosa turned his entire attention to
Japanese art in 1886, the chair of philosophy went first to
Ludwig Busse and then to Raphael Koeber. For these men
of German training philosophy meant primarily the then
popular writings of Schopenhauer, Lotze, and Hartmann.
From that time Japanese study and teaching of Western philosophy had a strong tone of philosophical idealism derived
from the Germans.[20]

To Japanese scholars the distinctively American philosophy of pragmatism has seemed casual and unsystematic.
Most of its influence has been outside the academic departments. A translation of William James' *Pragmatism*,
appearing in 1910 just at the time of his death, attracted
considerable interest.[21] In 1919 John Dewey delivered at
Tokyo University the series of lectures which were later published as *Reconstruction in Philosophy*. Since World War II
there has been a spate of books on both James and Dewey.
Tsurumi Shunsuke particularly has been publicizing pragmatism as a way of thought that will take philosophy away
from the professors and give it back to the people.[22]

Law. The study of law has always been the royal road into
the Japanese bureaucracy. In this field of education no foreign teacher compared in influence to the French jurist and
code-maker, Gustave Boissonade; but the chair of Anglo-
American law at Tokyo Imperial University was held by a
succession of Americans for forty years. The pioneer was

[20] Inoue Tetsujirō, "Fuenorosa oyobi Kēberu Shi no Kotodomo (Random Remarks about Fenollosa and Koeber)," in *Meiji Bunka Hasshō Kinenshi
(Papers Commemorating the Origins of Meiji Culture)* (Tokyo: Dai Nihon
Bummei Kyōkai, 1924), "Kaikoroku" section, pp. 47-52.
[21] *Saikin Shichō Jissai-shugi*, translated by Kitazawa Sadayoshi, Yoshida Kei,
and Nishiyama Tetsuji (Tokyo: Kōdōkan, 1910).
[22] Tsurumi Shunsuke, *Amerika Tetsugaku: Puragumateizumu o dō Kaishaku
shi Hatten saseru ka (American Philosophy: How can Pragmatism be Interpreted and Developed?)* (Tokyo: Sekai Hyōron-sha, 1950), pp. 266-290.

Henry Taylor Terry, whom Hearn described as "enormously self-sufficient and aggressive" but with "a rough plain goodness about him." [23] Terry began in 1878 by preparing a book which "set out in as plain and simple a manner as possible . . . the most general and elementary principles of the law." [24] Upon this foundation he built specialized courses in agency, partnership, maritime law, marine insurance, and public and private international law. In teaching contracts and sales he made use of the casebooks prepared at Harvard Law School by Christopher C. Langdell, thus introducing to a limited degree in Tokyo as early as 1880 a system of instruction which was not adopted by any other law school in the United States until a decade later. The case system never worked well in Japan, however, and was soon abandoned. Rather than working out principles of law for himself, the Japanese student wanted to take down from the professor prepared statements that he could learn verbatim.[25]

When Terry left Japan in 1884 he was succeeded first by Charles Bigelow Storrs and then by Alexander Tison. He returned to resume the chair in 1894, however, and by the time of his retirement in 1912 he had taught over one thousand Japanese lawyers, and through them exerted an incalculable influence upon legal thought and practice.[26]

Although the legal codes adopted by Japan during these years followed European models, there continued to be a remarkable interest in common law jurisprudence. John H. Wigmore, who himself taught law at Keiō and Tōkyō Semmon Gakkō from 1889 to 1892, attributed this popularity to the mental training gained from dealing with the concrete materials of Anglo-American law and to the preponderant com-

---

[23] Bisland, cited, V. 2, pp. 284, 316.
[24] *The First Principles of Law* (Tokyo: 1878).
[25] John H. Wigmore, "Legal Education in Modern Japan," *Japan Weekly Mail*, V. 19 (June 17, 1893), p. 711.
[26] It is easy to exaggerate the effectiveness of the foreign teacher. A Japanese colleague recalls that Terry spoke so rapidly that students had difficulty in understanding him. Since everything that they needed to know for examinations was included in printed notes that were distributed, they cut his lectures *en masse*. Most of Terry's energies were absorbed in preparation of an ambitious treatise on torts. Takayanagi Kenzō, *Bei-Ei no Hōritsu Shichō (Currents of Legal Thought in America and England)* (Tokyo: Unnokuchi Shoten, 1948), pp. 316-321.

mercial and political influence of the English-speaking peoples in the Orient.[27] To meet the demand Masujima Rokuichirō, a pupil of Terry's who had also studied at the Middle Temple, founded in 1885 the Igirisu Hōritsu Gakkō (English Law School). For several years courses on agency, partnership, personal property, and international law were given by Komura Jutarō, a graduate of Harvard Law School who was later to become Japan's Foreign Minister. G. H. Scidmore, the American Deputy Consul General in Yokohama, gave a series of lectures on procedure in the United States consular courts in Japan.[28] By 1893 the English Law School had 1,200 students, one-third of whom were studying directly from such American texts as Story on *Agency* and Kent on *Corporations*. In order to prepare its students for the realities of practice or administration, however, this school, which eventually became Chūō University, had to devote more and more time to the new Continental-type codes.

After Terry's retirement the fortunes of Anglo-American legal studies in Japan become more difficult to trace. The Tokyo chair was occupied from 1912 to 1918 by James Lee Kauffman. After that time no foreigners seem to have been appointed, although instruction was continued by Professor Takayanagi Kenzō. In 1926 Masujima established an Anglo-American Law Institute and Library on his Tokyo estate, to which Americans contributed many books. We know very little, however, about the use made of them.[29]

The Occupation reawakened interest in American law, although no effort was made to destroy the civil-law basis of Japanese jurisprudence. In recent years, Ben Bruce Blakeney has been conducting seminar courses at Tokyo University and lecturing in other law schools. He is also preparing a series of volumes of *Materials for the Study of American Law*. At least a dozen Japanese scholars are specializing in Anglo-American jurisprudence. They are seriously handi-

[27] *Japan Weekly Mail*, V. 19 (May 27, 1893), pp. 625-628.
[28] C. R. Greathouse to Department of State, April 14, 1887, Kanagawa Consular Dispatches, National Archives.
[29] "The Anglo-American Law Institute," *American Bar Association Journal*, V. 12 (September 1926), pp. 639-641; Alexander Tison to Douglas L. Dunbar, April 29, 1926, records of Japan Society, New York.

capped, however, by the lack of reports of recent decisions and other publications.[30]

Economics. In the 1890's economics was finally separated from philosophy and made part of the law curriculum of Tokyo Imperial University. The promising work as Lecturer on Political Economy and Finance that Charles S. Griffin began in 1899 was cut short by his accidental death in 1904, just when he was about to begin an extensive study of Japan's new industrial strength.[31] O. M. W. Sprague then interrupted his career at Harvard to spend the years 1905 to 1908 teaching in Tokyo. From 1913 to 1921 the post was held by William Hyde Price, who had previously taught at Wisconsin and Yale. The direct personal influence that Sprague and Price may have exerted upon future Japanese civil servants and businessmen is hard to assess. Neither one made an effort, however, to interpret for the American public the remarkable economic transformation that Japan was undergoing.

Private universities. This period also saw the development of Keiō and Waseda, the two private universities that have offered serious competition to Tokyo University. "Independence and self-respect" was the lifelong motto of the founder of Keiō, Fukuzawa Yukichi. The ultimate goal of national wealth and strength could best be attained, he felt, by maximum development of each individual. He urged his students, therefore, to make their own way in business or teaching, and not to rely upon the state for positions in the civil service. During the seventies and eighties Keiō-Gijuku was essentially an American-type high school that specialized in preparing native teachers of English. In 1889 a university course was added, and to start it off three recent graduates of Harvard were brought out as professors: J. H. Wigmore for the chair of law, Garrett Droppers for that of political economy, and William Liscomb as professor of literature. Literature was too impractical to enjoy real popularity; Liscomb's successor, Thomas Sergeant Perry, had only four students in 1900. "The rest," Perry wrote, "do not care for the study

[30] Suenobu Sanji, "Anglo-American Law," *Japan Science Review: Law and Politics,* No. 1 (1950), pp. 102-103.
[31] *Japan Weekly Mail,* September 17, 24, 1904.

of anything but political economy." [32] The latter subject, so important in the Keiō tradition, was carried on by a series of Americans: Enoch H. Vickers (1898–1910), W. W. McLaren (1908–1914), Robert J. Ray (1911–1914), Daniel H. Buchanan (1914–1925), Ralph C. Whitnack (1914–?), Will Goettling (1917–1921), and Thomas E. Jones (1921–1924).

In retrospect Professor Vickers has given one of those rare glimpses into the substance of the work of an American teacher in Japan.

My first classes were about 20 to 30 in number. In the later years of my tenure, I lectured to student groups ranging up to 200 and more in number. The total number of my Japanese students ran into the thousands. Subjects of the courses taught by me . . . were: Principles of Economics; Economic History; History of Economic Theory; Labor Problems and Policies; Commercial Policy; Money and Banking; Public Finance; also topical studies in Seminar. . . .

Besides my work within the system of technical education, I contributed more or less to many other pools of influence. Among them were scores of addresses each year; many articles for periodicals and newspapers, most of them published in Japanese translation; countless personal interviews and conferences with persons of eager and inquiring minds, [I] being often approached in public places with inquiries.[33]

At a time when the Japanese were trying feverishly to assimilate Western methods of creating wealth and power, the foreign teacher of economics was in a position to exert unusual influence.

Foreign teachers played a less important role at Waseda, the other great private center of training for politics and business. Ōkuma Shigenobu's primary motive when he founded the Tōkyō Semmon Gakkō in 1882 was to make advanced instruction available to Japanese students in their own language. Himself a great admirer of the parliamentary system, Ōkuma had no prejudice against foreign thought as such, but he wanted to have it assimilated by a native faculty. But because the literature available in translation was still

[32] John T. Morse, Jr., *Thomas Sergeant Perry: A Memoir* (Boston: Houghton Mifflin, 1929), p. 87.
[33] Letter from Vickers, August 25, 1949.

so limited, an English department had to be added in 1888. Aside from language teachers, however, Waseda employed only an occasional foreign lecturer. Wigmore gave part-time instruction in international law, and Hearn taught English literature there just before his death in 1904.[34]

Assessment of American influence. We can justifiably be proud of the work of American professors in the early development of so many fields of learning in Japan. But we should also ask whether, in the long run, their influence has been entirely good. Changes in the university system of Japan might be accomplished more easily today if both American critics and Japanese defenders of the *status quo* realized that many of the practices under debate are merely extreme developments of what were originally American influences. Certainly Japan has not copied the communal life and system of independent reading under the guidance of a tutor that distinguish Oxford and Cambridge. From the German universities she may have taken the pompous authority of the professor in the academic security of his chair, but not the corresponding independence of the student. Almost unconsciously these Americans molded Tokyo University during its formative years, and it set the pattern for the newer universities.

The American practice of course examinations set by the instructor, instead of general examinations by disinterested persons, has led in Japan to the most absurd parroting of lectures and a failure to integrate what is learned into original and meaningful wholes. The large number of courses taken by each student, which the British editor of the *Japan Mail* criticized in 1887 as an "American characteristic," is a legacy from the days when our college curriculum was struggling to encompass the whole of knowledge, before admitting defeat by adoption of either free electives or fields of concentration. The emphasis on lectures began when they were efficient ways of covering broad fields of knowledge not too crowded with either facts or concepts. As knowledge has been subdivided, lectures have become less synthetic and interpretive and deal with limited subjects that the student might

---

[34] *Han-seiki no Waseda (A Half-century of Waseda)* (Tokyo: Waseda Daigaku Shuppanbu, 1932), p. 40 and *passim.*

better approach directly through reading or laboratory experiments. In America these same dangers have been re-
lieved by the constant experimentation that goes on within
our decentralized system of higher education; in Japan practices of a bygone day have become fossilized and sanctified.

Period of Sensitive Nationalism, 1890–1910

The Imperial Rescript on Education of October 30, 1890
marked Japan's turn away from the values of the West to
the ancient virtues of "righteousness, loyalty, and filial
piety." Although the Rescript was much too vague to be an
accurate guide to policy, conservatives found it a powerful
weapon for use against Christian believers and liberal thinkers. Uchimura Kanzō was publicly disgraced in 1891 because
he refused to join the other teachers of the Tokyo Higher
Middle School in bowing to the Imperial signature on the
Rescript. Similarly, in 1896 the American teacher Christopher Carrothers lost his position at the Second Higher
School in Sendai because religious scruples kept him from
bowing to the portraits of the Emperor and Empress.

In the universities and higher schools the Japanese were
in many cases dispensing with the services of foreigners or
replacing Americans with Germans. The threat that his salary would be reduced because he had become a Japanese
citizen hung over Hearn's head, although it was not this but
the unauthorized intrusion of a foreign visitor into his classroom that precipitated his break with Tokyo Imperial University.[35] Of the thirty-two foreigners on the Tokyo faculty
during the decade 1902 to 1912, only four were Americans.
During this period the new Imperial University which
opened in Kyoto in 1897 employed only two Americans
part-time: Sidney L. Gulick as lecturer on Christian religion,
and Frank Lombard as teacher of Shakespeare.

The one educational development in this period that involved large numbers of Americans was an arrangement by
which the YMCA supplied teachers of English for the middle schools. The initiative seems to have come from the

---

[35] Vera McWilliams, *Lafcadio Hearn* (Boston: Houghton Mifflin, 1946), pp.
410-419.

Rev. J. H. DeForest of the American Board mission, who believed that the presence of Christian teachers in the inland cities would hasten evangelization of the country. Japanese educational authorities were interested in getting college graduates who would accept minimum salaries. DeForest first asked Dwight L. Moody if he could recruit some men from his Northfield summer school; and Moody, aware of the practical problem of financing passage to Japan, turned the request over to the International Committee of the YMCA. Three men were sent out in 1888, and in the next few years positions were found for eight others. John T. Swift combined direction of the movement with teaching and general YMCA work in Tokyo.[36]

A general reaction against Christianity and the desire of the schools to economize put an end to this first phase of the YMCA teacher movement in about 1894. By 1900, however, it was becoming evident that students entering the Higher Schools who had been taught English entirely by native teachers could hardly understand, much less speak, the language. The YMCA International Committee was again called upon to recruit college graduates, and by 1912 ninety-nine men had served in thirty-nine different cities.[37]

The YMCA teacher in a provincial middle or commercial school faced a lonely task. He might be the only foreigner in the community; if there were others, moral scruples sometimes forbade close association with them. His meager salary of 80 to 100 yen per month did not permit frequent trips to find companionship in the port cities. For sixteen to twenty-four hours each week he did fairly elementary teaching: English conversation and composition, perhaps a little geography and history. In his own work he had a fairly free hand, but he could not hope to exert any real influence upon curriculum formation or general educational policy. If he were discreet he could hold evening and Sunday Bible classes in his own house.[38] William Merrell Vories' efforts in this

[36] Young Men's Christian Association, International Committee, *Foreign Educational Committee* (Leaflet dated May 14, 1888); Galen M. Fisher, "The Association English Teacher Movement in Japan," in *The Christian Movement in Japan, 1912* (Yokohama: Conference of Federated Missions, 1912), p. 318.
[37] Fisher, cited, pp. 319-321.
[38] *The Association Teacher of English in Japan* (n.p., 1908).

direction in Hachiman from 1905 to 1907 provoked actual physical violence and cost him his job. (Vories stayed in Hachiman, however, and in time built up a remarkably successful self-supporting mission.) [39] The YMCA teacher tended to think of himself as primarily a lay missionary and judged his success more by Bible class attendance and number of baptisms than he did by academic standards.

Efforts to compensate for inexperience by group cooperation did in time build up a considerable degree of professional competence and esprit among the YMCA teachers. Each year they met in summer camp for a week or ten days to get a boost in morale, discuss problems of teaching, and orient new men. In 1907 they began to publish an *English Teachers' Magazine* and organized a small loan library of books on education. Realizing that basic improvement in English instruction depended upon better cooperation from Japanese teachers and administrators, they sponsored in 1913 the first of a series of National English Teachers' Conferences. [40]

This increasing professionalization spelled the end of the movement with definite "Y" connections. In 1923 the Ministry of Education created an Institute for Research in English Teaching which took responsibility for improvement of technical methods. Under the influence of Harold E. Palmer, the director of the Institute, more and more of the teaching positions went to Britishers. It is not clear just when the YMCA stopped recruiting new men, but the organization of a completely secular Association of Foreign Teachers in 1928 may be taken as the end of the movement. Over a period of forty years, the "Y" had directed to Japan 150 to 200 young teachers who worked quietly and effectively away from the main centers of foreign influence. Many stayed on in Japan as missionaries or YMCA workers; a few, Roy Smith and Harold Lane for example, are now back there again as teachers.

[39] W. M. Vories, *A Mustard-seed in Japan* (5th ed.; Omi-Hachiman: Omi Mission, 1925).
[40] *Japan Evangelist*, V. 20 (June 1913), pp. 290-292; *Japan Weekly Mail*, March 14, 1914.

*Exchange of Professors in a Period of Internationalism,
1910–1931*

In the twentieth century, alliance with Britain and victory
in the war with Russia brought Japan recognition as an important factor in world politics. Although her participation
in the First World War was definitely opportunistic, after
the war Japan entered the League of Nations and cooperated
in the first attempts to build a system of collective security.
The party cabinets of the twenties made a sincere effort to
find prosperity for Japan within a world of peaceful international trade. Until the militarists reasserted their power
by a coup in Manchuria, Japan seemed to be finding her
place in the world.

The coincidence is more than accidental that in this period exchanges of professors were developed that recognized
Japan as an equal partner. These exchanges were as much
political as educational in purpose; they reflected the concern of international-minded elements of the American public for peace and understanding. Although relations between
the two countries were never critical during these two decades, the festering questions of immigration and discriminatory treatment of Japanese citizens by West Coast states left
no room for complacency. The visiting professor was always
faced with the problem of either defending or apologizing
for his country's point of view.

Visits to Japan by leading American educators were nothing new, of course. Birdsey G. Northrop, former secretary
of the Connecticut State Board of Education, was invited to
give over thirty public addresses in Japan in 1895, and he
was appreciatively honored for his services to Japanese students during the 1870's. When George Trumbull Ladd came
to lecture on modern philosophy at Dōshisha in 1892, Nakashima Rikizō and other Yale alumni on the faculty of the
Imperial University arranged that he should also address
students in Tokyo. Ladd made a second visit in 1899, and
in 1906 he volunteered to come again to help check the ex-
travagance, licentiousness, and despondency among students
after the war with Russia. A disciple of Rudolf Hermann

Lotze, Ladd gladly accepted the findings of psychology, anthropology, and the other sciences, but insisted that the great variety of phenomena were merely means by which a higher ideal element expressed itself. In speaking to Japanese teachers, he emphasized inspirational and moral leadership. Although he made much of the abstract qualities of wisdom, justice, truthfulness, sympathy, and tenderness, he carefully avoided specifying the situations in which these should apply.[41] After inspecting the "benevolent" protectorate in Korea at the invitation of Itō Hirobumi, Ladd returned to America an apologist for Japanese imperialism. What a pity that the Japanese could not have been exposed to the more candid empiricism of his contemporary, William James.

Japanese professors who studied or traveled in the United States had hitherto been given few formal opportunities to teach Americans about Japan. In 1911 the Division of Intercourse and Education of the Carnegie Endowment for International Peace proposed an exchange of lecturers, who might be either scholars or men of affairs. A group of businessmen led by Shibusawa Eiichi agreed to pay the expenses of the speakers sent from Japan. Nitobe Inazō, a Johns Hopkins Ph.D., president of the First Higher School, authority on colonial development, and author of a book on *Bushidō* that had been widely read in the West, started the series. Besides giving lectures on "Characteristics of the Land and People of Japan" at six universities, Dr. Nitobe traveled extensively and made in all 166 addresses to over 40,000 people. In 1912–13 Hamilton Wright Mabie went to Japan to lecture on "American Ideals, Character, and Life." A Japanese journal commented that this was an "extremely difficult task, involving as it does an exposition of American freedom and American individualism that to the Japanese mind must border perilously on 'dangerous thoughts,' yet the essential genius of republican civilization is being presented by Dr. Mabie in a manner and spirit so tactful, sympathetic and graceful that every Japanese recognizes in it the truth spoken in love." [42]

[41] *Raddo-shi Kyōikugaku (Ladd's Pedagogy)* (Tokyo: Sanseidō, 1907). An English version of lectures given in Japan and Korea was published as *The Teacher's Practical Philosophy* (New York: Funk and Wagnalls, 1912).
[42] *Japan Magazine*, V. 3 (March 1913), p. 721.

The academic year 1913–14 saw two interpreters of Japanese life in America: Anesaki Masaharu as visiting professor at Harvard and Satō Shōsuke touring the country on the Carnegie lectureship. Satō was dean of the College of Agriculture at Sapporo and, like Nitobe, an alumnus of Johns Hopkins. His lectures stressed the economic and social progress of Japan in the half century since the opening of the country.[43] Plans for President John G. Hibben of Princeton to go to Japan in 1914–15 on the second American cycle of the exchange had to be canceled on account of war conditions.

The Endowment did not resume its support of exchanges with Japan until almost ten years after the war, and then only as part of a wider program of visiting Carnegie Professors of International Relations. Prominent American scholars were sent abroad to "multiply and strengthen the bonds of intellectual and scholarly understanding and friendship." Although they usually gave a few public lectures, the visitors did not teach courses, and most of their time was given to informal conferences with professors and students. Of the six men sent to Japan between 1927 and 1931, three were, quite naturally, specialists in Far Eastern affairs: George H. Blakeslee, George M. Dutcher, and Charles E. Martin. Philosopher William P. Montague, Shakespeare specialist Ashley H. Thorndike, and Clyde A. Duniway, professor of American history at Carleton College, made more indirect contributions to better bilateral relations. The Endowment did not in this period strive for an evenly balanced exchange; its efforts in behalf of Japanese scholars were limited to a semester at the University of Hawaii for Nakaseko Rokurō, professor of chemistry at Dōshisha University.

Deteriorating Relations, 1931–1941

The Americans still teaching in Japan during the thirties experienced in full measure that sense of frustration which is the fate of men of good will in times when the current of political events runs against them. They suffered not so

[43] Published as *Some Historical Phases of Modern Japan* (New York: Japan Society, 1916).

much from open hostility—there seems to have been remarkably little of that—but rather from a creeping loss of confidence and rapport. Even Japanese intellectuals oriented toward the United States by education or friendship were becoming bland apologists for Japan's Great East Asia Coprosperity Sphere. Japanese faculty members associated less and less with their foreign colleagues. The suspicion that informers sat in the classrooms put a restraint upon both teacher and students. By 1939 foreigners were forbidden to teach subjects like history and philosophy, even in private schools; so the American's only function was to conduct carefully sterilized drills in English conversation. The queries of the military police about the conduct and opinions of foreign teachers sometimes became so bothersome that schools decided that it would be simpler and safer to let them go. Of the 651 Americans still residing in Japan in August 1941, only 19 were classified as teachers.[44]

American Teachers in Japan's New Universities

In the future nearly every American teaching in Japan's public educational system will be working in an institution called a university, or *daigaku*. A reorganization that began to go into effect in 1949 has greatly changed the structure of higher education. In this the Japanese had two principal aims in view: (1) to expand opportunity for advanced training by increasing the number of universities; and (2) to reduce the dominance of the big cities by building up institutions in the prefectures that would resemble American state universities. Take as an example the new Kanazawa University in Ishikawa Prefecture, which has about a thousand students and faculties of law and letters, education, science, medicine, pharmacy, and engineering. Into it have been incorporated the old Fourth Higher School, Kanazawa College of Industrial Arts, Kanazawa University of Medicine, Ishikawa Normal School, Kanazawa Higher Normal School, and Ishikawa Youth School Teachers' Normal School.[45] By March

---

[44] *New York Times*, August 7, 1941.
[45] *Zenkoku Daigaku Ichiran* (*Tabular View of Japanese Universities*) (Tokyo: Mombushō Daigaku Gakujutsu-kyoku Daigaku-ka, 1952), pp. 15-16.

1953 there were 227 of these four-year institutions, at least one in each prefecture. The first two years are devoted largely to "general education" intended to give the student a basic understanding of the humanities, social sciences, and natural sciences. Specialized professional training is relegated to the last two years. The third year of the old university course has been transferred to the graduate school (*daigakuin*), of which there were 45. In addition, Japan in 1953 had 233 two- or three-year short-course universities, roughly equivalent to our junior colleges.[46]

Because of their involved structure and scattered facilities, many of the new units have been dubbed "octopus universities." During the confusion of the first few years, academic standards were often low. A majority of the faculty had never before taught at the college level. Libraries and laboratories were almost non-existent. Students took from fifteen to twenty lecture courses at one time, and did practically no work beyond memorizing their notes for examinations. But curricula are being revised, and if reasonably adequate funds are provided, great improvements can be expected. The National Association of University Professors formed in 1946 is working "to raise the standard of study and education . . . by mutual amity and cooperation of its members."

One of the requests that the Japanese made to the Educational Exchange Survey Mission in 1949 was that they be helped to obtain some competent American teachers. The U. S. Army then allocated funds for this purpose, and obtained the services of the Institute of International Education as administrative agent in the United States. The Institute invited about 100 of the more than 350 inquirers to submit applications, which were screened by a committee on which the State Department, the Department of the Army, and the principal professional organizations in the field of education were represented. Then Japanese universities were permitted to make their own selections. Thirty-five teachers were sent out, most of them in the spring of 1951. Four came home for various reasons, and one was replaced, making an

[46] *Jiji Nenkan, 1954*, p. 293.

effective total of thirty-two. They were scattered widely, most of them going to new prefectural universities.

The program might have been more successful if it had not tried to do too much with too little. The salaries offered —$2,000 per year at first, subsequently raised to $3,000, plus a yen salary to cover expenses in Japan—were not large enough to attract professors with established reputations. A few prewar teachers were glad to return to their former posts. But in several cases the younger teachers who went over had their rosy expectations shattered upon arrival. Some of the housing supplied by the universities failed to come up to Western standards of comfort. The U. S. Army did not allow them to buy at post exchanges, so they had to pay much higher prices for imported items at Overseas Supply Stores or order by mail from the United States.[47]

So many students wanted to learn English that the American teacher's efforts were spread thin and his physical endurance stretched to the breaking point. At the start one man was lecturing to every student in his university, at four separate locations.[48] Some teachers were disappointed because their recommendations on curricula and educational policy could not immediately be put into effect. Many of the university presidents were already acquainted with American education from past study in the United States, but they also recognized the practical obstacles to wholesale adoption of foreign techniques and standards.

In rather angry protest against the cost of living and teaching loads, the Americans formed an Association of University Professors in Japan for collective bargaining with the Ministry of Education and the University Accreditation Committee. The Ministry tried to meet legitimate demands, raised yen salaries, and even paid the professors' railroad fares and other expenses at meetings of the Association. As personal grievances were reduced, the group increasingly turned its attention to concrete problems of teaching.

As their two-year term passed, the teachers became better

[47] Of 24 professors who responded to a cost-of-living questionnaire in January 1952, eleven were able to live on the yen salary. The average excess cost was $55 per month.
[48] Letter from John P. Phillips, December 11, 1952.

aware of the opportunities as well as the limitations in their work. The American was regarded as an oracle on many subjects, and he enjoyed a status of importance higher than he could expect at home. He organized and judged literary and speaking contests, took a leading part in teachers' conferences, and gave lectures to various groups on life in America or on his special field. Japanese newspapers and magazines were eager to publish whatever he wrote; publishers were on the lookout for books in English. Some of the wives taught domestic science. The secretary of the Association of Professors evaluated the professional success of the program as follows:

Most of the universities are delighted with what the American professors are doing and are eager to have them continue if it is financially possible. The professors feel generally that they are doing some good but find it hard to judge just how much. Most of them are disturbed at the state of education in their universities and would like to see changes which would make their own teaching effective. Some have been able to bring about certain desired changes in their institutions, others despair of effecting any significant changes.[49]

For want of dollar support the program lapsed in April 1953, although the universities in most cases wanted to retain the teachers and the Ministry of Education agreed to try to increase yen salaries still further. At the end of the Occupation neither the Department of State nor private foundations were willing or able to take over fast enough to keep the program going. About fifteen of the professors, including the old hands, were able to make individual arrangements to stay on. Besides re-establishing the tradition of American teachers at places like Hokkaidō and Kōbe Universities, the 1951–53 experiment did make many new institutions aware of the role that foreigners could play on their faculties. In the long run, more flexible personnel arrangements that can take account of differences in experience and purpose will be more advantageous.

The funds derived from sale of surplus property in Japan under the Fulbright Act (Public Law 584, 79th Congress) will be the principal source of support for exchanges of

[49] Letter from William F. Marquardt, December 5, 1952.

teachers between the two countries during the next few years. Under an agreement concluded in August 1951, the Japanese government will make available the yen equivalent of $4,750,000, to be expended over a period of five years or longer. Administration is by a United States Educational Commission in Japan, made up of citizens of both countries.[50] During 1952 nine American lecturers and eight research scholars were brought to Japan. The program for 1954–55 provided for ten research awards on the faculty level and twenty lectureships in such varied subjects as American literature, home economics, music, and surgical anaesthesia.

Medicine and Dentistry in Japan

Training for the medical professions involves such special problems that it can best be considered separate from the rest of university education. American critics have in the last few years been trying to convince the Japanese of that very point. They think that Japanese medical training has been too academic, too much like the courses in law or literature. Reorienting the medical schools toward practical clinical work involves, however, reversal of strong historical trends.

After their country was opened to foreigners in the 1850's, Japanese doctors no longer had to rely on a few Dutch books for knowledge of Western medicine. Informal teaching through clinical demonstrations was an important part of the work of the first American physicians who came to Japan. Already in the 1860's Dr. J. C. Hepburn was training students in his dispensary at Yokohama, especially in the treatment of diseases of the eye.[51] At the Jūzen Hospital in the same city Dr. Duane B. Simmons conducted a voluntary class for medical practitioners. As foreign director of the Tokyo-fu Hospital during the 1870's, Dr. Albert S. Ashmead of Philadelphia trained student doctors and himself participated in the treatment of over 40,000 cases. In connection with his work at Hakodate for the Colonization Commission, Dr. Stuart Eldridge started the first medical journal in

[50] Report on the Operations of the Department of State (Under Public Law 584). 82nd Cong., 2d sess., H. Doc. 410 (Washington: GPO, 1952), pp. 16-22.
[51] Griffis, Hepburn of Japan, cited, p. 103.

Japan.[52] At Kōbe Dr. John C. Berry, medical missionary of the American Board, spent much of his time in teaching. He even prepared daily lesson sheets which were sent out to native doctors who lived at a distance.[53]

The outstanding practical work of these Americans, along with that of British doctors in the treaty ports, created a strong presumption in favor of use of the English language for academic training in medicine. But Guido Verbeck gave decisive support to the party led by Sagara Chian that wanted to follow German models. American physicians and surgeons, Verbeck reported, commonly went to Berlin and Vienna for advanced training. The use of German would have the added advantage of continuity with what had been learned through the Dutch. So the government engaged the first of a long series of German professors for the Tokyo University Medical School. The majority of Japan's leading doctors received training in their specialties in Austria or Germany. Noguchi Hideyo, who was to become world-famous for the work on syphilis and yellow fever that he did for the Rockefeller Institute for Medical Research, was practically unique in choosing an American university (Pennsylvania) for graduate work.[54]

As a result of long-sustained German influence, Japanese medicine has emphasized scientific research rather than clinical treatment. Teaching has been done largely through lectures, just as in other areas of education. The Japanese doctor may have a much more detailed knowledge of medical phenomena than does his American counterpart, but he is likely to be less adept in applying his knowledge to specific cases. "A disease is viewed as a stereotyped combination of certain signs and symptoms," an American professional observer reported recently, "not as a biologic problem or as a

[52] Sei-I-Kwai Medical Journal, V. 8 (April 1889), p. 86; W. N. Whitney, "Notes on the History of Medical Progress in Japan," Transactions of the Asiatic Society of Japan, V. 12 (1885), p. 348.
[53] John C. Berry, Medical Work in Japan (Boston: Woman's Board of Missions, Congregational House, n. d.), pp. 8-9; Katherine F. Berry, A Pioneer Doctor in Old Japan (New York: Revell, 1940), pp. 51-61.
[54] Meiji Ikō Kyōiku Seido Hattatsu Shi, cited, V. 1, pp. 143-144, 148, 198; Griffis, Verbeck of Japan, cited, pp. 210-211. Iseki Kurō, ed., Who's Who in Hakushi in Great Japan (Tokyo: Hattensha, 1921–1930), V. 2, gives biographical sketches of early medical leaders.

progressive physiological, biochemical and pathological process. Diagnosis is a matter of pulling the right term out of
the right pigeon-hole, not a logical deduction from available
evidence. Treatment is a memorized formula too often based
uncritically on some spoken or written pronouncement, not
on reasoned judgment and attempts to facilitate repair and
restoration of normal function." [55]

After World War II American Occupation officials found
the Japan Medical Association so resistant to change that
eventually they ordered it dissolved. Planning for reform of
medical education was entrusted to a Council on Medical
Education headed by Stanford-trained Dr. Kusama Yoshio.
The Council recommended, and the Ministry of Education
adopted on paper, a two-year program of premedical work
followed by four years of medical school, with emphasis on
practical methods of instruction.[56] To aid in the much more
difficult work of changing curricula and teaching procedures,
SCAP, with the assistance of the Unitarian Service Committee, brought parties of American medical educators to
Japan in 1950 and 1951. The first mission understandably
spent a great deal of time bringing the Japanese up to date
on new medical developments, but the second was able to
concentrate more effectively on problems of educational
method. The mission recommended that medical schools
concentrate on training physicians instead of on research,
that students should receive more experience in hospital
wards, and that an adequate system of intern and resident
training should be established. One result already apparent
is that several Japanese schools are using the clinical pathological conference to break down barriers between departments.[57]

Dentistry. A mission of five American dental experts that
visited Japan in the summer of 1951 had very similar criticisms to make. Theoretical phases of dental school curricula

[55] "Report of the Unitarian Service Committee's 1951 Medical Mission to
Japan," (mimeographed), pp. 32-33.
[56] Crawford F. Sams, "Medical Care Aspects of Public Health and Welfare in
Japan," *Journal of the American Medical Association*, V. 141 (October 22,
1949), p. 529.
[57] Same, pp. 47-52; "Report, Institutes of Medical Education, Japan, July 19-
September 5, 1950" (mimeographed), pp. 3-4.

were entirely adequate, but laboratory and clinical requirements were not. Too little effort was being made to apply the
results of research. "The work on patients," they reported,
"showed lack of fundamental knowledge with reference to
proper clinical procedures." [58]

In this case, however, faults cannot be blamed on German
influence, except as it may have been transmitted indirectly
from the medical profession. Modern dentistry in Japan has
from the beginning followed an American tradition. During
the 1870's and 1880's a number of Japanese served as ap-
prentices to American dentists practicing in Yokohama and
Tokyo. The first dental school was opened in 1889 by
Takayama Kisai, who had learned the art in the office of
Dr. Van Denburg of San Francisco during a seven-year stay
in the United States. A large proportion of Japan's practitioners have been trained at this Tokyo Dental College.
From 1890 to 1900 the Society for the Study of Dentistry
(Shika Kenkyū-kai) headed by Dr. Enomoto Sekiichi also did
much to introduce American methods. Texts like Garretson's
Oral Surgery and Fillebrown's *Operative Dentistry* were
translated.[59] Many of Japan's leading specialists and teachers
in dentistry studied in the United States, and until World
War II they were able to keep up with the latest American
technical literature. The problem the profession faces today
is partly one of catching up after almost a decade of isolation.

In 1951 the American mission found the Japanese eager
and determined "to better dental health services in every way
possible." In its report the mission made a number of constructive recommendations. It urged that dental colleges be
made part of recognized universities, but kept separate from
medical schools. Selection of faculty members on the basis
of experience and ability should replace the present system
of inbreeding. Students should be given more training in
technical operations and clinical procedures. Postgraduate
courses should be organized to keep practitioners abreast of

[58] "Mission to Japan: Report to Medical Section, Public Health and Welfare
Division, GHQ, SCAP," *Journal of the American Dental Association*, V. 43
(November 1951), pp. 593-595.
[59] Chiwaki Morinosuke, "Dentistry in Japan," in *Transactions of the Fourth
International Dental Congress held at St. Louis, Mo., U.S.A., August 29 to
September 3, 1904* (Philadelphia: Dental Cosmos, 1905), V. 3, pp. 427-436.

new advances. More attention should be given to preventive work, especially with children. Finally, the mission suggested that, for the sake of the aesthetic appearance that the Japanese people present to the world, metal be used less extensively in the restoration of front teeth.[60]

Student Personnel Services

In theory at least, the Japanese now subscribe to the view that the university exists primarily for the benefit of its students rather than for that of the faculty. With American guidance they are trying to expand non-academic services to students and to put these on a professional basis. Formerly the youth sitting at the feet of his teachers was assumed to be receiving adequate personal as well as intellectual guidance. Outside the classroom he was left pretty much to his own devices, subject only to the control of the ubiquitous police. Business offices of the university handled registration, health, food and lodging, and placement largely as clerical matters. But economic distress and rapid social change in postwar Japan have intensified the problems of students. The majority have to work to support themselves while they study. The breakdown of traditional channels of training leading directly to jobs throws upon the individual the responsibility for planning his career. Coeducation has brought new problems of social and sexual relations. Leftist leaders of student organizations have defied university administrators in strikes and demonstrations, often over purely political questions.

A mission of six specialists headed by Dean Wesley P. Lloyd of Brigham Young University spent the academic year 1951–52 in Japan advising on such problems. At three regional institutes they trained staff members from many universities in the philosophy and methods of "student personnel services"—a term that the Japanese adopted to describe the new concept. By use of discussion techniques and group projects, the mission demonstrated the virtues of non-authoritarian procedures in counseling. Through conferences with university presidents and deans of students they tried

[60] "Mission to Japan," cited, pp. 593-599.

to arouse enthusiasm in high quarters. The universities are now responding in various ways to the mission's recommendations that they establish separate personnel units, staffed by professionals, and that they allocate to these units from 7 to 11 percent of their total operating budgets. A number have set up their own programs for training faculty members in this field. A National Federation of Student Personnel Associations has been formed, with President Yanaihara of Tokyo University as head.[61]

So far as it focuses the attention of the university on the student and his problems, professional counseling will be a valuable innovation. But what seems to have sold the program to both SCAP and Japanese administrators was the hope that it would help to solve the problem of radicalism among students. The mission recognized in its report that this was "of most immediate and evident concern," and recommended that trained leaders assist student groups "to develop appropriate and constructive student activities." These activities would "demonstrate through effective group procedures the advantages of democracy in politics and economics." Adequate scholarships and opportunities for part-time employment would help to break down "the psychological resistance to capitalism." [62]

Certainly it is important to counteract the leadership initiative of a small minority of Communists. But the danger is that students will look upon an officially-sponsored program as a new form of thought control. Japan has a well-established tradition of campus radicalism, just as there is in many other countries where ideology and politics are of more burning concern to youth than they are in the United States. Problems that affect the whole society cannot be solved simply through manipulation by university personnel specialists. Neither psychological tests nor intramural baseball, for example, can erase the fact that Japan suffers from considerable white-collar unemployment.

[61] Wesley P. Lloyd, *Student Counseling in Japan: A Two-Nation Project in Higher Education* (Minneapolis: University of Minnesota Press, 1953) gives a complete report.
[62] Same, pp. 151-153.

Sports

Thanks in large part to the efforts of American teachers in the past, Japan already has a well-developed sports life closely resembling our own. This affords an opportunity for many exchanges and contacts that will receive wide public attention. In 1947, for example, a columnist for *Asahi Shimbun* noted with obvious pride that the only countries that really play baseball are Japan, the United States, and the Philippines.[63]

Horace Wilson and E. H. Mudgett were teaching baseball to students at the Kaisei Gakkō as early as 1875. In 1878 Hiraoka Ki, who had learned to play while studying in America, formed the Shimbashi Club, Japan's first organized team. It often played the American team from Yokohama, on which Henry Willard Denison was the star. By the late eighties, Keiō, Waseda, and the First Higher School, as well as several American mission schools, were holding spirited intercollegiate games. In 1905 the Waseda nine, coached by a former pitcher for the University of Chicago, made the first baseball tour of the United States. Although competition turned out to be tougher than expected, the Waseda men brought back new techniques which greatly raised the standard of performance in Japan. From that time, hardly a year passed without some Japanese team going to Hawaii or to the American mainland, or one or more of the American college teams going to Japan. On the whole, the Americans have had the edge, but competition has been close enough to arouse a great deal of interest in Japan.[64]

The Japanese first had a look at high-quality professional baseball in 1913, when McGraw and Comiskey brought the New York Giants and the Chicago White Sox to Tokyo as part of a world exhibition tour. Today many still remember the thrill of the 47 home runs hit by Babe Ruth, Lou Gehrig, Jimmy Foxx, Charley Gehringer and the other immortals

[63] Aragaki Hideo, *Shin Nihon no Ashioto (Footfalls of New Japan)* (Tokyo: Kawade Shobō, 1948), pp. 320-321.
[64] *Yakyū Taikan (Survey of Baseball)* (Tokyo: Ōbunsha, 1949), pp. 49-51; Fred Merrifield, "University Athletics in Japan," *University of Chicago Magazine,* V. 2 (January 1910), pp. 102-106.

whom Connie Mack brought over in 1934. Under this stimulus Japan's first successful professional team, the Tokyo Giants, was organized. In 1935 it made a very creditable showing in the United States, winning 75 out of 110 games.[65] In a "goodwill" exhibition series in America in the spring of 1953, the postwar Tokyo Giants won only 6 and lost 17.[66]

During the fall of 1953 both the New York Giants and an all-star major league team managed by Ed Lopat were in Japan as part of the Perry centennial celebrations. Japanese fans are still most interested, however, not in the professional teams, but in the Tokyo university championships and the secondary school tournaments held in Osaka. Exchange games between these Japanese amateur teams and American counterparts deserve support and encouragement.

Some of the other team sports are not so well suited to effective binational competition. This is particularly true of basketball, where the American advantage in height has proved decisive. This game was introduced about 1910 by the YMCA's and then taken up gradually by schools and colleges. When the Waseda team visited the West Coast in 1927–28 it defeated the best *nisei* teams but was unable to gain a single victory over American college teams. Likewise, an American all-star squad brought to Japan in 1935 made a clean sweep. A *nisei* team from Hawaii that won eight out of eight in 1950 demonstrated how far Japanese basketball players lag in technique. As a spectator sport, however, the showmanship of the Harlem Globetrotters and the Boston Celtics drew big crowds in Japan in the fall of 1952.[67]

Association football, or soccer, has long been played in Japan; but American-style football did not make its debut until 1934. George Marshall of the Rikkyō Department of Physical Education and *nisei* at Waseda and Meiji universities first got together a team to play the Yokohama Country and Cricket Club on Thanksgiving. A Tokyo Intercollegiate League of five teams was then organized. An American all-star squad brought to Japan in the spring of 1935 by the

[65] *Yakyū Taikan*, cited, pp. 67-77, 415.
[66] *The Mainichi*, April 6, 1953.
[67] I. J. Fisher, "Popular Sports in Japan," *New Japan*, V. 1 (March 1928), pp. 11-13; *Japan Today and Tomorrow, 1935–36*, p. 134; *Undō Nenkan, 1951 (Sports Yearbook, 1951)* (Tokyo: Asahi Shimbun-sha, 1951), p. 257.

Asahi gave valuable demonstrations of technique but thoroughly outclassed all Japanese players. The all-Japan team that went to the United States in 1936 lost to an all-California high school squad. In such international competition, the Japanese are at a decided disadvantage in weight and in size of hands. Just before the war, however, an effort was being made to increase the number of able players by introducing six-man football in the middle schools. Several private universities in the Tokyo area have revived American football teams since the end of the war, and have resumed their prewar rivalry in football. Although no postwar international games have been arranged, a game with a team of American servicemen is now a feature of Thanksgiving Day.[68]

The Japanese have also made remarkable progress in those Western-style sports which require individual prowess. Their record in swimming has been most striking. After they discovered in the 1920's that their traditional styles were too slow for international competition, the Japanese set out to master the crawl. In 1928 Johnny Weissmuller and other American champions came to take part in a meet at the new Meiji Shrine swimming stadium, and stayed to coach their Japanese opponents. The results of intensive training were revealed at the 1932 Olympics in Los Angeles, where a Japanese team made up largely of middle school boys won five out of the six men's events. The Japanese also defeated some of America's best swimmers in dual meets in 1931 and 1935.[69] In swimming, the Japanese have come back strongly since World War II. At the National AAU meet in Los Angeles in August 1949 a team paced by Furuhashi Hironoshin won four of five free-style events, swept the awards in three, and broke five world records. Thanks largely to the performance of *nisei* Ford Konno of Hawaii, the Americans were able to win a dual meet in Tokyo in 1950 by a score of 46-17. American coaches are now seriously considering, however, adop-

[68] *America Japan Society Bulletin*, V. 1 (Last quarter 1937), p. 5; *Japan Today and Tomorrow*, cited, p. 151; *Japan News-Week*, June 22, 1940; *Undō Nenkan, 1951*, cited, p. 278; *Nippon Times*, November 23, 1954.
[69] *Swimming in Japan* (Tokyo: International Young Women and Children's Society, 1935), pp. 4-27; Shimizu Tomesaburō and Unno Kazuma, *Modern Japan* (Tokyo: Modern Japan Kankōkai, 1933), pp. 522-524.

tion of the slower kick and other innovations that the Japanese have made in the crawl.[70]

In tennis the Japanese look back to 1921, their first year in Davis Cup competition, when Kumagai, Shimizu, and Kashio went to the challenge round, where they lost to the Americans. Never again have Japanese players reached the finals. They have been back in Davis Cup play since 1951, however, and have played a number of matches with American champions.[71] American track and field squads went to Japan for dual meets in 1934 and 1937, and won in both instances. More recently, Yamada Keizō set a new course record for the Boston Athletic Association marathon in 1953. In addition to their traditional styles of sumō and jūdō, the Japanese have taken up wrestling by Western rules. In 1937 and 1938 they won a majority of the matches with American amateur teams. In 1950, however, American visitors won seven matches and lost only one. American military attaché Warren J. Clear introduced boxing to Japanese army officers during the twenties. Professional bouts were first staged in 1922 by Watanabe Yūjirō, who had fought leading welterweights in California. It is reported that at first polite Japanese pugilists would not hit hard and apologized profusely if they did so accidentally.[72] Japan got its first boxing title in May 1952, when Shirai Yoshio defeated Dado Marino for the world flyweight championship.

The many contests between American and Japanese athletes over the years have translated national rivalry into good sportsmanship. They have also helped to break down the fairly common stereotype of Japanese physical inferiority. Unfortunately, Americans have not had equal opportunities to watch distinctive Japanese sports like sumō (Japanese wrestling) and kendō (fencing). Jūjitsu has attracted interest as a magical and rather unorthodox means of self-defense. A Japanese team was here in 1953. On the whole, Americans have overlooked the emphasis on self-control and perfection

[70] Japan Year Book, 1949–52, cited, pp. 743-744; New York Times, August 21, December 4, December 25, 1949, August 7, 1950.
[71] Japan Year Book, 1949–52, cited, pp. 742-743; Shimizu and Unno, cited, p. 529.
[72] Japan Today and Tomorrow, 1932–33, cited, p. 74; Shimizu and Unno, cited, p. 532; Undō Nenkan, 1951, cited, p. 307.

of individual style that runs through all Japanese sports. Certainly we should beware, in promoting athletic exchanges, of encouraging undesirable features of professionalism. Western sports in Japan started in most cases in the schools and universities, and they may best remain in such an amateur setting.

Problems of Language Teaching

Whether he is a scientist, a literature professor, or a part-time baseball coach, every American teaching in Japan will be faced, directly or indirectly, with technical problems of giving instruction in English language. One of the men there since World War II has written:

No matter what he teaches in the United States, the chief function of any American teacher in Japan will be to teach English. This generalization holds, I believe, for even such eminent universities as Tokyo University and Kyoto University. The students who take his courses will be there primarily because they are given in English and only incidentally because he has something special to say. And they will stay only if they find that they can follow what he is saying and if they feel that they are making progress in getting better control of English.[73]

In this postwar period, the desire of the Japanese to learn English is unbounded; but serious problems of method remain for solution.

We Americans have often laughed at choice specimens of Japanese English; but an objective view of the facts forces us to admit that the Japanese people are, on the whole, better linguists than we are. The Japanese have respect for linguistic ability; more time is spent on languages in their schools; and when they go abroad they usually try to speak the language of the country they are visiting. History explains their motivation, of course, just as geographical isolation over a long period accounts for our complacent indifference to language-skills. To the Japanese of the Restoration era languages were the codes in which the secrets of Western power were locked. They were tools to be acquired and used, not cultural embellishments.

[73] William F. Marquardt to Carl Bode, June 4, 1952.

The Kaisei Gakkō and other schools of early Meiji times were not strong on pedagogical theory, but they compensated for this by unconscious use of the direct method of language teaching. The student was thirsty for information that could be obtained only from foreign textbooks or from lectures in a foreign language. The teachers knew little or no Japanese, so the student was forced to communicate in the classroom in the language he was studying. In later years men trained by these rough-and-ready methods showed a much better practical grasp of English than those younger students who had used Japanese textbooks in most subjects and studied English only as an auxiliary language. In middle and higher schools most of the English has of necessity been taught by Japanese who are themselves not highly proficient. The pressure of a bulging curriculum kept students from learning much beyond what was required for the next set of entrance examinations, and the examinations have always emphasized literal translation at the expense of conversational ability.

The materials used for teaching English in Japan have been less standardized than those in any other subject. In the days before international copyright agreements halted pirating, enterprising Japanese printers reproduced Webster's *Spelling Book*, McGuffey's *New Eclectic Primer* and the *National Readers*, along with other textbooks, on cheap paper with only approximate accuracy. Choices of reading have often been determined by availability rather than quality. One recent teacher wondered how "such barnacles" as the works of Mrs. Gaskell and Charles Dudley Warner's *My Summer in a Garden* "have managed to keep fixed to the hull of English studies in Japan for a decade." [74]

A few American teachers have tried to devise materials specially adapted to Japanese needs. William Elliot Griffis, for example, prepared a *New Japan Primer* and a *First Reader* that were graded in difficulty but not juvenile in content. In 1900 C. M. Cady of the Third Higher School published *Foundation Exercises in English Composition*, which made use of intensive question and answer drills. During the twenties Harold Palmer, the British director of

[74] Marquardt to Bode, June 4, 1952.

the Institute for Research in English Teaching, tried to focus effort on the development of correct speech habits. His elaborate system of technical phonetics, with its talk about "alveolar obstructions" and a "three-syllable unbroken scandent head," encountered opposition, however, from both Japanese and conservative foreign teachers. In the thirties, at least, the emphasis on content and verbatim translation seems to have continued undiminished.

The hiatus of the war years, when schools were either closed or teaching very little language, damaged still further the English ability of both students and native instructors. William F. Marquardt reported that "the ability of audiences in Japan to grasp spoken English varies with the locality. In the metropolitan areas, where English teaching methods in the secondary schools are generally good, the students will be able to get along fairly comfortably in an English lecture. In the rural areas the students are generally quite incapable of getting more than a fourth of a very simple lecture." [75] The regional difference was confirmed by Henry C. Bush, who wrote from Hirosaki:

The teaching and study of English is incredibly bad; their art of *seeming* to understand English is perfect. Visiting Englishmen and Americans come and talk and leave without guessing that no one in that consummately polite audience understood a whole connected paragraph. Happens every week. [76]

Since so much of our information program in Japan assumes literacy in English, the methods of language teaching would seem to be a legitimate field for technical assistance, either by our government or by a private foundation.

At Niigata University Marquardt managed to get a meeting of minds by lecturing in Basic English. Basic offers great possibilities as an oral medium of limited vocabulary, but it does not solve the whole problem. The Japanese student does not want to read stories watered down into Basic; he wants to read William Faulkner and American textbooks on nuclear physics. We want educated Japanese citizens to be able to use the books and periodicals in our information libraries.

[75] Same.
[76] Letter dated December 4, 1952.

Effective teaching of English is essentially a problem for the secondary schools rather than for the universities. If the Japanese college student does not already have fundamental language skills, he will not be able to acquire them in the two or three hours per week of drill that his crowded course of study will allow. Nearly all the new secondary schools are offering English as an elective, and the percentage of students who enroll has in recent years been very high. It will obviously be impossible to have foreign teachers in all the 2,900 high schools, let alone in the 12,000 middle schools. American mission boards may be able to supply some people who will work in a spirit of humility, with the expectation of only moderate material rewards. A few American secondary teachers are being brought over under the Fulbright program to demonstrate new teaching methods. Recording equipment, motion pictures, and radio broadcasts could be used much more extensively. Since SCAP reported that "many teachers now in the schools simply do not have a sufficient command of English to use the new methods effectively," the training of native instructors might be the point at which American aid could do most to raise standards.[77]

The Goals of Teacher Interchange

Since financial resources for interchange of teachers cannot possibly cover all apparent needs, they ought to be allocated on some principle of the relation of means to ends. Do we want to give as many Japanese as possible direct personal contact with a representative of American culture and values? If so, a wide distribution of professors in prefectural universities has great advantages. In allocating Fulbright professors we should beware of increasing still further the advantage in standards and prestige of a few old-line institutions in the big cities. On the other hand, a strong intellectual influence upon leaders and potential leaders could probably be better exerted by sending over American professors of established reputation on brief lecture tours. In the American studies seminars that have been held at Tokyo and Kyoto Universities the past four summers, a number of

[77] *Postwar Developments in Japanese Education*, cited, V. 1, p. 20.

outstanding teachers have been able to reinforce each other's efforts. A third purpose might be to aid in the continuing reform of Japanese higher education. Here it is doubtful if any one individual could exert much leverage. The visiting educational mission would seem to be the most effective instrument for helping the Japanese to re-examine their own goals and methods. These three ways of working—permanent teachers, visiting lecturers, and special missions—should probably all be used in some proportion. Certainly we should be governed by the priorities felt and expressed by the Japanese themselves.

To keep exchanges fairly well balanced, we should be sure that Japanese teachers get sufficient chances to appear in their own role in the United States. A good start has been made in recent years. Suzuki Daisetsu lectured widely on Buddhism from 1950 to 1952, and philosopher Nakamura Hajime spent the year 1951–52 at Stanford. Professor Takeuchi Tatsuji of Kansai Gakuin University taught political science at Columbia from 1952 to 1954. A combination of Fulbright and Smith-Mundt funds is now being used to bring a number of Japanese scholars to our campuses. Abe Yoshishige, president of Gakushūin University, and geneticist Kihara Hitoshi were among the cultural leaders for whom Columbia University arranged short visits during 1952–53. But important as it is to recognize that Japan can teach us as well as learn from us, we should be careful not to drain away too much of her top talent for our own purposes. The Japanese were pleased to regain a Nobel Prize winner when nuclear physicist Yukawa Hideki relinquished a permanent appointment at Columbia to return and work in Japan.

CHAPTER SIX

EXCHANGE OF STUDENTS

THE UNITED STATES and Japan both have well-established traditions of students going abroad in search of knowledge. We share the experience of Western Europe, where scholars of the Middle Ages wandered from university to university, from Oxford to Paris to Bologna to Salamanca. Since colonial times Americans, too, have gone abroad for special training: to the law and medical schools of Great Britain, to the university seminars of Germany, to the art studios of Rome and Paris. In the twentieth century the forces of attraction have reversed their direction, and the United States has become a magnet drawing students from all parts of the world. In 1953–54 the total number of foreign students in our institutions of higher education reached 33,833.[1]

American thinking about foreign study has undergone a corresponding change. Formerly our emphasis was on cultural advantages for the individuals concerned. Now the much discussed programs of technical assistance use the diffusion of skills through education as one method of promoting economic development and world stability. We also assume, though perhaps without sufficient examination of the premise, that student migrations will serve as an antidote to poisonous nationalism by promoting mutual understanding and international cooperation. In this world of competing ideologies, it is hoped that students returning from America will be sympathetic interpreters of our point of view. These considerations have prompted the United States government to take an active part in encouraging and financing the exchange of students.

[1] *Education for One World: Annual Census of Foreign Students in Institutions of Higher Education in the United States, 1953–1954* (New York: Institute of International Education, 1954), Table II.

192

Japanese traditions of foreign study date back to the seventh century, when Shōtoku Taishi sent students to the mainland of Asia to bring back Chinese civilization. Despite continued contacts and strong Chinese influences, however, the Japanese have maintained a definite cultural autonomy. They have selectively assimilated elements of foreign culture and adapted them to their own needs. To the injunction in the Meiji Charter Oath that "knowledge shall be sought throughout the earth" was added the significant phrase "in order to establish firmly the foundations of the Empire." In this spirit the Japanese have been assiduous students of Western civilization. Today they again need to send out students to the most advanced countries, in order to catch up after their isolation during war and occupation. With the development of democracy, however, their emphasis should shift from benefit to the state to benefit for the individual.

Japanese Students in the United States

For ninety years Japanese students have been coming to America in significant numbers. Those who came in the decades immediately following the Meiji Restoration have already completed their careers. The students of the 1920's are now at full maturity. Those who have come here since World War II have carried on an old tradition; in many instances their parents or other relatives had attended American institutions. The case of Japan gives us an opportunity, therefore, to study the process of educational exchange over a long period of time. We can see what contributions Japanese trained in America have been able to make to their own society. We can also discern, although less clearly, their attitudes toward America and the roles they have played in bilateral relations.

Even before the Meiji Restoration a few Japanese managed to get to America despite the curtain of prohibitions lowered by the Shogunate. The captain of a New Bedford whaling ship picked up a drifting fisherman named Manjirō and placed him in school at Fairhaven, Massachusetts. After he returned to Japan in 1852, "John Munn," as he was known in America, was made a *hatamoto* (retainer of the Shogun) with the surname Nakahama. He rendered invaluable services as teacher and interpreter and also translated Bowditch's *Practical Navigator* into Japanese.[2] Niishima Jō slipped away from Japan in 1864 to obtain at Amherst College and Andover Seminary training for a life of Christian leadership.[3] Some young men sent out illegally by the *daimyō* of Satsuma came by way of England to Thomas L. Harris' strange socialist colony on Lake Erie, and from there to Rutgers Grammar School in 1867.[4] These scattered cases revealed one attitude already characteristic of the Japanese student, his conviction that America held knowledge worth almost any effort to obtain.

The flow of students to America could be established in volume, however, only by the encouragement and support of the Japanese government. When the leaders responsible for the Restoration realized that the threat from the West could be met only by developing modern technology, it was natural, in view of their traditions, that they should send out large numbers of *ryūgakusei*, or foreign students. In 1871 they directed the feudal lords to choose from one to three men, the number depending on the size of their domains. Two hundred fifty in all were sent abroad on stipends of about $1,000 gold a year. Half or more went to the United States. Unfortunately, few had any previous training in English; and at places like Monson (Massachusetts) Academy and the Preparatory School of Brooklyn Polytechnic Institute they were placed in classes with the youngest children. Supervision by the Japanese diplomatic representative proved merely nominal. Students chose their own schools and courses, and changed both at will. After official inspections revealed that many were not "following the road to learning," in the fall of 1873 all below college grade were ordered to return.[5]

[2] Nakahama Tōichirō, *Nakahama Manjirō Den* (*Biography of Nakahama Manjirō*) (Tokyo: Fuzambō, 1936), *passim*.
[3] Arthur Sherburne Hardy, *Life and Letters of Joseph Hardy Neesima* (Boston: Houghton Mifflin, 1891), pp. 1-100.
[4] William Elliot Griffis, "The Japanese Students in America," *Japanese Student*, V. 1 (October 1916), p. 11.
[5] *Meiji Ikō Kyōiku Seido Hattatsu Shi* (*History of the Development of the Educational System since the Beginning of Meiji*) (Tokyo: Mombushō Uchi

Japan did not abandon, however, her stated policy of seeking knowledge throughout the world. Thereafter, advanced students were chosen by rigid examinations from the new university in Tokyo. Megata Tanetarō, a graduate of the Harvard Law School in 1874, was empowered as Superintendent of Students in the United States to inspect their progress and order withdrawals in case of negligence or unsatisfactory work.[6] Until about 1880 the Japanese government continued to support students in America. By that time Tokyo University was beginning to supply the demand for specialists. In line with the shift in intellectual orientation then occurring, the few men sent abroad after 1880 by the ministries usually went to Germany.

The government-supported students in the United States were soon replaced, in number if not in eminence, by others who came without public support. Severe competition for a limited number of places in the higher schools and universities has been, until the recent expansion of facilities, an important feature of Japanese education. Disappointed candidates often turned to the United States as second choice. Some went as protégés of missionaries to small denominational colleges. Opportunities to combine work and study were glowingly described by Miyama Kanichi, one of the early emigrants to the San Francisco area, when he made a return visit to Japan in 1885. Many young men bought a steamship ticket for America, without any definite educational plans in mind, and set off with far more confidence than cash. When Katayama Sen arrived in 1884, he had only one Mexican dollar.[7] Most of their names will be found, not in the catalogues of major universities, but on the rosters of night schools and "commercial colleges." To Americans they became known as "Japanese schoolboys," no matter

Kyōiku Shi Hensankai, 1938–1939), V. 1, pp. 816-819, 826; *Itō Hirobumi Den* (*Biography of Itō Hirobumi*) (Tokyo: Tsumpo Kō Tsuishōkai, 1940), V. 1, pp. 675-676.

6 *Mombushō Dai San Nempō, Meiji Hachinen* (*Third Annual Report of the Ministry of Education, 1875*) (Tokyo: Ministry of Education, 1875), V. 1, pp. 17-20.

7 *Japan Weekly Chronicle,* April 17, 1924; Monica Sone, *Nisei Daughter* (Boston: Little Brown, 1953), p. 5, tells how her father came in 1904 intending to earn enough money to study law at the University of Michigan, but after a series of odd jobs he was diverted to operation of a waterfront hotel in Seattle.

what their age might be. While earning their way they often had unusual opportunities for realistic experience of American life. After 1907 strict observance by the Japanese government of the Gentleman's Agreement to issue no passports to laborers made it difficult for this type of student to come to America.[8]

Not until the First World War did the Japanese government again begin to send students to the United States. War with Germany cut off the previous source of specialized training just when the Japanese economy was undergoing great expansion. At first men were sent to America on a temporary basis, in the expectation that the war would end soon and that they could go on to Europe. Delayed longer than expected, they had a chance to witness our impressive preparedness and war effort. American prestige rose in official circles, and in 1919 eighty students were definitely assigned to the United States.[9] The number declined as European facilities were restored, but did not again dwindle to nothing. In 1928, for example, thirty persons came to the United States to study on government grants; in 1932 seventeen.[10] The great majority of Japanese students continued, of course, to be privately supported.

Almost from the beginning women have been included among the Japanese students coming to America. According to one estimate, about 200 had studied here up to 1934, half of them receiving degrees.[11] Two motives have been dominant. Until very recently women in Japan have been less well supplied with educational facilities than men, and only grudgingly were they given access to the leading universities. Many have turned to America, therefore, for advanced training in specialized fields. Others have had as their primary goal the experience of release and self-realization that they get by living in an atmosphere of greater social freedom and sex equality.

[8] Ichihashi Yamato, *Japanese in the United States: A Critical Study of the Problems of the Japanese Immigrants and their Children* (Stanford: Stanford University Press, 1932), pp. 88, 109-110.
[9] William L. Schwartz, "Japanese Government Students in America," *School and Society*, V. 10 (August 10, 1919), pp. 202-204.
[10] Institute of International Education, *News Bulletin*, April 1933, p. 7.
[11] Koizumi Ikuko, "Major Problems in Women's Education in Japan," *Mid-Pacific Magazine*, V. 47 (July-September 1934), p. 425.

The Colonization Commission sent over the first five young girls in 1871, on the theory that educated mothers were necessary if personnel were to be trained for economic development. Although none of them had any further connection with the Hokkaidō enterprise, the three girls who stayed had remarkable careers. After preparatory schooling Yamakawa Sutematsu and Nagai Shige entered Vassar College. Miss Yamakawa later married General Ōyama Iwao and was a leader in women's patriotic work during the Sino-Japanese War of 1894–95. Miss Nagai was one of Japan's first teachers of piano and the wife of Admiral Uryū Sotokichi. The youngest of the three, Tsuda Umeko, founded the well-known Tsuda Eigakujuku in 1900, in order to train girls for self-supporting careers as teachers of English.[12] In order to train female professors for the Tokyo Normal School for Women, the government also began in the late 1880's to send outstanding graduates to America to study.[13]

Most of the women have been privately supported, often with American aid. Mission schools have obtained funds from their home boards for a few of their promising pupils. Scholarships contributed by American friends enabled Miss Tsuda to direct several girls to her own alma mater, Bryn Mawr. Of these, Matsuda Michi, Hoshino Ai, and Kawai Michi all followed in her footsteps as educators of women. Several Japanese have benefited from the fund that Levi L. Barbour established to help young women from Eastern countries train at the University of Michigan for medical work or teaching. Of the 307 Japanese women studying here in 1952–53, only 44 were receiving United States government grants.

Only since World War II has the exchange of students with Japan come within the scope of United States government policy. At first SCAP restrictions on travel by Japanese nationals and on use of foreign currencies kept all but a few students from coming. Then gradually the potential

[12] B. G. Northrop, "The Three First Japanese Girls Educated in America: Their Influence in Japan," *Independent*, V. 48 (January 30, 1896), pp. 139-140; Tsuda Ume, "Teaching in Japan," *Bryn Mawr Alumnae Quarterly*, V. 1 (October 1907), pp. 16-21.
[13] Margaret E. Burton, *The Education of Women in Japan* (New York: Revell, 1914), p. 126.

contribution of foreign study to the occupation's reorientation program was recognized. An official exchange program began in 1949–50, when a portion of the GARIOA (Government and Relief in Occupied Areas) appropriation was used to send 50 teachers to the United States. The next year 300 students, including many government officials and businessmen, were chosen by a Japanese selection committee from over 6,000 applicants. From a peak of 500 students in 1951–52 the government program fell to 300 in 1952–53. Public funds for support of Japanese students in 1953–54 were limited to 74 Smith-Mundt grants covering full dollar expenses, 16 partial grants, and 150 Fulbright travel allowances.

The fact that over 900 Japanese were able to study here in 1952–53 without support from our government indicates that a normal flow has been reestablished. Scholarship aid is necessary, however, to provide some opportunities solely on the basis of merit and promise. Special funds designated for this purpose are not extensive. The Grew Foundation, established in 1950 with the Japanese royalties from Joseph C. Grew's *Ten Years in Japan* and an additional fifty-five million yen raised by his friends, sent its first party of four undergraduates in 1953. Before 1941 several students benefited from a fund left by another former ambassador, Edgar A. Bancroft. This Bancroft Fund, replenished by a residuary legacy, sent its first postwar scholar in September 1954. The Rotary International Clubs of Japan pay expenses and travel for one person each year. In recent years the YMCA and the YWCA, the Military Government Association, and the Seven Eastern Colleges Association in Japan have contributed to travel expenses. The Japanese Scholarship Foundation established through the untiring efforts of Malcolm Reed has given direct support to a few students, and has helped many more by directing their attention to the general scholarships and fellowships available at American colleges and universities. These unrestricted scholarship funds are the greatest potential sources of financial aid. Only careful attention to individual cases will keep an impressive number of Japanese in the annual census of foreign students.

Number of Japanese students in the United States. The following incomplete series gives the best statistics available:

1865–1885 total	290+	1935–36	1179 *
1904 a	105	1936–37	1713
1911–12 a	415	1937–38	1419
1915–16 b	568	1938–39	386
1918–19 c	555	1939–40	260
1921–22 d	532	1940–41	232
1922–23	658	1941–42	153
1923–24	708	1942–43	43
1924–25	793	1943–44	46
1925–26	685	1944–45	45
1926–27	619	1945–46	38
1927–28	743	1946–47	60+
1928–29	814	1947–48	29
1929–30	987 *	1948–49	86
1930–31	1004 *	1949–50	277
1931–32	1187	1950–51	732
1932–33	800 *	1951–52	1168
1933–34	1526	1952–53	1257
1934–35	1641	1953–54	1294

a. Commission on Survey of Foreign Students in the United States of America, *The Foreign Student in America* (New York: Association Press, 1925), pp. 11-12.

b. *Directory of Foreign Students in United States and Canada, 1915–1916.*

c. *Directory of Foreign Students in the United States of America, 1919.*

d. Statistics from 1921 on are from the records of the Committee on Friendly Relations among Foreign Students and the Institute of International Education. Inclusion of late reports and revisions in some instances accounts for variations from figures previously published.

　　Asterisks indicate figures revised by the Committee on Friendly Relations to exclude Japanese-Americans.

Except for recent years, these figures are merely approximate. In reporting the number of foreign students on their rolls, many institutions were not careful in the past to distinguish between students from Japan and Japanese-Americans. Another shortcoming is that only students at accredited institutions of higher education are included. In 1904, when our figures show 105 studying here, the Japanese government issued 1,267 passports to "students" bound for the United States. Many of these were undoubtedly emigrants concealing their true intentions, but others must have been bona fide students in preparatory, commercial, or unaccredited institutions. During the late twenties and thirties, in contrast, the number of student visas issued under section

4(e) of the Immigration Act of 1924, even taken cumulatively, does not account for the number reported as registered in colleges and universities. Many Japanese entering as tourists or businessmen must also have been carrying on formal studies. Again we have no way of knowing how many such persons may have been enrolled in non-reporting institutions. One conclusion is clear from the figures, however: only in the last four years, and with considerable pump priming through grants from the American government, has the flow of Japanese students to America reached the volume that was normal during the twenties and early thirties.

Distribution in institutions and courses. The choice of educational institution has been determined as often by circumstance as by logic. Guido Verbeck directed some of the earliest comers to Rutgers and to Hope College in Holland, Michigan, both connected with the Reformed Church in America. Likewise, Methodist missionary John Ing was responsible for directing two future ambassadors to the United States, Chinda Sutemi and Satō Aimaro, to De Pauw University in Greencastle, Indiana. The large samurai contingent that came in 1872 was distributed in private schools in the vicinity of Philadelphia, New York, and Boston. The prestige of Harvard and Yale has drawn the Japanese from the very beginning, and the attractions of life in New York City have helped to make Columbia and New York University favored places for study. The Johns Hopkins Graduate School has drawn some of the most scholarly, but few have gone farther into the South. In the Middle West, Michigan, Wisconsin, Illinois, and Chicago have been the favorite universities. West Coast institutions like California, Stanford, and Washington have offered the advantages of shorter distance from Japan and, since the 1920's, the supporting presence of many Japanese-American students.

Several of the Japanese who came in the late 1860's desired above all to enter the United States Naval Academy. Through the efforts of Senator Frederick Frelinghuysen of New Jersey, Congressional authorization was obtained in 1868; and in the next fifteen years twelve young Japanese trained at Annapolis. Among them were the future admirals Matsumura Junzō, Inoue Yoshitomo, Serada Tasuku, and

Uryū Sotokichi, all of whom played prominent parts in Japan's wars against China and Russia. During the mid-eighties, when the American navy was at a low point, Japan made no use of her privilege, but she began to send students again as soon as we began building modern cruisers and battleships. Suspicions that their primary purpose was espionage rather than education caused Congress to close Annapolis in 1906 to students "from any foreign country." [14]

A proposal to open West Point to Japanese students was defeated in 1872 because of concern over security and prestige. American military training never had a chance, therefore, to compete with the German models on which Japan built her army. Even more serious was the absence of direct personal relations, beyond those maintained by our military attachés, with high-ranking Japanese army officers. During the thirties we certainly needed inside channels through which to understand their motives and to make our own position clear. There were no old school ties, as there had been in 1922, when a reunion of the Annapolis class of 1881 in Japan, at the invitation of Admiral Uryū, did much to promote acceptance of the Washington Naval Treaty.[15] As Japan rebuilds her defense forces under American guidance, it may be wise to admit selected Japanese officers to our service academies and command schools.[16]

American administrators of postwar student exchanges have attempted to break the old prestige and popularity patterns and to scatter Japanese students much more widely over the United States. The 500 receiving government grants in 1951–52 were placed in 135 different institutions, with a maximum of ten to fifteen in any one place. The Grew Foundation deliberately places its students in colleges lo-

[14] Katō Katsuji, "Japanese Students at Annapolis," *Japanese Student,* V. 3 (November 1918), pp. 57-61; J. M. Ellicott, "Japanese Students at the United States Naval Academy," *United States Naval Institute Proceedings,* V. 73 (March 1947), pp. 302-307.
[15] *Views and Reviews of Japan,* V. 20 (August 1922), p. 47; "Beikoku Kaigun-kyō Dembi Shi Ikkō Shōtai Kankei Shorui (Documents relating to the Invitation of Denby, the United States Secretary of the Navy, and his Party)," Microfilms of Japanese Foreign Office Archives, Library of Congress, SP 206.
[16] In 1953 over 140 members of the Japanese Safety Forces were given technical training at Aberdeen Proving Ground, Fort Sill Armored School, and other military installations. *Mainichi Shimbun,* July 29, 1953.

cated in smaller cities in order that they may better "imbibe American principles of democracy and her spirit of justice and humanity." [17] It will be interesting to see if a wide geographical distribution continues when most students choose their own place of study. The advantages of a wider acquaintance with American life must be balanced, of course, against the quality of instruction received and the prestige-value of the institution in Japan.

Statistics for 1924–25 give what might be considered a normal distribution of Japanese students in various courses of study.[18]

	Number	Percent of Total		Number	Percent of Total
Liberal Arts	318	40.0	Pharmacy	13	1.6
Engineering	74	9.3	Agriculture	8	
Commerce	65	8.2	Chemistry	6	
Theology	57	7.2	Architecture	4	3.0
Medicine	30	3.8	Law	4	
Dentistry	29	3.7	Forestry	1	
Education	15	1.9	Unclassified	169	21.3
			Total	793	100.0

Study of law in America was much more popular in the 1870's and 1880's, before Japanese jurisprudence was definitely set in a European pattern. Although Japanese medicine in general followed German methods, during the twenties the Rockefeller Foundation was making a definite effort to bring Japanese doctors here for specialized training. Mission groups regularly gave their most promising native leaders opportunities to study in American theological seminaries.

The GARIOA student program continued to emphasize the social sciences and humanities rather than the natural sciences or engineering. Distribution of students by major areas of study was as follows: [19]

[17] *The Grew Foundation* (leaflet) (Tokyo: Foundation, 1952), p. 3. The first four Grew scholars went to Lafayette, Haverford, Knox, and Denison. Other institutions of a similar character may be used in the future.
[18] *Statistics regarding Foreign Students in the Institutions of Higher Learning in the United States* (Mimeographed; New York: Institute of International Education, 1925).
[19] Figures supplied by Institute of International Education.

	1951–52 Percent	*1952–53* Percent
Education, English language and literature	27	25
Economics, finance, business administration, industrial management, etc.	20	31
Political science, international relations, public administration, foreign trade	10	12
Engineering	8	13
Sociology, welfare, and psychology	5	5
Medicine and public health	5	4
Chemistry, physics, mathematics	3	4
Journalism	5	3
Library science	2	2
Miscellaneous	15	1

A return to free choice will show how well this allocation met the desires and needs of the Japanese themselves. Certainly some increase in the number in scientific and technical fields can be expected.

Adjustment in the United States. Except for Wallace Irwin's vicious caricature of Hashimura Togo, "Japanese Schoolboy age 35 years," who had "come to this Free Country for some following reason: 1. To save up money for old age; 2. To learn so much I can; 3. To wait on table 14 hours Daily at Boarding house of Mrs. C. W. O'Brien, honourable lady," we have had no striking picture of Japanese students in America.[20] On the whole they have been quiet and unobtrusive. A strong sense of obligation to family and country has kept them hard at work. During the thirties their tension was heightened by the necessity either to defend or to dissociate themselves from their country's policies. Their characteristic politeness and restraint has kept from view both their own problems of adjustment and their opinions of America.

The earliest Japanese students had the advantage of being social curiosities. The presence of about a dozen heirs to *daimyō* titles contributed to the impression that all should be treated as "princes" and "princesses." Close personal friendships often had direct results in education. Oliver Wendell Holmes, Jr., steered Kaneko Kentarō to the study

[20] *Letters of a Japanese Schoolboy* (New York: Doubleday Page, 1909), p. 3.

of law; and Komura Jutarō was able to get practical legal experience in the office of Edwards Pierrepont, one of New York's leading attorneys. The homes of John S. C. Abbott at New Haven and Mrs. Wistar Morris at Philadelphia became social centers for Japanese students in those areas. Edward S. Morse at Salem, Massachusetts, welcomed and counseled many a young Japanese scientist. Such personal contacts are still as possible as they are desirable, but now a much larger group of Japanese must compete for attention with thousands of students from other parts of the world.

The experiences of the many self-supporting students were probably not so happy. Many stayed on the West Coast, where they were subject to prejudice against Orientals. One wonders, for example, what was the effect upon statesman Matsuoka Yōsuke of being put ashore here to fend for himself at the age of fourteen, surviving only through the kindness of a Seattle working-class woman, and finally working his way through college and law school. His professed affection for America could not hide a marked cynicism and opportunism. On the credit side, the chance to study while working, sometimes even to send money back to the family in Japan, confirmed for many Japanese America's reputation as a land of great opportunity.

Since the First World War extensive facilities have been developed in the United States for handling and counseling foreign students. The Institute of International Education, founded in 1919, is now the leading agency for administration of student exchanges, but only in the last few years has it dealt with Japanese. The one agency that paid them particular attention was the Committee on Friendly Relations among Foreign Students, founded in 1911 by Dr. John R. Mott, Cleveland Dodge, George W. Perkins, Andrew Carnegie and others as an outgrowth of the work of the International Committee of the YMCA. The Committee's purpose was to see that "the student shall get what he has come for, and that, returning, he shall entertain feelings of affection for America and that he shall devote his energies to the promotion of international friendship and goodwill." [21] The

21 *The Directory of Japanese Students in North America, 1923–1924* (New York: Committee on Friendly Relations Among Foreign Students, n.d.), p. 11.

basic aim of developing a Christian character led to organization in 1924 of a Japanese Student Christian Movement, but the Committee also rendered various services to all Japanese, without regard to religion. A special Japanese secretary gave information about colleges, courses, and expenses, met students at the ports and helped with travelling arrangements, and helped them find employment. Local Japanese YMCA chapters and student clubs provided a focus for social life. In criticism it should be said that this method of working encouraged segregation by making the Japanese student busy and content within his own group.

Shorn almost entirely of its religious orientation and no longer working along national lines, the Committee on Friendly Relations still performs extensive services for foreign students. On the theory that the first hours and days in America may be vital in determining attitudes, it provides assistance and orientation at all ports of entry. The Committee mobilizes and directs the vast resources of individuals and organizations throughout the country for hospitality and informal education. The goal is at least one "sustained relationship," with an American family if possible, for each student. The Japan Society of New York, for example, takes responsibility for home hospitality to Japanese in that area. In eighteen cities coordinating committees have been set up to make available to foreigners the pertinent opportunities for learning that exist in the community.[22]

Almost every college and university has at least one person assigned to deal with the special problems of foreign students. The work of over a thousand counselors is coordinated and their experience shared through a National Association of Foreign Student Advisers (NAFSA). In general, Japanese students have posed some baffling problems for these advisers. The Japanese are too polite, too docile, too reluctant to form and express opinions. They carry out obediently, but rather mechanically, all the suggestions given merely as possible alternatives. Because they want to be told how to solve their problems, they do not respond well to techniques

[22] Statement by J. Benjamin Schmoker, general secretary of the Committee, in *Overseas Information Programs of the United States*, Hearings, U. S. Senate Committee on Foreign Relations Subcommittee, 83rd Cong., 1st sess. (Washington: GPO, 1953), Pt. 2, pp. 521-531.

of nondirective counseling. The adviser quite often ends by deciding that the Oriental is, indeed, inscrutable.[23]

To the usual problems of adjustment there has been added since the war the possibility of conflict in objectives between the students themselves and their American sponsors. This proved particularly true of the first group of fifty who came on GARIOA grants in 1949–50. From the point of view of the Army the goal was "reorientation," defined as "changing the mental outlook and habits of operation of those whose past years have given them undemocratic concepts." But the first group sent over were nearly all young academicians, assistant professors in universities and normal schools, whose ambitions centered on advancement in rather narrow specialties. One boasted that he was the only person in the American university to which he was assigned who was taking all his work with one professor. Most were not fortunate enough to find even one instructor who knew or cared much about their narrow fields of research. The result was severe frustration, usually expressed in a request to change to another university. A few plunged into progressively deeper bitterness, vented in savage and indiscriminate criticism of everything American. After considerable counseling most of the men changed their expectations and managed to have a fairly pleasant time the rest of the year. But one wonders whether the "awareness of what the democratic process means in terms of status of the individual," the measure of success adopted for the evaluation interviews at the end of the year, indicated deep convictions or merely the common Japanese desire to give the response that is expected.[24]

This conflict of objectives was somewhat reduced in later groups of GARIOA grantees. For one thing, government officials and businessmen were more accustomed to learning through observation and conversation. The later comers were also given six-week orientation courses, designed, first

[23] Based in part on an interview with J. B. Schmoker, who is also executive Secretary of NAFSA. Studies made by John W. Bennett at Ohio State showed that, by the yardstick of effective interaction, Japanese adjusted less well than other foreign students.

[24] *Evaluation of Japanese Student Program* (Mimeographed; Office of the Secretary of the Army, Office for Occupied Areas, Reorientation Branch, 1951).

of all, "to convey to the student precisely why he is here, what is expected of him, and what is not expected of him." The emphasis was put on what we thought they should learn. The Japanese undoubtedly felt much more comfortable knowing these things, but a few may have been subtle enough to see that the method was not compatible with the lesson: "the supremacy and inviolability of the individual." [25]

The opinions that Japanese students have formed about America would fill a broad spectrum from uncritical enthusiasm to intense revulsion. Highly specific experiences are likely to be generalized into sweeping judgments. Miss Kawai was distressed by rude behavior in college classes. "Was it the accepted thing for students to challenge their teachers' statements and make haste to point out mistakes?" [26] Others have criticized American students as lacking in serious purpose and political consciousness.[27] On the other hand, the friendliness, the generosity and the sincerity of their college friends has made a deep impression.

Successful adjustment may depend as much upon the relation between expectation and reality as it does upon the objective qualities of a person's experience. If hopes are pitched too high, even a relatively pleasant stay may be a keen disappointment. Uchimura Kanzō, for example, came to the United States in 1884 convinced by missionary friends that he was entering heaven on earth. "I dreamed of its templed hills," he recalled, "and rocks that rang with hymns and praises. Hebraisms, I thought to be the prevailing speech of the American commonality, and cherub and cherubim, hallelujahs and amens, the common language of its streets." No sooner had he reached San Francisco than his pocket was picked. The only Hebraisms he heard were curses. Soon the ugly realities of gambling, lynching, and race prejudice forced themselves upon his attention. Continued disillusionment drove him into an intellectual position hostile to both

[25] *Report of the Conference on Orientation of Japanese and Ryukyuan Students* (New York: Institute of International Education, 1950), pp. 5-6.
[26] Kawai Michi, *My Lantern* (Tokyo: Kyōbunkan, 1939), p. 84.
[27] For an example, see Ko Hisashi and Laurence Critchell, "What You Americans Did to Me," *Saturday Evening Post*, December 20, 1952, p. 65.

the United States and missionaries, although he became an influential Christian leader.[28]

Tsurumi Yūsuke has written about his first visit in 1911: "I had learned to admire the America of Washington Irving, of Emerson, of Longfellow and of Abraham Lincoln. But a land of politics, automobiles, sky-scrapers, trusts and Tammany Hall was rather distasteful to me."[29] In recent years Japanese who thought of the United States as a paragon of democracy have been disillusioned to find class distinctions, political corruption, and an uninformed electorate. Since our faults are not likely to disappear in the near future, the problem becomes one of the image of America current in Japan. If our information program emphasizes the democratic process rather than the ideal goal, diversity of standards rather than uniformity, self-criticism rather than self-congratulation, future students may come better prepared to appreciate the real conditions of American life.

The question whether we should make a conscious organized effort to give foreign visitors an understanding of American values will provoke a lively debate in any group concerned with cultural relations. Some argue that students will react negatively to any attempts at indoctrination. With Japanese there is the opposite danger of confirming their tendency to accept statements on authority rather than to draw their own conclusions. Others will insist that a foreigner needs some help in order to penetrate beneath the surface of our complex and heterogeneous society. Americans tend to be reticent about their values. Young people who are outspoken about their radicalisms may be basically very conservative and conformist. Japanese, particularly, may have difficulty in seeing the relation between our individualism and our sense of community responsibility. Perhaps foreign students should be told in orientation courses, not what to believe, but what to look for.

Length of stay is undoubtedly a key factor in both personal adjustment and formation of attitudes. Formerly most

---

[28] Uchimura Kanzō, *The Diary of a Japanese Convert* (New York: Revell, 1895), pp. 101-118.

[29] Tsurumi Yūsuke, "What America Means to Me," *New East*, V. 1 (June 1917), p. 32.

Japanese came for several years, sometimes taking longer than the normal time to complete a course or degree. In order to give as many people as possible experience in America, the United States Government has made most of its postwar grants for one year, in rare instances extending them for a second year. The student feels, as a result, a sense of urgency about his academic task, especially if he has language difficulties. He does not have much time for social life and informal learning. If his initial attitudes toward America were critical, they are not tempered appreciably by cumulative experience. On the other hand, enthusiasm does not have time to mellow into real understanding. The student may go back after a year with only a sense of rich confusion. For this reason the Japan Society of New York has been making grants-in-aid, about twenty-five each year, which enable graduate students to complete their programs satisfactorily by staying another year. A stay of four or five years is an essential feature of the Grew scholarships.

Readjustment upon return to Japan. Until the full results of the intensive interviews of former students that Herbert Passin conducted in Japan for the Social Science Research Council are available, our knowledge of the psychological problems connected with fitting again into the old society must necessarily be fragmentary and superficial.[30] To judge by a few personal narratives, the shock of return after several years in America is severe. Japanese women, particularly, have found it difficult to submit again to the restraints upon their activities, upon their personal movements, even upon their thoughts. A man often feels frustrated when no one in his government office or business firm shares his enthusiasm for new ideals or new methods. For the sake of professional success, many of the men seem to submerge their newly acquired attitudes and to conform, perhaps more closely than usual, to the general pattern of thought and behavior. Those who do not bend may accentuate American mannerisms and opinions to the point of eccentricity, thereby forfeiting their chance for influence.

[30] The preliminary report in Herbert Passin and J. W. Bennett, "The America-educated Japanese," *Annals of the American Academy of Political and Social Science*, V. 295 (September 1954), pp. 83-107, will be amplified greatly in a forthcoming book.

We can draw more definite conclusions about vocational adjustment and success. The record of the earliest students is almost certainly better than that of those who came later. In the rapidly changing society of the early Meiji period, youthful talent easily attained responsible position and rapid advancement. Of 293 Japanese known to have studied in the United States between 1865 and 1885, it has been possible to trace the later careers of 197 (67 percent). Of these 162 (55 percent of the total number) occupied positions of responsibility and influence in government, academic, and business life. Many of those who could not be traced were in that group of poorly-qualified samurai sent over in 1872. Changes of name through adoption and *yōshi*-marriages [31] undoubtedly account for some of the others.

Many of the early students turned to teaching and helped to build a modern educational system for Japan. Toyama Masakazu (Michigan '76), Yamakawa Kenjirō (Yale '75) and Matsui Naokichi (Columbia and Yale) became presidents of Tokyo Imperial University. Yamakawa was also the first head of Kyūshū Imperial University. Niishima Jō (Amherst '70) founded the Dōshisha, Japan's leading Christian college. Fukuzawa Ichitarō (Oberlin and Cornell) succeeded his famous father as proprietor of Keiō, and Waseda University was headed from 1898 to 1908 by Hatoyama Kazuo (Columbia and Yale Law Schools). Kikuchi Takeo (Boston University Law School) directed the training of other lawyers at Chūō University. The leader in the development of technical education was Teshima Seiichi (Lafayette). President of the First Higher School in Tokyo was only one of many important posts held by Nitobe Inazō (Johns Hopkins). For twenty years Orita Hikoichi (Princeton) headed the Third Higher School in Kyoto. Kanda Naibu (Amherst '79) and Nakashima Rikizō (Western Reserve '84, Yale Graduate School) were only two in a long list of influential teachers.

Although the leading positions in government were long monopolized by the original group of oligarchs, several men trained in America were able to rise to second rank. Komura Jutarō (Harvard Law '77) was twice Minister of Foreign Af-

---

[31] When a family had no male heirs, the husband of a daughter often took her name and succeeded as head of the house.

fairs. In addition to long service as Minister of Finance, Takahashi Korekiyo, who had been a self-supporting student in San Francisco in the late sixties, became Premier for a brief period in 1921 and 1922. Makino Nobuaki held a number of ministerial posts and was one of Japan's delegates to the Paris Peace Conference. In recognition of his work in drafting the Constitution of 1889, Kaneko Kentarō (Harvard Law '78) was appointed a Privy Councillor. Matsumoto Sōichirō (R.P.I. '76) was president of the Imperial Government Railways from 1893 to 1897. The House of Peers had a sizable number of members who had studied in America, and Shiba Shirō (Pennsylvania '84) and Nemoto Shō (Vermont '89) were influential in the House of Representatives. Other graduates were scattered throughout the bureaucracy.

The careers of several men prominent in finance lay on the border line between government and private enterprise. Hara Rokurō (Yale), Sōma Nagatane (Columbia and Yale) and Mishima Yatarō (Massachusetts Agricultural College '88 and Cornell), were each in turn president of the Yokohama Specie Bank, Japan's leading institution for foreign exchange transactions. Mishima was also Governor of the Bank of Japan from 1913 to 1919. Tominaga Fuyuki (M.I.T.) stepped down from the Supreme Court to become director of the Tokyo Stock Exchange. For almost fifteen years Ono Eijirō (Oberlin '87, Michigan) was president of the Industrial Bank of Japan.

The *zaibatsu* strongholds of business power were not exempt from American influence. At least two of the five members of the Mitsui family who were sent abroad for study in 1874 spent some time at the Rutgers Grammar School. At a later date the family sent several of its scions to Dartmouth. Baron Iwasaki Hisaya, who headed the Mitsubishi enterprises from 1896 to 1917, received a Bachelor of Science from the University of Pennsylvania. It was the hired managers, however, who held the real positions of power in these *zaibatsu* firms. Dan Takuma (M.I.T. '78) rose in Mitsui service until he was chairman of the board at the time of his assassination. Kushida Manzō (Pennsylvania '90) held a comparable position in the Mitsubishi empire.

The role of these men in the development of modern

Japan is clear; their contribution to Japanese-American relations is much harder to assess. Although their success was probably due more to personal qualities of leadership than to their American training, nevertheless a large number of men in high position did have intimate experience of American life. Kaneko was a leading spirit in the Friends of America Society (Beiyū Kyōkai) and later in the America-Japan Society. Megata Tanetarō headed an important financial mission to the United States in 1917. Yoshida Kiyonari, Kurino Shinichirō, Komura Jutarō, Chinda Sutemi, and Satō Aimaro were all diplomatic chiefs of mission at Washington; and a number of other former students have served on the embassy staff. One danger is, of course, that such sympathetic spokesmen will hesitate to communicate the full force of unfriendly sentiment in Japan.

The much larger number of Japanese students in later years makes difficult similar detailed analyses of careers. In our enthusiasm for new exchanges, however, we should not underestimate the potential influence of those who studied here before 1941. To get a rough index of their importance I have analyzed the entries in *The Japan Who's Who, 1950–51* [32] under three common initials of Japanese surnames. Of 506 biographies under "K," 39 or 7.7 percent indicated some education in the United States; of 260 under "O," 24 or 9.2 percent; of 349 under "S," 26 or 7.4 percent. Exclusion of all former officers of the Japanese Army or Navy probably makes this a somewhat warped sample of Japan's élite. But an analysis for comparison of *Who's Who in Japan 1940–41* [33] shows that 32 biographies out of 375 (8.5 percent) under "O" and 65 out of 555 (11.7 percent) under "S" indicated study here, and many others had traveled in America on business or official inspections.

To maintain meaningful contact with these past students will be one of the principal tasks of a continuing program of cultural relations. In this endeavor the regular university alumni organizations have not been particularly successful. Their activities are pointed at the graduates near at hand; the foreign alumnus can seldom attend a football game or a

[32] Tokyo: Tokyo News Service, 1950.
[33] Tokyo: Who's Who in Japan, 1941.

reunion. There has been, it is true, a Harvard Club in Japan, a Columbia Club, a Yale Dōsōkai, an Ann Arbor Club and a Tokyo Princeton Club, but these organizations have lapsed after moments of enthusiasm into long periods of inactivity. Too often a university has one or two "pet" alumni in Japan, persons who immediately come to mind because of their eminence or eagerness, and who always are on hand to greet prominent American visitors. The vast majority of the Japanese alumni remain unknown or unnoticed.

New and broader types of alumni organizations may fill the gap. The Institute of International Education is now attempting to build up a Central Alumni File on all foreign students. If the records on the Japanese can be made reasonably complete, this file should be of great value in many phases of cultural work. The GARIOA students formed their own Exchange Student Association (Beikoku Ryugakusei Kai) in 1952. The organization in Tokyo of an alumni chapter of the International House Association is another promising development. The regular members have all had the experience in common of residence in one of the International Houses while studying in America. Other persons with "common interests" may become associate members. Such a group can be of great aid both in orienting new students bound for America and in smoothing their readjustment when they return. Avoiding a bilateral emphasis, it strives to be a center for truly international discussion and fellowship. It remains to be seen, however, whether it can bring in the many Japanese alumni who were not International House members.

Three Continuing Problems. Future relations with Japanese students will involve, then, three general problems. The first is to maintain a flow of able Japanese into our colleges and universities. The wise allocation of scholarship funds can play a part, but in the long run success may depend upon the situation in Japan. If training in the United States opens doors to prestige and position, the best young Japanese will find ways and means to come. If Japanese society becomes less fluid; if, for example, the former near-monopoly of Tokyo University in training for government service should be restored, we will get more of the second-best, and those who do study here will be barred from important fields of influence. The second problem is to make sure that the student, while here, both achieves his own objectives and gets an accurate and meaningful impression of American life. The third problem is to maintain contact with him after he returns to Japan, not in order to use him as a tool for our political purposes, but to sustain and reinforce the knowledge and the attitudes that he has gained from his experience in America.

American Students in Japan

The story of American students in Japan can be quickly told, because there has never been a true exchange in anything like equal volume. The necessity for knowing the Japanese language has kept Caucasians, with the exception of a few members of missionary families, out of the regular courses in Japanese schools and universities. There has never been, therefore, anything like a "Junior Year in Japan." Earlham College did experiment in this direction by sending Wilfred Jones to spend the year 1927–28 at Tokyo Imperial University. Several thousand Japanese-Americans have returned to Japan for intermediate or higher education, but they have contributed more to Japanese knowledge about American life than to our understanding of Japan.[34] These *kibei* are in a peculiar position of cultural isolation, even among their own people. In the past most of our public information about Japan has come from those who have gone there as teachers, missionaries, or businessmen, rather than from ex-students.

Luckily, during the 1930's a few American graduate students—E. O. Reischauer, Hugh Borton, Charles B. Fahs, and Yanaga Chitoshi, for example—were able to carry on systematic studies in Japan. Their knowledge of Japanese affairs proved invaluable during the war and has provided a foundation for the development of Japanese studies in this country. During the same period the Japanese Society for International Cultural Relations (Kokusai Bunka Shinkōkai)

[34] *Foreign Students in Japan, 1896–1947* (Mimeographed; Education Research Branch, CI & E, SCAP, 1948), p. iv.

granted fellowships for study of cultural arts to a few Americans.

The experience of our own students in Japan during the 1930's suggests that we should be cautious about directed orientation in values. Interested as these Americans were in Japan, they would have resented any concerted effort to explain the official militaristic ideology or to convince them of its virtues. Their appreciation and affection for the Japanese people came not from lectures but from the experience of living and working with them. They gained cultural understanding as much by osmosis as by analysis.

One of the ironies of war is that it stimulates efforts to understand the enemy and his culture that are neglected in times of peace and friendship. After Pearl Harbor our military services found themselves with only a handful of former attachés who knew either the Japanese language or much about the country. Using Japanese-Americans and former missionaries as teachers, the Army and Navy hurriedly set up schools to give young officers intensive language training. The graduates were used primarily for prisoner-of-war interrogation, translation work, and intelligence evaluation. In expectation of war's end, other men in ASTP programs and civil affairs training schools were given a broad orientation for Occupation duty, training which in many cases was never put to use.[35] By improvisation we had to compensate for the lack of a sufficient number of people who had studied in Japan.

Since World War II Japanese studies have expanded greatly in America. To supplement established academic programs at California, Columbia, Harvard, Stanford, Washington, and Yale, the Rockefeller Foundation provided funds for a new Center of Japanese Studies at the University of Michigan. Its general goal is to determine "the impact of Western civilization upon Japan." A field station at Okayama provides research facilities for faculty and students of the Center and for a few associated scholars. The Social Science Research Council has also been providing area training

---

[35] As a result of decisions that left Occupation functions largely in the hands of field forces, most of the men given special training were never used in Japan.

grants for individuals who need to do research in Japan. Fulbright funds are now available for similar purposes. The Ford Foundation fellowships for Asian studies make it possible for persons in business, agriculture, labor relations, and other professions, as well as scholars, to become acquainted with Japan. Emphasis on diverse backgrounds and purposes is particularly important if we wish fresh and accurate information about Japan to be disseminated widely in America.

Now that more Americans are going to Japan to study, careful attention should be given to relations with the Japanese academic community. Few students will want to take a conventional course of studies in a Japanese university. But we should avoid what might be called academic extraterritoriality: strictly American projects or even research centers operating with no relation to recognized Japanese scholars in their field. On the other hand, Americans should not expect gratuitous use of facilities or extensive guidance from heavily burdened professors. Arrangements flexible enough to meet special needs can be worked out by which Americans become contributing members of some university. The Fulbright Commission in Japan now arranges for each of its research grantees to be attached to a sponsoring institution.

Will it be possible to maintain interest in Japanese studies as World War II recedes into the distance and Japan lies farther from the focus of attention? This may depend upon the success with which persons with highly specialized area training are absorbed into teaching, research, government service, and other occupations. Ideally, the area programs should produce generally competent economists, anthropologists, political scientists, etc., who have special interest and experience in Japan. In practice, however, learning the language and surmounting the difficulties of using Japanese materials take so much time that the major discipline suffers. Fellowship funds should be made available to permit a longer total period of training for the area specialist.

So long as American students cross the Pacific only to study Japan itself—its history, its arts, its religion—their number will necessarily be limited. In contrast, Japanese come here to study all the arts and sciences; indeed, we have difficulty persuading them to take a systematic look at American life. Does Japan offer Americans similar opportunities for liberal education? Tsurumi Yūsuke's suggestion during the twenties that there ought to be a Japanese equivalent of the Rhodes Scholarships certainly had some merit, but the language problem still stands in the way. In art, communication is more direct and graphic, and American students might well develop both technique and appreciation by work with Japanese masters. There may be other fields in which true reciprocity is possible.

Geographically compact scenic beauties and a variety of cultural attractions make Japan an ideal place for summer travel and study. In prewar days organized study tours were quite a common practice. In the summer of 1929, for example, one party of 117 teachers and students went under the leadership of Professor Josef W. Hall ("Upton Close") of the University of Washington. Beginning in 1930 the Oriental Culture Summer College of Tokyo, organized by Nakamura Kaju, presented lectures and demonstrations on Japanese life for such parties and for unattached tourists. By 1941 over 4,000 visitors had attended.[36] In 1940 the war in Europe forced the Experiment in International Living to shift to Japan temporarily its plan of placing American students in homes abroad. Such brief trips cannot give any deep knowledge of Japan, but they do create a receptive and appreciative basis for further learning.

Relations between Student Groups

College students learn as much, it is commonly said, from their contemporaries as from their professors. Young people often believe that by greater honesty and idealism they can find solutions to problems when their elders have failed. Successive crises in Japanese-American relations have, therefore, stimulated students in the two countries to establish direct

---

[36] *Japanese Abroad*, V. 15 (July 1941), p. 4. Nakamura was a former student at New York University, a member of the Diet, and proprietor of the magazine *Kaigai no Nihon* (*Japanese Abroad*). During the 1920's he took several parties of Japanese students on summer trips to the United States. He started the Summer College when he became convinced that Americans and Europeans were more ignorant of Japan than Japanese were of the West.

relations with each other. Fifteen college students from the West Coast made a "Pilgrimage of Friendship" to Japan at the time that the law excluding Oriental immigrants went into effect in 1924. Student groups find it difficult, however, to turn their goodwill into effect on policy. Frank discussion of interracial relations may have dissipated some of the resentment in Japan, but it did nothing to get the offending legislation repealed. Similarly, three goodwill student lecturers sent to the United States in the spring of 1933 by the Oriental Culture Society, the Rotary Clubs of Japan, and the America-Japan Society were inevitably put in the position of apologists for their country's Manchurian policy.

The most ambitious ventures in student relations were the Japan-America Student Conferences that began in 1934. The idea originated with two young men, Nakayama Kōi and Itabashi Namiji, who attended the World Council of Youth held in connection with the Olympic Games at Los Angeles in 1932. They persuaded the Japan Student English Association to raise funds for a binational meeting of similar nature. In the summer of 1934, 98 Americans from 28 colleges and about 100 Japanese met for a week behind closed doors and had a "full and frank discussion of all important topics in the field of American-Japanese relations." The government saw to it, however, that the guests were taken on a "show-window tour" of Manchuria.[37]

In 1935 American students, with financial help from the Carnegie Endowment for International Peace, acted as hosts at a conference at Reed College. Thereafter sponsorship and location were alternated regularly. Each year, however, the intellectual problems became more difficult. The Foreign Office tried to control the Japanese delegations. For protection of individuals the meetings were closed to all but actual student members, and after 1936 no proceedings were published. No effort was made to reach agreement, but points of view diverged more and more. The Americans could not accept Japan's China policy, but they had their own liability

[37] G. Carpenter Barker, "The America-Japan Student Conference: An Experiment in Understanding," School and Society, V. 51 (June 1, 1940), pp. 707-708; letter from Hoshino Satoshi to Russell L. Durgin, January 1, 1952; Matsumoto Toru and Marion O. Lerrigo, A Brother Is a Stranger (New York: John Day, 1946), pp. 106-113.

in the exclusion of Japanese immigrants. The pious hope that, despite these conflicts, good relations would be maintained could have little practical effect.

This series of Japan-America Student Conferences was resumed in 1947 under the auspices of the International Student Association of Japan. The American delegations have of necessity been made up almost entirely of persons already in Japan with the occupation forces or on other business. In 1953 the Japan Society of New York provided funds to help pay the travel expenses of two representatives of the National Student Association of America. A *nisei* delegate also came from Hawaii. Although the theme of the week-long conference at Sophia University was "The Unity of East and West," differences of opinion were sometimes vehemently expressed. The Japanese delegates stressed their need for restored trade with China and, for fear of military involvement, opposed almost without exception the acceptance of mutual defense assistance from the United States. The Americans urged the overwhelming danger from Soviet imperialism as reason for a more active policy in pursuit of peace.[38]

In these bilateral conferences, in the International Student Seminars that the American Friends Service Committee has organized in Tokyo, and in the Japanese student movement at large, the sentiment of peace has evoked enthusiastic response. In part peace talk has been inspired by Communist leadership in the National Federation of Student Self-government Associations (Zengakuren). But we must recognize that it also rests upon genuine youthful idealism, upon the conviction that only by some sort of neutrality can Japan avoid a revival of totalitarianism from within. Student conferences offer an opportunity for better understanding of the context in which these problems appear to the Japanese themselves.

The Goal: Friendship or Citizenship?

Before we leave the subject of student exchange, we must again face the difficult question of goals. What do we want

[38] *The Mainichi*, July 13, 14, 16, 1953. A delegation of fifteen students from Japan came to the United States during November and December 1954, for conferences on several campuses.

to accomplish by promoting exchange of students with Japan and with other countries of the world?

Answers to this question are often phrased in terms of friendship. We want Japanese who study here to learn to like us and to share American objectives. But the fallacy in friendship becomes apparent as soon as we invert the relation. We do not want Americans who learn to like the Japanese and to share their objectives to become special pleaders in their behalf. It is inconsistent, then, to expect ex-students to repay us with speeches or articles in unqualified support of the latest policy of our State Department. The role that our own Japan experts played during World War II shows that the person best qualified for friendship is potentially the most effective enemy.

The psychological satisfactions of friendship apply better to relations between individuals than to those between nations. We should never undervalue the pleasures of friendship between individual Americans and Japanese that may result from study abroad. Like beauty, friendship is its own excuse for being. But nations must be held together by a more substantial community of interest. Mere admiration for American freedom will not keep Japan free. She must be able to attain a viable and satisfactory place in the free world. For Japan her own objectives have priority.

Let us stress, instead, the contributions that student exchange can make to citizenship. In the long run, what the Japanese who have studied here do for Japan is far more important than their feelings about America. First of all, we should give them the technical training—whether it be in electrical engineering, public administration, or English teaching—that they want and their country needs. We cannot expect to educate as many of Japan's leaders as we did in early Meiji times, but we can help to fill the need for specialists. Second, if the education we give is really imbued with democratic values, we may simultaneously enlarge their concept of citizenship from one of unquestioning service to the state to one of constant concern and responsibility for public policy. Such lessons are taught by example rather than by preaching, and unfortunately our examples are not always faultless. But our efforts will be more clearly focused if, instead of making our student visitors over into Americans, we concentrate on making them more effective citizens of their own land.

The benefits that Americans gain from study abroad can also be expressed in terms of citizenship. Again the first dimension is vocational. We can gain much usable knowledge from Japan, if only we explore the possibilities seriously. Experience abroad has most lasting and functional effects when it is closely integrated with a person's vocation. On a broader plane, study abroad can make Americans better qualified to handle the world responsibilities of citizenship. By learning to know Japan (or any other country) we will realize better how complex international problems are, how real divergences in objective may be, and that progress toward peace and harmony can come only through the hard patient work involved in reconciliation of interests.

CHAPTER SEVEN

EXCHANGE OF CULTURAL MATERIALS

THE VAST majority of Americans and Japanese are not able to cross the Pacific Ocean and savor fully the life of their distant neighbor. Their first-hand impressions are limited to the transportable evidences of culture—to books, to art objects, to the occasional performances of music and drama. As a young nation, we Americans strive self-consciously for a culture that will be different from that of Europe. The Japanese were among the first to admit the distinction; hence the term *Ō-Bei*—Europe and America. The Japanese, on the other hand, really have two cultures, their ancient traditional arts and a modern Westernized culture. In arranging cultural exchanges we must not forget that they have both *The Tale of Genji* and naturalistic novels, *nō* dramas and symphony orchestras.

Japan has drawn upon many sources, European as well as American, for elements in her modern culture. But it is fair to say that Japanese have paid as much attention to American cultural productions as to those of any other single Western nation. Although here it is hard to separate British from American influences, English has definitely become the second language of the country. The heightened interest in cultural as well as material aspects of American life since World War II has been far more than a desire to flatter the conqueror. Out of a sense of isolation and deprivation, the Japanese have explored enthusiastically the creative manifestation of the American spirit. Japanese intellectuals with a broad interest in Western culture but without vested interest in any particular national tradition may, in fact, be in an ideal position to see American production in fresh perspective.

In contrast, cultural materials have never flowed from Japan to America as easily or in such volume as those from, let us say, France or Germany. Things Japanese remain an exotic interest for Americans, outside the main cultural tradition. For that very reason, deliberate encouragement is necessary to increase the cultural traffic down the other side of the "two-way street."

Exchange of cultural materials on any large scale does not just happen by accident. Trans-Pacific art exhibitions and theatrical performances involve many problems of financing and arrangement. Books are published either from expectation of profit or because someone provides a subsidy. To reach many people, a foreign book must be translated. The individuals who have the interests of fruitful cultural relations between the United States and Japan at heart must take positive action to overcome the obstacles to exchange. In this chapter we shall discuss some of the opportunities and difficulties in exchange of printed materials, movies, drama, music, and art. As in other areas of cultural relations the experience of the past century provides a base upon which to build. But we cannot rest content with history. The experience of another culture must constantly be renewed, for each individual and for each new generation.

Books and other Printed Materials

Over the past century the printed word has been one of the most important channels for transmission of information about the West to Japan. General literacy created by the public educational system in Japan has been accompanied by a widespread eagerness to learn through reading. The teaching of English in the higher Japanese schools has meant that a small but influential part of the population has been able to read American books in the original language. Despite the necessity for manual type-setting of the cumbersome Chinese characters, Japan has become one of the most voluminous publishers among modern nations. Many foreign books have been made available by translation or by adaptation of their contents.

In the early years the language barrier was circumvented

by using books on modern subjects printed in Chinese by
the mission presses. Townsend Harris obtained over a hundred geographies from Dr. W. A. P. Martin for distribution
among officials in Edo, and Martin's own *Ko wu ju mên*
(*Introduction to Natural Philosophy*) unlocked the secrets
of nature for many educated Japanese. In 1860 Guido Verbeck distributed 486 books and almost 900 pamphlets, on
science, medicine, and history as well as on religion.[1]

When Fukuzawa Yukichi visited the United States in 1867,
he bought large quantities of books, some for his own Keiō
school and others for the Sendai and Kishū clans.[2] For many
years American schoolbooks were widely used in Japan.
Peter Parley's Universal History by Samuel G. Goodrich, for
example, was a standard text in middle schools and a favorite for general reading.[3] McGuffey's, Sargent's and Willson's series of readers were reprinted in pirated editions.
Both Shibusawa Hideo and Abe Yoshishige have commented
on the pleasure they received from the American fare of the
National Readers.[4]

Until about 1890 Japanese intellectuals were primarily
concerned with catching up with the West, with its practical
knowledge and material success. A list of books translated
during the latter part of 1879 included such utilitarian items
as Asa Gray's *Botany,* H. N. Robinson's *Conic Sections and
Analytical Geometry,* and Richard Henry Dana's *Seaman's
Friend.* I have not discovered any Japanese editions of Ho-
ratio Alger, but the popularity of O. S. Marden's "Pushing
to the Front," Sarah K. Bolton's *Poor Boys who Became
Famous* and Lorimer's *Letters from a Self-made Merchant*
showed that Nakamura Nasanao's famous translation of *Self-
Help* by Samuel Smiles had not sated the demand for guides

[1] Otis Cary, *A History of Christianity in Japan,* cited, V. 2, p. 51; *Twenty-
ninth Annual Report of the Board of Foreign Missions of the Reformed
Protestant Dutch Church . . . for the year ending April 30th, 1861* (New
York: Board of Publication, 1861), pp. 18-19.
[2] Ishikawa Kammei. *Fukuzawa Yukichi Den (Biography of Fukuzawa Yukichi)*
(Tokyo: Iwanami Shoten, 1932), V. 1, pp. 510-517.
[3] Kumashiro Tanesuke, "Paarei Bankoku Shi Kangae (Thoughts on Parley's
Universal History)," in Meiji Bunka Kenkyūkai, *Meiji Bunka Kenkyū Ronsō
(Collection of Studies on Meiji Culture)* (Tokyo: Ichigensha, 1934), p. 327.
[4] Shibusawa Hideo, *Amerika Ōrai (To and From America)* (Tokyo: Tōhō
Shoten, 1948), pp. 24-25; statement by Abe, December 1, 1952.

to personal success. Mitarai Masakazu's *Meika no Yokun* (1887) was only the first of several translations of Benjamin Franklin's *Autobiography*.

During the nineteenth century American literature, in the sense of *belles lettres*, could not rival the popularity in Japan of the works of Scott, Bulwer-Lytton, Dickens, Disraeli, and Wilkie Collins. The first American novels translated into Japanese were such now-forgotten titles as Edward King's *The Gentle Savage*, John Esten Cooke's *My Lady Pokahontas*, and *The Crime of Christmas-day: A Tale of the Latin Quarter*. The "Old Sleuth Library" also had a coterie of admirers. During 1887 the *Yomiuri Shimbun* published translations of Bret Harte's "M'liss" and of Poe's "Murders in the Rue Morgue" and "The Black Cat." [5] Emerson's essays were admired by philosopher Nakamura Masanao and novelist Kitamura Tōkoku, as well as by leaders in English studies like Kanda Naibu and Tsuda Umeko. A recent bibliography of 228 items by or about Emerson published in Japan testifies to his continued popularity. [6] Somewhat later, during the democratic movement of the Taishō era, Walt Whitman became the inspiration for novelist Arishima Takeo and for poets Shiratori Shōgo, Tomita Saika, Fukuda Masao, and Momota Sōji. [7]

About 1910 Japanese taste in foreign books began to shift from British and American works to those from European countries. But the fact that Russian and French works were the favorites, instead of German literature, suggests that this shift may have been tied more closely to world literary trends, shared even in England and the United States, than it was to Japan's political orientation toward Germany. World War I stimulated imports of books from the United States, but most of these were of a technical nature. Many of the American books translated during the twenties and thirties appealed

---

[5] Toyoda Minoru, *Nihon Eigaku Shi no Kenkyū* (*Essays in the History of English Studies in Japan*) (Tokyo: Iwanami Shoten, 1939), pp. 459-467; *Japan Weekly Mail*, March 17, 1894.
[6] Jugaku Bunshō, *A Bibliography of Ralph Waldo Emerson in Japan from 1878 to 1935* (Kyoto: Sunward Press, 1947).
[7] See Nishikawa Masami, "Amerika Bungaku no Eikyō (The Influence of American Literature)," in *Nihon Bungaku Daijiten* (*Encyclopedia of Japanese Literature*) (Tokyo: Shinchōsha, 1951–1952), V. 8, pp. 5-7.

only to special groups. The works of John Dewey were popular among educators. Self-consciously proletarian intellectuals made translations of Upton Sinclair and Jack London. The police permitted Paul Whiteman's book on *Jazz* but ruled that *The Rampant Age*, Robert S. Carr's account of the foibles of American youth, was an unhealthy encouragement to "modern boys" and "modern girls." Pearl Buck's novels about China were popular, as were the detective stories of Erle Stanley Gardner and Ellery Queen. In the absence of any copyright protection for translations, several Japanese publishers would compete to get hasty versions of best sellers like *Gone with the Wind* and *The Yearling* before the public.[8] Considering the vogue of cowboy films, the absence of Western stories is surprising. In general, serious nonfiction and *avant-garde* American literature were not tranlated.

After World War II a Japanese public eager to read about the United States was frustrated far too long by SCAP red tape. Exchange restrictions made it practically impossible to buy books from the United States. Not until May 1948 did the Civil Information and Education Section establish procedures for obtaining rights of translation and publication. The rights to ninety-one "approved" American and British books were then opened to competitive bidding. In their speculative eagerness Japanese publishers made exorbitant bids, and as a result have since found it difficult to cut back to realistic rates. A 36 percent royalty was paid on Joseph C. Grew's *Ten Years in Japan;* the average for the first list was about 15 percent.[9] SCAP later approved supplementary lists of books, including a few from France and Russia. By 1949 it was possible for Japanese publishers to make contracts directly with foreign copyright proprietors who had met certain SCAP licensing requirements.

A few definite lines of interest can be discerned if one searches the new national bibliography published by the Diet Library for American books translated since 1949.[10] From

---

[8] *Japan Times Weekly,* September 21, 1939.
[9] *New York Times,* June 15, 1948.
[10] *Zen Nihon Shuppanbutsu Sō-mokuroku (General Catalogue of Japanese Publications)* (Tokyo: Kokuritsu Kokkai Toshokan, annual since 1948). Current publications are listed in *Shuppan Nenkan (Publishing Yearbook)*

Ernie Pyle's *This is War,* J. A. Field's *The Battle of Leyte Gulf,* John Hersey's *Hiroshima,* Admiral Zacharias' *Secret Missions,* and Norman Mailer's *The Naked and the Dead* the Japanese got varied American accounts of the recent war. They enjoyed reading in Mark Gayn's *Japan Diary* strictures on the Occupation which they would hardly have dared to express themselves. Translations of Ruth Benedict's *The Chrysanthemum and the Sword* and Jerome B. Cohen's *Japan's Economy in War and Reconstruction* reflected a self-conscious concern about American opinion of them and their problems.

Books about the United States quite naturally bulked large among the translations. The range was wide: Charles Beard's *The Republic,* Van Wyck Brooks' *Flowering of New England,* Catherine Drinker Bowen's *Yankee from Olympus,* F. L. Allen's *Only Yesterday* and *Since Yesterday,* Florence Peterson's *American Labor Unions,* among others. Harold Laski's *American Democracy* has been translated as a five-volume set. In literature, attention was first paid to popular novels like *Anthony Adverse,* Lloyd C. Douglas' *The Robe,* and a new authorized edition of *Gone With the Wind.* During 1951, however, translations were published of works by Dreiser, Dos Passos, Faulkner, Hemingway, Saroyan, Steinbeck, and Thornton Wilder, as well as older items like *The Last of the Mohicans, Walden, Innocents Abroad,* and *Ben Hur.* The standard Iwanami Library series has recently included such varied American classics as *Tom Sawyer, Huckleberry Finn,* Hawthorne's *The Scarlet Letter,* and Henry James' *Daisy Miller.*

Japan's new-found freedom in the study of social and economic questions has brought a rash of translations of Marx, Lenin, and Stalin. It is significant that among the few translated American books in this field there should be two by Paul M. Sweezy, *The Theory of Capitalist Development* and *Socialism,* both written from an avowed Marxist point of view. One can balance against these Schumpeter's weighty *Capitalism, Socialism, and Democracy* and the technical *Survey of Contemporary Economics* edited by Howard S. Ellis.

(Tokyo: Shuppan Nyūsu-sha, annual) and in *Shuppan Nyūsu* (*Publishing News*).

Direct defenses of democracy were available in Jacques Barzun's *Of Human Freedom* and David Lilienthal's *This I Do Believe.*

Americans may want to encourage the publication of specific books in Japan, but the problem of translation in general promises to take care of itself. The copyright agreement with Japan signed on November 10, 1953, extending protection to translation rights, provides a legal framework for contracts. The Charles E. Tuttle Co. is now acting as the Japan agent for a number of American publishers. Translators are abundant and reasonably competent. The market for translations of American books may, in fact, be a good barometer of our cultural relations.

Paradoxically, we are losing out most seriously in competition with the Communists in distribution of books printed in English. Volumes imported from the United States are too expensive for students and many other Japanese who would like to use them to improve their language ability. Communist book stores offer handsome books in English at prices that are varied to fit the pocket of the customer. Their publications have the added allure of world famous authors—Lenin, Stalin, Mao Tse-tung. Stalin's *Problems of Leninism,* for example, offers over 800 pages of reading for the equivalent of fifty-five cents.[11] A countermeasure that would not require an entirely new publishing enterprise would be to promote the distribution of pocket-sized editions of outstanding American books in Japan.

Ideological competition is also strong in magazines. The special editions of *Time* and *Newsweek* published in Japan together do not sell as many copies as the Moscow *New Times.*[12] In addition to flourishing journals like *Heiwa* and *Ashi* devoted entirely to the "world peace movement," three of Japan's leading general magazines—*Chūō Kōron, Sekai,* and, to a lesser extent, *Kaizō*—are inclined to be neutralist or anti-American in tone. Americans might consider giving support to a rival journal of opinion of the same high quality that *Der Monat* has provided in Germany. But we already

11 *United States News and World Report,* October 23, 1953, pp. 109-111.
12 Same, p. 110.

have certain assets. By concise and lively presentation of material with much human interest, the Japanese-language *Reader's Digest* has built a record circulation.[13] The picture of America that avid Japanese readers get from *True Story* is of more doubtful value. Perhaps the most encouraging sign is that the circulation of *Bungei Shunjū*, which has followed either a pro-American or balanced editorial policy, has far outstripped that of the neutralist journals and is still climbing above 550,000.[14]

The opportunities for Americans to become acquainted with Japanese writing are less encouraging. Very little Japanese literature, especially modern literature, is available in English translation. A list that Glenn Shaw prepared in 1936 gave seventy-one titles, half of them pre-1850 works. Many were published in Tokyo by the Hokuseido Press and can be found in only a few American libraries.[15] Although the Japanese themselves tend to overemphasize the esoteric, incommunicable qualities of their literature, there is some truth in the comment that it is "a literature of form without much substance, and, when pressed into the mold of a foreign language, the peculiar beauties are apt to disappear like the opal tints from a squeezed jellyfish."[16] This is particularly true of poetry and drama. The strict syllable patterns of the terse, sophisticated Japanese poems called *tanka* and *hokku*, which exerted such a strong influence upon American poets of the imagist school, are lost in translation.

Modern Japanese novels probably offer the best possibilities for translation, although even here the market is quite uncertain. Japanese reviews are so uncritical that it is hard for American publishers to judge theme and quality. Few translators have had experience with literary work. The Japan Society of New York is now taking the initiative to

---

[13] In 1953 circulation stood at about 650,000, a considerable decline from a peak of 1,500,000 in 1949.

[14] *Shuppan Nenkan: 1953 Nen Han (Publishing Yearbook: 1953 Edition)* (Tokyo: Shuppan Nyūsu-sha, 1953), pp. 1389-1390; Sasaki Senichi, "Magazines in Postwar Japan," *Contemporary Japan*, V. 19 (July-September 1950), pp. 378-388.

[15] Glenn Shaw, *Living in Japan* (Tokyo: Hokuseido Press, 1936), pp. 189-210.

[16] Roger Riordan and Takayanagi Tozō, *Sunrise Stories: A Glance at the Literature of Japan* (New York: Scribner, 1896), p. v.

break down these obstacles. It will circulate accurate information about selected novels to publishers. If they show definite interest, the Society will then finance experimental translations.

Besides the few books that publishers will ever undertake to issue in translation, there must be in both Japan and America adequate reference collections of the materials printed in the other country. In 1921 the Carnegie Endowment presented 1,800 volumes on American civilization to the Hibiya Public Library of the City of Tokyo. This collection was added to later, but little is known about the extent to which it has been used. In 1947 the American Library Association presented a similar collection of Americana to the National Library (formerly the Imperial Library) at Ueno. This library has now been incorporated into a new National Diet Library patterned after our own Library of Congress.

The American Library Mission that went to Japan at the end of 1947 urged that this Diet Library be given a basic collection of American books. The Social Science Research Council asked Hugh Borton to choose recent works in the social sciences, and René Wellek made similar choices for the humanities. In 1949 the Rockefeller Foundation asked the Council on Foreign Relations to expend $10,000 for additional books in the social sciences. A Division of International Affairs has been established in the Diet Library to handle international exchanges, chiefly of government documents. American advisers and teachers of library science at the new library school of Keiō University have been trying to inculcate in the minds of Japanese librarians our attitude that books are meant to be used, not to be kept carefully and displayed. So far, however, the Japanese have been very slow in developing systems of interlibrary loan that would make these special collections available to users throughout the country.

Before World War II American libraries were not keeping pace with the torrential output of the Japanese presses. University collections followed the scholarly interests of the few specialists in Japanese studies. The Japan Institute Library in New York, although small, was unique in that its primary purpose was to answer inquiries from the public.[17]

Since 1945 American holdings of Japanese books have been greatly expanded. At the end of the war several large collections belonging to military and colonial development organizations in Japan were confiscated and made available, first to the Library of Congress, and in case of duplication to other libraries. The Library of Congress is now trying to purchase all serious current publications. Columbia, Harvard, Michigan, Washington, and the University of California have made significant additions to their Japanese collections. The Hoover Library at Stanford is attempting to collect all material "which would shed light on the movements and forces within Japan which had plunged the nation into total war and complete defeat." [17a]

The big question is how effectively these large collections will be used to increase our knowledge and understanding of Japan. Staffs in the Oriental libraries are too small; the Japanese Section of the Library of Congress estimates that it has a cataloging backlog of about fifty years. Union cataloging has only been begun in a small way. Too few Americans can read Japanese well enough to unlock the material in the books we already have, not to mention the thousands of new ones being published each year. Coöperative effort could do much more to save time and to make the substance of Japanese materials available to scholars who do not have command of the language. The Center for Japanese Studies at the University of Michigan is taking the lead by preparing annotated bibliographies and by publishing as part of its *Occasional Papers* a series of "Abstracts of Japanese Materials in the Social Sciences and Humanities."

Movies

By the end of the nineteenth century Japan was so completely a part of the modern world that the newest form of entertainment and informal education, the moving picture,

[17] The Japan Institute collection has now been deposited in the East Asiatic Library of Columbia University.

[17a] Higashiuchi Yoshio, *Literature on Contemporary Japan* (Tokyo: Hoover Institute and Library, 1951), p. i.

was introduced with hardly any time lag. In 1896, only a year after public announcement of the invention, the Edison-Armat Vitascope and the Lumière Cinématographe machines were imported almost simultaneously from America and France and exhibited around the country. Before long the Japanese were filming performances by actors of the traditional theater like Danjurō and Kikugorō. Eventually the Japanese film industry developed two distinctive genres: the historical plays (*jidaigeki*) produced in the Kyoto area and the modern plays (*gendaigeki*) associated with Tokyo studios.

Before the First World War most of the imported films came from Europe rather than the United States. This reflected the condition of the industry as much as a conscious choice by the Japanese. When American studios were still turning out action features and comedies of about 1,000 feet, the French and the Italians were already making six- and eight-reel historical dramas, with elaborate scenery and careful acting. When the war cut off supplies from Europe, Japanese exhibitors turned to American films. One source mentions *The Broken Coin*, a 1911 release that reached Japan in 1915, as the first American hit. By 1919 we were exporting 5½ million feet of film to Japan, who quickly became our third best customer for this type of entertainment. Japanese movie makers now began to break free of the stage and to imitate the American free-ranging camera technique. By 1924 American films were so popular that an attempt to boycott them as a protest against the Immigration Act failed to rally public support.[18]

The shift from silent to sound movies at the end of the twenties threatened temporarily the position of foreign films in Japan. By providing a narrator, known as the *katsuben* or *benshi*, who stood or sat at the side of the screen to translate the titles and interpret the action, the Japanese had actually raised the silent film to a higher pitch of artistry than it attained in the West. Many of the *katsuben* were excellent

18 Yoshioka Chōsaburō, *Eiga* (*Motion Pictures*) (Tokyo: Daiyamondo-sha, 1938), pp. 99-104; A. N. Vardac, *Stage to Screen: Theatrical Method from Garrick to Griffith* (Cambridge: Harvard University Press, 1949), pp. 211-212; International Cinema Association of Japan, *Cinema Year Book of Japan, 1936–1937* (Tokyo: Sanseidō, 1937), pp. 1-3.

actors, whose monologues were in demand as phonograph records. Their role was now superseded by unintelligible dialogue which also slowed down the action. Predictions that talkies would never succeed in Japan proved incorrect, however. The problem was solved, just as in other countries, by superimposing titles in Japanese on foreign films. By 1931 about 85 percent of the footage imported from the United States carried sound, and Japanese studios were experimenting with various recording techniques.

American films were able to hold their market in Japan during the 'thirties in spite of the deterioration in political relations. In 1933, 217 American films were released, compared to 19 from other countries and a native production of 490. Even in 1937, after Japan had signed cultural pacts with Germany and Italy, only 56 pictures came from Europe and 239 from the United States.[19] As the war with China became more intense the whole industry was severely restricted by government regulations. But at the time of Pearl Harbor approximately ten million yen due American distributors was in blocked funds in Japan.

For better or for worse, the average Japanese obtained his most vivid and specific ideas about the United States from the movies. The total impression is difficult to assess. Government censorship cut out lengthy kisses, bedroom scenes, revolutionary violence, and everything that could be construed as reflecting even remotely upon the Imperial system. Some of the most popular imports were historical or fantastic in setting and had little direct relevance to America; Douglas Fairbanks' *The Thief of Bagdad,* for example, was shown year after year. Cowboy pictures apparently created a romantic impression; many Japanese soldiers captured during the war said that they would like to start life anew on a ranch in the Wild West.

In 1933 a student goodwill envoy from Dōshisha University put his finger on the two worst distortions when he said that the movies had given Japanese the idea that life in America consisted entirely of rounds of cocktail parties in cities ruled by gangsters. American movies were commonly blamed for the fast life of the *mobo* (modern boys) and *moga*

[19] *Motion Picture Herald,* December 13, 1941.

(modern girls). "Foreign clothes, rouge, shingled hair, short thick parasols, greased hair, huge spectacles à la Harold Lloyd, Oxford bags, and so on" were the outward marks of urban youth conspicuously bent on pleasure. Their tendency toward radical socialism, however, was certainly not the result of Hollywood influence.[20] On the score of violence, Kermit Eby has told how he sat through a Tokyo screening of *Scarface,* after which a student asked him if it would be physically safe to attend Northwestern University Dental School.[21] Another unfortunate occurrence was the showing in Japan in 1932 of *Hell Divers,* which suggested strongly that the Japanese were the potential targets of the U. S. Navy planes.[22]

Condemnation of American commercial films for their effects abroad tends to become a cliché, however, which does not necessarily fit the facts. In part it rests on assumptions by intellectuals that people ought to have more refined tastes than they do. A comparative study of French, British, and American films by Martha Wolfenstein and Nathan Leites has shown that our movies do reveal a fairly definite pattern of American values—emphasis on competition and winning, confidence in future success and happiness, the belief that virtue is heightened by exciting temptations, confidence in the amateur rather than the official expert.[23] But we have the uncomfortable feeling that these values are not ideal enough for export. During the years that the Army was able to choose for release in Japan the films that it thought best suited for reorientation, much the same complaints were heard from Americans. The Japanese point of view, however, may be quite different. One recent newspaper editorial characterized American pictures as more wholesome and better suited for family viewing than those produced in Japan.[24]

20 *New York Times,* February 2, 1933; *Trans-Pacific,* October 8, 1927.
21 *Interchange of Knowledge and Skills between People of the United States and Peoples of other Countries.* Hearings, Committee on Foreign Affairs, House of Representatives, 79th Congress, 1st and 2d Sessions, on H. R. 4368 and H. R. 4982 (Washington: GPO, 1946), p. 36.
22 *New York Times,* October 2, 1932.
23 *Movies: A Psychological Study* (Glencoe, Ill.: Free Press, 1950), pp. 298-301.
24 *The Mainichi,* August 20, 1953.

With between 40 and 50 percent of their revenue coming from foreign rentals, American picture companies are extremely careful not to give positive offense to audiences abroad. In Japan they are now subject to a government-imposed quota which allowed importation in the fiscal year ending March 31, 1954 of 146 American features, 84 shorts, and 4 weekly newsreel series. Since quotas are allocated according to past earnings, competition is keen and the companies use pictures with the best box-office potential. In what may have been an unusual week early in October 1952, *Gone With the Wind, A Place in the Sun, Ivanhoe,* and *For Whom the Bell Tolls* were vying for attention in Tokyo.[25]

The factors determining popularity of our films abroad are always rather unpredictable, however. Viewers project into each picture their own concerns and aspirations. One reason that *Gone With the Wind* broke records may have been that the Japanese found in this story of a South devastated by war and carpetbaggers a parallel to their own recent history. Romantic pictures, now shown with kisses and clinches intact, help those who are groping for modern attitudes toward love and marriage. Commenting on the hysterical reception that Marilyn Monroe received when she came to Japan in February 1954, a woman designer said, "The popularity of Miss Monroe for Japanese girls was an explosion of emotion among people pursued by the instinct of wanting to become beautiful, tied up with the liberation of sex." [26] The psychology involved in an experience of entertainment is so complex that commercial films are a very undependable medium for carrying a positive message.

Documentary films with an avowed purpose of giving information or education can do much more to correct distortions of fact or opinion. The Japanese Ministry of Education had made a considerable start in educational cinema before the war, using foreign as well as native films. During the Occupation SCAP documentaries were estimated to have reached every Japanese, on the average, once in nine months. Projectors originally loaned by CI & E have now been do-

25 Information supplied by Herbert J. Erlanger of the Motion Picture Export Association, April 29, 1953; *Paramount International News,* January 7, 1953.
26 *Nippon Times,* February 16, 1954.

nated permanently to prefectural boards of education. The American Cultural Centers both show and distribute American documentaries. At the end of 1954 the United States Information Service in Japan had in stock from 20 to 160 prints of 390 films with Japanese-language narration, also single prints of 500 different titles with sound tracks in English.[27]

The few attempts to show Japanese films to the general American public before World War II had discouraging results. In 1930 *Jūjiro* (*Crossroads*) achieved a short run in New York under the lurid title "The Slums of Tokyo, a Story of the Yoshiwara." No sound picture was shown outside the Japanese-American communities until 1937, when *Kimiko* was given a try at the Filmarte in New York. Some University of Chicago professors had recommended it as representative of modern life in Japan. The *Variety* critic gave this realistic appraisal:

Has little entertainment value for average film audiences. May draw in few arties, but chiefly as novelty. . . . And that despite certain unaffected charm of the pic and genuine direction and production. Film's chief flaw is its dreary pace. Also fact that Japanese are racially not emotionally demonstrative, as result of which performances are agonizingly underplayed.[27a]

This difference in dramatic standards is an unfortunate barrier, for films have great potentialities for giving an understanding of Japanese customs and psychology. But few of the 300-odd films coming out of Japanese studios each year can possibly find a receptive audience in the United States. The Japanese themselves admit that their practice of one-week first runs leads to cheap and hasty production.[28]

Even under severe limitations of time and money, however, a few outstanding directors, especially those working with producer Nagata Masaichi of the Daiei Studios, have been able to turn out work of high artistic quality. Yoshimura Kimisaburo's *Tales of Genji* took the award for best photography and composition at the Cannes Film Festival

[27] *Nippon Times*, January 29, 1955.
[27a] *Variety*, April 14, 1937.
[28] *New York Times*, February 21, 1954; Ueno Ichirō, "Motion Picture Industry," *Contemporary Japan*, V. 23 (1954), p. 57-65.

in 1952, and in 1954 *Jigokumon* (*Gate of Hell*) won the grand
prize there. At the Venice Festival *Rashomon,* Kurosawa
Akira's version of a story by Akutagawa Ryūnosuke, won
similar top honors in 1951, and in 1952 Mizoguchi Kenji
received a director's award for his *Saikaku Ichidai Onna.* In
1953 *Ugetsu* was judged the best foreign film shown at
Venice.

With this international acclaim behind them, a few outstanding Japanese films are gradually finding a place on the
American art circuit. *Rashomon* was shown with fair success
in the winter of 1951–52. The violent action, swordplay,
and tone of sadness so typical of the *jidaigeki* were readily
understandable. But many Americans found the deeper
meaning puzzling: the cynicism about truth implied in the
four unreconciled versions of the violent act, followed by a
plea for faith in humanity. When *Ugetsu* was brought to the
United States in the fall of 1954, critics praised its weird
beauty, but found the symbolism unfamiliar, the meaning
"strangely obscure, inferential, almost studiously perplex-
ing." The immediate effect may be to emphasize the differences, rather than the common ground, in Japanese and
American taste and thought.[29] With *Jigokumon* the Daiei
studio demonstrated its ability to use the Eastman color
process to create original effects of striking beauty. But all
three of these pictures have been historical in theme. What
we now need is an equally powerful film that will communicate the tone of life in present-day Japan.

Theatre

A successful five-week engagement of the Azuma Kabuki
Dancers and Musicians in New York early in 1954 suggests
that differences in theatrical tradition can be bridged if first
class performers are brought here with the best sponsorship
and publicity. Each of the principals, Azuma Tokuho, Onoe
Kikunojō, and Fujima Masaya, was head of a leading school
of *kabuki* dancing in Japan. Prince Takamatsu and the Japanese Ministry of Foreign Affairs endorsed the show as an
important venture in cultural relations. Sol Hurok gave it

[29] *New York Times,* September 8, 12, 1954.

the benefit of his vast experience in theatrical management, while Joshua Logan and James Michener had a part in the preliminary arrangements. Audiences liked it and critics hailed it as an exciting "fusion of music, movement, dramatic impulse, creative costuming and decorative milieu." [30] Though it was not the full *kabuki* program of drama and dance as presented in Tokyo, Americans were given an extensive demonstration of genuine Japanese theatrical arts.

Hurok plans to send Miss Azuma's own troupe on a world tour in 1955–56, and it is hoped that American audiences will be able to see professional *kabuki* performances at least once in five years. Interest in Japanese drama can be kept alive in the intervals by the informed work of amateur or semi-professional groups. The presence of even one talented native performer can be a powerful stimulus. Itō Michio, for example, came to New York in 1916 after studying dance in Europe. Besides giving recitals of Japanese dances, Itō helped the Washington Square Players to present a piece called *Bushidō,* one act from the classic *kabuki* sequence *Sugawara Denju.* In 1921 he and Komori Toshi joined the Neighborhood Players in a Japanese program which included the *nō* drama *Tamura.* Two years later Itō staged the *nō* drama *Hagoromo* for the Thursday Evening Club.[31] To take another example, part of the *Chūshingura,* a *kabuki,* was presented at the University of Washington in 1936. If only they had expert advice and direction, American theater groups today might be willing to try other experiments with traditional Japanese plays.

Too often Japan has been represented in our theaters by spurious items. Gilbert and Sullivan's well-known light opera *The Mikado* reveals more about British taste than it does about Japan. Instead of sending a *bunraku* puppet show to the expositions at New York and San Francisco in 1939, as originally planned, Japan sent the Takarazuka Cherry Blossom Ballet. "It is a girl show, frankly billed as such," commented the *New York Times,* "and whether in Nippon-

[30] *New York Times,* February 28, 1954.
[31] Students of Moravian College for Women, Bethlehem, Pa., presented the same play in English as part of Columbia University's "Festival of Japanese Theatre," on April 19, 1953.

ese or any other language, the aroma of honky-tonk is virtually the same the world over." [32]

Japanese interest in Western drama goes back to the period immediately following the Russo-Japanese War. Professor Tsubouchi Shōyō of Waseda University then organized the Bungei Kyōkai (Arts Society), which put on his translation of *Hamlet* and gave a performance of Ibsen's *A Doll's House*. In 1909 Osanai Kaoru and Ichikawa Sadanji formed a *Jiyū Gekijo* (Free Theatre) group which put on plays by Ibsen, Gorky, Hauptmann, and Andreyev. During the twenties Osanai was the leader in the Tsukiji Little Theatre, which received some inspiration from the corresponding movement in the United States. Russian influence was equally as important, however, and most of the plays produced were European. The Japanese like their drama heavy, and the American theatre at this time was just beginning to move away from the elaborate staging developed by Dion Boucicault and David Belasco to a real concern with intellectual content. Eugene O'Neill's plays did attract considerable interest during the twenties and early thirties. *Desire under the Elms* ran afoul of the censor, but *Beyond the Horizon, Before Breakfast, The Long Voyage Home, The Great God Brown, Bound East for Cardiff,* and *The Hairy Ape* were all produced successfully. Several of Elmer Rice's plays were also given on Japanese stages. Interest in American drama was actually on the upswing in the years before 1941. Maxwell Anderson's *Winterset,* Odets' *Awake and Sing,* Sidney Kingsley's *Dead End,* Robert Sherwood's *The Petrified Forest,* and the Kaufman and Hart comedy *You Can't Take It With You* were all presented after the outbreak of the "China incident" in 1937.[33]

At the end of World War II the "new drama" (*shingeki*) enjoyed for the first time real financial support and the use of large theaters like the Tokyo, the Imperial, and the Yūrakuza. In the first half of 1946 the Zenshinza troupe gave highly successful performances of Lillian Hellman's *Watch*

[32] *New York Times,* May 22, 1939.
[33] Sekiguchi Jirō, "The New Theatre Movement," *Contemporary Japan,* V. 7 (December 1938), pp. 478-487; Sano Saki, "The Tokyo Left Theatre and Its Relation to the Japanese Stage," *Theatre Arts Monthly,* V. 15 (October 1931), pp. 836-842.

on the Rhine and John Drinkwater's *Abraham Lincoln.* Two years then passed before rights to any more American plays could be obtained through the tangles of SCAP red tape.[34] In the meantime, an American Drama Study Society of playwrights and translators was formed in December 1947 to discuss "methods of presentation to insure full comprehension by Japanese audiences." [35]

At irregular intervals a considerable number of American plays have appeared on Tokyo stages in recent years. By June 1948 SCAP had set a policy on royalties, and Thornton Wilder's *Our Town* and Holm and Abbott's *Three Men on a Horse* played to full houses. In December 1948 the Haiyūza troupe gave nine performances of O'Neill's *Ah! Wilderness.* The next year CI & E encouraged the formation of a new experimental group, the Picadilly Theatre, partly to counter the increasingly radical tendencies of the Zenshinza. Starting in October 1949 with *The Voice of the Turtle,* which played for thirty-nine days to a total of 21,443 people, the Picadilly troupe went on to give Steinbeck's *Of Mice and Men* and Tennessee Williams' *The Glass Menagerie.* For the next two years the *shingeki* stage presented original plays by Japanese authors and revived plays by Ibsen, Strindberg, Gorki, Chekhov, and Rostand. A new flurry of interest in American plays began in early 1953. The Bungakuza troupe presented Wilder's one-act *The Long Christmas Dinner* in combination with a Japanese play, and the Young Actors' Group put on Maxwell Anderson's *Winterset.* In March the Shinkyō Gekidan revived *Dead End.* F. Hugh Herbert's witty handling of sex in *The Moon is Blue* lost its point when Japanese critics and audiences took the play as a serious study of the "new woman." In contrast, the Bungakuza's production of *A Streetcar Named Desire* in April 1953 was a great success. Japanese reception of American plays will always be somewhat unpredictable, but in general heavy straight dramas are the most successful.[36]

[34] *Bungei Nenkan, 1949 (Yearbook of the Arts, 1949)* (Tokyo: Shinchōsha, 1949), pp. 24-25; *New York Times,* May 16, 1948, sect. 2.
[35] SCAP, *Summation of Non-military Activities in Japan,* no. 27 (December 1947), p. 34.
[36] The annual volumes of the *Asahi Nenkan* give the best summary of *shingeki* activities.

Except for Army shows, American plays have thus far been produced in Japan only in translation. Japanese actors and liberal adaptations to fit native scenes and customs have blurred their real American character. Perhaps there would be some virtue in having an American company go to Japan to give an outstanding play in English. At one point the *Asahi Shimbun* was negotiating to send an American cast in *Death of a Salesman,* which the Japanese regard as a play of great social significance, on a tour of six cities.[37] But the language problem is serious, particularly so when we realize how much our theater depends on word play and innuendo. Difficulties might be less in the case of a musical comedy, and it is reported that the Japanese long ago set their sights for *Oklahoma.* Ballet also makes a direct appeal to eye and ear; and in November and December of 1953 Nora Kaye, star of the New York City Ballet, made a highly successful tour of Japan.

Music

The performances by the Azuma Kabuki troupe early in 1954 gave Americans their best chance to hear traditional Japanese music in an authentic setting, for the old Japanese music is usually not performed alone in a concert hall, but in close combination with other theatrical arts. "Seated on the stage, the orchestra as a whole fills a function beyond that of a mere accompaniment for the dance. Now narrating, now describing, now commenting on the scene and action, the ensemble gives to one familiar with its musical language a wealth of subtle atmospheric and emotional detail." [38] As one is transported simultaneously into a new world of sight and sound, the unfamiliar pentatonic scale and harmonic combinations of Japanese music cease to jar upon the Western ear.

Except for occasional performances by individual amateurs, previous attempts to present Japanese music here have been very limited. During the winter of 1931–32 the Yoshida Trio made a concert tour under the auspices of Pro Musica

37 *New York Times,* October 4, 1953.
38 *The Azuma Kabuki Dancers and Musicians* (Washington: Information Section of the Embassy of Japan, 1954), p. 16.

of New York and the various Japan Societies.[39] In 1935 Leopold Stokowski, who has been very interested in the Orient, performed with several leading American orchestras a piece of old Japanese court music (*gagaku*) entitled *Etenraku*.[40] And we should not overlook the work of American composers like Henry Eichheim and Claude Lapham, who have tried to capture the spirit of Japanese music in Western forms.

Although the traditional skills handed down from teacher to pupil preserve much that is ancient, Japanese music has not had a rich or varied development. The instruments used are practically limited to the flute, drums and other percussion devices, the thirteen-stringed *koto,* and the three-stringed *samisen.* Modern Japanese governments have recognized the thinness of the musical heritage by encouraging the development of Western-style music. Impressed by the band concerts given by Commodore Perry's fleet and by foreign military units stationed in Japan, they employed foreign bandmasters for the Japanese army and navy. In response to Taguchi Ukichi's public suggestion that Japan needed new songs, the Ministry of Education created in 1879 a Commission for the Investigation of Music.[41]

The head of this commission, Isawa Shuji, invited to Japan as his adviser Luther Whiting Mason, the Director of Music in the primary schools of Boston. Besides creating new songs and other teaching materials for Japanese schools, Mason began to train some of the court musicians to play Western-style wind and stringed instruments. Progress was slow, however, because of the unfamiliar principles of harmony involved. This phase of the work was carried on by the Tokyo Academy of Music, where Mason was succeeded by a series of Europeans—Franz Eckert, Rudolf Dittrich, Raphael von Koeber, and August Junker. At the time Japa-

---

[39] Mabel T. Johnson, "Japan Society Activities in San Francisco," *Japan,* January 1932, p. 47; *New York Times,* December 20, 1931, January 18, 1932.
[40] KBS Quarterly, V. 1 (October–December 1935), p. 14.
[41] Nihon Kyōiku Ongaku Kyōkai (Japan Educational Music Society), *Hompō Ongaku Kyōiku Shi (History of Music Education in Japan)* (Tokyo: Ongaku Kyōikusho Shuppan Kyōkai, 1938), pp. 50-52; Miura Toshisaburō, *Hompō Yōgaku Hensen Shi (History of the Changes in Western Music in Japan)* (Tokyo: Nittō Shoin, 1931), pp. 107-114.

nese music could hardly have done better than to draw directly from the German symphonic tradition.[42] For a time a competing influence was exerted by E. H. House, an American, formerly a teacher at the Kaisei Gakkō and editor of the *Tokio Times*. After his return to Japan in 1891, House served as an instructor in the Bureau of Ceremonial Music of the Imperial Household Ministry. Finding that atmosphere too conservative, he joined with Uehara Rokushirō in the organization of an independent Meiji Musical Society, which gave an ambitious series of concerts.[43]

At the beginning of the Taishō era Japan first really entered the main stream of world music. Yamada Kōsaku returned from study in Germany in 1914 and organized the Tokyo Philharmonic Orchestra. He came to New York in 1918 and 1919 to give two Carnegie Hall concerts, chiefly of his own compositions, under the auspices of the Japan Society. His music was more suggestive of Debussy and Strauss, however, than of the Orient.[44] When World War I closed the concert halls of Europe, noted artists like Mischa Elman, Efrem Zimbalist, Fritz Kreisler, and Madame Schumann-Heink sought new audiences in Japan.[45]

Between the wars Japan developed a rich musical life. Outstanding foreign artists like Leonid Kreutzer, John MacCormack, and Amelita Galli-Curci, along with many others, continued to appear in her concert halls. The sale of classical records and the popularity of radio concerts testified to the widespread interest in serious music. Henry Hadley of the Manhattan Symphony went to Japan in 1930 as guest conductor of the New Symphony Orchestra that Viscount Konoe Hidemaro had organized in 1926. Hadley introduced several American works, including his own suite entitled "Streets of Pekin." After Joseph Rosenstock came from Germany in 1936 to be its conductor, the New Symphony concentrated heavily on the works of Beethoven. Japan was represented

[42] *Hompō Kyōiku Ongaku Shi*, pp. 105-106, 154, 210.
[43] Ebihara Hachirō, "E. H. Hausu ni tsuite (Concerning E. H. House)," *Meiji Bunka Kenkyū*, cited, V. 1 (February 1934), pp. 154-155; Miura, cited, p. 388.
[44] *New York Evening Post*, October 17, 1918.
[45] *Gendai Ongaku Taikan (Survey of Contemporary Music)* (Tokyo: Nihon Meikan Kyōkai, 1927), section entitled "Seiyō Ongaku no Hattatsu (The Development of Western Music)," pp. 54-57.

abroad by an opera company for which Madame Miura Tamaki did a famous rendition of "Madame Butterfly." Music was, in fact, one facet of Western culture that did not fall victim to the growing trend of nationalism and militarism. The Japanese government encouraged band and orchestral music as better suited "to arouse groups to action" than traditional Japanese music which appealed only "to individual taste or preference." [46]

During the occupation, Clarence Davies, music officer in CI & E and a prewar critic for the *Japan Advertiser*, concentrated on making the Japanese aware of American creativity in music. On May 17, 1947 a program devoted to works by Wallingford Riegger, Daniel Mason, Godfrey Turner, and Roy Harris was given at the Tokyo Academy of Music. Two months later the *Yomiuri Shimbun* sponsored the organization of a Japanese American Music Study Association, which soon had a membership of 350. Recordings of modern American works were furnished to the Broadcasting Corporation of Japan and made available to individual listeners at SCAP information centers. In 1948 there were over fifty performances of contemporary American music in Tokyo. Included were Gershwin's famous *Rhapsody in Blue* and the music of Aaron Copland's ballet *Appalachian Spring*. This forced interest could hardly be maintained, and Japanese orchestras have since returned to more standard repertories.[47]

But America's musical reputation around the world rests primarily on jazz, rather than on serious orchestral music. Japanese musicians began to copy the jazz rhythms during the 1920's, when places like the Florida Dance Hall in Tokyo and the Higashiyama Cabaret in Kyoto became favorite haunts of the *mobo* and *moga*. Hillbilly and Hawaiian bands were also popular. The militarists frowned upon such foreign frivolities, but immediately after the surrender in 1945 jazz bands reassembled to play outdated tunes for the American troops. Catching on fast to new styles, Japanese musicians were soon producing "jungle boogie-woogie" and many

---

[46] *Japan Year Book, 1938–9* (Tokyo: Foreign Affairs Association of Japan, 1938), pp. 866-870; *Nippon Today and Tomorrow, 1941*, p. 70.
[47] "Western Music in Japan," *Music Educators Journal*, January 1950, pp. 33, 37, 45-46; SCAP, *Summation of Non-military Activities in Japan*, no. 20 (May 1947), pp. 248-249; no. 21 (June 1947), p. 268.

variations. They have been particularly inspired by the visit of Norman Granz's famous "Jazz at the Philharmonic" group of big-name players in November 1953. Japanese jazz now has its "combos," its star vocalists, even knowing critics.[47a]

Now that America's musical inferiority complexes are being dispelled, we should be careful about our attitudes toward Japanese achievement in this field. Americans often show a rather patronizing surprise that Japanese artists can come up—well, almost—to the Western standard. Is the often heard generalization that Japanese musicians are technically competent but weak on interpretation really true? Critic Olin Downes asserted the very opposite about violinist Etō Toshiya, who made his American debut at Carnegie Hall in 1951. "The fact that he has a prodigious technique is accessory to the beauty and vitality of his tone, which is exceptionally warm, rich and vibrant, and [to] his taste and musicianship." [48] Does Japan now have other soloists, conductors, or composers who need only a wider hearing to gain a prominent place in world music? Meanwhile, when will a concert of *koto* music receive as informed and appreciative a hearing in the United States as some of our difficult modern music gets in Tokyo?

Art and Architecture

From the time of the earliest contacts, Americans have been impressed with the aesthetic sensitivity and creative ability of the Japanese. At first, interest in Japanese art took the form of a rather indiscriminate enthusiasm for what were popularly known as "curios." The articles of Japanese manufacture displayed at the Philadelphia Centennial Exhibition of 1876 attracted so much attention that in 1877 Tiffany & Co. offered for sale 1900 lots of curios selected for them in Japan by Dr. Christopher Dresser. The same year the Kiritsu Kōshō Kaisha, chartered by the Japanese government for the encouragement of native art industries, established a branch office in New York. Although much of

[47a] Katō Eimei, "There's Music in the Air," *New Japan*, V. 7 (1954), part 2, pp. 36-38.
[48] *New York Times*, November 10, 1951.

the Oriental goods sold in this country has been too ornate to be representative of the best taste, the cultural value of the curio trade should not be dismissed summarily. Ownership of an honest piece of workmanship in lacquer, ceramics, or textiles may do more to foster admiration and respect for Japanese artistry than occasional glimpses of masterpieces in a museum.

Japanese historians recognize that it was an American, Ernest F. Fenollosa, who was largely responsible for the preservation and revived appreciation of their best art traditions.[49] When Fenollosa went to Japan in 1878 to teach at Tokyo University, the craze for Westernization was at its height. The government employed Italian artists to teach pencil sketching and oil painting. An artist of the old school like Hashimoto Gahō could make a precarious living only by painting fans and making bridges for *samisen*.[50]

Fenollosa's eye, too, was first caught by the cheap curios of the market place, until friends like Kaneko Kentarō opened new vistas of appreciation by showing him in private collections the work of Sesshū, Shūbun, Kano Tanyū, and Maruyama Ōkyo. Impressed by the bold strength of line, marked contrast of dark and light masses, and rich color texture in these pictures, Fenollosa became eager to learn more. He set two of his students to work translating biographies of artists and books on Oriental painting. He sought lessons from the surviving masters of the Kano and Tosa schools. During academic vacations he traveled through the country, buying undervalued masterpieces for his own collection. For ten years he employed two artists to copy works of art and inscriptions.[51]

By 1882 Fenollosa was ready to speak out publicly in defense of native traditions and techniques. In a famous speech

[49] Odakane Tarō, "Ānesuto Efu Fuenorosa no Bijutsu Undō (Ernest F. Fenollosa's Activities in the Field of Art)," *Bijutsu Kenkyū*, nos. 110-112 (February to April, 1941) is the most complete and accurate account.

[50] Fenollosa, "Contemporary Japanese Art," *Century Magazine*, V. 46 (August 1893), pp. 577-579; *Shinsen Dai Jimmei Jiten* (*New Biographical Dictionary*), V. 5, p. 102.

[51] Kaneko Kentarō, "How Professor Fenollosa Came to Appreciate the Art of Japan," *Asian Review*, V. 2 (January 1921), pp. 139-142; Fenollosa, *Epochs of Chinese and Japanese Art: An Outline History of East Asiatic Design* (New York: Frederick A. Stokes, n.d.), V. 1, p. xxviii; V. 2, p. 118.

before a new art society called the Ryūchikai, he castigated the attempts of self-consciously modern Japanese to paint in oils in the Western manner. At the same time he deplored as decadent the taste for *bunjinga,* a pallid and sentimental form of landscape painting borrowed from China in the eighteenth century. A return to traditional Japanese principles of design would produce works of unique aesthetic value, he said, for export to all the world.[52] In 1884 Fenollosa took a leading part in the organization of the Kangakai, a group of artists and critics who met once a month "to study ancient works of art in a new spirit of scientific and historical criticism." To counter the influence of both modernists and formalistic conservatives, the Kangakai began holding its own exhibitions in 1886. The lively controversy attracted the attention of the government, and in the fall of that year, Fenollosa was sent abroad with a commission to study art education. The result was the establishment of the Tokyo Art School, at which Kano Hōgai and Hashimoto Gahō were instructors in painting. Fenollosa himself lectured on aesthetics. He also helped the Japanese government to appraise and register national art treasures in temples throughout the country.[53]

After he returned to America in 1890, Fenollosa did more than any other person to stimulate an appreciation of Oriental art. His monumental work on *Epochs of Chinese and Japanese Art,* though not free of errors and faulty judgments, gave the whole subject badly needed breadth of historical perspective. His lectures on art education and the methods of teaching composition that he worked out with Arthur Wesley Dow had a great influence on rising young American artists.[54]

Dr. Charles G. Weld purchased Fenollosa's own magnificent collection of paintings for deposit in the Museum of Fine Arts at Boston. To it were eventually added the ceramics collected by E. S. Morse and 3,634 paintings, over 20,000

[52] This address is reprinted in *Meiji Bunka Zenshū* (*Collection of Works on Meiji Culture*) (Tokyo: Nihon Hyōron-sha, 1928–1930), V. 12, pp. 157-174, under the title *Bijutsu Shinsetsu* (New Theory of Art).

[53] *Japan Weekly Mail,* April 10, 24, 1886; Kiyomi Rokurō, *Okakura Tenshin* [Biography of Okakura Kakuzo] (Tokyo: Heibonsha, 1934), pp. 24-47.

[54] See Arthur W. Dow, *Composition* (12th ed., New York: Doubleday, 1924).

prints, and 25,000 drawings assembled by Fenollosa's friend, William Sturgis Bigelow.[55] The noted critic and artist Okakura Kakuzō has said of the Boston collection: "In point of size it is unique, and . . . in quality it can only be inferior to the Imperial Museums of Nara and Kyoto, while for the schools of Tokugawa painting it is unrivalled anywhere. . . . The splendid Kōrin screen, known as the Wave Screen, and the superb Banku, are both masterpieces." [56]

Luckily, sizable collections of Japanese art are within reach of people in several parts of our country. Thanks to gifts from Samuel Colman, Brayton Ives, Charles Stewart Smith, Dr. I. W. Drummond, and Mrs. V. Everit Macy, among others, the Metropolitan Museum in New York has notable examples of Japanese work in almost every medium. The New York Public Library has about 1,500 prints that once belonged to Captain Frank Brinkley. The fine items assembled by Charles L. Freer, under the inspiration and guidance of Fenollosa, are now in the Freer Gallery in Washington, D.C. The Chicago Art Institute has the outstanding Clarence Buckingham collection of prints. Henry P. Bowie and Katherine M. Ball helped to stimulate interest in Japanese art in San Francisco. In recent years the Seattle Art Museum has been rapidly building up its Japanese holdings. The interests of individual collectors have brought small collections, often not balanced in scope or quality, to museums in many smaller cities throughout the country.[57]

Certain limitations of the material available in the United States must be recognized, however. Immoderate emphasis has been placed by collectors on *ukiyoe* prints depicting scenes from common life, because they were colorful, available in quantity, and at relatively moderate prices.[58] Since

[55] *Museum of Fine Arts Bulletin*, V. 9 (1911), pp. 34, 48, 50. Interest in art led Fenollosa and Bigelow to study of Buddhism, and both now lie buried in the grounds of the Miidera Temple, above Lake Biwa.

[56] Okakura Kakuzō, *The Heart of Heaven*. . . . (Tokyo: Nippon Bijutsuin, 1922), pp. 205-206.

[57] Howard Mansfield, "American Appreciation of Japanese Art," in Lindsay Russell, ed., *America to Japan* (New York: Putnam, 1915), pp. 239-250; Benjamin March, *China and Japan in Our Museums* (New York: American Council, I.P.R., 1929).

[58] Louis V. Ledoux, *Japanese Prints in the Occident* (Tokyo: Kokusai Bunka Shinkōkai, 1941) gives a brief account of print collecting in America.

the late eighties, when Fenollosa persuaded the Japanese government to register its national art treasures, real masterpieces could not be brought out of Japan for any amount of money. During the Occupation, however, Americans were able to purchase a few first-rate unregistered items from private collectors.

Outstanding collections of historical treasures have been brought here on three occasions. The first came to the Boston Museum in the fall of 1936, in connection with the Harvard Tercentenary. Picked to complement the Boston collection, this exhibition was particularly strong in ancient Buddhist sculpture and early Ashikaga-period painting.[59] In 1951 the Cultural Properties Protection Commission of Japan cooperated to send a broad selection of sculpture, painting, ceramics, metal work, prints, and dolls for exhibition at the M. H. de Young Memorial Museum in San Francisco during the peace treaty conference. Although limited to only one month, this exhibition had a total attendance of over 200,000.[60] Since the restrictions under which some articles were loaned made it impossible to bring this collection to the east coast, John D. Rockefeller, 3rd, and others began to urge the Japanese to assemble a similar collection for wider showing. Three American experts—Archibald G. Wenley, Langdon Warner, and Alan Priest—helped to choose ninety-one pieces of painting and sculpture that surpassed in overall quality any selection previously exhibited in America. The items ranged in age from the sixth to the nineteenth century and included outstanding secular as well as religious works. Japanese culture was in the spotlight of publicity throughout 1953 as this exhibition moved from Washington to New York, Seattle, Chicago, and Boston.[61]

Americans are less well informed about Japan's contemporary art, much of which is strongly influenced by Parisian

[59] *Illustrated Catalogue of a Special Loan Exhibition of Art Treasures from Japan Held in Conjunction with the Tercentenary Celebration of Harvard University, September–October 1936.* (Boston: Museum of Fine Arts, 1936); *Bosuton Nihon Ko-bijutsu Tenrankai Hōkoku-sho (Reports on the Exhibition of Japanese Ancient Art in Boston)* (Tokyo: Kokusai Bunka Shinkōkai, 1937).
[60] Harada Jirō, "Exhibition of Japanese Art Treasures in San Francisco," *Contemporary Japan,* V. 20 (October–December 1951), pp. 509-523.
[61] The exhibition was elaborately catalogued in *Exhibition of Japanese Painting and Sculpture sponsored by the Government of Japan* (N.p., 1953).

schools and techniques. During 1953, it is true, works by Okamoto Tarō, Okada Kenzō, and Takata Biichi were exhibited in commercial galleries in New York. The California Palace of the Legion of Honor and Le Salon de Printemps sponsored a travelling loan exhibition of "Contemporary Japanese Painting" which showed the range of current work in Japan. Another contribution in this regard was the recent American tour by Yoshida Tōshi, who demonstrated how his family is using traditional techniques of wood-block printmaking to turn out work that is distinctly modern.

Through its profound impact on European, especially French, art since 1870, Japanese art has strongly influenced modern American painting. Sadakichi Hartmann sees Japanese influence

in Manet's ambition to see things flat; in the peculiar space composition of Degas, Skarbina, the German secessionists, and the poster painters; in the parallelism of vertical lines as practised by Puvis de Chavannes, and the parallelism of horizontal lines in D. W. Tryon's landscapes; in the frugal Kano-school-like colouring of Steinlen's Gil Blas illustrations, which have caused a revolution in modern illustration; in the disregard for symmetrical composition of the impressionists; in the eccentric drawing of the symbolists; and in the serial treatment of one phase of nature, as practised by Monet.[62]

John LaFarge found in the Japanese landscape the background for his great mural altarpiece of the Ascension of our Lord.[63] The bridge in the background of Hiroshige's "Boating" triptych is the direct prototype for Whistler's "Battersea Bridge." The work of other American impressionists like Childe Hassam, Thomas W. Dewing, and J. Alden Weir closely resembled that of the Japanese in spirit.[64] Painter Kuniyoshi Yasuo and sculptor Noguchi Isamu have stood be-

---

[62] Sadakichi Hartmann, *Japanese Art* (Boston: L. C. Page, 1904), pp. 162-163; Gotō Sueo, *Tōzai no Bunka Ryūtsū* (*The Circulation of Culture between East and West*) (Tokyo: Dai Ichi Shobō, 1938), p. 25 ff. discusses Japanese influence on French art.

[63] John LaFarge, *The Manner Is Ordinary* (New York: Harcourt, Brace, 1954), p. 6.

[64] Wilfred B. Shaw, "The Relation of Modern American Art to That of China and Japan: Demonstrated at the Recent Exhibition at Ann Arbor," *Craftsman*, V. 18 (August 1910), pp. 528-529.

tween the two cultures and combined elements from both in their work. Noguchi has gone to Japan in recent years to design the "Peace Bridges" at Hiroshima and to exhibit new sculptures and ceramics. Although one critic acclaimed his "perfect and spontaneous freedom" as "a deep lesson for Japanese artists," many have found his work to be too primitive, indeed, too Japanese.[65] Likewise, the water-colors and gouaches by Americans exhibited in Japan in 1953 were actually closer to traditional Japanese styles than the heavy work in oils being produced by Japanese painters today.[66]

Interrelations in creative work have been most direct and active in the field of architecture. Frank Lloyd Wright's Imperial Hotel won the admiration of the Japanese by its ability to withstand the great earthquake of 1923. In rebuilding Tokyo and Yokohama, the Japanese turned away from ponderous brick and stone construction in a style that Ralph Adams Cram dubbed "Potsdam Renaissance," to reinforced concrete and American-type steel-frame skyscapers. During practice in Japan between 1921 and 1937 Antonin Raymond, a pupil of Wright, built the American Embassy, the Socony and Rising Sun Buildings, St. Luke's International Hospital, and other structures that attracted international attention. Since the war Raymond's firm has designed the striking Reader's Digest Building in Tokyo.

Wright returned to America to apply the secret of "elimination of the insignificant" that he found in both the color print and the Japanese house. He did not want Americans to live on *tatami* (straw mats), but he thought that the same ideal of organic functional construction should be worked out in materials native to this country.[67]

Severe simplicity and emphasis on outdoor living in integrated house and garden have become important elements of some modern homes, especially on the West Coast and in Hawaii. Some actually do use straw mats of the *tatami* type for floor coverings. The model Japanese house designed by Yoshimura Junzō, shown in the garden of the Museum of

[65] *Scene,* V. 4 (March 1953), pp. 26-29.
[66] Wallace S. Baldinger, "Takeuchi Seihō: Painter of Post-Meiji Japan," *Art Bulletin,* V. 36 (March 1954), p. 56n.
[67] Frank Lloyd Wright, *An Autobiography* (New York: Duell, Sloan & Pearce, 1943), pp. 196-205.

Modern Art in New York since July 1954, has attracted attention by its general graciousness and serenity. Japanese influence can be seen in Bernard Maybeck's emphasis on wood textures, in Harwell Harris' use of removable panels, in Charles Eames' functional furnishings. In the last few years many Americans have shown interest in Japanese ceramics, textiles, and other folk arts—what might be called curios for practical use in the home.[68]

The most urgent need at present is to give the Japanese a better understanding of American work in art and architecture. At the international display called UNESCO Village, in Murayama Park, thirty miles west of Tokyo, the United States is represented only by a "mongrel mixture of Mount Vernon and a Vermont farmhouse." [69] Some modern American painting has been shown. Early in 1951, John Denman, a Northwest Airlines pilot flying to Japan, helped the *Mainichi* to arrange an exhibition of work by fifteen Americans, including Georgia O'Keefe, Stuart Davis, Ben Shahn, and Jack Levine. In the summer of 1952, 39 paintings by 31 contemporaries, chosen by the American Federation of Arts to cover the whole range from romantic realism to extreme abstraction, toured the major cities of Japan as part of an International Exhibition. The Museum of Modern Art in New York sent 42 works by Morris Graves, Lyonel Feininger, John Marin, Mark Tobey, Charles Demuth, Maurice Prendergast, and Charles Burchfield to the Second International in 1953. For a balanced view of American painting, the Japanese should also be shown some older work, like the exhibition of nineteenth century canvases that the United States Information Service sponsored in Germany and Italy.

Cherry Blossoms and Dogwood:
A Note on Floral Exchanges

To discuss flowers as cultural materials along with music, drama, and art may at first seem strange. But for many Americans mention of Japan calls up visions of luxuriant

[68] *Nippon Times*, January 9, 1953; Hamaguchi Ryuichi, "Japanese Architecture and the West," *Architectural Forum*, January 1953, pp. 138-149.
[69] *Nippon Times*, January 12, 1953.

but ephemeral cherry blossoms, gardens of austere simplicity, and ingenious flower arrangements. Proud of their floral heritage, the Japanese have used it as a sentimental bond and symbol of binational friendship. Botanical exploration and borrowing goes on all the time, of course, without creating any special feeling of indebtedness. For a cultural effect there must be flowers plus publicity.

The famous Japanese cherry trees in Washington, D.C., are the outstanding example. Early in 1909 Eliza Scidmore reminded the new First Lady, Mrs. Taft, of the beautiful cherry blossoms that they both had seen in Japan. Mrs. Taft ordered some trees from an American nursery and planted them near the present site of the Lincoln Memorial. Hearing of this, the noted chemist Takamine Jōkichi offered to give enough trees for planting around the whole Tidal Basin. He modestly arranged that the gift should come officially from the city of Tokyo. But when the first lot of trees arrived, they were found to be so infected with insect parasites that they had to be burned.[70] Selected trees of eleven of the finest varieties of flowering cherry were then carefully decontaminated and shipped to Washington in time for planting in the spring of 1912. The delay only heightened the publicity.[71] In 1929 the Cherry Blossom Society of Japan (Sakura no Kai) presented 500 trees to replace those that had died when Potomac Park was flooded the preceding summer.[72] After surviving demands during World War II that they be torn out or renamed Korean cherries, the Japanese cherry trees still form one of the springtime glories of our national capital.

In several other cities Japanese cherries have been given special meaning by the circumstances of presentation. Following the Hudson-Fulton Celebration in 1909, Japanese residents of New York, led by Dr. Takamine, gave the city 2,000 trees. Some were set in Central Park, others along the

[70] When an American diplomat told him about the mishap, Mayor Ozaki Yukio replied with tactful humor: "Destroying cherry trees and then telling the truth about it is a traditional American custom begun by Washington. So instead of worrying about it, you should be proud." Isa Hideo, *Ozaki Yukio Den (Biography of Ozaki Yukio)* (Tokyo: Ozaki Yukio Den Kankōkai, 1951), pp. 760-761.
[71] Paul Russell, "Japanese Spring in America," *Asia*, V. 30 (May 1930), pp. 315-318.
[72] *New York Times*, March 31, 1929.

Hudson bank from Grant's Tomb north to 154th Street.[73] During the twenties Ambassador Matsudaira Tsuneo arranged that some cherry trees should be given to Philadelphia for Fairmount Park. Columbus, Ohio, also received some trees from the city of Tokyo in 1928. If the 100,000 seeds presented in 1953 by the Japanese Parent-Teachers Association, the Friends of the World, Inc., the Japan Travel Bureau, and the United Nations Association of Japan are planted successfully, many other parts of our country will be able to enjoy the flowering cherry.[74]

Americans have returned some of these floral tributes in kind. The United States Government sent the city of Tokyo a large number of young dogwood trees in 1915, as thanks for the Washington cherries.[75] In 1936 the Garden Clubs of America sent 4,650 plants to Japan in appreciation of the reception given a party of their members the preceding summer.[76] Despite all these gestures of floral diplomacy, however, an important difference remains. For Americans gardening is primarily horticulture; for the Japanese it is part of art and poetry.

The Bond of Culture

Theatrical performances and art exhibitions are not of themselves sufficient to solve international conflicts of interest or to prevent wars. But once the minimum conditions for political and economic coöperation have been attained, the exchange of cultural materials can be a powerful force in building mutual respect and appreciation.

This potential bond of culture can be illustrated by an incident that happened immediately after the war. It was widely reported in Japan that Nara and Kyoto had been spared from bombing in deference to their great treasures of art. Many Japanese ascribed the decision to the personal

---

[73] *Takamine Hakushi* (Tokyo: Shiobara Matasaku, 1926), pp. 89-91.
[74] *Christian Science Monitor*, April 18, 1953.
[75] Japan Society, New York, *Bulletin* no. 22, June 22, 1915.
[76] *America-Japan Society Bulletin*, V. 2 (1938), p. 10. In the spring of 1952, the Committee for Free Asia presented a box of redwood seeds which were planted in Inokashira Park near Tokyo. *Christian Science Monitor*, July 19, 1952.

influence of Dr. Langdon Warner. "In the fact that the powerful American military force yielded immediately to the counsel of one man of culture," Aragaki Hideo wrote in the *Asahi*,
"is seen the inexpressible goodness of a cultured people. . . .
Suddenly we cannot suppress a great gust of emotion. For the
first time since we lost the war we feel as if the Japanese people are respected. People of high culture pay sincere respect
without distinction between victor and vanquished." [77]

[77] Aragaki Hideo, *Shin Nihon no Ashioto* (*Footfalls of the New Japan*)
(Tokyo: Kawade Shobō, 1948), pp. 280-281.

CHAPTER EIGHT

THE ROLE OF AMERICAN MISSIONARIES

MEASURED BY the number of persons participating, missionary work has been the most ambitious of the American cultural activities in Japan. From the handful of representatives of the Episcopalian and Presbyterian Churches and of the Reformed Church in America who began work there in 1859, the Protestant mission force grew to 138 (counting wives but not children) by 1883 and to 723 in 1900. A peak of 1,355 was reached in 1925, and during the thirties mission strength averaged just short of a thousand. At least 75 percent of these Protestant missionaries came from the United States, and part of the remaining quarter from Canada.[1] These American missionaries were forced out of Japan during World War II, but since 1945 strength has been rebuilt rapidly. With the influx of many new missions of a revivalistic character the total number of Protestant workers has now reached new heights. By the middle of 1953 there were 2,040 adults connected with 120 different groups, plus 128 missionaries working independently.[2]

The early stages of modern Roman Catholic missions in Japan are not so pertinent to the history of American-Japanese relations. These missionaries came largely from Europe, with only a few scattered Americans attached to foreign congregations. In 1933 the Vatican assigned to the Catholic Foreign Mission Society of America, commonly known as the Maryknoll Mission, a territory around Kyoto, in which it had eighteen workers in 1940. Since the war Maryknoll activities

[1] Statistics are taken from the mission yearbook published under the title *The Christian Movement in Japan*, 1903–1926, *Japan Mission Year Book*, 1927–1931; and *Japan Christian Year Book*, 1932–1941, 1950–current.
[2] *Japan Christian Year Book*, *1953* (Tokyo: Christian Literature Society, 1953), pp. 378-441.

have expanded, and American Jesuits, Franciscans, and other orders have entered the field in Japan. In 1951, 182 Americans made up about 15 percent of the total Roman Catholic foreign force of 1,200.[3]

Even if full statistics were available, the mission effort could not be measured adequately in financial terms. The aggregate sum expended by Americans on behalf of Japanese missions from 1859 to the present would exceed, I should estimate, $100,000,000. The mission boards of the Methodist churches in the United States, North and South, spent almost $10,000,000 for work in Japan between 1873 and 1922.[4] Even in 1934, a depression year, the churches affiliated with the Foreign Missions Conference of North America were laying out $1,625,000.[5] At present the eight churches working through the Interboard Committee for Christian Work in Japan are spending about $2,000,000 per year. To name only a few of the independent bodies, the Southern Baptists are putting in over $700,000, and the Protestant Episcopal Church and United Lutheran Church each about $100,000.[6] Perhaps more significant than any aggregate sum is the fact that these funds do not come merely from a few large donors, but are collected from a broad church membership which thereby acquires some knowledge about and interest in Japan.

An estimate of the number of Japanese involved in contacts with American missionaries, Catholic or Protestant, is practically impossible. By the very nature of his task, however, the missionary works more closely with the native population than the average foreigner residing in Japan. Missionaries are, as Dr. Henry Bovenkerk has aptly said, presumptuous people, who go into a country to sell an intangible, with the conscious purpose of changing the beliefs

[3] Everett F. Briggs, *New Dawn in Japan* (New York: Longmans Green, 1948), pp. 223-228; *U. S. Catholic Missionary Personnel Overseas in 1951* (Washington: Mission Secretariat, n.d.), pp. 29-30.
[4] David S. Spencer, "The Present Accomplishment—What the Missionaries Have Done," *Japan Christian Quarterly*, V. 1 (July 1926), p. 211.
[5] *Japan Christian Year Book, 1937*, cited, p. 129.
[6] *Annual of the Southern Baptist Convention, 1953*, p. 198; National Council of the Protestant Episcopal Church, *1952 Annual Report*, p. 23; *Lutheran Global Missions, 1951*, p. 127.

and values of the people.[6a] In this chapter we shall survey what they have accomplished in almost a century of work in Japan, and try to assess their potential role in future cultural relations.

The Missionary as American

In assessing the role of this extensive mission effort in Japanese-American relations, we must remember that the missionary's primary motive and emphasis is religious. He is an ambassador of Christ, first of all, and only incidentally a representative of his country. In 1893 the Rev. Judson Smith defined the aim of mission work as being "to bring to lost nations our one great treasure—the glorious Gospel of the Blessed God. When this is done, so that Jesus Christ is revealed to the pagan world . . . and his Gospel is received as the power of God unto salvation to everyone that believeth, the main work of the missionary is accomplished. All else is the carrying out of this work to greater fullness or the preparation for it." [7] The optimistic hope of the American missionary crusade was probably best expressed in the slogan adopted by the Student Volunteer Movement for Foreign Missions: "The Evangelization of the World in this Generation."

The literature produced by the missions indicates that over the years American workers in Japan have spent far more time expounding the institutions and life of Biblical lands and times than those of their own country. Like most other Americans, until recently they found little reason to be conscious of, or defensive about, their national culture. At first, learning the Japanese language and getting an intimate understanding of Japanese life was an engrossing task. After long years of service, with only brief furloughs at home, missionaries often found themselves out of touch with develop-

[6a] Statement before Council on Foreign Relations Study Group on American Cultural Relations with Japan, March 30, 1953. Dr. Bovenkerk, now treasurer of the Reformed Church Foreign Mission Board, was at the time chairman of the Interboard Committee for Christian Work in Japan.

[7] *Interdenominational Conference of Foreign Missionary Boards and Societies in the United States and Canada, held in New York, January 12, 1893* (New York: E. O. Jenkins' Son's, n.d.), p. 35.

ments in the United States. From their experience some gained a pronounced belief that Japanese culture had its own unique advantages and values.

In general the missionaries have maintained a careful neutrality in political issues between Japan and the United States. When the immigration law of 1924 threatened to undermine their work, they took the position that discriminatory exclusion did not represent the true feeling of the people of the United States. As individuals most missionaries certainly had misgivings about the course of events in Japan during the 1930's, but they refrained from open criticism. An editorial on "The Missionary's Dilemma" in the July 1938 number of the *Japan Christian Quarterly* accepted the view that Christianity in Japan must adapt itself to a non-democratic environment. The missionary "must forego every temptation to dwell upon the important and challenging corollaries and applications of the faith, and like his great predecessor, determine to know nothing among these people 'save Christ Jesus and Him crucified'."

Concentration on the abstract principle of separation of church and state, rather than on its practical aspects, can easily put the missionary in a false position. True, he does not want to identify the world religion of Christianity with any particular set of political institutions. But he must recognize that free and democratic systems provide a more favorable environment for his own work and for the values for which he stands than does totalitarianism. The missionaries driven out of China by the Communists are bringing a badly needed sense of political realism to work in Japan. Although Americans engaged in religious work abroad are under no obligation to agree with or defend all the policies of their government, they should understand what those policies are. Both government and missionaries could profit from more active consultation on developments abroad.

Beyond the level of explicit denials of political identification, however, American missionaries have not been able to escape their national heritage. The Protestant churches have had such a strong American coloring that converts have sometimes naively assumed that Christ, too, was an American.[8] Despite periodic demands for a "Japanese Christianity," little progress has been made in adapting church institutions to the social habits and traditional customs of the people. Christianity has been part of the imitative Westernized sector of the life of urban Japanese, who are themselves quick to reject attempts at accommodation to indigenous ways. The situation described by Charles W. Iglehart in 1936 is still fairly common:

> Almost no use has been made of native music in the churches. The composition of lyric poetry, so common in Japan, has not been taken into the church life. Architecture still owes but little to Asiatic traditions, and Japanese Christian art has made only a bare beginning. The liturgy of worship and the forms of service in most of the denominations are direct importations. The traditional church year of American Protestantism has been adopted—even to Mother's Day and Children's Day—and but slight rapprochement has yet been made with the immemorial festivals of Japanese everyday life.[9]

Through the informal contacts of daily living, missionary families also demonstrate constantly American values, manners, and material possessions. The danger is that the difference in standards of living may become a barrier to understanding rather than a stimulus to improvement. Sherard Vines' unfriendly picture of "self-sacrificing" missionaries setting out in their Ford cars to favorite summer resorts in the mountains, where they had "perfect orgies" of tennis, communal prayer, ice-cream soda, and dances punctuated with rowdy hymns and bright little addresses, contains a measure of truth. The relative affluence and leisure of the foreigner contrasts strongly with the straitened circumstances of the Japanese ministry. According to a recent survey, the average Japanese pastorate in the Church of Christ in Japan (Nihon Kirisuto Kyōdan) was a part-time job paying only 4,500 yen a month.[10] The Roman Catholic missions are spared this problem by the celibacy of their members, who live in communi-

---

[8] Matsuoka Yoko, *Daughter of the Pacific* (New York: Harper, 1952), p. 23.
[9] *Japan Christian Year Book, 1936,* cited, p. 126.
[10] Sherard Vines, *Yofuku; or, Japan in Trousers* (London: Wishart, 1931), p. 124. Missionary T. T. Brumbaugh was also critical of the leisurely pattern of life. *Japan Christian Quarterly,* V. 3 (October 1928), pp. 323-324.

ties under almost exactly the same conditions as native priests, brothers, and sisters.

One of the most direct contributions of the missionaries to better American-Japanese relations is made on this side of the ocean. For millions of Americans the only meaningful contact with Japan is through the mission work of their church. Accounts of life in Japan by missionaries in the field are published in Sunday School leaflets and church magazines. Much of this literature is elementary and repetitious, but it reaches a wide public that would never read the most authoritative of trade books. On several occasions, most recently in 1949–50, the Missionary Education Movement has chosen Japan as its foreign study topic and distributed large quantities of carefully prepared literature. Missionaries on furlough customarily travel about their home areas giving vivid accounts of their experience. On the scholarly level, D. C. Holtom and A. K. Reischauer, among others, have contributed greatly to our understanding of Japanese philosophy and religions. Our knowledge and appreciation of Japan still need to be extended greatly, but without our missionaries we would be even less well informed.

The Influence of Christianity in Japan

The fact that only one-half of one percent of the Japanese people are members of Christian churches is not an adequate measure of the influence of Christianity. The Japanese themselves generally recognize that it now ranks with Buddhism and Shintō as one of the "three religions" of the country. Christianity is an inextricable part of the Western cultural complex that has had such a revolutionary effect upon Japan over the past century. During the 1880's, when treaty revision was the paramount issue, many influential Japanese seriously proposed that their country should adopt the Christian religion in order to gain recognition of equal status from the West. A better understanding of the separation of church and state and the realization that there were important divisions in thought and belief within the West itself soon dispelled this idea. But the continuing desire of the Japanese for Western knowledge and patterns of life has unavoidably brought them into contact with Christian principles.

Although intellectual interest in Christianity has been widespread, the doctrines and polity of the Western churches have involved certain difficulties. The theological disputes of the denominations have been merely confusing and have enlisted no strong loyalties. Harada Tasuku has pointed out that the central doctrine of Christ's atonement for man's sins is difficult for the Japanese to accept. The very notion of sin as a basic inward unworthiness is new to a people whose standards of conduct are determined primarily by etiquette or social duty. The life of Christ is better understood as the triumph of *giri* (obligation) over *ninjō* (human feelings).[11] The concept of the church as a selective voluntary organization of limited functions is also somewhat strange. In Japan, participation in shrine and temple functions is part of life in a community, binding a man to his neighbors rather than setting him apart from them.

One response to these difficulties has been a *Mukyōkai,* or non-church, Christian movement of an estimated fifty to one hundred thousand members. It stems largely from the teaching of Uchimura Kanzō, who thought that the materialistic Americans had little to offer the Japanese in the realm of spiritual experience.[12] Present adherents to this type of intellectual Christianity include Nambara Shigeru and Yanaihara Tadao, presidents in turn of Tokyo University; Professor Takagi Yasaka; and Mitani Takanobu, Grand Chamberlain of the Imperial Household. *Mukyōkai* groups meet informally for study and discussion, but maintain no ministry or definite organization. Whatever cohesion they have comes from the use of the same Bible study magazines. The sale of 7,000 copies of an edition of the Greek New Testament in six months is evidence of the earnestness and high level of this intellectual interest.[13]

[11] Harada Tasuku, "Japanese Character and Christianity: A Study of Japanese Ethical Ideas as Compared with the Teachings of Christianity," *Pacific Affairs,* V. 2 (November 1929), p. 693.

[12] *Japan Christian Intelligencer,* V. 1 (November 5, 1926), pp. 358-360.

[13] H. Van Straelen, "Christian Influence on Japanese Non-Christians," *Worldmission,* V. 3 (Autumn 1952), p. 293; Nakazawa Kōki, "The Mukyokai or Non-Church Movement in Japan," Missionary Research Library, *Occasional Bulletin,* V. 3, no. 1 (January 15, 1952).

The YMCA and YWCA movements have also had a strong appeal in Japan precisely because of their non-denominational emphasis upon personal fellowship and practical service. The first association was formed in Tokyo in 1880 by a group of young men which included such rising Christian leaders as Kozaki Hiromichi, Ibuka Kajinosuke, Uemura Masahisa, and Honda Yoitsu. John T. Swift came out in 1889 as the first of a long series of American secretaries who have guided the movement in Japan, always on a fraternal basis that left essential control in the hands of the Japanese themselves. At the universities the "Y" has supplied clubhouse and dormitory facilities. Its annual summer conference for Bible study became an outstanding feature of student Christian work. The city associations have taught English, commercial subjects, and sports to thousands of young men in business. Since about 1900 the YWCA has been of service to the growing number of Japanese women who have left the home for work or higher education.[14]

The effect of Christianity has been not to supersede the older religions of Japan, but to stimulate them to greater activity. The reaction of State Shintō was defensive, in the shape of formulation of a more explicit philosophy of the *kokutai* (national polity). Buddhism has tended to assimilate the methods and attitudes of its foreign competitors. The Nishi Honganji branch of the Shin sect, for example, made it a rule that all temples under its control should have Sunday schools for the instruction of children. Young Men's Buddhist Associations and Young Women's Buddhist Associations were established. Theological seminaries on the western model were established for the training of priests; in some of them study of the Bible for comparative purposes was required. In the 1890's Inoue Enryō and Nakanishi Gyūrō began a "New Buddhist" movement which sought to restate Buddhist thought in Western philosophical terms.[15]

Immediately after World War II some Americans thought hopefully that Buddhism and especially Shintō had been

[14] *Japan Weekly Mail*, December 25, 1915, Social Reform Supplement; *Japan Christian Year Book, 1953*, cited, pp. 292-295.
[15] Ebina Danjō, "The Evangelization of Japan Viewed in Its Intellectual Aspect," *Harvard Theological Review*, V. 2 (April 1909), p. 197; J. Takakusu, "What Buddhists are Doing in Japan," *Young East*, V. 1 (June 8, 1925), p. 4.

discredited by Japan's defeat and would wither in strength without the support of the state. But indications are that the older religions are adjusting quite successfully to the new condition of complete equality and free competition. SCAP made a small contribution to reorientation in this field by sending eight non-Christian religious leaders to the United States to study the legal position of religion in America and "to discover some of the problems, difficulties and failures of religious organizations in a democratic society." According to a report evaluating the project, the visitors remained unconvinced of the values of lay leadership or social action, but concluded that "the basic Buddhist and Shintoist view of man, as having divine possibilities, possessed the essential postulate for a religious basis for democracy." [16]

Non-Christians like Ichimada Hisato, financial leader and former governor of the Bank of Japan, have expressed concern whether their country will be able to maintain democratic institutions without the foundation of Christian thought and ethics that exists in the West.[17] Over the years Christianity has certainly been a preparation and support for democracy through its emphasis on individualism and equality. It has taught that all men are equal before God, and that each is responsible for his own salvation and personal conduct. Reinhold Niebuhr has emphasized that the Christian view that all men are subject to sin and error underlines the need for checks and safeguards against absolute authority.

In a country like Japan where most people are closely bound by group responsibility and social convention, the Christian emphasis on the individual opens great possibilities of conflict. Since the early part of the Meiji era enemies of Christianity have cited Bible verses like "He that loveth father and mother more than me is not worthy of me," to show that it destroys filial piety and the family system. In many cases this was true. Bishop Naide of the Nihon Seikōkai has told how upon conversion he was required to burn his ancestral tablets. "It was an easy matter in those

[16] *Japan Christian Quarterly*, V. 17 (Autumn 1951), pp. 182-183; Emily C. Keeffe and Elizabeth Converse, *The Japanese Leaders Program of the Department of the Army* (New York: Institute of International Education, 1952), p. 102.
[17] *Christian Century*, V. 68 (November 14, 1951), p. 1310.

days to recognize a Christian's grave, for it was overgrown with weeds!" Christianity had greatest success among students and younger middle-class people in big cities, the very groups that were free, at least temporarily, from family control.[18]

The Christian churches in Japan have been criticized, both from within and from without, as too individualistic, too bourgeois, lacking in social consciousness. Members have been most comfortable in small closely-knit congregations, a sort of family-substitute, and have not been eager to bring the Christian message to the multitude. As a leading socialist put it, Japanese Christians did not "seek sufficiently to help the unfortunate, they do not sympathize with the working-man as Christ did; they are satisfied rather to gather about their organs and sing and pray and sentimentalize." [19] The failure of the Japanese churches to take forthright social action is explainable, however, on at least two grounds. When most churches were either dependent on subsidies from abroad or barely self-supporting, their resources seemed far too small in proportion to the task. Secondly, during the "suppression of dangerous thought" campaign of the twenties and the militaristic control of the thirties, Christian groups were fearful of inviting suspicion that they were radical. It was much more politic for individual Christians to take part in secular reform movements that enlisted wider support.

Familiarity with the name and work of Kagawa Toyohiko has led Americans to overestimate the strength of the "social gospel" in Japan. Few Japanese have been willing to follow this graduate of Princeton Seminary in his work among the poorest people in the slums of Kobe. Although Kagawa was a staunch anti-Marxian, his activity in organizing labor and farmers' unions, his insistence that a cooperative form of economic organization must supersede capitalism, smacked

[18] Kishimoto Nobuta, "How I Came into Christianity," *New World*, V. 1 (June 1892), p. 316; Naide Yasutarō, "The Christian Message and Ancestors," *Japan Christian Quarterly*, cited, V. 2 (July 1927), pp. 222-224. Literally "the Holy Catholic Church in Japan," the Nihon Seikōkai has drawn from both Anglican and American Episcopalian traditions.
[19] Quoted in C. B. Olds, "The Christian Message and the Educated Classes in Japan," *Japan Christian Quarterly*, V. 5 (July 1930), p. 234.

of radicalism. In 1927 he was expelled from the National Religious Conference because of his bitter accusations that Shintō and Buddhism, as well as Christianity, were socially irresponsible. Kagawa could never be accused of neglecting souls for bodies, however, for his preaching was the mainstay of the Kingdom of God evangelistic campaign of the early thirties. But his social emphasis evoked no great enthusiasm among his fellow Christians. Although a few of the missionaries organized a Kagawa Fellowship to support his work, many were openly or tacitly critical.[20]

Since World War II Kagawa's point of view has been coming to the fore in the Kyōdan and the other older Protestant churches. Freed from legal restraints on thought and speech, many Christians are searching for an acceptable substitute for Japan's still rather feudalistic capitalism. They would welcome more visitors like Professor John C. Bennett of Union Seminary to give them guidance in this field. They would like some missionaries with special competence in labor relations and problems of the workingman. Unfortunately, the mission boards have difficulty in finding personnel to fill this bill. From the standpoint of cultural relations the question is this: are American missions able and willing to be the vehicle for developing creative leadership for the solution of Japan's economic and social problems? What contributions have they made to the larger life of the nation?

The Missionary's Contribution Through Education and Social Work

Unless he is clearly a specialist, the missionary faces a problem of how to divide his effort between preaching the gospel and ministering to the minds and bodies of the people. American thinking on the relation between the central evangelistic aim of missions and the subsidiary means of education, philanthropy, and social improvement has shifted with the temper of the times. Joseph Cook's statement before the World's Congress of Missions held in connection

---

[20] William Axling, *Kagawa* (Rev. ed.; New York: Harper, 1946), *passim;* Kozaki Michio, "Dr. Kagawa and 'The Kingdom of God Movement'," *International Review of Missions,* V. 18 (October 1929), pp. 573-583.

with the Columbian Exposition of 1893 is representative of the older view:

> It is wrong to carry to a nation as an adequate religious message any directions that can be obeyed and leave the souls that obey unsaved. I might say to an unevangelized nation: introduce improved methods of agriculture, railways, telegraphs, telephones, telautographs; improve your methods of transportation and commerce. The nation might do all that and die without deliverance from the love of sin and the guilt of it. . . . Let him [the missionary] teach the nation the necessity of immediate repentance; let him emphasize the truth of Scripture, that it is never safe for any man to die in his sins.[21]

The social gospel movement in the American churches inevitably had a reflexive effect upon the philosophy of missions. In 1914 a leading mission board executive, Robert E. Speer, told the Student Volunteer convention that education and philanthropy, if properly conducted, were not just means of contact but a part of evangelism itself.[22] The height of the trend toward a humanistic and humanitarian definition of a mission task was reached in *Re-thinking Missions,* the report that Laymen's Foreign Missions Inquiry made in 1932. The Inquiry urged, in the words of its official reporter, Professor William E. Hocking, that missions in the Orient be freed from "organized responsibility to the work of conscious and direct evangelization."

> We must be willing to give largely without any preaching; to cooperate with non-Christian agencies for social improvement; and to foster the initiative of the Orient in defining the ways in which we shall be invited to help. This means that we must work with *greater faith* in invisible successes. We must count it a gain when without addition to our institutional strength, the societies of the East are slowly permeated with the spirit of Christian service.[23]

[21] *Missions at Home and Abroad: Papers and Addresses presented at the World's Congress of Missions, October 2–4, 1893* (New York: American Tract Society, 1895), p. 481.

[22] *Students and the World-wide Expansion of Christianity. . . .* (New York: Student Volunteer Movement, 1914), p. 107.

[23] Laymen's Foreign Missions Inquiry Commission of Appraisal, *Re-thinking Missions: A Laymen's Inquiry after One Hundred Years* (New York: Harper, 1932), p. 70.

Many American churchmen rejected the humanistic views of the lay leaders, however, in favor of a new enthusiasm for evangelism that found intellectual justification in Barthian terms in Hendrik Kraemer's *The Christian Message in the Non-Christian World*.[24] Since World War II the most authoritative statement is the report of the National Council's Commission on "The Missionary Task in the Present Day." Relief is expressed that the most urgent social and economic problems are being handled by the United Nations or national aid programs, leaving mission resources free for the central religious task. On the other hand, the Communist menace to both Christianity and free institutions has, in a sense, reunited secular and religious interests.[25]

In Japan special circumstances turned the missionaries toward subsidiary activities from the beginning. The treaty concluded by Townsend Harris in 1858 gained them rights of residence in certain ports and freedom of personal worship, but the laws of Japan barred them from propagandizing. So Guido Verbeck and Samuel R. Brown turned to teaching in government schools, and Dr. J. C. Hepburn opened a dispensary at Yokohama. Even after open proselyting became possible in 1873, private Christian schools that catered to the widespread desire for Western knowledge proved to be one of the best methods of making contact with potential converts. By 1882 there were seventy Christian schools. The total enrollment, however, was only 2,611, an indication that most were extremely small.[26]

As Japan developed a thorough system of public education, the Christian schools were forced to find spheres in which their religious work could be a supplement. Primary education was surrendered to the state, but kindergartens were an open field that offered contact with both impressionable children and their parents. In 1940 there were 349

[24] New York: Harper, 1938.

[25] *The Missionary Obligation of the Church: The Missionary Task in the Present Day, Report of Commission IV* (New York: Committee on Research in Foreign Missions of the Division of Foreign Missions and the Central Department of Research and Survey, National Council of the Churches of Christ in the U.S.A., 1952).

[26] Otis Cary, *A History of Christianity in Japan* (New York: Revell, 1909), V. 2, p. 163.

Protestant kindergartens with about 12,500 pupils. Middle schools for boys at one time were the point of emphasis, but by the thirties there were only about a dozen under Protestant auspices. Girls were less well provided for publicly, which helps to explain the fact that in 1935 Protestant missions were operating 37 girls' high schools (kōtō jogakkō) with over 14,000 students. A shortage of facilities at the level of higher school (kōtō gakkō) and college (semmon gakkō) gave scope for such institutions as Aoyama Gakuin, Tōhoku Gakuin, Meiji Gakuin, and Kobe College for Women.

The shortcomings of the Christian higher schools were recognized by many missionaries and carefully defined by a joint Japanese-American Commission on Christian Education that surveyed the situation in 1931. Far too many of the students were inferior, those who had been unable to make the next step on the public ladder. Physical equipment and, on the average, the teaching force did not come up to the standard of the national schools. Most serious was the charge that the Christian schools did not show leadership in experimentation with curriculum or teaching methods, but were pale imitations of the Ministry of Education standard.[27]

Statistical analysis has shown recently that the Christian schools have not been as influential as many supposed who had given attention only to conspicuous examples. Of 27,615 persons listed in the latest edition of Bunka Jimmeiroku, the national directory of cultural leaders, only 429, or 1.5 percent, are graduates of church-connected schools. Only 1,570 of the 6,700 teachers in such schools are themselves graduates of Christian colleges.[28]

Since 1947 Christian schools have been readjusting to the new division of school years into a 6-3-3-4 pattern. In 1953 sixteen colleges and universities (four with graduate schools), twenty-eight junior colleges, seventy-two senior high schools, sixty-three junior high schools, nine primary schools, and two theological seminaries were members of the Japan Christian Educational Association. The total number of students

[27] Japan Mission Year Book, 1929, pp. 150-151; Commission on Christian Education in Japan, Christian Education in Japan (New York: International Missionary Council, 1932).
[28] Study by the Japan Christian Educational Association, reported in Christian Century, V. 71 (April 7, 1954), p. 440.

was 103,096.[29] Strenuous efforts have been made to raise standards. The mission boards have contributed substantial sums for rebuilding and extending physical facilities. Even yet, however, many schools cannot provide their students with an adequate dormitory life. The Japan Christian Educational Association has published excellent textbooks reflecting a religious point of view. Teaching staffs were bolstered by the eighty-seven young American college graduates who came to Japan in 1948 and 1950 under the so-called J-3 (three years in Japan) program.[30] Far from being prepared for leadership, however, most of the Christian institutions have difficulty in even coming up to legal standards. Japanese students need above all to break away from reliance on a single textbook. But Meiji Gakuin, for example, with a library of only 37,000 volumes as of 1953, did not allow borrowing for outside use; and its reading room seated only fifty. Unless it increases its library to 100,000 volumes by 1955, it is in danger of losing its authorization to operate as a four-year college.[31]

Before World War II the Christian educational pyramid was truncated, with no university at the top that had general recognition for scholarship. Dōshisha University came the closest, but its religious connections had become more and more attenuated after the death of Niishima Jō, the founder. Rikkyō (St. Paul's), Kansei Gakuin, and Jōchi (Sophia) obtained government recognition of *daigaku* status, but could not compete in prestige with the Imperial universities. Only in English, commerce, and political science were the Christian universities adequately equipped to train teachers.

For a number of years after the hope was first raised at the World Missionary Conference held in Edinburgh in 1910, plans for a Central Christian University in Japan were under active discussion; but they were never realized. Since 1945 funds have been raised both in Japan and in North America for a new International Christian University located at

[29] *Japan Christian Year Book, 1953*, cited, p. 116.
[30] *Japan Christian Quarterly*, V. 17 (Summer 1951), pp. 32-35.
[31] Matsumoto Tōru, "The Meiji Gakuin Story," *Japan Christian Quarterly*, V. 19 (Winter 1953), p. 33.

Mitaka, near Tokyo. From the undergraduate course that began in April 1953, and from the graduate school of education to be headed by Hidaka Daishirō, former vice-minister of education, improvement in teaching should rapidly permeate downward to the lower mission schools. It remains to be seen, however, whether graduates of ICU will be able to overcome old school ties and deeply founded habits of academic inbreeding so as to obtain really important positions of leadership in the country at large.

ICU's planned graduate school of social work will place on a better scientific basis many activities which Christian missionaries first introduced in Japan. In pre-modern times there had been unfortunate people, of course, but they were cared for in a minimum way by the family group or by the local community. But industrialization and growth of cities shook people loose from their traditional moorings, and at the same time vastly increased the problems of health and morals. In instance after instance missionaries perceived a social need and provided a Western-type institution to meet it.

Early in the 1870's, for example, Dr. John C. Berry of the American Board urged the need for improvement of prisons and for reform rather than mere punishment of criminals. After two years of observation and study in the United States, one of Berry's disciples, Tomeoka Kōsuke, established the Katei Gakkō, a model reformatory for delinquent youth. He also served as adviser on penology to the Home Ministry and instructor at the Police Prison School. Miss Caroline MacDonald and Hara Inshō took the lead in rehabilitation of released convicts.[32]

The Catholics first established orphanages in Japan, and it was an ex-Catholic, Ishii Jūji, who founded the best known Protestant institution, the Okayama Kojiin. Daniel C. Greene of the American Board Mission helped Katayama Sen to establish Kingsley Hall in Tokyo, a settlement house patterned after Toynbee Hall in London. Under the direction of the Rev. Clay MacCauley, the Unitarian center in Tokyo

[32] Matsumiya Kazuya, Nihon Kirisutokyō Shakai Bunka Shi (History of Christian Society and Culture in Japan) (Tokyo: Shin Kigen-sha, 1948), pp. 120-124; Japan Weekly Mail, October 18, 1902.

also became a focus for many reform and relief activities. The tuberculosis sanatorium that William Merrell Vories opened at Omi in 1918 was small in size, but it demonstrated the most advanced housing, equipment, and methods of treatment for one of Japan's greatest scourges. Specific mention of these pioneers should not obscure, of course, the contributions of many other missionaries and Japanese Christians who have extended and carried on their work. In addition to their long-term work, the Christian bodies have always stood ready to help the unfortunate when disasters of earthquake, fire, and flood have struck Japan.

The Japanese themselves were quick to follow the Christian lead in social work. Buddhists, with the Shin sect in the lead, were stimulated to substitute programs of constructive social service for mere alms-giving. Mitsui, Mitsubishi, and other large corporations established foundations for charitable work. But as the magnitude of social problems became apparent, the Japanese Government found it necessary to coordinate and supplement these private efforts. A Bureau of Social Affairs was set up in the Home Ministry in 1920, and in 1937 a separate Ministry of Welfare was created. In 1951 this ministry disbursed over forty-four billion yen for social work. Since the war the American-type Community Chest drive has been adopted for coordinated financing of private charities.[33]

The day of the strictly missionary-supported and operated social service institution in Japan has largely passed. Since World War II American contributions for welfare have gone through broader channels. Between 1946 and 1952 eleven million dollars worth of relief and rehabilitation supplies were imported through Licensed Agencies for Relief in Asia (LARA), a joint committee of Protestant and Catholic welfare agencies. Distributed through the Ministry of Welfare, these supplies went to public and Buddhist as well as to strictly Christian institutions. Along with more direct contributions by individuals through CARE, they were an impressive demonstration of the American spirit of forgiveness

[33] Mildred Anne Paine, "Social Movements and Christian Projects in Japan," in *Japan Christian Year Book, 1938,* cited, pp. 183-197; James Thayer Addison, "Social Service in Japanese Buddhism," *International Review of Missions,* V. 15 (October 1926), pp. 704-713; *Japan Year Book, 1949-52,* pp. 683-689.

and sympathy for a defeated enemy. In most cases foreign mission boards now contribute less than 5 percent of the budget of Christian welfare institutions; the rest comes from the Japanese churches, local community chests, and government grants. The Christians are still supplying leadership, but they cannot hope to command resources large enough to meet all needs.[34]

The Christians have been less successful in stimulating the conscience of the Japanese nation on matters of social morality. It was inevitable that the temperance crusade, which occupied the attention of so many American Protestants in the late nineteenth century, should be transferred to Japan. Almost every advance in the Japanese movement has been directly stimulated by the visit of some American. The first society was formed in 1875 in the pioneer Kaigan Church at Yokohama, but disbanded because members failed to keep pledges of abstinence. In 1886 Mrs. Mary Leavitt of the World's WCTU stimulated the formation of the Kirisutokyō Fujin Kyōfukai, which was headed for thirty-five years by Yajima Kajiko. The visit of energetic Miss Jennie Ackermann in 1890 led to the organization of the Tokyo Temperance Society, in which Andō Tarō and Nemoto Shō were the leading spirits. In 1898 Miss Clara Parrish, another "round-the-world" WCTU missionary, brought various local societies together in the Nihon Kinshū Dōmeikai (Japan Temperance League). A colorful note was added in 1917 when Captain W. H. Hardy, a member of the Perry expedition, came to Japan to give gospel and temperance lectures. In 1920 Dr. D. M. Gandier of the Anti-Saloon League of California contributed to the organization of a non-sectarian National Temperance League intended to appeal to non-Christians. Mark R. Shaw of the Methodist Board of Temperance sparked the formation of the Japan Intercollegiate Anti-Alcohol League in 1923.[35]

[34] Japan Christian Year Book, 1950, cited, pp. 131-133; same, 1953, pp. 129-131; Henry G. Bovenkerk, "A Century of Protestantism in Japan," Far Eastern Survey, V. 22 (December 1953), p. 178.
[35] Yamamoto Kyohei, "Temperance Movement in Japan," Japan Christian Intelligencer, V. 1 (April 5, 1926), pp. 62-64; Standard Encyclopedia of the Alcohol Problem (Westerville, Ohio: American Issue Publishing Co., 1925-1930), V. 3, pp. 1388-1390.

The coolness of public reaction can be seen from the fact that the bill forbidding sale of liquors to persons under twenty, which Nemoto first introduced in the Diet in 1910, did not pass until 1921. Later attempts to raise the age to twenty-five were unsuccessful. A few villages exercised a sort of local option, but Japan did not follow the United States in prohibition legislation. Nagao Hampei did have some success in getting pledges from railroad workers, using arguments of safety, and there was a small movement within Buddhism; but on the whole the temperance movement was one of the by-products of Christian belief. For the Christian, abstinence was a test of self-control and another mark of distinction; for the average Japanese, *sake* was an important part of the ceremonial occasions of birth, marriage, and death. The spiced variety called *o-toso* was used almost universally as part of the New Year celebration. Foreign-style beer and whisky have grown rapidly in popularity. Despite the shortage in domestic food supplies, in 1952 precious grain was used to produce 66.5 million gallons of sake and 78 million gallons of beer.

Japan's extensive system of licensed prostitution naturally clashed with Christian standards of monogamy and personal purity. The fight against it proceeded along two fronts. The first goal was to get court rulings that women could not legally be bound to such service for the satisfaction of debts. British and Australian personnel in the Salvation Army took the lead in rescuing prostitutes and rehabilitating them for normal life. Christian leaders like Shimada Saburō, Abe Iso-o, and Yajima Kajiko fought for the second objective, legislation to ban the whole licensing system. Their first success came in Gumma prefecture about 1890. A big drive during the 1920's took advantage of public resentment over the burning of prostitutes locked in *Yoshiwara* quarters during the earthquake fire, and obtained abolition measures in eight prefectures. Enforcement was another matter, however, which required the constant vigilance of the National Purity League (Kokumin Junketsu Dōmei).[36] Both organized and amateur vice have increased so markedly under the system of local autonomy since the war that Christians are

[36] Matsumiya, cited, pp. 138-143.

now urging national control of prostitution. The Christian argument on sexual morality has, however, been seriously damaged by the conduct of occupation soldiers and the resulting Eurasian children.

Christian education and social work have both been directed primarily toward the problems of urban Japan. Perhaps the greatest shortcoming of the missions has been their failure to get a real foothold in the rural areas. Ninety-nine percent of the villages and a majority of the rural towns still have no organized Christian church. A survey made in 1927 showed that 75 percent of the converts that were made in the country soon migrated to cities. Either as cause or as symptom, acceptance of Christianity was part of the break from old social moorings.[37] Missionaries and native pastors oriented by training to the city had difficulty in making Christianity meaningful in the rural pattern of life.

Kagawa did try to combine instruction in religion and in better methods of agriculture at short term Farmers' Gospel Schools, patterned after the Grundtvigian folk schools of Denmark.[38] In 1931 the International Missionary Council sent its specialist on rural life, Dr. Kenyon L. Butterfield, to survey the Japan field and draw plans for true "rural community parishes." His recommendations were too ambitious in terms of budget and activities, however, and up to 1941 only a half-dozen pilot projects had been set up.[39]

In twenty-five years, rural work begun since the war may show real results. As yet, however, only 1 percent of new converts are country people. The Church of Christ (Kyōdan), with help from the Interboard Committee for Christian Work in Japan, established in 1948 a central Christian Rural Service and Training Center at Hino, near Tokyo. The Kyōdan now has five similar regional centers and small local centers in all the prefectures. The Brotherhood of St. Andrew of the Nihon Seikōkai (Anglican) also maintains a model Christian rural community at Kiyosato,

---

[37] *Japan Mission Year Book, 1927*, pp. 65-66.
[38] Edward M. Clark, *The Other Half of Japan (A Rural Perspective)* (Harrisburg, Pa.: Evangelical Press, 1934), pp. 41-50.
[39] *Japan Christian Year Book, 1932*, cited, pp. 110-111; Ralph A. Felton, *The Rural Church in the Far East* (New York: Department of Social and Industrial Research, International Missionary Council, 1938), pp. 76-77.

in Yamanashi prefecture, and is planning to set up branch centers on Hokkaido, Shikoku, and Kyushu. At these centers native workers are thoroughly trained in the technical, economic, and social problems of farmers, as well as in new methods of rural evangelism.[40]

Japanese Christians and the Test of War

It is fair to ask, as we did about our business and technical contacts, how well the cultural relations developed through missions stood the test of political divergence and war. At the outset, we must recognize that Christians were far too small a minority in Japan to check the dominant trend toward militarism. Even in Western countries Christian ideals of pacificism and world brotherhood give way in times of crisis to the demands of national patriotism. Over a whole decade Japanese Christians were subjected to pressure for conformity that was well-nigh irresistible.[41]

In the Manchurian crisis and the subsequent discussion of the case before the League of Nations, Japanese Christians stood, on the whole, on the side of peace and moderation. Looking back in 1935, William Axling appraised the results as follows:

> There has been no out-and-out persecution of Christians. But their failure to march with the masses has raised a question mark against them in the minds of many. . . . Over-zealous public school teachers have made remarks in their classes unfavorable to Christianity. This has resulted in a terrific slump in Sunday School attendance clear across the Empire.[42]

As a refuge from the reality of current problems, the crisis theology of Karl Barth, with its concentration on the inviolate relation of the individual soul to a transcendent Divinity, became very popular among the intellectuals. The emphasis on personal holiness of the early stages of the Moral

[40] Japan Christian Year Book, 1953, cited, pp. 83-84; Japan Christian Activity News (National Christian Council), June 1, 1953, p. 4; Chronicle of an Idea (Chicago: American Committee for the Brotherhood of St. Andrew in Japan, n.d.), p. 3.

[41] Charles Iglehart, "The Church and War Time Pressures," Japan Christian Quarterly V. 18 (Winter 1952), pp. 34-42, places the Japanese experience in a broad context.

[42] "Trends of the Time," Japan Christian Quarterly, V. 10 (July 1935), p. 250.

Rearmament movement also attracted the attention of both Japanese and missionaries.[43]

When the China incident began in 1937 the National Christian Council decided not to offer resistance to national policy. Instead it placed emphasis on spiritual mobilization for the sacrifices ahead. In 1939 the Council resolved "to make plain the official purposes for the establishment of a new order in East Asia and to cooperate in their realization." An East Asia Bureau was set up to handle missionary work in the occupied areas.[44] Professor Hiyane Antei of Aoyama Gakuin Theological Seminary even suggested in the January 1940 *Japan Christian Quarterly* that "perhaps it is not a dream to hope that we Japanese may be able to propagate and preach the Gospel to the world more vigorously than others."[45]

The shrinkage in church membership by a third to a half during the war was due more to military service, war work that recognized no Sundays, and the disruption of travel and communications than it was to any active persecution. Except for arresting Holiness and Seventh-day Adventist leaders, whose doctrine of the second coming of Christ was regarded as a threat to the imperial system, the Japanese government used rather than abused the Christians. Pro-American elements in the Foreign Office had a part in sending Japanese Christian leaders to the United States in the spring of 1941 for a conference at Riverside, California, that touched on political problems. In September Prime Minister Konoe asked Kagawa to appeal to American leaders in an effort to to avert war.[46] After the wider Pacific war began, Japanese clergymen and priests were used to help control the local population in conquered areas like the Philippines.

In fairness to the Japanese Christians, it should be said that their predominant attitude was one of perilous persistence in faith rather than of easy compliance with the demands of patriotism. In the face of community pressures

[43] Willis C. Lamott, "Calvin in Japan," same, V. 7 (January 1932), pp. 9-16.
[44] J. W. Decker, "The Sino-Japanese Conflict and the Christian Movement in Japan," *International Review of Missions*, V. 29 (1940), pp. 519-532.
[45] V. 15, p. 49.
[46] Kakehi Mitsuaki, "Nine Years After," *Contemporary Japan*, V. 19 (July-September 1950) pp. 389-402.

against those who shared "the enemy's religion," it took courage to continue church attendance or family worship. The principal of Kinjo Women's College in Nagoya, for example, stubbornly refused to strike the words "according to Christian principles" from the charter of his school. "This is my faith," he said, "and I am unable to teach anything but Christian principles. You can take my life if you wish but I cannot give up my faith." [47]

One by-product of the crisis was consummation of the union of Protestant churches. This move had been under active discussion since about 1925, when the United Church of Canada furnished an example. The decisive stimulus came from the Religious Bodies Law of 1940, which required that units be of a certain size to obtain full legal privileges. The more jingoistic elements organized as the Christian Brotherhood (Kirisutokyō Dōshikai) also pushed the union movement as a way of getting rid of the missionaries. The issue of freedom from foreign control was more emotional than practical, however, for in most denominations administrative and financial control had already been turned over to the Japanese members. "Extraterritorial Christianity," as the Rev. J. H. De Forest once called it, had already been wiped out by a gradual devolution of responsibility. But the feeling that they were no longer really wanted made many missionaries decide to leave Japan during 1940 and early 1941, even before the diplomatic situation became truly critical.[48]

After over a year of discussion and negotiation, the Church of Christ in Japan (Nihon Kirisuto Kyōdan) came into being on November 24, 1941. Thirty-four denominations came in. Whatever the future of the Kyōdan may be, most Japanese Christians would agree that without this strength in unity the Protestant church would have suffered even more under the test of war.[49] The Roman Catholic communion was more fortunate, since it was already a large united group and most of its European personnel were able to continue work undisturbed.

---

[47] Walter W. Van Kirk, "Japan's Christians Stood Firm!" *Christian Century,* V. 62 (December 19, 1945), pp. 1409-1411.
[48] *Japan Christian Year Book, 1941,* cited, pp. 59-60.
[49] Same, 1950, p. 4.

The bitter experience of being double losers, of losing first their sense of integrity and then losing the war, helps to explain the strong support that many Japanese Christian leaders now give to pacifism and neutralism. Fifty pastors and professors in western Japan, organized as the Kinki Christian Peace Society, have made this public statement:

> We deeply repent of our failure, at the time of the Second World War, to carry out our Christian duty, and feel the more keenly our responsibility to conduct ourselves without again committing the same error in the present dreadful situation. . . . Holding fast to the spirit of Christ, we adhere to the peace constitution and oppose rearmament and the stationing of foreign troops in Japan.[50]

In February 1952 a Council of the Christian Peace Movement was formed to coordinate the action of various groups against rearmament. Some have since withdrawn from the Council, however, as the steam-roller tactics of Communist infiltrators became apparent. It is significant that the Peace Problems Committee of the Kyōdan decided in 1953 not to take a position on rearmament. "So long as it is not a question of faith," it stated, "we cannot help having a variety of opinions among church members, especially on political issues." [51] But the American policy of supporting Japanese rearmament is clearly creating new dilemmas for many Christians who are predisposed to be our friends.

Christianity in Postwar Japan

Since 1945 Christianity, as the religion of the majority of the conquerors, has enjoyed great prestige in Japan.[52] To this General MacArthur contributed greatly by his endorsement of Bible distribution ("Make it ten million"), his call for more missionaries, and frequent public statements in praise of Christian principles. Katayama Tetsu, when he be-

[50] "Our Attitude towards the Peace Treaty," *Japan Christian Quarterly*, V. 18 (Spring 1952), p. 107.
[51] *Japan Christian Quarterly*, V. 20 (January 1954), p. 79.
[52] Russell L. Durgin, "Christianity in Postwar Japan," *Far Eastern Survey*, V. 22 (January 28, 1953), pp. 13-18, discusses several aspects of postwar mission work more thoroughly than I am able to do here.

came premier in 1947, declared that the Japanese government "must be guided by a Christian spirit of morality" and
called a Christian Round Table Conference on Culture and
Peace to advise on public problems.[53] The number of Christian members in the Diet has consistently been well beyond
the proportion in the general population, although in the
general election of April 1953 the number in the lower
house fell from nineteen to thirteen. Through the influence
of Mrs. Elizabeth Vining, tutor to the Crown Prince, the
Empress and the imperial princesses took Bible lessons.
Prince Akihito himself was given lectures on Christianity
as preparation for his trip to the West in 1953.

Interest has not necessarily meant acceptance, however.
The theory that Christianity could pour in to fill a "spiritual
vacuum" in Japan has proved to be an illusion. Attendance
at the temples and shrines has grown steadily as the people
recovered from the paralysis of defeat. Statistics for 1953
show only 438,960 members of Christian churches (234,286
Protestants, 171,785 Catholics, and 32,889 Eastern Ortho-
dox).[54] Growth is barely keeping up with population; today
as in 1927 only one Japanese in 200 is Christian. Practically
none of the recent converts are in the age range thirty to
fifty, the generation most deeply affected by the war and the
one which will be in control in the years immediately ahead.
The churches are feeling the reaction against foreign control
that followed the restoration of sovereignty. The Communists are attacking them as agencies of American imperialism. The road ahead is uncertain, though not necessarily
dark.[55]

Tagawa Daikichirō made a prophetic statement in 1927
when he cast the responsibility for church union back upon
the West.

If we united all the Japanese churches, other new denominations would come from western countries, which would not unite.
Even if that did not happen some Japanese who had studied in

---

[53] SCAP, *Summation of Non-military Activities in Japan*, No. 21 (June 1947),
p. 258; No. 29 (February 1948), p. 298.
[54] *Japan Christian Year Book, 1953*, cited, table on church statistics.
[55] Michael H. Yashiro, "Christianity in Japan since the War," *International
Review of Missions*, V. 41 (July 1952), p. 277.

a foreign country might bring back a new one . . . we cannot
help looking at the growth and attainment of the unity movement in foreign churches, because it seems difficult for us to
secure it unless the foreign churches realize it first.[56]

To avoid denominational disruption of the united Church
of Christ, ten mission boards in the United States and Canada decided at the end of the war to channel their activities
through an Interboard Committee for Christian Work in
Japan. But the Nihon Seikōkai (Anglican) never joined the
Kyōdan as a body; and the Lutherans, some Baptists and
Presbyterians, and several other small groups have seceded
from it. The Kyōdan now includes only 63 percent of Protestant strength.[57]

To complicate the picture further, many new groups of a
fundamentalist and revivalist character have begun work in
Japan since the war. Organizations like the Bethel Pente-
costal Temple, Jehovah's Witnesses, and the Worldwide
Evangelization Crusade have each sent a number of missionaries.[58] The largest group is The Evangelical Alliance Mission (known as TEAM), which had 158 adult representatives
in Japan in February 1954 and 26 more home on furlough.[59]
The Far Eastern Gospel Crusade is made up of twenty-odd
chaplains and GI's with Occupation experience. In the
United States these fundamentalist groups are affiliated in
the National Association of Evangelicals and the Evangelical
Foreign Missions Association, which are in active opposition
to the National Council of Churches. In Japan they have
refused to enter the National Christian Council and the
Fellowship of Christian Missionaries, and instead have
formed their own Japan Evangelical Alliance. In 1952 the
Alliance reported 854 affiliated missionaries in over fifty
different missions.

Many observers feel that by concentrating on street preaching, radio broadcasting, and wholesale tract distribution the
revivalists put too much emphasis on the offer of salvation

---

[56] *Japan Christian Quarterly*, V. 2 (January 1927), pp. 59-60.
[57] *World Christian Handbook, 1952* (London: World Dominion Press, 1952),
p. 4.
[58] For a full list, see *Japan Christian Year Book, 1953*, cited, pp. 378-441.
[59] *Missionary Broadcaster*, March 1954.

and the declaration of decision, and pay too little attention to follow-up education and organization of churches. Charles W. Iglehart is more charitable: "Perhaps this is the real 'grass-roots' Christian transplanting," he writes, "that is to reach the common people in large numbers and blossom into a church that is truly indigenous while also passionately evangelical." [60] Their potential influence on both the cultural and the religious level should not be underestimated. The TEAM representatives, for example, appear to be healthy young American extroverts without intellectual pretensions. They are eagerly learning the Japanese language and will probably have much better rapport with the common man than a seminary graduate. So long as general prosperity continues in the United States they will have ample financial resources.

Past experience indicates that a simple evangelistic faith may have a wide appeal in Japan. Before the war the indigenous healing cult called Tenrikyō had gained about five million followers, especially among farmers and workers. In postwar Japan Tenrikyō retains its vitality, and many new sects are springing up around leaders who claim direct divine inspiration.[61] With the help of only a few American evangelists, the Japan Holiness Church had organized by 1935 437 congregations, all self-supporting, with 315 ministers (including 127 women) and almost 20,000 members.[62] In their revived form the Holiness Churches may be able to gather up many of those who are first reached by the evangelists. At any rate, the new missions offer a challenge to the older churches really to carry their message to the masses.

Intellectually, Japanese Christians are just beginning to emerge from the confusion that followed isolation and defeat. The Roman Catholics are showing interest in neo-Thomism, and a Japanese businessman has endowed a chair of scholastic philosophy at Kyoto University. The National Christian Council has described the dominant trend in

---

[60] Charles W. Iglehart, "The Christian Church in Japan," *International Review of Missions*, V. 41 (July 1952), p. 284.
[61] Osaka Motokichirō, "Tenrikyo, One of Japan's New Religions," *Japan Christian Quarterly*, V. 5 (October 1930), pp. 363-370.
[62] *Japan Christian Year Book, 1940*, cited, pp. 165-166.

Protestantism as being toward greater social consciousness, away from Barth to Emil Brunner and John C. Bennett. Much of the thinking about social questions takes place within a framework of Marxism, and one of the men who commands respect is economist Ōtsuka Hisao of Tokyo University, who has struggled valiantly to combine Marx and Christ. Interest in democracy has led Takagi Yasaka, Abe Kōzō, and Natori Junichi to study the history of American Protestantism, particularly of Puritanism.[63]

At this moment of intellectual and spiritual ferment, mission work is one of the most promising aspects of our cultural relations with Japan. Motive and interest are firmly based; the churches will not abandon Japan in favor of some new enthusiasm. The missions recognize the need for thorough training in the Japanese language, for understanding and appreciation of the Japanese way of life. Time and again during the Occupation it was necessary to call upon the great fund of experience accumulated by the missionaries. They are almost the only Americans who are willing to spend long years in Japan, working with the people and for the people.

Professor F. S. C. Northrop's warning that "nothing in any culture is more dangerous and destructive than the acceptance of new philosophical and religious beliefs . . . at the cost of the rejection of native beliefs which may be equally true and valuable" [64] does not apply, it seems to me, to Japan. The balance has already been upset by the wholesale importation of the material side of Western civilization. Japan shares in a world-culture. Her ancient faiths are more anachronistic than the new. If she is to achieve a new peaceful synthesis, she must be exposed to the religious values that are the checks to the materialism of the West.

[63] *Japan Christian Activity News* (National Christian Council), November 15, 1952, p. 3; December 15, 1952, p. 2; Takeda Kyoko, "The University Christian Community in Japan," *Student World*, V. 42 (1949), p. 217; Robert Considine, *The Maryknoll Story* (New York: Doubleday, 1950), p. 69.

[64] Northrop, *The Meeting of East and West: An Inquiry Concerning World Understanding* (New York: Macmillan, 1946), p. 431.

CHAPTER NINE

COORDINATION, PRIVATE AND PUBLIC

TODAY THE world has become acutely conscious of the age-old process of cultural contact between nations. The impact of one people upon another now seems too important a matter to be left entirely to chance or to personal whim. In this chapter we shall consider cultural relations between Japan and the United States from the standpoint of conscious direction, of coordination. To what extent do private voluntary organizations fill the need for planned action? What things can better be done through a government-sponsored and supported program? How can government and private efforts be coordinated?

If our cultural relations are to measure up to the ideal of "peoples speaking to peoples" for mutual enrichment and benefit, the presumption is in favor of maximum scope for private organizations. Organization should never be an end in itself, of course, but without it no extensive program of action is possible. When strictly cultural activities are tied too closely to government policy, they may be suspect as being propaganda or cultural imperialism. Furthermore, the continuity of government programs is likely to be broken by tactical turns in foreign policy or political maneuvering for domestic effect. Certainly the information program of the United States government has not been exempt from such influences during its short history.

Voluntary groups for the pursuit of common purposes have long been one of the outstanding features of American life. The Japanese, too, especially the city-dwellers, have in modern times been "joiners." They have formed a multitude of *kyōkai* (societies) and *kurabu* (clubs) that cut across the primary structures of family, community, and state. Most of the groups on both sides of the Pacific have been highly specific in purpose: associations of scholars, clubs of stamp and coin collectors, societies to foster a pet social reform. Whatever international relations these specialized groups may have are concerned primarily with their particular interests. Japanese and American scientists have met, for example, at periodic Pan-Pacific Science Congresses, educators at meetings of the World Federation of Education Associations. Personal friendships and growing mutual respect may have been important byproducts, but such groups address themselves primarily to professional problems rather than to cultural understanding.

Special organizations that we may call loosely the Japan Societies have, in contrast, been directly concerned with bilateral relations. Their purpose has been to promote friendship between the United States and Japan, and to diffuse knowledge and understanding of each other's culture. But in the face of limited resources and fluctuating interest, the Japan Societies have often found it hard to translate these lofty aims into sustained programs of effective action. In some cases, it may not be too severe to say that existence was a substitute for action. As one editorial critic put it, membership often served as "a balm to consciousness of the fact that things are not as they should be." [1] For too many Americans in Tokyo, for example, belonging to the America-Japan Society was the only gesture toward meeting the Japanese on a basis of real equality and friendship.

After a decade of inactivity during the war and its aftermath, the Japan Societies are now reorganizing and drawing up new programs of action. Now that we are more conscious of the problems of cultural relations, their usefulness as catalysts and coordinators can be greatly expanded. Their broad terms of reference allow them to undertake any project that will contribute to better relations between the United States and Japan. They can initiate activities that are being neglected, then hand these over to others once they are successfully launched. They can engage in cultural subcontracting. We shall first survey the organizations that have

[1] *Far East*, V. 11 (May 26, 1917), p. 203.

existed, both here and in Japan, and then suggest some of the opportunities for action.

Binational Organizations in Japan

The first society specifically intended "to promote and cultivate friendship between the people of the United States and Japan" was the Friends of America Association (Beiyū Kyōkai). It was organized in Tokyo in 1898 by Japanese who had spent some time in America as students, business representatives, or government officials. Viscount Kaneko Kentarō was the president and leading spirit. By 1910 the Association had over 400 members. The formal tone of its activities has been characteristic of most subsequent binational cultural organizations. On July 14, 1901 the Association unveiled with great ceremony the monument at Kurihama commemorating Commodore Perry's landing. It gave dinners for prominent American visitors and entertained on occasions like the signing of a new commercial treaty with the United States in 1911. After 1917 the Beiyū Kyōkai was apparently absorbed by the new America-Japan Society (Nichi-Bei Kyōkai).[2]

Early in 1917 B. W. Fleisher, publisher of the *Japan Advertiser,* suggested to Viscount Kaneko the need for a society that would bring together prominent Japanese and Americans living in Japan. Responding with enthusiasm, Kaneko called a meeting on Washington's Birthday to organize an America-Japan Society. An inaugural banquet was held on May 11 at the Bankers Club. By June 1917, the Society already had about 500 members. Viscount Shibusawa, the Mitsui and Iwasaki families, and other wealthy persons contributed securities to establish an endowment.[3] Kaneko served as president until 1924, when he resigned in protest against the American immigration act. From 1924 until his death in 1940, Prince Tokugawa Iesato headed the Society. Count Kabayama Aisuke then took the helm until the out-

---

[2] Kaneko Kentarō, "The American Friends' Association," *Overland Monthly,* V. 55 (February 1910), pp. 159-161; *Mid-Pacific Magazine,* V. 3 (January 1912), p. 91.

[3] America-Japan Society, *List of Members* (Tokyo: the Society, 1935), p. 1.

break of war. The American Ambassador was customarily named Honorary President. In 1940 the Society had about 775 members—425 Japanese and 350 Americans. Many former residents continued to belong after they returned to America.[4]

Formal hospitality was the keynote of the Society's activities. Visiting celebrities were given special dinners or garden parties, while run-of-the-mill notables were honored at the regular monthly luncheons. For several years the Society gave medals for the best essays on Abraham Lincoln written by Japanese school children. In the late thirties a Young People's Committee was supporting the work of the Japan-America Young People's Federation, made up of about a dozen clubs organized by American-born Japanese who had come to Japan for education or employment.[5]

Since World War II the America-Japan Society has resumed activities under the leadership of Komatsu Takashi. Even in 1947, when the food shortage made it necessary for members to bring their own sandwiches to Society meetings, a brave show was made of fellowship. Now the normal pattern has been restored, with luncheons at the Industrial Club, speeches of welcome and reply. The Young People's Subcommittee is now primarily concerned with counseling Japanese going to America to study and maintaining contact with them when they return.

Comparable prewar societies in western Japan have apparently not yet been revived. The Japan-America Society of Kobe was organized in 1921 in order to promote "mutual intimacy among the members and a better understanding between America and Japan." Although it cooperated closely with the American Association of Kobe, only a limited number of Americans were invited to become associate or honorary members. Tazaki Shinji, president of the Kobe University of Commerce, headed the Society in 1939. At that time the Japan-America Society of Kansai, established in nearby

[4] "Hompō ni okeru Kyōkai oyobi Bunka Dantai Kankei Zakken: Nichi-Bei Kyōkai Kankei (Miscellaneous Documents relating to Associations and Cultural Organizations in Japan: The America-Japan Society)," Foreign Office Archives, Library of Congress, S 9.1.10.0-6, contains for the most part documents assembled when the Society reorganized as a "juridical person" in 1934.
[5] *Bulletin of the America-Japan Society of Tokyo*, V. 3 (July 1, 1939), p. 9.

Osaka in 1922, had about 200 members. The president was Ogura Masatsune, a leading executive in Sumitomo enterprises. Lectures, formal dinners, and garden parties on appropriate occasions were the principal activities of both organizations.

The initiative of the Public Affairs Officer of the American Consulate-General in Yokohama in organizing a Japan-America Society in that port city shows continued faith in the value of this type of local binational organization. At an organization meeting on September 10, 1952, Nomura Yōzō, president of the New Grand Hotel and former head of the Yokohama Chamber of Commerce and Industry, was elected president. The objectives of the Society were stated in the familiar terms of promoting mutual understanding and friendly relations "through association and through the study of the aims of the national life of the people of both Japan and the United States, their ideals, learning, culture, industries, and economic conditions." [6] At the inaugural meeting on October 10, 1952, Ambassador Robert Murphy spoke in acknowledgment of a gift of historical documents that the Kanazawa Library was making to the University of California and the Library of Congress.

Other groups have had more specialized aims. The America-Hawaii-Japan Society (Nihon Bei-Fu Kyōkai) was organized in 1932 by two prominent Buddhist leaders, Takakusu Junjirō and Ōtani Sonyū. It was concerned with the welfare of children of emigrants when they returned to Japan for education. The Society maintained a Japan-America dormitory, also an Institute that taught *nisei* Japanese culture and tutored them for entrance examinations.[7] The Black Ship Association (Kurofune Kyōkai) was formed in 1933 under the leadership of Hayashi Jinnojō, a prominent businessman who had studied in America. Each year it sponsored a Black Ship Festival at either Shimoda or Kurihama. The Association has now been revived, with eighty-year-old Nakajima Kumakichi as president. It contributes to American-Japanese cultural relations by keeping alive memories of the contribu-

---

[6] *Nippon Times*, September 12, 1952.
[7] *Academic and Cultural Organizations in Japan, 1939* (Tokyo: Kokusai Bunka Shinkōkai, 1939), pp. 85-87.

tions that Commodore Perry and Townsend Harris made to Japanese history.

Although its scope was international rather than binational, the Society for International Cultural Relations (Kokusai Bunka Shinkōkai) played an important role in promoting contacts between Japan and America prior to World War II. This Society was organized in April 1934 as a vehicle for Japanese cultural leaders who had been active in the International Committee on Intellectual Cooperation so long as Japan was a member of the League of Nations.[8] Count Kabayama Aisuke was chairman of the board of directors until 1939. KBS prepared bibliographies and introductory surveys of various aspects of Japanese life. It sent Japanese professors abroad on lecture tours, and granted fellowships to a number of young Westerners, Americans among them, who wished to study Japanese culture. The Society also gave financial support to the Japan Institute Library in New York.

Since the Japanese government provided funds and a degree of policy guidance, the work of KBS was in a sense an official cultural program directed to Europe and America. Connection with an aggressive foreign policy inevitably cast suspicion upon activities that were in themselves meritorious. All officially-sponsored programs, including our own, run the danger of being judged by the political policies with which they are associated. Access to government funds must be balanced against independence. The Society for International Cultural Relations has had difficulty, since it resumed in 1949, in financing its activities solely from contributions by individuals and corporations. Many foreigners living in Japan have paid an annual fee for membership in a group called "Friends of KBS." But in fiscal year 1953 the Society accepted a subsidy of ¥2,500,000 from the Foreign Office for special projects like production of a series of color films on "Present-day Japan."[9]

[8] *K. B. S. Quarterly,* V. 1 (April-June 1935), p. 3.
[9] *Nippon Times,* September 24, 1953. The work of the Society is described in the *KBS Bulletin,* published at irregular intervals. A group called "KBS Friends in the United States," centering in the Los Angeles area, has cooperated in several projects.

Binational Organizations in the United States

The oldest organization of its kind in the United States is the Japan Society of San Francisco, founded in October 1905. Until 1932 it used the name Japan Society of America. The organizer and first president was Henry P. Bowie, a businessman who late in life became an accomplished painter in the Japanese classical style. Over the years Wallace M. Alexander, of the Hawaiian sugar and commission firm of Alexander and Baldwin, was one of the leading spirits. After rather intermittent activity the Society reorganized in April 1931, employed a permanent executive secretary, and set up an office in the Fairmont Hotel. In 1932 it had 284 members, 182 Americans and 102 Japanese.

The Society's activities during 1931 included a formal dinner for Prince and Princess Takamatsu and luncheons for Ozaki Yukio, a liberal politician, and Count Hayashi Hirotarō, President of the Imperial Educational Association. The party of Japanese students brought over by Nakamura Kaju for a summer visit were taken on an automobile tour of the city. The Society also sponsored a transcribed broadcast by the Tokyo Symphony Orchestra and Chorus, a concert of classical Japanese music by the Yoshida Trio, a costume exhibit, and a lecture on Japanese prints by John Stewart Happer. Members participated in the Chrysanthemum Festival at Redwood City. The enthusiasm generated by reorganization was probably not maintained, but the range of activities was typical.[10]

The Japan Society of San Francisco was reactivated in 1952, with Joseph A. Moore, Jr., of the Moore Dry Dock Co., as president. Dinners have been given in honor of Ambassador Araki Eikichi and John M. Allison, the American representative in Japan. In addition, the Society has sponsored a demonstration of ceramics by Hamada Shoji, and an exhibition of Japanese folk and provincial art. In 1953 George Killion, president of the American President Lines, succeeded Moore as president. Mrs. Wallace M. Alexander was designated Honorary President.

[10] Mabel T. Johnson, "Annual Meeting of Japan Society of San Francisco," *Japan*, May 1932, pp. 37, 42-43.

The occasion that led to the founding of the Japan Society of New York was the visit in 1907 of the Japanese warships *Tsukuba* and *Chitose*. Jacob H. Schiff, General Stewart L. Woodford, John H. Finley, and others responsible for arranging a dinner in honor of Admiral Ijuin and General Kuroki saw the need for a permanent organization which could act on similar occasions in the future. Under the presidency of Lindsay Russell, from 1910 to 1919, the Society broadened its functions to include continuous "diffusion among the American people of a more accurate knowledge of the people of Japan, their aims, arts, sciences, industries, and economic conditions."

Throughout most of its history the Society was under the administrative direction of either Eugene C. Worden or Douglas L. Dunbar.[11] For several years during the twenties it supplied a trade information service to contributing business firms. The Society also distributed publications for the Japan Tourist Bureau. An Earthquake Relief Fund was collected in 1923 and 1924. In 1932 the Society bought for the new American Embassy in Tokyo a Japanese painting to hang beside one contributed by the America-Japan Society. The next year it gave five hundred yen to help set up the Hearn Memorial Museum in Matsue. Most of the Society's activities, however, were directed toward its own members. The high points were the annual dinners, usually given in honor of the Japanese Ambassador.

In 1920, under the leadership of Kobayashi Masanao of the Mitsui Company, several of the large Japanese firms doing business in New York joined together to present to the Society securities with a redemption value of about $74,000. The income from this Townsend Harris Permanent Endowment Fund was to be devoted to "educational work along the broadest lines among Americans to disseminate a knowledge about Japan and the Japanese." Some money was used to finance lectures, concerts, and art exhibitions. Sets of lantern slides with explanatory text were loaned to teachers and clubs. The Society's syllabus on Japan was given a wide distribution—over 10,000 copies, in all, of

11 Douglas W. Overton, the present executive director, has kindly permitted me to examine the records of the Society.

the eight editions. Most of the funds were used, however, for distribution of handsome books on Japan to members and to selected libraries.

The Society apparently did not consider the threat of war with Japan serious enough in 1941 to warrant advance planning. December 8th and the days following brought a flood of resignations, including that of the President, Henry W. Taft. After an interval of confusion, enough members were rallied to allow a skeleton organization and the formal business meeting required by the charter. All other activities were suspended. The Society's endowment was in Japanese securities and produced no income.

Reorganization was effected in 1952, in a different climate of opinion, with John D. Rockefeller, 3rd, as President and Douglas W. Overton as Executive Director. Now that payments on Japanese external debts have been resumed, the Society has a substantial income from investments. This is being spent for a variety of cultural interchange projects. The Society's grants-in-aid to Japanese students, college lectureships on Japan, and plans for translation of recent literature have already been mentioned in previous chapters. A revised edition of the syllabus on Japanese history and culture has been prepared. During 1954–55 the Society planned to acquire films, slides, and other exhibit materials for circulation to schools, clubs, and other organizations. Grants will be available for distinguished Japanese academic and cultural visitors who need to make field trips, purchase special materials, or extend their stay in the United States. The Society is also sending Tsunoda Ryūsaku of Columbia University to Japan to give a series of lectures on American thought. In addition to these special projects, the Society is always alert to supply information about Japan and to assist relevant activities by other groups.

Formal efforts by citizens of Los Angeles to promote friendship between America and Japan date back to 1909, although there is some question about continuity between the various groups of which we have record. In 1913 a group of Americans and Japanese calling itself the Japanese Fraternity was giving dinners about four times a year for prominent visitors.[12] A Trans-Pacific Society was organized in 1916 "to foster a better feeling and just relations between America and Japan." Dr. Norman Bridge, a prominent civic leader, was president; and President James A. B. Scherer of the Throop Institute of Technology, formerly a teacher at Saga Middle School, was vice-president.[13] In 1919 a Japan Society headed by Edward C. Bellows, formerly consul-general in Yokohama, had over 100 members.[14] Just before World War II the name Japan-America Society was used, and a postwar society under the same name was formed in 1953.

In Boston a Japan Society was organized on October 4, 1920, at the initiative of the Rev. Thomas Van Ness of the Old North Church, who had just returned from a trip to the Orient. It brought together the many people in religious, academic, and social life around Boston who had an interest in Japan. In 1937 it had about 350 members. Reconstituted after the end of the war, The Boston Japan Society gave a dinner for Crown Prince Akihito and Ambassador Araki in September 1953.

The visit in 1923 of Itō Nitarō, a member of the Tokyo City Council who had come to America to study municipal government, stimulated organization in Seattle. The constitution and by-laws of the Japan Society of Seattle were consciously patterned after those of the New York Society. The Mokuyō Kai (Thursday Society), an organization of Japanese businessmen, offered to share its club rooms. The Japan Society maintained a library there and issued a bulletin at irregular intervals. A student branch was organized at the University of Washington.[15] In 1937 the Seattle Society reported about 170 active members and 80 members of a Women's Auxiliary.

The Seattle Society reorganized in 1952, with former mayor William F. Devin as president and Ralph A. Johansen of Pan American World Airways as secretary. Two hun-

---

[12] Neeta Marquis, "Inter-racial Amity in California: Personal Observations on the Life of the Japanese in Los Angeles," *Independent*, V. 75 (July 17, 1913), p. 140.

[13] *Japanese Student*, V. 1 (October 1916), p. 44.

[14] *Nanka Nihonjin Nenkan, 1918–1919 (The Southern California Japanese Year Book)* (Los Angeles: Teikoku Insatsusho Shuppanbu, 1919), pp. 13-35.

[15] *Japan Society Bulletin*, No. 1 (December 6, 1923).

dred and forty persons attended the second annual meeting on February 12, 1954, at which Rear Admiral Albert M. Bledsoe, commandant of the Thirteenth Naval District, gave an address; and students from the University of Washington sang parts of the musical drama "Atsumori" composed by Professor Charles W. Lawrence. At this meeting Lane Summers, a lawyer, was elected new president. The Society has again begun to publish its newsletter. In early 1954 it cooperated with the Japanese Community Service and the local consulate in sponsoring Japanese programs and exhibits at the International Trade Fair held in Seattle.

Prewar societies in four other American cities had not yet been revived by the middle of 1954. The Japan Society organized in New Orleans in 1928 drew members from the whole Gulf area, which was tied to Japan by the cotton trade. Its principal activities seem to have been entertainment of Japanese business representatives. By 1937 the membership had grown to about 175. In that same year a Nippon Society operating under the wing of the Chamber of Commerce in Portland, Oregon, had 54 members. The Japan American Society in Santa Barbara, California, had more local aims of fostering good relations with residents of Japanese blood in that area.

The Japan-America Society of Chicago was launched with great enthusiasm in 1930 under the leadership of Charles H. Chandler. Horace E. Coleman, a long-time resident of Japan, served as executive secretary. But ambitious plans for maintaining a large reference and loan library and a permanent art exhibition were stillborn. One of the handicaps was the absence of a strong Japanese community in the city. The large Japanese banks and business houses did not maintain representatives there, and the socially prominent leaders of the Society found little in common with the few Japanese small businessmen. Therefore, the secretary wrote in 1935, "the work of the Society has to be more in the nature of offering lectures on subjects related to Japanese culture; to the entertainment of Japanese visitors who pass through the city; and in keeping our members more or less well informed on the latest books and articles which have to do with all forms of Japanese culture." [16] A change of consul in 1940 gave occasion for a banquet—the "first big function in nearly four years."

What the Japan Societies Might Be

Some limitations of the Japan Societies in the past are apparent. Yet they possess traditions of great value. The problem is not how to replace them, but how to expand their usefulness. The outstanding possibilities would seem to lie in four major areas.

First of all, the Societies should be more effective channels for the cooperation of all persons interested in Japan. This means a broad membership. At the end of 1953 the New York Society had 674 members; and the groups in Boston, San Francisco, Seattle, and Los Angeles were resuming activities. Although definite statistics are not available in all cases, I should estimate that in 1937 the total membership of the nine societies in the United States was about 2,400. In view of the large number of people who became genuinely interested in Japan during the war or the occupation, the potential total membership today should be at least 5,000. Persons living outside the cities in which societies are located should be offered a meaningful non-resident affiliation. The criterion for membership should be genuine interest in Japan, not social standing, political opinion, or concern with some preferred form of cultural activity.

Expansion in size would make necessary a new conception of membership. In a New York Society of 2,000, let us say, no member could expect to be invited to every function. Activities would have to be directed to different interests. By questionnaire or other means, information should be collected about the past experience and present interests of all members. Such a questionnaire would also serve as a census of resources, showing persons who could be called upon to serve the Society in concrete ways. Positive contribution to the cause of Japanese-American relations through membership should be stressed, rather than the benefits to be gained

---

[16] Ruth F. Everett to Douglas L. Dunbar, December 3, 1935, Records of the Japan Society of New York.

by the individual. For financial reasons, the days when a member would more than get his dues back in free books and an annual complimentary dinner are gone. The accompanying state of mind should also go.

Cooperation among the Japan Societies in various parts of the country should be improved. In most prewar years no more than four or five letters passed between the Japan Society of New York and the groups in other cities. Unfortunately, a plan of the America-Japan Society to bring representatives of all the groups in the United States together in Tokyo in 1940 had to be abandoned on account of the international situation. An organic federation of the societies would be wise only if it served a definite purpose, but certainly there could be more exchange of information and coordination of activities. Perhaps a common news bulletin or a small magazine on things Japanese would tie them together sufficiently.

If the Japan Societies are to contribute to the ideal of "peoples speaking to peoples," there must be more direct communication between Japan and America. Before the war the New York Society short-circuited most requests for information back to the local consul-general, instead of helping to establish direct contacts with the appropriate sources in Japan. In case a reference or introduction cannot be made immediately, the request might better be routed through one of the cultural organizations in Japan. The Japan Society of New York, for example, expects that in time International House in Tokyo will become its closest correspondent.

Secondly, the Japan Societies might serve as agencies for widespread distribution of information about Japan. Today developments in Japan are being poorly reported in the United States. Only major political events like cabinet dissolutions and elections can compete for attention with the major power struggle with the Soviet bloc. The success of Japan's experiment in democracy, her struggles for economic health, and her active cultural life go almost entirely unanalyzed. Only the Emperor and former Prime Minister Yoshida are well enough known to emerge in the American consciousness as distinct personalities. The rest of Japan's leaders are merely hard-to-remember names, without color, without pasts or predictable futures. At the same time, there is a latent appreciation of the importance of Japan as a nation on our side in the world power struggle.

One or more of the Japan Societies might move to fill this need by supplying an information service on Japan. In today's battle for space and attention, handouts must be matched by handouts. Japan suffers from some natural disadvantages that must be compensated for. Because of the language barrier, most of what is currently published in Japan is not noticed and adapted here. Unusual stories about Japan involve names and facts that are hard to check and background information that is relatively hard to get. Japan is too far away in time and dollars to attract many competent free-lance writers. But correspondents or writers already in Japan might be engaged to supply cultural news on a stringer basis. The Society could fill this out and supplement it by research in Japanese-language sources. In addition to a general clipsheet given wide distribution, stories of local interest could be directed to papers that would otherwise seldom notice Japan. Material with a potential market in popular magazines could be turned over to writers of established reputation. In time the Societies would be able to establish their position as a ready source of authoritative and interesting information on Japan.

The third suggestion is that the Japan Societies should do more to encourage scholarly and authoritative studies of Japan and its culture. Unlike the Japan Society of London, which grew out of the International Congress of Orientalists, none of the Societies in America has placed emphasis on scholarship. None has maintained a library or museum comparable to that of the Hispanic Society of America. Original studies of Japan have been made chiefly in the universities or under the sponsorship of the Institute of Pacific Relations. During the 1930's the Society of Japanese Studies headed by Louis V. Ledoux and Harold G. Henderson worked for the development of Japanese studies in American universities. Japan specialists now find their best professional focus in the broader Far Eastern Association established in 1947.

Between 1922 and 1941 the New York Society did support

from its Townsend Harris Fund, either by direct subsidy or by purchase of copies, the publication of twenty-five books. Fifteen of these are included in the bibliography of best books on Japan compiled by Borton, Elisséeff, Lockwood, and Pelzel.[17] Preference was shown for works on art in which the cost of illustration was an obstacle to publication. But the Townsend Harris Committee rejected other technical and expert books on the ground that they would not appeal to the general membership of the Society. Little or nothing was done to encourage writing on neglected facets of Japanese life.

As a result of the stimulus given to Japanese studies by World War II, a sufficient number of Americans now have the linguistic and scholarly equipment to do serious work on Japan. Library resources have been vastly increased. But at the same time research support and cost of publication have become increasingly serious problems. The Japan Societies might well support a number of projects which promise to make real contributions to knowledge. In the long run, the serious book which will be drawn upon for years by writers, teachers, and students will make a greater contribution to public interest in Japan than another ephemeral rehash of the same familiar information. No better way of presenting the psychology and values of the Japanese could be found, for example, than through the careful and artistic translation of their best literature.

Fourth and last, the Japan Societies should be more effective forums for frank discussion of Japanese-American relations. Sooner or later any binational organization is faced with serious divergences in the political or economic interests of the two countries. It is useless to ignore these differences or to deny their existence, in the hope of maintaining a factitious cultural amity. The problem is rather how to use the accumulated resources of mutual understanding to expose the exact nature of the dispute, to assess the merits of the opposing points of view, and to contribute to a solution. When necessary, the Japan Societies should be political, but not partisan.

[17] *A Selected List of Books and Articles on Japan in English, French and German* (Revised ed.; Cambridge, Mass.: Harvard University Press, 1954).

Among the leading advocates of friendship between Japan and America, Viscount Shibushawa Eiichi was unique in his appreciation of the essential priority of political questions. For over twenty years he strove to find solutions to such questions through "people's diplomacy." In 1909 he headed a large party of Japanese businessmen which visited 53 American cities. When anti-alien land legislation was under discussion in California in 1913, he organized a Nichi-Bei Dōshikai (Japan-America Friendship Society), the members of which were drawn largely from the Associated Chambers of Commerce of Japan. This Society decided to send Soeda Juichi, president of the Industrial Bank of Japan, and Kamiya Tadao to America as unofficial envoys. Unfortunately, the land law passed before they arrived. But they stayed to investigate conditions in California and to advise their countrymen not to make a wholesale return to Japan. In Washington they had interviews with Wilson and Bryan, who explained that the federal system made it difficult for the national government to prevent a state from taking such action. Meanwhile, members of the Dōshikai worked to calm public opinion in Japan. The *ad hoc* organization did not continue beyond this immediate crisis, however.[18]

When Shibusawa came back to America in 1915 to attend the Panama-Pacific Exposition, he was pleased to learn that the San Francisco Chamber of Commerce had set up a special committee to consider the growing problems in Japanese-American relations.[19] In February of the next year, the Viscount organized a comparable Japanese-American Relations Committee (Nichi-Bei Kankei Iinkai) in Tokyo for the express purpose of "continuous study and reconciliation of disputes between the two countries." Membership was limited to a carefully-picked group of thirty. Included were such prominent businessmen as Ōkura Kihachirō, Hayakawa Senkichirō of the Mitsui Bank, Furukawa Toranosuke, Asano Sōichirō, Baron Kondō Rempei of the Japan Mail

[18] Shiraishi Yoshitarō, *Shibusawa Eiichi Ō (The Venerable Shibusawa Eiichi)* (Tokyo: Tōkō Shoin, 1933), pp. 603-605; *New York Japan Review*, V. 1 (August 1913), p. 58.
[19] An account of Shibusawa's discussions with this committee is found in Microfilms of Archives in the Japanese Ministry of Foreign Affairs, Library of Congress, MT 3.8.2.287-2, pp. 28-32.

Steamship Co., and Kushida Manzō. Kaneko, Nitobe, and Admiral Uryū—all old friends of the United States—were also charter members.[20]

This Committee made an ambitious effort to find solutions to all pending problems through unofficial bilateral conferences held in Tokyo in 1920. In March Committee members had eight days of discussions with a group from the Pacific coast of America headed by President Benjamin Ide Wheeler of the University of California and Wallace M. Alexander, Chairman of the San Francisco Japanese Relations Committee. A party from the East Coast led by Frank A. Vanderlip, president of the Japan Society of New York, came in April for similar talks. All agreed to use their influence with the two governments to get the burning questions of immigration and Japanese ownership of land referred to a Joint High Commission patterned after the one used in the dispute between Britain and America over the Newfoundland fisheries. In this they did not succeed, and in the fall of 1920 California voters approved an initiative measure further restricting property holding by aliens.[21]

Throughout the 1920's the Japanese-American Relations Committee provided a sort of collective backing for Shibusawa's continued personal negotiations with American friends. In addition to the San Francisco Committee, it cooperated with the National Committee on American-Japanese Relations in New York, headed by George W. Wickersham and Sidney L. Gulick. After the Viscount died in 1931, the work of the Nichi-Bei Kankei Iinkai carried on under the joint leadership of his son-in-law, Baron Sakatani Yoshirō, former ambassador to America Ishii Kikujirō, and Fujiyama Raita, a prominent sugar manufacturer. Formal organization continued as late as 1939.

In their earlier days, the Societies in the United States did not seek to avoid political questions. The Japan Society of

[20] Obata Kyūgorō, An Interpretation of the Life of Viscount Shibusawa (Tokyo: Shibusawa Seien Ō Kinenkai, 1937), pp. vii, 208-217; Shibusawa Hideo, Amerika Ōrai (To and From America) (Tokyo: Tōhō Shoten, 1948), pp. 80-86, 98-99.
[21] Japan Review, V. 4 (May 1920), pp. 213-214; Henry W. Taft, Japan and America: A Journey and a Political Survey (New York: Macmillan, 1932), pp. 5-50.

America was organized in San Francisco in 1905 partly as a counterweight against the growing anti-Japanese sentiment in the West. Until the question of legality was decided by the U.S. Supreme Court in the Ozawa case in 1922, this Society publicly advocated naturalization of Japanese immigrants. Similarly, on April 25, 1913, the executive committee of the New York Society adopted a resolution expressing concern over "the gravity of the issue raised by the proposal of the California legislature to enact measures [the Webb-Haney alien land bill] which ignore the treaty obligations of the United States," and supporting President Wilson "in all he is doing to maintain the honor of the nation." Distribution of Professor H. A. Millis' *The Japanese Problem in the United States* and the symposia *Japan to America* and *America to Japan* to Congressmen, chambers of commerce, and public libraries was certainly intended to have a political effect.

The Societies in these years did run the danger of being discredited for advocating a partisan point of view. This was recognized in 1920, when anti-Japanese land legislation was again pending in California. In answer to a plea for action from Viscount Kaneko and the America-Japan Society, the New York group stated that anything they might say or do could not possibly affect the results and would only be resented by the people of California and used for partisan purposes.

This abstention from action on grounds of expediency seems to have slipped over imperceptibly into the view that political questions were entirely outside the scope of the Society. The leaders privately deplored but publicly ignored the immigration act of 1924. By 1934 the official position had come to be that "The Japan Society takes no part in political controversies nor does it engage in political activities. Understanding between the peoples of Japan and the United States can profitably and effectively be promoted by concentrating on the dissemination of a broader knowledge of cultural relationship." The records of the Society during those years between 1931 and 1941 certainly give the picture of an ostrich hiding its corporate head under a bundle of prints. Many members who were critical of Japan's aggression against China found no choice but to resign.

The course that I would propose lies between the extreme of partisan pleading and timid isolation. When a political or economic question arises between Japan and the United States, the Japan Societies should sponsor a thorough exploration and frank airing of the issues. Who are better qualified than their own members to supply the information and analysis around which public opinion will form? Under conditions of democratic control, discussions of the sort that the party of prominent Americans led by Frank A. Vanderlip had in Japan in 1920 may effect a modification of positions. "That we effected or attempted to achieve any definite diplomatic result cannot be said," wrote one member of the Vanderlip party, "that we contributed something to the imponderable elements which later entered into diplomatic interchanges and such conferences as that held in Washington in 1921, can, perhaps, without undue assumption, be asserted." [22] Even during the thirties, something might have been achieved if the concern over Japan's aggression felt by even those Americans predisposed to be sympathetic had been fully brought home to the Japanese. The Societies cannot solve all political problems, but they ignore them only at peril of their own integrity.

Broader Patterns of Organization

Few problems or issues are any longer strictly binational in character. Any tug along the tangled skein of world politics puts strain upon the interests of many nations. Modern communications bring to bear upon each nation a variety of competing cultural influences. In cultural interchange, therefore, we may expect some of the most significant results to come from groups that have transcended the binational pattern of organization.

From its origin in 1925 the Institute of Pacific Relations has been an international organization concerned with study and discussion of the problems of the whole Pacific area. But within this framework have occurred some of the most sig-

[22] Taft, cited, p. 66.

nificant intellectual contacts between the United States and
Japan. Many eminent Americans have visited Japan under
the auspices of the Institute and enjoyed outstanding cooperation from the Japanese Council. In turn the American
Council has been of service to scholars and publicists coming
from Japan. In 1929 and again in 1954 the general conference of the IPR was held in Kyoto. In preparation for this
latest meeting, discussions on Japanese-American relations
were held in a number of American cities and a bilateral
conference convened in Honolulu in January 1953. Add to
these things the many excellent research studies that the Institute has sponsored and the attention it has given to teaching about the Orient in American schools, and its role in
cultural relations will be apparent. Without making a judgment on the justice of the charges brought against the IPR
in recent congressional investigations, one can recognize that
the usefulness of one of our principal channels for relations
with Japan has been seriously impaired.

The Asia Foundation is the newest and most experimental organization in the field. In March 1951 a group of private American citizens set up the Committee for Free Asia
in order to help Asian peoples to develop free democratic
institutions. The original project of short-wave broadcasting,
patterned after "Radio Free Europe," was abandoned after
trial. Instead the Committee shifted its efforts to direct contacts and financial aid which would strengthen voluntary
organizations and civic participation in Asian countries.
Youth groups, particularly, were helped to develop dynamic
and constructive activities free of Communist influence. In
an effort to protect indigenous cultures against the disinte-
grating effect of Communism, the Committee has encouraged creative writing, art, and other forms of expression,
and the exchange of cultural productions within Asia. For
example, it helped to produce a documentary film on the
conference of the World Fellowship of Buddhists, held in
Tokyo in 1952, for showing to Buddhist groups throughout
the world. The emphasis has been on supporting and encouraging Asian initiative rather than trying to sell American ideas. Faith in the long-term value of this approach was

shown when the Committee was reconstituted as a broader Asia Foundation in November 1954.

In Japan, where voluntary organization and cultural activity were already well advanced, the Asia Foundation has found it relatively easy to develop an extensive program. It is using Japan's experience with 4-H work as an example for rural organization in other Asian lands. The Foundation often brings Japanese and American groups with related interests into direct cooperation, but its basic outlook is regional rather than binational. It aims to help Japan to cooperate with her Asian neighbors, intellectually and economically, rather than to develop exclusive ties with America. The role of mediator in this process is for Americans a new level of sophistication in cultural relations.

Government Cultural Programs

Two limitations to the work of private binational organizations prompt governments to take a hand in the promotion of cultural relations at times when they become vital to the national interest. First of all, private groups do not have funds for an extensive program. The best endowed of the Japan Societies, the one in New York, is budgeting no more than $60,000 per year for cultural interchange projects. The Societies must operate with very small staffs or on volunteer labor. They cannot afford to spend much money on publication or to purchase radio and television time. Even a modest government appropriation is gigantic by comparison. Expenditures for the United States government's information program in Japan during the fiscal year 1953 were $1,761,066.

The second factor encouraging government action is the ineffectiveness of private groups, as we have noted, in handling basic political problems. Private organizations understandably try to avoid the taint of propaganda. Even when they agree fully with the foreign policy goals of their government, coordination of private activities with the details of policy execution is an almost insuperable problem. Whenever cultural activities are to be used in direct support of national policy, they must be directed, coordinated, and financed by the government.

Compared to other nations, the United States was slow in accepting the responsibility for official action. By 1900 France had already spent over 20 million francs to "maintain her moral influence in the Near East and to extend it to the Far East." Most of the money went to support educational and philanthropic institutions in those areas. In later years even the United States benefited from official funds spent for exchange professors, support of *maisons françaises* on university campuses, and other means of encouraging the study of French language and culture. In Germany, long-established official concern that *Deutschtum* be preserved among emigrants abroad was intensified and given sinister political implications during the 1930's by the *Auslandsorganisation* of the Nazi Party. The Italian government propagated the view that "Culture is Fascism." In self-defense the British government organized in 1934 the British Council for Relations with Other Countries. Largely through the teaching of English language, the Council hoped to spread an understanding of British institutions and ideals.[23]

The United States government program of cultural activities was also improvised to meet this crisis of the 1930's. The first steps were taken in an effort to hold the friendship of our "good neighbors" in South and Central America against the blandishments of German and Italian propaganda. Instead of trying to fight the totalitarians with their own weapons, we hoped to give a convincing demonstration of our American tradition of "intellectual freedom and educational integrity." [24] In May 1938 the President set up an Interdepartmental Committee for Scientific and Cultural Cooperation to facilitate exchanges through existing government agencies. A Division of Cultural Relations created in the Department of State that same year stimulated and coordinated the efforts of private cultural groups. By

[23] Ruth Emily McMurry and Muna Lee, *The Cultural Approach: Another Way in International Relations* (Chapel Hill: University of North Carolina Press, 1947), pp. 9-32, 39-73, 137-157.
[24] Ben M. Cherrington, "Ten Years After: Ten Years of International Cultural Relations," *Association of American Colleges Bulletin*, V. 34 (December 1948), p. 500.

1940 this division was also administering direct exchange of students, professors, and specialists with Latin-American countries.[25]

World War II brought further improvisation at accelerated tempo. State Department cultural activities in Latin America were overshadowed by the more ambitious ones of the Office of the Coordinator of Inter-American Affairs, headed by Nelson Rockefeller. The Overseas Branch of the Office of War Information disseminated information about the United States to allies, neutrals, and enemies. In OWI operations Americans gained their first extensive experience in the use of mass media like the radio and motion pictures to achieve definite political goals abroad.[26]

Since 1945 we have been experimenting—some would say fumbling—to find the appropriate position and scope for cultural and information activities in a world neither at peace nor at war.[27] At first a decision was made, rather reluctantly, to concentrate them in the State Department under an Assistant Secretary for Public and Cultural Affairs. There they remained, through several administrative reorganizations and distressingly frequent changes in top personnel, until 1953. Then all information work was placed in charge of a separate United States Information Agency, responsible to the President through the National Security Council. Educational exchange was left under the direct control of the State Department.

Turns in world events have forced a constant reshaping of the policy underlying American cultural and information work. Immediately after the war the dominant hope was that our official program could be dignified, neutral, and long-range in its objectives. President Truman placed emphasis on giving other peoples a "full and fair picture of American life and of the aims and policies of the United

25 McMurry and Lee, cited, pp. 208-229; *The Cultural-Cooperation Program, 1938–1943* (Department of State Publication 2137) (Washington: GPO, 1944); Charles A. H. Thomson, *Overseas Information Service of the United States Government* (Washington: Brookings Institution, 1948), pp. 1-3, 158-171.
26 Thomson, cited, pp. 4-6, 17-147.
27 Edward W. Barrett, *Truth Is Our Weapon* (New York: Funk & Wagnalls, 1953), is an indispensable guide to both the history and the issues.

States Government." [28] On one occasion Assistant Secretary of State William Benton explicitly rejected his own long experience in public relations as inapplicable. "The Department's program, as contrastd with one of persuasion, is a program aimed at expansion of direct communications between peoples, of personal contacts among them, and of candid and unbiased information flowing freely to them." [29] But it soon developed that any picture of American life, once it was made official, became bitterly controversial at home. Liberals and conservatives alike attacked the Voice of America, particularly, for broadcasting distortions of the true image of America. As the power struggle between the West and the Soviet bloc became the dominant fact in world affairs, the need for a narrower focus was realized. To talk was not enough: we had to answer back. On April 20, 1950 Truman called for "a sustained, intensified program to promote the cause of freedom against the propaganda of slavery. We must make ourselves heard round the world in a campaign of truth." [30] Public-relations technique came into its own as Congress, under the impact of the Korean attack, came through with appropriations large enough to permit a threefold expansion of activities.

During the early months of 1953 information policy seemed about to enter a new phase. The Eisenhower administration had high hopes of using propaganda and psychological warfare as powerful positive weapons in the world struggle. After careful study, however, the President's Committee on International Information Activities, headed by William H. Jackson, reached the wise conclusion that psychological strategy could produce no magic results apart from other official policies and actions. Creation of the new United States Information Agency actually involved a reduction, rather than an expansion, of activities and personnel. The auxiliary status of the Agency was implicit in the President's definition of its mission: "to submit evidence

[28] Statement of August 31, 1945, *Department of State Bulletin*, V. 13 (September 2, 1945), pp. 306-307.
[29] Address to American Public Relations Association, March 29, 1946, State Department Press Release No. 201, March 28, 1946.
[30] Speech to the American Society of Newspaper Editors, *Department of State Bulletin*, V. 22 (May 1, 1950), p. 672.

to peoples of other nations by means of communication techniques that the objectives and policies of the United States are in harmony with and will advance their legitimate aspirations for freedom, progress, and peace." [31] Although remnants of long-range cultural goals remain, notably in the library program, attention is focused on support for the day-to-day policies outlined by the State Department.

The Government Program for Japan

The American cultural program for Japan has naturally been affected by policies and techniques developed within the State Department, but administratively its history has been somewhat different. From 1945 until the end of April 1952 the United States Army had direct control. Information and cultural exchange were merely part of the broader objectives of the military occupation. The Civil Information and Education Section within the general headquarters of the Supreme Commander for the Allied Powers was charged with responsibility for thoroughgoing reorientation and reeducation of the Japanese people.

For this ambitious task CI & E had powers far beyond those enjoyed by American information specialists working in sovereign countries. It could direct the reform of the Japanese school system, censor the press and other communications channels, and make authoritative "suggestions" to cultural groups of all kinds. Precisely because it could work through the Japanese in so many ways, the Occupation did not need to use the whole gamut of communications techniques. It did not engage in direct radio broadcasting to the Japanese people. Documentary films could be distributed through prefectural centers run by the Japanese themselves. No newspapers or magazines were sponsored by the Occupation, as had been done in Germany.

CI & E did introduce to Japan the information center, which has become one of the hallmarks of American cultural work around the world. Books, magazines, records, and other cultural materials are made available cafeteria-style. This system was an outgrowth of the OWI libraries and of

[31] *New York Times,* October 29, 1953.

the cultural institutes set up during the war in Latin-American countries.[32] In November 1945 CI & E set up its first information library in Tokyo. Besides giving special service to Japanese editors, scholars, and government officials, the library was popular with the general public. In the twelve-month period beginning March 17, 1946, 125,000 people made use of its facilities.[33] SCAP was unexplainably slow, however, in extending the same opportunities to people in the rest of Japan. Robert Textor has charged that books and librarians waited idly in Japan for close to a year.[34] In September 1947 the logjam was finally broken, and centers opened in quick succession in Kyoto, Osaka, and the leading provincial cities. By the time the Occupation ended in April 1952, 23 were in operation.

In order to ease the transition when the peace treaty came into effect, the State Department took responsibility in January 1952 for supplying materials to these Army centers. A department planning mission that went to Japan also studied the future of the cultural program. The State Department concluded that it could not hope to get funds to support all existing activities, and closed some of the centers soon after it took over in April. Under USIA there have been further reductions, until in early 1954 only fourteen centers remained in operation. Each has an American director—a man in most cases rather than the woman librarians employed by SCAP—and ten to twelve Japanese employees. Since the direct equivalent for "information" in Japanese—jōhō—has strong connotations of underhanded intelligence work, they are called Amerika Bunka Senta (American Cultural Centers). Nine former centers are being continued on a binational basis, with the Japanese supplying space and staff to handle American materials.

For a typical example, let us see how the Cultural Center at Kobe fits its program to the needs of the community.[35] A

[32] The example of British Council libraries was probably also influential.
[33] SCAP, *Summation of Non-Military Activities in Japan*, No. 18 (March 1947), p. 276.
[34] Robert B. Textor, *Failure in Japan, with Keystones for a Positive Policy* (New York: John Day, 1951), p. 159.
[35] I am greatly indebted to Frank Tenney, former director of the Kobe Center, for a detailed account of its activities. A speech by William K. Bunce before

commercial and industrial metropolis on the Inland Sea just west of Osaka, Kobe is Japan's sixth largest city, with a population of over three-quarters of a million. As a foreign trade port, it is second only to Yokohama. Although cultural influences from Osaka are strong, Kobe has its own daily newspaper and radio station. Besides a full system of public schools, it has both a national and a municipal university. The Center easily makes contacts with local leaders in all fields through the senior Japanese member of its staff, a woman from a prominent Kobe family who received part of her education at Columbia University.

The information library inherited from CI & E continues to be the basic activity at Kobe, as it is at other centers. Although the book collection grew from 11,000 to 14,000 volumes during the first two years after the peace treaty came into effect, the primary emphasis has been on improving the quality of materials. Popular fiction in Armed Forces Editions has been replaced by more substantial fare. Besides books, the library has many pamphlets, periodicals, and United States government documents. Specialized items can be obtained on loan from other centers through the union catalogue at USIS headquarters in Tokyo. High school and university students eager to learn English form the majority of the readers. Teachers and professional people also come to use the library's collection of scientific books and technical journals. The Japanese appreciate the privilege of borrowing books for home use, something their own public libraries usually do not permit. The Kobe Center also maintains deposits of books in Japanese libraries at Himeji and other cities in Hyogo prefecture. Through the book presentation program, selected individuals receive as gifts volumes for which they have particular need.

Since the audiovisual libraries run by the prefectural governments contain a great deal of American material, USIA does not maintain as many mobile film units in Japan as it does in many other countries. The cultural centers do have projectors and collections of films, however, which are in great demand. With the personnel and transportation available

---

the America-Japan Society, published in the *Nippon Times*, January 29, 1955, surveys the whole USIA program in Japan.

the Kobe Center is able to arrange an average of one showing each day. Most of these take place outside the center
building, in schools and factories. Films on time-and-motion
study and on industrial developments in America, for example, have been very popular with both employers and
workers.

Several activities of the Kobe Center are designed to
counteract the stereotyped opinion that Americans are not
interested in the higher forms of cultural expression. Three
or four record concerts are held each week. In most instances
Japanese cultural leaders from the community take responsibility for the programming and commentary. The *Kobe
Shimbun* joined in sponsoring an exhibition of American
silk-screen prints. Many more people saw it at the newspaper
building, where such exhibitions are customarily held, than
would have come to the cultural center. Other displays of
American arts and crafts could be used advantageously.

In order to keep a varied and effective program going, the
busy center director must call upon other Americans in the
community for help and cooperation. Much of his own time
is taken up by requests for speeches and ceremonial appearances. Tokyo headquarters may call upon him for special services like giving all local candidates for fellowships
for study in America a preliminary screening for ability to
speak English. At the Kobe Center American volunteers,
some of them from the security forces, teach fifteen classes
each week in English conversation and American history and
civilization. A jazz band from the cruiser *Quincy* agreed to
give a show at the Chamber of Commerce auditorium, under
the sponsorship of the local radio station. In the larger cities,
certainly, the function of the center director should increasingly be that of a coordinator, working to bring Japanese
and Americans together in meaningful relations.

Although the United States Information Service headquarters in Tokyo is now organized as a unit separate from
the embassy, it operates under the direct control of the American Ambassador. The Tokyo office provides certain central
services to local cultural centers and to public affairs officers
attached to consulates at Sapporo, Nagoya, Kobe, and Fukuoka. Five days a week it issues to the Japanese press a "wire-

less file" of United States government press releases, accompanied by background information and editorial material. Documented articles have been prepared, for example, which contrast Soviet claims of advanced labor and social practices with true conditions. According to a survey by *New York Times* reporters late in 1952, however, "in Japan propaganda handouts were resented and rarely used by newspapers and magazines." [36] Speeches and articles of outstanding interest are translated into Japanese for wide distribution as pamphlets. Each month USIS publishes reviews of new American books in a magazine called *Beisho Tayori,* and it tries to help Japanese publishers obtain translation rights. During the 1954–55 fiscal year it planned to use local facilities to produce films on Japanese and free-world labor problems.

Realistic estimates of the situation have limited Voice of America broadcasts to Japan. No attempt is made to match in quantity the output, 13½ hours per day in 1953, that Communist stations in Russia, China, and North Korea beam toward the islands. American broadcasting in Japanese began in September 1951, during the San Francisco peace conference. For two years, however, potential reception was limited to the 250,000 shortwave sets in Japan. A powerful new transmitter on Okinawa now reaches all the ten million medium wave receivers in the country. Since January 1954 VOA has been sending a 15-minute program of straight news from 6:15 to 6:30 A.M., Tokyo time. This is followed immediately by a half-hour of news commentary, interviews, special events, and features. The half-hour program is repeated later in the morning and in the evening. In addition, each week 3½ hours of the Far East English service is specially tailored for Japan.[37]

It is difficult to gauge the extent to which Japanese listen to the Voice. They are already well supplied with good domestic programs, from new commercial stations as well as

36 *New York Times,* November 24, 1952. Leading dailies like the *Asahi* and *Mainichi* find that their own correspondents abroad supply materials better suited to their limited space.
37 *Overseas Information Program of the United States,* Hearings before a Subcommittee of the U. S. Senate Committee on Foreign Relations, 83rd Cong. 1st sess., Part 2 (Washington: GPO, 1953), pp. 1325-1333; *Nippon Times,* January 7, 1954.

from the semi-official Nihon Hōsō Kyōkai (Broadcasting Corporation of Japan). The largest audience is undoubtedly reached through NHK's rebroadcast of Voice material on its evening overseas hour. Japanese stations have also been glad to use music programs and special events like the world series and Eisenhower's inauguration. Opportunities to supply American program material may become even greater in Japan's burgeoning television industry.

Our cultural program must constantly be sensitive and responsive to new needs and opportunities. Policy suggestions are supposed to flow upward to Washington from the people who have intimate knowledge of the requirements of the field. There they are embodied in an over-all "country plan." The Area Assistant Director is a personal link between USIA headquarters and the posts overseas, which he visits at frequent intervals. Japan's problems were assured expert and sympathetic attention by the fact that Saxton Bradford, formerly cultural attaché in Tokyo, was appointed the first Assistant Director for the Far East.

What really matters, of course, is not administrative tidiness but the impact of the program upon the Japanese. Evaluation of such an intangible matter is always difficult. But the Japanese seem to accept the USIS program as an established institution of real utility. Few protests or demands for its termination are heard. On the contrary, regrets were widely expressed when the Tokyo Cultural Center had to be closed during most of 1952 for lack of a suitable building. In Hakodate 40,000 signatures were collected on petitions that the local center be continued. The willingness of some communities to provide financial support for binational centers is an indication that they are really valued.

Outlook for the Future

In the years ahead the United States will need to maintain a strong information and cultural program in Japan. Situated as it is on the periphery of the Communist bloc, Japan is one of the areas which it is crucial to hold for the free world. We hope that the Japanese themselves will share our objective of creating there "a politically stable, economically

viable nation that is capable of defense against internal subversion and external aggression and allied to the United
States and the free world." But Communist propagandists
systematically plant doubts and suspicions: that defense and
prosperity are not compatible, that Japan will be the tool
and not the beneficiary of a Western alliance. Our day-by-
day tacks into the shifting winds of world politics are sometimes hard for the Japanese to follow. If we are not to lose
their support by default, we must explain our actions and
our purposes, openly and frankly. The Voice of America
and government press services must put the American position on record, clearly and forcefully. Here as elsewhere, the
first and foremost objective of our information services must
be to support and publicize our foreign policy.

Unless a basic change in policy leads to over-all expansion
of official cultural activities, some reduction in the size and
scope of the program in Japan seems likely. The feeling of
special responsibility for the tutelage of the Japanese that
survives from the military occupation will gradually dimin-
ish. At the end of 1953 the mission in Japan was the third
largest field operation of the United States Information
Agency, measured by the total number of personnel. The
much larger program in Germany was also a carryover from
occupation. In India, a much more extensive country with
four times the population of Japan, the Agency used fewer
Americans to supervise and support a somewhat larger staff
of local employees.[38] The cuts in Japan are most likely to
come in the long-range, strictly cultural aspects of the program. The number of cultural centers may even be reduced
still further.

Limiting operations to a few of the largest cities may not,
however, be the wisest course. The citizens of Tokyo, Yokohama, Osaka, and Kobe are already best supplied with opportunities for education and information. They are more
likely to have contact with America and Americans in the
normal course of life. The community leaders there tend already to have an international outlook. Many smaller prefectural capitals offer better chances for pioneering work.

[38] U. S. Information Agency, *First Review of Operations, August-December
1953* (Washington: GPO, 1954), pp. 24-26.

There we are less likely to be talking to those who are already convinced. The new universities and libraries in these cities need help and support. By maintaining cultural centers throughout the country, we can give the Japanese a practical demonstration of our faith in the grassroots from which democracy is supposed to spring.

Private organizations will have to assume responsibility, therefore, for much of the long-range work of cultural cooperation. The Information Agency recognized this fact by doubling the allocation to its Office of Private Cooperation in 1953–54, despite an over-all budget cut. To name only a few of its diverse activities, this office stimulates private letter-writing to friends abroad, arranges for collection and redistribution of books and magazines, and obtains publications and exhibit materials from business firms. Early in 1953 it helped to arrange an exchange of musical salutes by recorded tape between Kansas City and Osaka. A number of American newspapers and syndicates have been persuaded to allow republication of anti-Communist cartoons in Japan.[39]

Both the Information Agency and the Japan Societies have a part to play, then, in coordinating private efforts. The two should be complementary rather than in conflict. From the broad perspective of policy, government officials can give assurance that projects will be in the national interest. From the narrower focus of bilateral relations, the Japan societies can advise on channels and contacts, on the interests and needs of the Japanese. But above all, in the constant flow of cultural relations between the two countries, coordinating agencies should be pumps rather than bottlenecks. We should count it fortunate when the spontaneous interests of the two peoples overflow beyond established channels.

[39] *Overseas Information Programs,* cited, pp. 1087-1101, 1209-1214.

PART IV
CONCLUSION

CHAPTER TEN

EXPERIENCE AND EXPECTATION

FROM A multitude of details we have tried to build up a composite picture of one hundred years of American cultural relations with Japan. In Part II we saw how these cultural contacts were related to Japan's persistent problems of economic growth, development of political and social institutions, and education. Part III traced the principal channels of communication and influence: through exchanges of teachers and students, through American missionaries, through acquaintance with each other's artistic heritage, and in recent years through government information programs. We must now attempt to assess the broader meaning of this century of experience. The choice of the historical approach to questions of cultural policy has involved a tacit assumption that the past has some meaning for the present.

Unfortunately, it is never easy to discern the meaning of any segment of human history. Meaning cannot be completely objective; it involves the values and interests of the interpreter. We run the danger of "salting" our own mine, of putting in the gold of interpretation that we triumphantly draw out again. By careful selection of evidence, the dogmatist can readily make history prove almost anything. The first obligation of the careful historian is to establish his facts according to the best standards of knowledge, to winnow out mythology and wishful thinking, to describe events in the context in which they occurred. Even in this we may not have been completely successful, for the modern history of Japan is a wilderness of data in which students are only beginning to map out paths of order.

How satisfying it would be if we could now establish definite positive correlations between the historical phenomena that we have studied. Some historians strive hopefully for the precision of a simple formula for causation:

"whenever A, then B." Do peaceful relations result whenever there is significant interchange of persons between two
countries? Does knowledge of the literature and art of another people lead to sharing of values and goals? If we could
be sure that these things are true, then a concerted effort at
cultural interchange might be the most direct way of building
a peaceful international society.

This case study of Japanese-American cultural relations
offers little evidence, alas, to support such optimistic generalizations. Analysis of our experience from this narrow point of
view would more likely lead to conclusions of cynicism or
despair. Cultural relations between Japan and America before 1941 were quite extensive and, on balance, clearly a positive contribution toward peace and cooperation. One could
hardly find a better instance of mutual influence between two
nations so different in basic culture. Race prejudice and the
immigration question did cast shadows. But of the thousands
of Japanese and Americans who had a chance to visit the other
country most brought back impressions that were favorable.
As teachers and technicians several hundred Americans had
played important roles in the modernization of Japan. Many
Japanese who were educated here found important places in
their own society. The Christian churches in Japan begun by
American missionaries exerted an intellectual force far out
of proportion to their size. Despite all these cultural bonds,
however, the essential policies of the two nations diverged
more and more widely, until in 1941 there came the splitting
rupture of war. Indeed, there had never been more conscious
attention to cultural relations than in the downhill decade
of the thirties. The stream of goodwill envoys from Japan
met a return flow of Americans bent upon serious study of
Japanese life and culture. The knowledge they gained did not
necessarily bring with it agreement; personal friendships
were submerged in national enmity. Add to this the experience of two wars with Germany, a country with which Americans had even closer ties, and one must conclude that cultural
interchange is certainly no guarantee of peace or political
coöperation.

The meaning that we draw from this past experience with
cultural relations is more likely to be usable if we focus

attention on the continuity of history instead of trying to establish formulas for cause and effect. As the philosopher Morris R. Cohen once said, "The past literally continues into the present. Past conditions, such as old ideas and habits, buildings, fields, and laws, continue to operate." [1] The problems that Japan faces today have been shaped by her past history. America's relation to Japan has been part of the growing involvement of the United States in world affairs. Our expectations for the future are related to historical experience, not through cyclical repetition, but through the persistence of past conditions and problems.

This sense of continuity between past and present is an essential basis for human action. The historical past provides a stable foundation upon which innovations can be made. One of the weaknesses of the American military occupation was that it tended to reject all of the Japanese past as bad and unusable. It did not take full advantage of the cultural ties that we have just reviewed. The Japanese themselves have had to grope for new continuities, chiefly with their experience in Meiji times, that would provide meaningful guides to reconstruction. For economy of effort they often seize upon salient parts of the past as symbols of a larger whole. Thus Commodore Perry and Townsend Harris, embellished somewhat by myth, became symbols of Japanese-American friendship. For the immediate practical purpose of establishing rapport and stimulating response, therefore, it is important that Americans be familiar with the record of past relations with the Japanese.

Far more important to our pursuit of meaning is the basic continuity in modern Japanese history. Since the opening of the country in 1854 Japan has been trying to find her place in a world of nation-states competing for power. In this process cultural relations with the United States clearly did not play anything like a decisive role. This emphasis on international power-politics may not be the perspective in which historians will ultimately see the events of the past century, but it is the interpretation according to which the Japanese nation has lived and acted. It also fits the events of

[1] Morris R. Cohen, *The Meaning of Human History* (La Salle, Ill.: Open Court Publishing Co., 1947), p. 107.

today. Japan is again—or still—seeking a secure place for herself, this time in a world dominated by two great power blocs.

A century ago the Japanese were keenly aware of the competing imperialistic drives of the European nations who urged the opening of their ports. The concessions forced from China as a result of the Opium War were an omen of their own possible fate. Commodore Perry's embassy simply offered an opportunity to yield to a more disinterested nation. For the next decade the crumbling regime of the Tokugawa Shoguns clung to the hope of again "driving away the barbarians." But the more resolute leaders who took control at the Meiji Restoration realized that Japan's only hope for independence lay in building up her unity and strength. This they sought to attain by a dynamic policy of Westernization.

The Meiji leaders naturally gave primary attention to the material bases of national power. With the help of British advisers, they built up a modern navy. For Japan's new conscript army they looked first to France for models, then to Germany. The government assumed primary responsibility for the heavy industries and communication systems vital to national defense. Agricultural development in Hokkaidō, in which General Capron, William S. Clark, and other Americans played an important part, was intended to secure the northern frontier against Russia, as well as to add to the supply of food. Even the system of public elementary education adapted from the American one was valued primarily as a way of mobilizing the energy and skills of all classes in the race for modernization and survival, rather than as a foundation for political democracy. Although Japanese intellectuals had a lively interest in the political and social ideas of the West, the national leaders gave a low priority to changes in these spheres. New legal codes and a constitution providing for parliamentary government might help to convince foreign powers that they could safely relinquish extraterritoriality, but such reforms were not intended to change the basic structure of power and control. Even so-called "liberal" politicians like Itagaki and Ōkuma put the national honor first. In the vital field of political institutions and ideology, therefore, American influence was at best superficial.

Until the century's end Americans watched with pride the

progress of the nation which was, in a sense, their protégé. In the protracted negotiations over revision of the unequal treaties, the United States tended to take the lead in support of full sovereignty for Japan. Individual Americans who had an appreciation of cultural relativity—Verbeck, Murray, Fenollosa, Hearn—cautioned the Japanese against modernizing too fast and indiscriminately, lest they lose their whole cultural heritage. By hard work and self-denial the Japanese seemed to be finding a secure place in the world. Only when this newly-created power became aggressive did we realize that it might threaten the *status quo* in China which Americans defended under the slogan of the Open Door. But American sentiment continued on the whole to support Japan through her first two military ventures. After the Chinese war of 1894–95 Japan could claim that she had been robbed by the intervention of three powers who were themselves far from disinterested. In the Russo-Japanese War she appeared only to be despoiling one of the robbers. Americans accepted the Japanese absorption of Korea with hardly a murmur of protest.

Speculations about the might-have-beens in Japanese history center on the quarter century from 1906 to 1931. In this period Japan's chances of attaining a satisfactory equilibrium were good. Acquisition of Formosa, Korea, the former Russian concessions in Manchuria, and the German islands in the Pacific that she received under League of Nations mandate gave her room for dynamic growth. Under pressure Japan abandoned her dubious venture in Siberia and returned Shantung to China. Despite strong authoritarian tendencies in the military services, business, and the parties themselves, Japan seemed during the twenties to be struggling toward real parliamentary government. The grant of suffrage to all adult males pointed the way to increased democratic control. Under the stimulus of World War I Japan's industrial plant had expanded greatly. The ties that American electrical manufacturers made with Japanese companies, described in Chapter Two, were merely one indication of her ability to compete in world trade. But heavy dependence on exports made the Japanese economy highly vulnerable to the onset of world depression. The breakdown of prosperity gave Japanese militarists a chance to try their plans for autarkic exploitation of all East Asia.

With Japan's future course of development suspended so delicately in the balance during this quarter-century, the weight of American influence in international affairs fell, it seems fair to say, on the wrong side. By remaining outside the League of Nations, the United States diminished the chances for success of an experiment in international order in which Japan joined in good faith. Our political life in the era of Harding and Coolidge was hardly a model that would evoke enthusiasm. In various fields of cultural relations one senses a decline, not in volume of activity but in relevance to essential problems. American teachers, for example, were being cast in the role of drill masters in English language, instead of being able to open up exciting new vistas of thought. Whatever gratitude Americans earned by their aid at the time of the great earthquake and fire of 1923 was wiped out by the insult of excluding all Japanese immigrants. If during the twenties the Western powers had been able to hold a less chaotic China to observance of her legal obligations, Japan might have had less provocation—and less temptation.[2] Finally, had American economic policies in the 1920's been wiser and more farsighted, they might have checked or mitigated the Great Depression of the 1930's, which helped to push the world down the path to war.

Mention of our own contributory negligence does not, however, excuse Japanese aggression during the 1930's as being a mere reaction to intolerable deprivation. In large part her action was a ruthless pursuit of ambitions for control over Asia that dated far back in Japanese history. Leadership was gravitating to elements in the population who were least affected by Western influence or inclined to interpret it cynically as cultural imperialism. By the end of the decade many Japanese were convinced that international political power was being radically redistributed, and that Germany and Italy should not be allowed to get all the spoils. Japan's place in the world was easily exaggerated and, with the

[2] John V. A. MacMurray emphasized this point in a memorandum he submitted to the State Department in 1935. Joseph C. Grew, *Turbulent Era: A Diplomatic Record of Forty Years, 1904–1945* (Boston: Houghton Mifflin, 1952), V. 2, pp. 929-930.

help of neo-Shintō mythology, given an aura of divine destiny. Perhaps the most serious miscalculation was the belief that the American people were so committed to ostrich-like neutrality that they would make no objection. Or, alternatively, that by a lightning blow at Pearl Harbor American power could be made ineffective long enough for Japanese hegemony over East Asia to become a *fait accompli*.

During the long years of World War II few Americans bothered to think seriously about the future of their Japanese adversary. Minds, men, and matériel were concentrated on checking and destroying the military might of the Axis. Most would have said that by their folly the Japanese had earned whatever fate befell them, whether it be atomic death or starvation. Although the American military occupation could hardly be called vindictive, it postponed the question of ultimate goals until by repentance and reform the Japanese had re-established their claim for consideration. Japan was to be, as Reischauer has aptly put it, "on probation, living apart from the rest of the world and having no influence on it." [8] Events since 1945 have destroyed the illusion that a permanently powerless Japan is desirable, or even possible. A power vacuum there would be a standing invitation to the new Communist imperialism of the Soviet Union and Red China. In a bipolar world the industrial capacity and technical skills of Japan become a valuable prize for either side. Once again we face the question that has been central since 1854: what is Japan's position to be in a world of power struggle?

Americans have not yet fully faced up to this question. Those who still think in terms of the "Initial Post-Surrender Policy" of 1945, which set the guide lines for the Occupation, hope wishfully that Japan's infant democracy can somehow be sheltered from the stern realities of world politics. Others assume too easily that we can manipulate Japan at will, that she will do whatever we want her to do. But Japan will be nobody's puppet; she will be working to re-establish her own position and prestige. If we are to have her co-operation, a common ground of policy must be found that

[8] Edwin O. Reischauer, *The United States and Japan* (Cambridge, Mass.: Harvard University Press, 1950), p. 37.

will satisfy the national interests of both the Americans and the Japanese.

First, let us define minimum requirements from the American point of view. Japan must contribute to her own defense against aggression from without. She must maintain a regime stable enough, and just enough, to reduce the danger of subversion from within. Her political and social institutions should be based on democratic participation and human dignity, although in form they need not resemble our own. Her economic resources and skills must be available for development of the rest of free Asia, without reviving the danger of imperialistic domination.

The Japanese see the essentials of policy from a somewhat different point of view. They recognize the necessity for defense, but fear that America will use Asians as mercenaries to fight Asians. Opinions on security against subversion go to two extremes: desire for tight government controls and fear that anti-Communism will be the entering wedge for resurgent totalitarianism. Above all, the Japanese want a self-sustaining, expanding economy, not merely a hand-to-mouth existence dependent upon American favors. The opportunity to trade on favorable terms they regard as vital. A nation just released from occupation is understandably sensitive about sovereignty and resents the fact that the United States, by virtue of her power and leadership in the free world, is able to control many of Japan's actions. To regain their country's bargaining power, the more calculating among the Japanese will not hesitate to make moves toward a Communist alternative that they do not really want.

The Japanese will turn our own arguments and actions against us. They point out that General MacArthur himself wrote renunciation of military force into their constitution. President Yanaihara Tadao of Tokyo University bases his absolute pacifism upon Christianity. "The words 'In God We Trust' are cut on the face of American coins," he writes. "If Americans really understood the meaning of that motto, they would know that what the Japanese people need today as they set out toward self-support and independence is not rearmament supported by America but the faith in God to preserve the truth." [4] Intellectuals like Tsuru Shigeto, Minami Hiroshi, and Ōyama Ikuo, who are presenting in articles and speeches a picture of America on the road to fascism, gain credence because in each case they have spent a long period in the United States. All our inconsistencies, our own sins against democracy, are quickly noted.

Inside all these fringes of difference, however, the Japanese and the American people do have a core of common interest. They want to live in essentially the same kind of free dynamic world. The problem is to expand the area of overlap in specific policy goals. The most urgent need is a material one—to find for Japan a prosperous place in the world economy. Direct American financial aid will help, but it promises to be limited in extent. The solution is more likely to come by a slow process of adjustment in which Americans can help the Japanese to stand on their own feet. Reductions in American import duties would give the Japanese an expanded dollar market. Domestic food production in Japan can be increased slightly, industrial efficiency improved, and new trade relations established with Southeast Asia and other parts of the non-Communist world. On questions of international politics Japanese and Americans need a much better understanding of each other's attitudes and goals. Differences resulting from misinterpretation of facts can be separated from those that are real. The real differences then may or may not be susceptible to compromise. Only so far as the two peoples find a community of interest on basic questions will they be able to experience the rich psychological rewards of cultural amity.

Cultural interchange can play an important part in improvement of bilateral relations, provided it contributes to the solution of basic political and economic problems, instead of seeking to evade them. Thanks to the continuity of history, the means available are already broadly familiar. In some cases the same sort of relations have been going on for close to a century. Let us recapitulate them briefly:

First, we are now better aware of the ways in which a relatively small input of *technical assistance* can produce sub-

[4] Yanaihara Tadao, "Minzoku to Heiwa (The People and Peace)," *Chūō Kōron*, V. 69 (January 1954), p. 144.

stantial economic results. Assistance can be transmitted either through governments or by contracts between private companies that will be mutually profitable.

Second, skills and special knowledge can be transmitted by *exchange of students*. At the same time, by living abroad both Americans and Japanese get a more detached view of their own interests and can make a more realistic appraisal of their neighbors. Personal friendships and favorable attitudes toward the host country may also result, but these should not be considered the primary goals.

Third, both knowledge and perspective can be brought to a much greater number of people by *interchange of teachers*. Movement of educators in both directions is particularly needed while Japan's new educational system is still adjusting its curricula, methods, and organization.

Fourth, *Christian missionaries* from America bring to Japan valuable resources for education, humanitarian work, and intellectual stimulation, which they are ready to place at the disposal of the leaders of the native churches. Now that emphasis is no longer exclusively on "conversion of heathens," the missionaries are more ready to recognize the inherent values of Japan's Buddhist and Shintō faiths.

Fifth, extensive *exchange of cultural materials* will help the two peoples to know and appreciate each other. Here traffic down the other side of the street, from Japan to America, is especially important. Japan can teach us a great deal about the place of simplicity, restraint, and aesthetic values in human living. Her advantages in cultural maturity and tradition will counterbalance America's material superiority.

Sixth, the only real innovations in methods are the *modern communications techniques* that governments now use to explain their actions and purposes to the people at large in foreign countries. The United States is speaking to Japan through the Voice of America, press releases, and the many sources of information supplied by the cultural centers. Through the Information Section of its embassy in Washington, the Japanese Government is beginning to speak openly and candidly in reply.

Will media like the film, radio, and television accelerate the whole process of cultural interchange, perhaps to the point where it can have more decisive influence? They do enable people in the mass to share directly, across barriers of distance and time, their cultural heritage and point of view. They carry messages of remarkable vividness and verisimilitude. But so many voices clamor for attention, each impression is so quickly blurred and supplanted by another, that the residue of understanding may actually be smaller than comes from indirect sources of information. In addition, these media have been so readily perverted to purposes of propaganda that they are already widely suspect. Governments and private parties alike bear a heavy responsibility for their proper use in the service of international understanding.

The newness of this sixth method of cultural communication is a reminder that history is emergent as well as continuous. Experience grows and changes by accretion. Japan does not have the same past today that she did fifty years ago. Those who look only at the feudal and authoritarian elements in Japan's heritage are inclined to be pessimistic about her future. But they ignore the more hopeful tendencies of the 1920's. In addition, the experience of defeat and occupation has changed Japan profoundly. Nearly seven years of American tutelage altered significantly the balance of internal forces, even if it did not produce complete democratization and social transformation. Workers and farmers, for example, greatly improved their position. Opportunities for education and social mobility have been broadened. On this new past the moving present can build toward the future.

One reason, therefore, for looking carefully at history is to determine how a current situation differs from previous ones. Along with new problems, there may be new possibilities, new resources that can be used in working out a solution.

Changes in the American role in world affairs and progress in international organization, for example, mean that our relations with Japan can now be placed in a broader framework than was ever possible before World War II. What really counts is Japan's relation to the free world, not exclusive ties to the United States. Other countries may be better suited than we are to offer Japan help and guidance. The economic experience of Britain, or of the Netherlands, or of Switzerland may be more relevant to Japan's problems than the American story of great resources and relative self-sufficiency. Europeans are better able to drive home the dangers of Communism. Japanese are inclined to discount American statements on this subject as the product of uninformed hysteria. Dr. Ferenc Nagy, former Prime Minister of the Hungarian Republic, and two other East European exiles who toured Japan in the spring of 1954 made a deep impression by their accounts of bitter personal experience with Communist rule. The Japanese need frequent opportunities to hear the opinions of politically-experienced and sophisticated Europeans of other than leftist convictions. In many cases a visit to Berlin might be more valuable for Japanese leaders than one to the United States.

Although Japan is blocked for the time being from full membership in the United Nations by the opposition of the Soviet Union, she has been able to profit from participation in the work of some of the specialized agencies. In the Economic Commission for Asia and the Far East she cooperates with Asian neighbors on problems of trade and development. Some of her requests for financial aid are better handled through the impartial scrutiny of the World Bank than by the political tests for direct American aid. The work and ideals of the United Nations Educational, Scientific and Cultural Organization have aroused particular enthusiasm in Japan. In addition to the official national commission, over one hundred cooperating organizations are united in a Federation of Unesco Associations (Nihon Unesco Kyōryoku-kai Remmei). In 1952 there were over 170 Unesco Student Clubs. Unesco's project for "translation of works representative of national culture" plans to make forty-one outstanding items of Japanese literature available in Western languages.[5] Cultural exchange that is world wide appeals to Japanese intellectuals, many of whom think that interest in American

[5] United Nations' Educational, Scientific and Cultural Organization, *Records of the General Conference, Seventh Session, Paris, 1952: Proceedings*, pp. 86-87; Haruki Takeshi, "Unesco Activities in Japan," *World Affairs Interpreter*, V. 22 (Spring 1951), pp. 76-87; *Nippon Times*, April 11, 1954.

literature and art was much overplayed during the occupation.

Cooperation between Japan and America within a world community might well be the keynote of future policy. Both common interests and differences of opinion now extend beyond the narrow limits of strictly bilateral relations. The basic economic and political problems require an over-all solution. As we work toward this, there will be ample opportunities for extension of the direct ties between the two peoples that have developed during a century of cultural relations.

Today Americans have a growing volume of cultural relations with Asian nations much newer than Japan, equally different in language and heritage, equally desirous of modernization and development in order to obtain a secure place in the world. This case study can produce no easy solutions for the problems involved. It can, perhaps, suggest some of the complexities and the patterns into which they may fall. It can underline the need for study of the particular cultural context in a spirit of humility and faith in humanity.

Despite the urgency of the current world crisis, we must not lose sight of the values in cultural relations that transcend collective national interest. As relations of men to men, they involve a rich range of motives and satisfactions. The desires of men to learn and to share are precious things that extend beyond national boundaries. In dealing with peoples throughout the world, Americans can give no better demonstration of their belief in supremacy of the individual, of their faith in free inquiry, than by a broad and spontaneous flood of cultural interchange that will overflow the main channel of official policy.

BIBLIOGRAPHICAL ESSAY

THE PURPOSE of this bibliography is to indicate the materials that have been most valuable for a study of cultural relations between the United States and Japan. Many items cited in the footnotes in order to document specific points are not repeated here. On the other hand, I have included a number of books and articles to which I have a general indebtedness for information and ideas. The ground that I have attempted to cover has been so broad that some pertinent material inevitably will have escaped my attention. Although I have tried to make extensive use of publications in the Japanese language, by force of circumstances I have been limited to what is available in the larger collections in the eastern United States.

GENERAL WORKS

No single work covers exactly the same ground as this study. Edwin O. Reischauer's excellent *The United States and Japan* (Cambridge, Mass.: Harvard University Press, 1950) is written from a broad cultural point of view, but on a higher level of generalization. In *The Western World and Japan: A Study in the Interaction of European and Asiatic Cultures* (New York: Knopf, 1950), George B. Sansom has chosen a much broader canvas—Japanese relations with the whole West up to about 1895. The essays by Nitobe Inazō and others in *Western Influences in Modern Japan: A Series of Papers on Cultural Relations* (Chicago: University of Chicago Press, 1931) are uneven in quality, but they contain much useful information. The Kaikoku Hyakunen Kinen Bunka Jigyōkai in Japan is now preparing a five-volume work entitled *Nichi-Bei Bunka Kōshō Shi (History of Japa-*

nese-American Cultural Relations), but unfortunately it was not available in time for use in writing this book.

Richard Heindel surveyed some of the high points in an article on "American Influence on Japan," *Social Studies,* V. 33 (May 1942), pp. 214-224. Two older articles suggested subjects for further study: J. Ingram Bryan, "Americans who have Helped to Make Japan," *Japan Magazine,* V. 2 (February 1912), pp. 560-563, and William Elliot Griffis, "American Makers of the New Japan," *Century Magazine,* V. 86 (August 1913), pp. 597-605. Shigehisa Tokutarō and Amano Keitarō, "Meiji Bunka Kankei Ō-Beijin Meiroku (List of Europeans and Americans who Contributed to Meiji Culture)," *Toshokan Kenkyū,* V. 10 (October 1937), pp. 547-572, was another fruitful source of leads.

Japanese-American cultural relations have been discussed more often in enthusiastic essays than in serious scholarly studies. The collections *Japan to America,* edited by Masaoka Naoichi (New York: Putnam, 1914), and *America to Japan,* edited by Lindsay Russell (New York: Putnam, 1915), combine reminiscences with exhortation. George H. Blakeslee, ed., *Japan and Japanese-American Relations: Clark University Addresses* (New York: Stechert, 1912) is more scholarly. Frank Livingstone Huntley, "Ideological Patterns: Japan and the United States," in William B. Willcox and Robert R. Hall, eds., *The United States in the Postwar World: Addresses Given at the 1945 Summer Conference of the University of Michigan* (Ann Arbor: University of Michigan Press, 1947), pp. 217-232, is a useful essay by a former teacher in Japan.

My information about modern Japanese history has come from many sources, but a few books have been particularly valuable for giving the flavor of life at different periods. William Elliot Griffis' *The Mikado's Empire* (New York: Harper, 1876; later editions with additions) is based on personal experience of the exciting days of early Meiji. Kiyohara Sadao, *Meiji Shoki Bunka Shi (Cultural History of the Early Meiji Period)* (Tokyo: Kembunkan, 1935) surveys the intellectual life of the same period. Japanese leaders sum up the achievements of the first half century in Ōkuma Shigenobu, ed., *Fifty Years of New Japan* (2 v.; London: Smith,

Elder & Co., 1909). *Meiji Taishō Shi (History of the Meiji and Taishō Periods)* (15 v.; Tokyo: Jitsugyō no Sekai-sha, 1929–1930) is a mine of detailed factual information. By virtue of its very impressionism, Miriam Beard, *Realism in Romantic Japan* (New York: Macmillan, 1930) gives an excellent picture of life during the 1920's. Shimizu Tomesaburō and Unno Kazuma, *Modern Japan* (Tokyo: Modern Japan Kankōkai, 1933) is very uneven but contains information not readily available elsewhere. The basic source for data on the early phases of the Occupation is the monthly *Summation of Non-Military Activities in Japan* (Tokyo: SCAP, September 1945 to August 1948). Harry Emerson Wildes, *Typhoon in Tokyo: The Occupation and Its Aftermath* (New York: Macmillan, 1954) is a critical summary by a participant.

As guides to the literature in western languages I have used the standard comprehensive bibliographies compiled by Wenckstern, Nachod, Praesent, and Haenisch and the annual lists published in the *Far Eastern Quarterly*. Hugh Borton, Serge Elisséeff, William W. Lockwood, and John C. Pelzel, *A Selected List of Books and Articles on Japan in English, French and German* (Cambridge, Mass.: Harvard University Press, 1954) is carefully chosen and up-to-date. Dorothy Purviance Miller, *Japanese-American Relations: A List of Works in the New York Public Library* (New York: the Library, 1921) opened up much of the material in older periodicals.

Like other workers in modern Japanese materials, I have felt the need for more adequate subject bibliographies but have been very grateful for those that do exist. Amano Keitarō's *Hōsei Keizai Shakai Rombun Sōran (Guide to Articles on Law, Politics, Economics, and Sociology)* (2 v.; Tokyo: Tōkō Shoin, 1927–1928) covers those fields through 1927. *Sōgō Kokushi Rombun Yōmoku (Catalogue of Selected Articles on Japanese History)*, compiled by the Ōtsuka Shigakkai, is rather difficult to use because the titles are grouped in such broad categories. Higashiuchi Yoshio, *Literature on Contemporary Japan* (Tokyo: 1951) lists materials collected for the Hoover Library at Stanford. The National Diet Library's *Zasshi Kiji Sakuin* now fills the crying need for a general index to periodicals.

PERIODICALS

English-language newspapers and magazines published in Japan have yielded a rich variety of material. By far the most useful was the *Japan Weekly Mail* (Yokohama), especially during the 1880's and 1890's when Captain Frank Brinkley was the active editor. The *Tokio Times* (Tokyo, 1877–1880) was edited by E. H. House. For the 1920's and early 1930's *Trans-Pacific,* the weekly edition of the *Japan Advertiser,* was searched for pertinent items. The *Japan Times Weekly* (1937–1941) and the *Japan News-Week* contained many feature articles on cultural subjects. The *Japan Magazine* (Tokyo, 1910–1935) has many articles on pertinent subjects, but they are often disappointingly sketchy and superficial. The daily *Nippon Times* and the English edition of *The Mainichi* have provided news articles on many developments in recent years.

A few short-lived periodicals have been devoted specifically to friendship between Japan and America. The America-Japan Society in Tokyo published *America-Japan* from July 1920 to July 1922. *Japan and America* was published monthly in New York from July 1901 to November 1903. The *New York Japan Review* (1913–1914) was intended "to interpret Japan to America and America to Japan."

For events in recent years I have used the *Mainichi Shimbun* and *Asahi Shimbun* in reduced-size monthly volumes with indexes, but I have made no effort to search Japanese-language papers for a longer period. The annual English supplements that the leading newspapers published before 1941, however, contained a good deal on cultural matters. The Asahi's volume was entitled *Present-day Japan.* The *Ōsaka Mainichi* published *Japan Today and Tomorrow,* and in 1938 put out a special supplement called *America and Japan in Amity and Trade.* This tradition is being continued in the postwar volumes called *New Japan* published by the Mainichi Newspapers. Many Japanese-language periodicals have been used for specific articles, some of which will be cited separately.

MANUSCRIPTS

The paucity of material on cultural relations in the dispatches and post records of United States ministers and consuls in Japan, now preserved in the National Archives, is added evidence of how little official attention was given such matters until recent years. The letterbooks of the United States Commissioner of Education (National Archives) during the 1870's contain some correspondence with Mori Arinori and Tanaka Fujimaro on matters pertaining to education. The confiscated records of the Japanese Navy Ministry, also in the National Archives, contain some papers on students sent to Annapolis. I have used limited portions of the microfilms of archives of the Japanese Ministry of Foreign Affairs, now in the custody of the Library of Congress.

In the absence of any historical society especially interested in locating and preserving material on relations with Japan, the number of available private papers is rather limited. The William Elliot Griffis Papers in the Rutgers University Library is perhaps the richest collection. Griffis carried on extensive correspondence with the *yatoi*—foreigners employed by Japan—and their relatives in preparation for a book that he never found time to write. The David Murray Papers in the Library of Congress contain copies of reports and speeches but no correspondence. The Connecticut Historical Society has letters written by Henry S. Munroe during his stay in Japan, 1872 to 1876, and papers concerning his teaching at the Kaitakushi Temporary School and the Kaisei Gakkō. My concerns were so general that I was not able to make full use of the detailed records in the hands of mission boards of various churches. I have examined some of the reports and letters from the Japan Mission of the American Board of Commissioners for Foreign Missions, now preserved in excellent order in the Houghton Library of Harvard University.

TOPICAL BIBLIOGRAPHY

Chapter 1. Eyes Across the Pacific

The theory of national character study is discussed by Margaret Mead in International Symposium on Anthropology, *Anthropology Today: An Encyclopedic Inventory* (Chicago: University of Chicago Press, 1953), pp. 642-647 and in David G. Mandelbaum, "On the Study of National Character," *American Anthropologist*, V. 55 (April-June 1953), pp. 174-187. Yabuki Keiki and others, *Gaijin no mitaru Nihon Kokuminsei (Japanese National Characteristics as seen by Foreigners)* (Tokyo: Chūō Kyōka Dantai Rengōkai, 1934) gives bibliographies and summaries of older works. Herman M. Spitzer, *Bibliography of Articles and Books Relating to Japanese Psychology* (Washington: Office of War Information, 1945) lists material in scholarly journals, in both Japanese and Western languages.

From the earlier American attempts to assess Japanese national character, I have chosen the following as both typical and systematic:

Lyman, Benjamin Smith. "The Character of the Japanese: A Study of Human Nature," *Journal of Speculative Philosophy*, V. 19 (April 1885), pp. 133-172.

Lowell, Percival. *The Soul of the Far East*. Boston: Houghton Mifflin, 1888.

Lowell, Percival. *Occult Japan, or the Way of the Gods. An Esoteric Study of Japanese Personality and Possession*. Boston: Houghton Mifflin, 1895.

Hearn, Lafcadio. *Japan: An Attempt at Interpretation*. New York: Macmillan, 1904.

Nitobe Inazo's *Bushido, the Soul of Japan: An Exposition of Japanese Thought* (Rev. ed.; New York: Putnam, 1905) strongly influenced the American image of Japan. So did the lectures that Nitobe gave while he was exchange professor in the United States, printed as *The Japanese Nation: Its Land, Its People, and Its Life, with Special Consideration to Its Relations with the United States* (New York: Putnam, 1912).

Ruth Benedict's *The Chrysanthemum and the Sword: Patterns of Japanese Culture* (Boston: Houghton Mifflin, 1946), was far the best of the attempts made during World War II to explain the enemy's behavior. John F. Embree, *The Japanese Nation: A Social Survey* (New York: Farrar & Rinehart, 1945) and Frederick S. Hulse, "A Sketch of Japanese Society," *Journal of the American Oriental Society*, V. 66 (July-September 1946), pp. 219-229, are both judicious attempts at generalization. The psychoanalytical approach is best represented by Geoffrey Gorer, "Themes in Japanese Culture," *Transactions of the New York Academy of Sciences,* Series 2, V. 5 (March 1943), pp. 106-124, and Weston La Barre, "Some Observations on Character Structure in the Orient: the Japanese," *Psychiatry,* V. 8 (August 1945), pp. 319-342. Lily Abegg's *The Mind of East Asia* (London: Thames & Hudson, 1952) is a more recent attempt to apply concepts borrowed from C. G. Jung to Oriental personality.

The more extreme pretensions of national character analysis have received professional criticism in John F. Embree, "Standardized Error and Japanese Character: A Note on Political Interpretation," *World Politics,* V. 2 (April 1950), pp. 439-443; Fred N. Kerlinger, "Behavior and Personality in Japan: A Critique of Three Studies of Japanese Personality," *Social Forces,* V. 31 (March 1953), pp. 250-258; and Douglas G. Haring, "Japanese National Character: Cultural Anthropology, Psychoanalysis, and History," *Yale Review,* V. 42 (Spring 1953), pp. 375-392. For Japanese criticism and amplification of Ruth Benedict's work see the papers in *Minzokugaku Kenkyū,* V. 14 (1949), pp. 263-297; Kawashima Takeyoshi's "Giri," in *Shisō,* No. 327 (September 1951), pp. 21-28, and his " 'On' no Ishiki no Jittai (A Field Study of Consciousness of 'On')," *Chūō Kōron,* V. 66 (March 1951), pp. 119-129. Hasegawa Nyozekan's *Nihonjin Kishitsu (The Japanese Temperament)* (Tokyo: O-cha-no-mizu Shobō, 1950) is an interesting analysis in more traditional terms.

Japanese analysis of the United States and of American character has been less systematic. I have found these accounts to be particularly useful:

Kanzaki Kiichi. "Beikoku Kokuminsei Kanken (A Personal View of American National Character)," *Gaihō Jihō,* no. 539 (May 15, 1927), pp. 36-46.
Kawashima Takeyoshi. "Amerikajin no Seikatsu Ishiki (Daily Life Consciousness of Americans)," *Kaizō,* V. 31 (July 1950), pp. 64-67.
Matsuzawa Atsushi. *Amerika no 'Wairudo Uesuto' wo Tembō shite (A View of the American Wild West).* Tokyo: Aikōdō, 1933.
Natori Junichi. *Amerika no Seishin Bunka: Amerika Tamashii*

no *Kenkyū* (*The Spiritual Culture of America: A Study of the American Spirit*). Nagano: Shinyūsha, 1948.

Noguchi Yonejirō. "Beikokujin ni Atau (To the Americans)," *Kaizō*, V. 3 (October 1921), pp. 111-122.

Suma Yakichirō. *Beikoku oyobi Beikokujin* (*America and Americans*). Tokyo: Dai Nihon Yūbenkai Kōdansha, 1941.

Suzuki Hanzaburō. *Beikoku Kokuminsei no Shin Kenkyū* (*A New Study of American National Character*). Tokyo: Rakuyōdō, 1916.

Takagi Yasaka. *Amerika*. Tokyo: Meizen Shobō, 1948.

Tsurumi Yūsuke. *Hokubei Yūzeiki* (*Account of a Lecture Tour in North America*). 2d ed. Tokyo: Dai Nihon Yūbenkai Kōdansha, 1928.

Tsurumi Yūsuke. *Ō-Bei Tairiku Yūki* (*Travels on the European and American Continents*). Tokyo: Dai Nihon Yūbenkai Kōdansha, 1933.

No study exists which explores carefully the relations between anti-Japanese prejudice in the United States and the broader course of relations between the two countries. The historical portion of Carey McWilliams' *Prejudice: Japanese-Americans; Symbol of Racial Intolerance* (Boston: Little Brown, 1945) is suggestive, but it is strongly colored by his self-conscious liberalism. Ichihashi Yamato, *Japanese in the United States: A Critical Study of the Problems of the Japanese Immigrants and Their Children* (Stanford: Stanford University Press, 1932) summarizes much factual information.

Richard L.-G. Deverall, *The Great Seduction: Red China's Drive to Bring Free Japan behind the Iron Curtain* (Tokyo: Author, 1953) gives some striking examples of anti-American propaganda current in Japan. For a Japanese view of its causes and strength, see Fukuda Sadayoshi, "Han-Bei Shisō (Anti-American Thought)," *Bungei Shunjū*, V. 31 (September 1953), pp. 76-82. Usui Yoshimi, "Uchinada," *Kaizō*, V. 34 (August 1953), pp. 116-122, gives a quite detailed account of that key incident.

Chapter 2. Economic Cooperation

For careful analysis of Japan's current economic dilemmas, I am greatly indebted to the series of discussions of

"Japanese Trade and Investment Problems" at the Council during the winter of 1952–53, and to the working papers that Jerome B. Cohen prepared for that group. The annual *Economic Survey of Japan* prepared by the Economic Counsel Board of the Japanese government summarizes both trends and statistics. Edward A. Ackerman appraises Japan's potentialities in resource development in *Japan's Natural Resources and Their Relation to Japan's Economic Future* (Chicago: University of Chicago Press, 1953).

The historical work of broadest scope is G. C. Allen's *A Short Economic History of Modern Japan, 1867–1937* (London: Allen & Unwin, 1946). G. C. Allen and Audrey G. Donnithorne, *Western Enterprise in Far Eastern Economic Development: China and Japan* (London: Allen & Unwin, 1954) summarizes much material but makes no detailed original researches. Japan's prewar economy is analyzed from several angles in E. B. Schumpeter, ed., *The Industrialization of Japan and Manchukuo, 1930–1940; Population, Raw Materials and Industry* (New York: Macmillan, 1940), Jerome B. Cohen's *Japan's Economy in War and Reconstruction* (Minneapolis: University of Minnesota Press, 1949) covers the war and immediate postwar period very thoroughly. T. A. Bisson reports on SCAP's experiment in deconcentration of Japanese industry and finance in *Zaibatsu Dissolution in Japan* (Berkeley: University of California Press, 1954).

Bruce F. Johnston interprets the key role of agricultural development since the beginning of the Meiji era in "Agricultural Productivity and Economic Development in Japan," *Journal of Political Economy*, V. 59 (December 1951), pp. 498-513. Documents concerning government action are collected in *Meiji Zenki Kannō Jiseki Shūroku (Archives concerning the Promotion of Agriculture during the Early Meiji Period)* (2 v.; Tokyo: Dai Nihon Nōkai, 1939). Azuma Tōsaku, *Meiji Zenki Nōsei Shi no Sho-mondai (Problems in the History of Agricultural Policy in Early Meiji)* (Tokyo: Jinsei Shoin, 1936) and Okutani Matsuharu, *Kindai Nihon Nōsei Shiron (Essays on the History of Agricultural Policy in Modern Japan)* (Tokyo: Ikuseisha, 1938) interpret some of this material. The importation of foreign books, plants, tools, and techniques is treated in Tsuge Tsuyoshi, *Kindai Nihon Nōshi Kenkyū (Studies in the Agricultural History of Modern Japan)* (Tokyo: Hikari Shobō, 1943) and in Koike Motoyuki, "Meiji Shoki ni okeru Nōgyō Gijutsu no Hattatsu (The Development of Agricultural Techniques in Early Meiji)," in Keiō Gijuku Keizai-shi Gakkai, *Meiji Shoki Keizai-shi Kenkyū*, V. 1, pp. 29-77.

There is an abundance of good material on the Hokkaidō experiment and the part that Americans played in it. I have used the general accounts in Takeuchi Umpei, *Hokkaidō Shiyō (A Summary History of Hokkaidō)* (Hakodate: Hakodate Public Library, 1933) and in the third volume of *Shinsen Hokkaidō Shi (New History of Hokkaidō)* (7 v.; Tokyo: Hokkaidō Chō, 1937). John A. Harrison's *Japan's Northern Frontier: A Preliminary Study in Colonization and Expansion with Special Reference to the Relations of Japan and Russia* (Gainesville, Fla.: University of Florida Press, 1953) is the best account in English. *American Influence upon the Agriculture of Hokkaidō, Japan* (Sapporo: Tōhoku Imperial University College of Agriculture, 1915) is an important pamphlet. Wakabayashi Isao, *Hokkaidō Kaitaku Hiroku (Secret Records of the Colonization of Hokkaidō)* (2 v.; Sapporo: Gekkan Gakuin, 1949) adds some new information.

Reports and Official Letters to the Kaitakushi (Tokyo: Kaitakushi, 1875) is the official account of the work of General Horace Capron and other members of the American mission. Capron's career is discussed in Merritt Starr, "General Horace Capron, 1804-1885," *Journal of the Illinois State Historical Society*, V. 18 (July 1925), pp. 259-349, and in Tanimura Issa, *Kēpuron Shōgun (General Capron)* (Tokyo: 1937). John A. Harrison, "The Capron Mission and the Colonization of Hokkaidō, 1868-1875," *Agricultural History*, V. 25 (July 1951), pp. 135-142, is more realistic about the shortcomings of the mission.

The work of William Smith Clark and his successors at Sapporo is described in *A Historical Sketch of the College of Agriculture, Tohoku Imperial University: What America has done for a Japanese Government College* (Sapporo: Tōhoku Imperial University, 1915) and in *The Semi-Centennial of the Hokkaidō Imperial University, Japan, 1876-1926*

(Sapporo: Hokkaidō Imperial University, 1927). Ōshima Masatake has written from personal recollection about *Kurāku Sensei to sono Deshitachi (Professor Clark and his Pupils)* (Tokyo: Shinkyō Shuppansha, 1948). The *Fifth Annual Report of Sapporo Agricultural College, Japan* and the *Sixth Report of the Sapporo Agricultural College, covering the years 1881–1886 inclusive* contain much information on curriculum and extension work. D. H. Davis, "Agricultural Occupation of Hokkaidō," *Economic Geography*, V. 10 (October 1934) appraises the lasting American influence upon agricultural patterns in the northern island.

For current problems of Japanese agriculture I have used Ackerman's book on resources and several articles on land reform:

Campbell, Colin D. "Weak Points in the Japanese Land Reform Program," *Journal of Farm Economics*, V. 34 (August 1952), pp. 361-368.

Gilmartin, William M. and W. I. Ladejinsky "The Promise of Agrarian Reform in Japan," *Foreign Affairs*, V. 26 (January 1948), pp. 312-324.

"Japan's Land Reform." *Fuji Bank Bulletin*, V. 4 (May 1953), pp. 22-34.

Trewartha, Glenn T. "Land Reform and Land Reclamation in Japan," *Geographical Review*, V. 40 (July 1950), pp. 376-396.

The Livestock Industry of Japan, Foreign Agriculture Circular, FLM 1-52 (Washington: Office of Foreign Agricultural Relations, U.S. Department of Agriculture, 1952) weighs the possibilities of increased production of animal products.

The industrial history of modern Japan has received much less attention than agricultural history. Horie Yasuzō has published two important articles: "An Outline of the Rise of Modern Capitalism in Japan," *Kyoto University Economic Review*, V. 11 (July 1936), pp. 99-115, and "Government Industries in the Early Years of the Meiji Era," same, V. 14 (January 1939), pp. 67-87. Edwin P. Reubens' "Foreign Capital in Economic Development: A Case Study of Japan," *Milbank Memorial Fund Quarterly*, V. 28 (April 1950), pp. 173-190, is excellent. The most detailed work is the *Meiji Kōgyō Shi (Industrial History of the Meiji Era)* (Tokyo:

Kōgakkai Meiji Kōgyō Shi Hakkōsho, 1929-1931). The fifth volume concerns the electrical industries that I have used as a case study. Details on American-linked firms are given in D. F. G. Eliot, "Twenty-five Years of Successful Cooperation in Japan," *Far Eastern Review*, V. 20 (February 1924), pp. 83-87, and "Linked with America in Big Industry: Success of the Shibaura Engineering Works," same, V. 18 (November 1922), pp. 665-669. Terashima Masashi, *Creative Nippon: An Epic of Japan's Scientific Achievements* (Tokyo: *Nippon Times*, 1943) makes extravagant claims of invention but has some useful information about prewar science and technology.

Jerome B. Cohen's "Private Point Four in Japan," *Fortune*, V. 47 (April 1953), pp. 148-149, 184-188, is the best summary of the current phase of American technical assistance. *Japanese Industry Today: Foreign Investment Possibilities, 1952* (Tokyo: Foreign Capital Research Society, 1952), and Takita Kazuo, "Air Transportation Today," *Contemporary Japan*, V. 22 (1954), pp. 612-632, add some details. Most of my information about the number and type of assistance contracts came from Japanese and American newspapers.

For the history of the Japanese labor movement I have used Hattori Korefusa, *Monogatari Nihon no Rōdō Undō (Narrative History of the Japanese Labor Movement)* (Tokyo: Riron-sha, 1953) and the first volume of Hosotani Matsuta's *Nihon Rōdō Undō Shi (History of the Japanese Labor Movement)* (Tokyo: Dōyūsha, 1948). *Saikin no Shakai Undō (Social Movements in Recent Times)* (Tokyo: Kyōchō-kai, 1929) is an invaluable compilation of facts. *The Socialist and Labour Movement in Japan* (Kobe: Japan Chronicle, 1921) gives a picture of expansion during World War I. Paul Scharrenberg, "The Labor Movement in Japan," *American Federationist*, V. 37 (July 1930), pp. 809-818, is an assessment by an American labor leader who had mixed feelings about the Japanese.

SCAP action in the labor field is discussed in the *Final Report of the Advisory Committee on Labor: Labor Policies and Programs in Japan,* and in Miriam S. Farley's *Aspects of Japan's Labor Problems* (New York: John Day, 1950). Ayusawa Iwao surveys postwar "Developments in Organized Labor" in *Contemporary Japan*, V. 21 (1952–1953), pp. 225-245, 410-424, 541-554. Various short articles by Richard Deverall published in the *American Federationist* and *International Free Trade Union News* during 1953 and 1954 gave eyewitness accounts of developments in Japan. Lewis L. Lorwin's *The International Labor Movement: History, Policies, Outlook* (New York: Harper, 1953) provided a broader context. Solomon B. Levine's "Prospects of Japanese Labor," *Far Eastern Survey*, V. 23 (May 1954), pp. 65-70, (July 1954), pp. 107-110, was the latest account available at the time of writing.

Chapter 3. Institutions and Ideology

My problem in writing this chapter has been to find, amid the plethora of material on Japanese political and social development *per se,* information which would indicate the extent and nature of American influence. Before World War II the relations were often tenuous. With the military occupation American influence and guidance became pervasive, but as yet we have only interim reports on the success and durability of the many reforms and changes.

The most thoughtful, and thought-provoking, account of modern Japanese political history is Robert A. Scalapino's *Democracy and the Party Movement in Prewar Japan: The Failure of the First Attempt* (Berkeley: University of California Press, 1953). In *The Beginnings of Political Democracy in Japan* (Baltimore: Johns Hopkins Press, 1950), Ike Nobutaka discusses the events of early Meiji in greater detail and from a more optimistic point of view. Three books were useful for the history of social and political thought:

Kada Tetsuji. *Meiji Shoki Shakai Keizai Shisō Shi (History of Social and Political Thought in the Early Meiji Period).* Tokyo: Iwanami Shoten, 1937.

Rōyama Masamichi. *Nihon ni okeru Kindai Seijigaku no Hattatsu (The Development of Modern Political Science in Japan).* 2d ed. Tokyo: Jitsugyō no Nihon-sha, 1949.

Shimoide Junkichi. *Meiji Shakai Shisō Kenkyū (Studies in Meiji Social Thought).* Tokyo: Asano Shoten, 1932.

For constitutional development I have drawn upon the encyclopedic *Dai Nihon Kensei Shi (Constitutional History of Japan)* (10 v.; Tokyo: Hōbunkan, 1927–1928) by Ōtsu Junichirō, and two works by Osatake Takeshi: *Nihon Kensei Shi Taikō (Outline of Japanese Constitutional History)* (2 v.; Tokyo: Nihon Hyōron-sha, 1938–1939), and *Nihon Kensei Shi no Kenkyū (Studies in Japanese Constitutional History)* (Tokyo: Ichigensha, 1943).

Several works discuss American influence more explicitly. Robert A. Wilson has given a careful account of "The Seitaisho: A Constitutional Experiment," in *Far Eastern Quarterly*, V. 11 (May 1952), pp. 297-304. William Elliot Griffis' *Verbeck of Japan, A Citizen of No Country* (New York: Revell, 1900), is the only biography of that important American, but it is disappointingly vague about his work as political adviser. President Grant's visit in 1879 is described in John Russell Young, *Around the World with General Grant* (2 v.; New York: American News Co., 1879). *Guranto Shōgun to no Go-taiwa Hikki (Memorandum of the Conversation between His Majesty and General Grant)* (Tokyo: Kokumin Seishin Bunka Kenkyūjo, 1937) is an important document. Kaneko Kentarō's *Kempō Seitei to Ō-Beijin no Hyōron (The Establishment of the Constitution and the Opinions of Europeans and Americans)* (Tokyo: Nihon Aonenkam, 1937) gives American reactions to the Meiji constitution. Kaneko's own role is detailed in *Teikoku Kempō to Kaneko Haku (The Imperial Constitution and Count Kaneko)* (Tokyo: Dai Nihon Yūbenkai Kōdansha, 1942). Inada Masatsugu, "Kempō Kisō no Sankō Shiryō ni tsuite (Reference Materials for Drafting the Constitution)," *Kokka Gakkai Zasshi*, V. 55 (October 1941), pp. 1170-1194; (November 1941), pp. 1327-1357, added some details about literary influences. Ebihara Hachirō's "Sōkō Nihonjin Aikoku Dōmei Shimatsu (An Account of the Japanese Patriotic League in San Francisco)," *Meiji Bunka Kenkyū*, no. 2 (1934), pp. 98-117, pointed out the significance of America as a haven for political refugees. American connections with the early Socialist movement in Japan are discussed in Kakehi Mitsuaki, "Protestantism and Socialist Movement in Japan," *Contemporary Japan*, V. 16 (July-September 1947), pp. 285-291, and Abe Kōzō, "Meiji Kōki ni okeru Kirisuto-kyō to Shakai-shugi (Christianity and Socialism in the Latter Part of Meiji)," *Riron,* V. 4 (January 1950), pp. 1-13.

A good account of the enthusiasm for democracy during World War I and immediately after is found in Sugiyama Kenji, "Social Thinking in Japanese Universities and Colleges," *Japan Mission Year Book, 1930,* pp. 195-208. The essays that started the controversy are reprinted in the first volume of *Yoshino Sakuzō Hakushi Minshu-shugi Ronshū (Collected Essays on Democracy by Dr. Yoshino Sakuzō)* (Tokyo: Shin Kigen-sha, 1946). Yoshino's address on "Japan's Trend to Democracy," *Living Age,* V. 309 (May 28, 1921), pp. 512-518, is an interesting statement. The *Chūō Kōron* for May 1933 published a number of articles commemorating Yoshino's career, of which Sasa Hiroo's "Yoshino Sakuzō Hakushi to Demokurashī (Dr. Yoshino Sakuzō and Democracy)" is most informative. Kikukawa Tadao's *Gakusei Shakai Undō Shi (History of Student Social Movements)* (Tokyo: Kaiguchi Shoten, 1947) shows how more extreme leftist elements took over the democratic movement. The standard work on counter-movements to the right is now Kinoshita Hanji, *Nihon Fashizumu Shi (History of Japanese Fascism)* (3 v.; Tokyo: Iwasaki Shoten, 1950–1951).

The few studies of American government and politics that Japanese made before 1941 tend to be formal and legalistic. Minobe Tatsukichi's *Beikoku Kempō no Yurai oyobi Tokushitsu (Origin and Special Characteristics of the American Constitution)* (5th ed.; Tokyo: Yuhikaku, 1946) is an outstanding example. Fujii Shinichi's *Beikoku Seitō Seiji no Kansoku (A Survey of American Party Government)* (Tokyo: Waseda Daigaku Shuppanbu, 1927) explores our political history. Professor Takagi Yasaka's *Beikoku Seiji Shi Jōsetsu (Introduction to American Political History)* is limited almost entirely to the period before 1800.

Political Reorientation of Japan: September 1945 to September 1948: Report of Government Section, Supreme Commander for the Allied Powers (2 v.; Washington: GPO, 1949) is an official history with a valuable companion volume of documents. Written in 1948, it is more frank about matters like American responsibility for drafting the new Japanese constitution than might be expected. The vital question is whether in practice the new political forms really are representative and democratic. The postwar parties were studied by Kenneth E. Colton, "Pre-war Political Influences in Post-war Conservative Parties," *American Political Science Review,* V. 42 (October 1948), pp. 940-957; John Saffell, "Japan's Post-war Socialist Party," same, pp. 957-969; and Justin Williams, "Party Politics in the New Japanese Diet," same (December 1948), pp. 1163-1180. Two reports by Robert A. Scalapino are extremely perceptive: "Politics and Public Opinion in Japan," *Foreign Policy Reports,* V. 27 (March 15, 1951), pp. 2-11; and "Japan and the General Elections," *Far Eastern Survey,* V. 21 (October 29, 1952), pp. 149-154. Robert E. Ward gives a valuable account of "Patterns of Stability and Change in Rural Japanese Politics" in University of Michigan, Center for Japanese Studies, *Occasional Papers,* no. 1, pp. 1-6.

The character and methods of the traditional Japanese bureaucracy are described in Milton J. Esman, "Japanese Administration—A Comparative View," *Public Administration Review,* V. 7 (Spring 1947), pp. 100-112. Foster Roser writes of his own experience in "Establishing a Modern Merit System in Japan," in *Public Personnel Review,* V. 11 (October 1950), pp. 199-206. Another important contribution to the subject of public administration is Ardath W. Burks' "A Note on the Emerging Administrative Structure of the Post-Treaty Japanese National Government," University of Michigan, Center for Japanese Studies, *Occasional Papers,* no. 3, pp. 47-58.

Miyake Masatarō, *An Outline of the Japanese Judiciary* (2d ed.; Tokyo: Japan Times and Mail, 1935) describes the prewar legal system. Alfred C. Oppler, Chief of the Legal Section of SCAP, gives general accounts of postwar changes in "Courts and Law in Transition," *Contemporary Japan,* V. 21 (1952), pp. 19-55; and "The Reform of Japan's Legal and Judicial System under Allied Occupation," *Washington Law Review,* V. 24 (August 1949), pp. 290-324. Special phases of code revision are discussed in Richard B. Appleton, "Reforms in Japanese Criminal Procedure under Allied Occupation," *Washington Law Review,* V. 24 (November 1949), pp. 401-430, and Kurt Steiner, "Postwar Changes in the Japanese Civil Code," same, V. 25 (August 1950), pp. 286-312. Wagatsuma Sakae, "Guarantee of Fundamental Human Rights under the Japanese Constitution," *Washington Law Review*, V. 26 (May 1951), pp. 145-165, is another authoritative article in the same series. *Recent Developments in the Field of Criminal Justice of Japan* (Tokyo: Criminal Affairs Bureau, General Secretariat, Supreme Court of Japan, 1950) describes the actual working of the courts under the new rules of procedure.

American influence upon local government before 1945 came almost exclusively through the Tokyo Institute of Municipal Research. *Tōkyō Shisei Chōsakai to sono Jigyō (The Tōkyō Institute of Municipal Research and Its Work)* (Tokyo: Tokyo Shisei Chōsakai, 1948) gives a brief summary of its history and achievements. Tsurumi Yūsuke, "Gotō Haku to Biādo Hakushi (Count Gotō and Dr. Beard)," *Toshi Mondai*, V. 8 (June 1929), pp. 1267-1280, relates the circumstances under which Charles A. Beard came to Japan as a consultant. Beard gives his own version in "American Influence on Municipal Government in the Orient," *National Municipal Review*, V. 14 (January 1925), pp. 7-11. His book on *The Administration and Politics of Tokyo: A Survey and Opinions* (New York: Macmillan, 1923) and "Memorandum Relative to the Reconstruction of Tokyo, presented to Viscount S. Goto," *Far Eastern Review*, V. 21 (June-July 1925), pp. 252-256, are important documents.

The intent of Occupation reforms in local government is stated in *Political Reorientation of Japan*, V. 1, pp. 260-290. Professor George A. Warp of the University of Minnesota makes a survey of results in "Nihon no Chihō Gyōsei ni kansuru Jakkan no Kōsatsu (Some Reflections in Regard to Local Administration in Japan)," *Toshi Mondai*, V. 43 (October 1952), pp. 1-33. His critical conclusions are summarized in " 'Americanization' in Japan," *National Municipal Review*, V. 41 (October 1952), pp. 443-448, and "In Our Image and Likeness," same, V. 42 (April 1953), pp. 175-178, 188. Okuno Seiryō, *Amerika no Tabi (American Travels)* (Tokyo: Chihō Zaimu Kyōkai, 1951), describes a visit to America to study local government and finance. *Report on Japan-American*

Pacific Coast Mayor's Conference, Tokyo Metropolis, October 30th-November 10th, 1951 (Tokyo: Liaison Office, Tokyo Metropolitan Government, 1952) is a record of another bilateral venture in this field. The most recent survey of tendencies is Kurt Steiner's "Local Government in Japan: Reform and Reaction," *Far Eastern Survey*, V. 23 (July 1954), pp. 97-102.

For a general account of the women's rights movement in Japan I have used Takamure Itsue, *Nihon Josei Shakai Shi (Social History of Japanese Women)* (Ōsaka: Shin Nihonsha, 1948). *Women of the Pacific: Being a Record of the Proceedings of the First Pan-Pacific Women's Conference . . .* (Honolulu: Pan-Pacific Union, 1928), contains some good material, including a paper by Ichikawa Fusae on the "Woman Suffrage Movement in Japan." Ide Kikue's "History and Problems of the Women's Suffrage Movement in Japan," *Mid-Pacific Magazine*, V. 36 (September 1928), pp. 217-222, was prepared for the same conference. Tanaka Sumiko, *Advance of Women in Japan the Past Six Years* (Washington: Women's Bureau: U.S. Department of Labor, 1952) summarizes the postwar changes. The new legal relations are described by Wagatsuma Sakae in "Democratization of the Family Relation in Japan," *Washington Law Review*, V. 25 (November 1950), pp. 405-426. By far the most perceptive account of women's experiences during the post-war years is Mishima Sumie's *The Broader Way: A Woman's Life in the New Japan* (New York: John Day, 1953).

Chapter 4. New Education for Japan?

I have used two general histories of Japanese education: Tsuji Kōzaburō, *Dai Nihon Kyōiku Tsūshi (General History of Japanese Education)* (Tokyo: Meguro Shoten, 1933) and Takahashi Shunjō, *Zōtei Kaihan Nihon Kyōiku Shi (History of Japanese Education, Revised and Enlarged)* (Tokyo: Kyōiku Kenkyūkai, 1929). Fujihara Kiyozō's *Meiji Taishō Shōwa Kyōiku Shisō Gakusetsu Jimbutsu Shi (History of Educational Thought, Systems, and Personalities during Meiji, Taishō, and Shōwa)* (4 v.; Tokyo: Tōa Seikeisha and Nihon Keikokusha, 1942–1944) is a far more comprehensive work, but it was obtained only when research was already well advanced. *Meiji Ikō Kyōiku Seido Hattatsu Shi (History of the Development of the Educational System since the Beginning of Meiji)* (12 v.; Tokyo: Mombushō Uchi Kyōiku Shi Hensankai, 1938–1939) prints a wealth of material from official archives. The most systematic historical accounts in English, Kikuchi Dairoku's *Japanese Education: Lectures Delivered in the University of London* (London: John Murray, 1909) and Hugh L. Keenleyside and A. F. Thomas, *History of Japanese Education and Present Educational System* (Tokyo: Hokuseido, 1937) are both disappointingly formal and impersonal. The fourth and fifth volumes of the *Proceedings of the Seventh Biennial Conference of the World Federation of Education Associations, Tokyo, Japan, August 2-7 1937* (5 v.; Tokyo: WFEA, 1938) contain many valuable papers presented by the Japanese delegates. The only attempt at general treatment of the subject of this chapter is Kaigo Tokiomi's "The American Influence in the Education of Japan," *Journal of Educational Sociology*, V. 26 (September 1952), pp. 9-15.

For the first phase of American influence I have drawn heavily from my unpublished doctoral dissertation, "American Influence in the Education of Meiji Japan, 1868–1912" (Harvard University, 1950). Fujihara Kiyozō, *Meiji Kyōiku Shisō Shi (History of Meiji Educational Thought)* (Tokyo: n.p., 1909) and Inatomi Eijirō, *Meiji Shoki Kyōiku Shisō no Kenkyū (A Study of the Educational Thought of the Early Meiji Period)* (Tokyo: Sōgansha, 1944) are both good specialized treatments of this period. Yanagida Izumi, "Mori Arinori to sono Kyōiku Shisō (Mori Arinori and his Educational Thought)," *Atarashii Kyōshitsu*, V. 3 (January 1948), pp. 48-58, covers new ground. Material on the work of David Murray, in addition to the Murray papers in the Library of Congress, is found in *In Memoriam: David Murray, Ph.D. . . .* (New York: Privately printed, 1915) and in the *Mombushō Nempō (Annual Reports of the Department of Education)* for 1874 to 1877. *Education in Japan: A Series of Letters Addressed by Prominent Americans to Arinori Mori* (New York: Appleton, 1873) contains opinions that may have had some influence. W. E. Griffis describes

"The Tokei Normal School" in *College Courant*, V. 14 (January 3, 1874), pp. 3-4. *Hompō Ongaku Kyōiku Shi (History of Music Education in Japan)* (Tokyo: Ongaku Kyōikusho Shuppan Kyōkai, 1938), compiled by the Nihon Kyōiku Ongaku Kai, discusses Luther Whiting Mason's work in introducing music in Japanese schools. For the beginnings of physical education instruction, see Paul C. Phillips, "George A. Leland," *Amherst Graduates' Quarterly*, V. 14 (November 1924), pp. 29-33.

The influence of American progressive education in Japan during the 1920's is much less well documented. The third volume of Fujihara's *Meiji Taishō Shōwa Kyōiku Shisō Gakusetsu Jimbutsu Shi* contains some good material, and Umene Satoru surveys the subject in "Nihon no Shin-kyōiku Undō: Taishōki Shingakkō ni tsuite no Jakkan no Nōto (The New Education Movement in Japan: Some Notes on the New Schools of the Taishō Period)," in Tōkyō Kyōiku Daigaku Kyōikugaku Kenkyūshitsu, *Nihon Kyōiku Shi* (Tokyo: Kaneko Shobō, 1951), pp. 161-291. Carleton Washburne, *Remakers of Mankind* (New York: John Day, 1932), pp. 12-40, gives the impressions of one of America's leading progressive educators. Marie Swabey's "The Pan Pacific New Education Conference," *School and Society*, V. 42 (November 9, 1935), pp. 653-654, describes the declining phases of the movement. Influence surviving even the war is apparent, however, in the comments by Japanese reported in Alice Miel, "Education's Part in Democratizing Japan," *Teachers College Record*, V. 55 (October 1953), pp. 10-19.

Education from the middle thirties through 1945 was dominated by official nationalistic ideology. Ienaga Saburō has explored the origins of the Imperial Rescript on Education in "Kyōiku Chokugo Seiritsu no Shisōshi-teki Kōsatsu (A Study of the Drafting of the Imperial Rescript on Education from the Point of View of Intellectual History)," *Shigaku Zasshi*, V. 56 (December 1946), pp. 1173-1191. Charles Nelson Spinks, "Indoctrination and Re-education of Japan's Youth," *Pacific Affairs*, V. 17 (March 1944), pp. 56-70, is a useful article by a one-time teacher at the Tokyo University of Commerce. Examples of the official line are found in Robert K. Hall, ed., *Kokutai no Hongi: Cardinal Principles of the National Entity of Japan* (Cambridge, Mass: Harvard University Press, 1949) and Robert King Hall, *Shushin: The Ethics of a Defeated Nation* (New York: Teachers College, Columbia University, 1949). R. P. Dore, "The Ethics of the New Japan," *Pacific Affairs*, V. 25 (June 1952), pp. 147-159 reports an unsuccessful postwar attempt to promulgate an official ethic.

The philosophy behind Occupation reforms in the field of education is stated in the *Report of the United States Education Mission to Japan, submitted to the Supreme Commander for the Allied Powers, Tokyo, March 1946* (Washington: GPO, 1946), and in the *Report of the Second United States Education Mission to Japan, submitted to the Supreme Commander for the Allied Powers, Tokyo, 22 September 1950* (Washington: GPO, 1950). The following SCAP reports tend optimistically to equate statement of objectives with accomplishment, but they do contain a great deal of detailed information:

SCAP. Civil Information and Education Section. Education Division. *Education in the New Japan*, Tokyo: SCAP, 1948. 2 v.

SCAP. Civil Information and Education Section. *Mission and Accomplishments of the Occupation in the Civil Information and Education Fields*. N.P., 1949.

SCAP. Civil Information and Education Section. Education Division. *Post-war Developments in Japanese Education*. Tokyo: SCAP, 1952. 2 v.

Harold E. Snyder and Margretta S. Austin, eds., *Educational Progress in Japan and the Ryukyus* (Washington: American Council on Education, 1950) contains some similar material. *Education Reform in Japan: The Present Status and the Problems Involved, 1950* (Tokyo: Education Reform Council, 1950) and *Progress of Educational Reform in Japan* (mimeographed; Tokyo: Ministry of Education, 1950) are two official reports from the Japanese side. In "The Ideals of Educational Reforms in Japan," *Educational Record*, V. 31 (January 1950), pp. 5-13, Nambara Shigeru speaks as chairman of the Education Reform Council.

For more realistic views of what has actually happened, one must look to reports by individuals. Robert King Hall's

Education for a New Japan (New Haven: Yale University Press, 1949) was written after he had left SCAP. He puts immoderate emphasis on language reform. *The Development and Present Status of Romaji in Japan* (Mimeographed; Tokyo: SCAP, 1950) reports further on the slow progress in that field. Kaigo Tokiomi, *Nihon Kyōiku no Shinten (New Developments in Japanese Education)* (Tokyo: Tokyo Daigaku Shuppanbu, 1951) is by a leading professor of education at Tokyo University. I have found other objective summaries by Japanese authorities in the 1950 and 1951 volumes of the *Nihon Kyōiku Nenkan (Japanese Yearbook of Education)* (Tokyo: Meiji Shoin, annual). Dallas Finn, "Reform and Japan's Lower Schools," *Far Eastern Survey,* V. 20 November 7, 1951), pp. 193-199, is by an American woman now teaching in Japan.

The difficulties, dissatisfactions, and doubts felt by the Japanese themselves are expressed in a number of magazine articles:

Irie Michio. "Ao-jashin no Roku-sansei (The 6-3 System of the Blueprint)," *Kaizō,* V. 33 (April 1952), pp. 146-147.
Katsuta Shuichi. "Kiro ni Tatsu Kyōiku (Education at the Crossroads)," *Sekai,* no. 74 (February 1952), pp. 88-97.
Murayama Osamu. "Roku-san Sei no Sho-dammen (Some Aspects of the 6-3 System)," *Reference,* no. 13 (1952), pp. 92-110.
Rōyama Masamichi. "Whether Educational System?" *Oriental Economist,* V. 21 (April 1953), pp. 193-195.
Tamaki Hajime. "PTA no Jittai (The Status of the PTA)," *Chūō Kōron,* V. 68 (July 1953), pp. 218-227.

In "Seisan-shugi Kyōiku Ron (The Productionism Theory of Education)," *Chūō Kōron,* V. 64 (October 1949), pp. 45-52, Professor Miyahara Seiichi proposes more vocational and less cultural education.

Chapter 5. Interchange of Teachers

International exchange of teachers has received little general study or analysis. Two documents discuss Japanese needs specifically: *Report of the United States Cultural Science Mission to Japan* (Tokyo: SCAP, 1949), and *Report of the Education Exchange Survey to the Supreme Commander for the Allied Powers* (Tokyo: SCAP, 1949).

Into this chapter is woven an account of the development of modern higher education in Japan. The standard source for the history of what is now Tokyo University is *Tōkyō Teikoku Daigaku Gojūnen Shi (Fifty Year History of Tokyo Imperial University)* (2 v.; Tokyo: Tokyo Teikoku Daigaku, 1932). For Keiō I have used *Keiō Gijuku Shichi-jū-go-nen Shi (Seventy-five Year History of Keiō Gijuku)* (Tokyo: Keiō Gijuku, 1932); *The Keiogijuku University: A Brief Account of Its History, Aims and Equipment* (Tokyo: Keiogijuku University, 1936); and the biography of the founder—Ishikawa Kammei, *Fukuzawa Yukichi Den (Biography of Fukuzawa Yukichi)* (4 v.; Tokyo: Iwanami Shoten, 1932). The development of Waseda is chronicled somewhat less satisfactorily in *Han-seiki no Waseda(A Half-Century of Waseda)* (Tokyo: Waseda Daigaku Shuppanbu, 1932) and in *Waseda University: Its History, Aims and Regulations* (Tokyo: Waseda University, 1936).

Several articles have reported on the postwar expansion and reorganization of the university system. Walter Crosby Eells, "Recent Higher Educational Developments in Japan," *Educational Record,* V. 32 (October 1951), pp. 380-392, is an excellent statement of facts. Dallas Finn's "Reform and Japanese Higher Education," *Far Eastern Survey,* V. 20 (November 21, 1951), pp. 201-206, is brought up-to-date in her "Japanese Universities Today," *Yale Review,* V. 43 (June 1954), pp. 559-573. Hugh and Mabel Smythe, both of whom were exchange professors in Japan, point out some of the shortcomings of the new system in "Shackled Scholarship in Japan," *American Scholar,* V. 21 (Summer 1952), pp. 326-334. Wesley P. Lloyd's *Student Counseling in Japan: A Two-Nation Project in Higher Education* (Minneapolis: University of Minnesota Press, 1953) is more than a report of an American mission to help the Japanese establish student personnel services; it makes revealing comments on many aspects of university life.

Details about American teachers and their work in Japan have come from a wide variety of sources. The following are extended accounts by or about individuals:

Bisland, Elizabeth, ed. *The Life and Letters of Lafcadio Hearn*. Boston: Houghton Mifflin, 1906. 2 v.

Bisland, Elizabeth, ed. *The Japanese Letters of Lafcadio Hearn*. Boston: Houghton Mifflin, 1910.

Clark, E. Warren. *Life and Adventures in Japan*. New York: American Tract Society, 1878.

Crew, Henry. "Thomas Corwin Mendenhall, 1841–1924," in National Academy of Sciences, *Biographical Memoirs*, V. 16 (1936), pp. 331-351.

Ebihara, Hachirō. "E. H. Hausu ni tsuite (Concerning E. H. House)," in *Meiji Bunka Kenkyū*, no. 1 (February 1934), pp. 149-159.

Inouo, Tetsujirō. "Fuenorosa Oyobi Kēberu Shi no Kotodomo (Random Remarks about Fenollosa and Koeber)," in *Meiji Bunka Hasshō Kinenshi (Papers Commemorating the Origins of Meiji Culture)* (Tokyo: Dai Nihon Bummei Kyōkai, 1924), pp. 47-57.

Ladd, George Trumbull. *Rare Days in Japan*. New York: Dodd Mead, 1910.

Maclay, Arthur Collins. *A Budget of Letters from Japan: Reminiscences of Work and Travel in Japan*. New York: A. C. Armstrong and Son, 1886.

Morse, Edward S. "Biographical Memoir of Charles Otis Whitman, 1842–1910," in National Academy of Sciences, *Biographical Memoirs*, V. 7 (August 1912), pp. 269-288.

Morse, Edward S. *Japan Day by Day: 1877, 1878–79, 1882–83*. Boston: Houghton Mifflin, 1917. 2 v.

Scherer, James A. B. "With the Passing of Four Decades," *Japan*, V. 21 (December 1932), pp. 17-19, 38-40.

Shigehisa Tokutarō. "Meiji Shoki no Eibungaku Kenkyū ni Kiyo seru Eibeijin (An Englishman and an American who Contributed to the Study of English Literature in Early Meiji," *Eibungaku Kenkyū*, V. 15 (April 1935), pp. 245-254. (William A. Houghton).

Vining, Elizabeth Gray. *Windows for the Crown Prince*. Philadelphia: J. B. Lippincott, 1952.

Vories, William Merrell. *A Mustard-seed in Japan*. 5th ed. Omi-Hachiman: Omi Mission, 1925.

Wayman, Dorothy G. *Edward Sylvester Morse: A Biography*. Cambridge, Mass.: Harvard University Press, 1942.

Whitman, C. O. *Zoology in the University of Tokio*. Yokohama: Author, 1881.

I found pamphlets and other miscellaneous material about the large group of YMCA teachers in the Historical Library at Springfield College, Springfield, Massachusetts. Luther D. Wishard, *A New Programme of Missions: A Movement to Make the Colleges in all Lands Centers of Evangelization* (New York: Revell, 1895) is an official statement about the early phases of the movement. A later summary by Galen M. Fisher, "The Association English Teacher Movement in Japan," appears in *The Christian Movement in Japan, 1912,* pp. 316-328. The annual volumes of this publication give names and locations of teachers. W. M. Vories, "Opportunities of Teachers in Japanese Government Schools," *Intercollegian,* V. 28 (January 1906), pp. 89-90, is by a teacher who has had a long and colorful career as an independent missionary.

The literature on higher education in Japan is stronger on the administrative aspects than on curriculum and content, but there are a few good monographs and articles on teaching in special fields. Araki Ibei, *Nihon Eigogaku Shoshi (Annotated Bibliography of the Study of English in Japan)* (Tokyo: Sogansha, 1931) and Shigehisa Tokutarō, *Nihon Kinsei Eigaku Shi (History of Modern English Studies in Japan)* (Kyoto: Kyōiku Tosho K.K. 1941) discuss primarily the early period of disorderly enthusiasm. Oda Masanobu's "Remarks on the Study of Meiji Literature," *Monumenta Nipponica,* V. 5 (January 1942), pp. 203-207 contains some interesting remarks about William A. Houghton's influence on the study and writing of literature. The emphasis on phonetic analysis under the leadership of Harold Palmer is described in *The Institute for Research in English Teaching, Its History and Work* (Tokyo: Institute, 1936).

Takayanagi Kenzō's "Occidental Legal Ideas: Their Reception and Influence," in Nitobe and others, *Western Influences in Modern Japan,* pp. 70-88, is a brief basic account of modern legal education. His *Bei-Ei no Hōritsu Shichō (Currents of Legal Thought in America and England)* (Tokyo: Unnokuchi Shoten, 1948) contains a revealing memoir of Henry Terry. John H. Wigmore, "Legal Education in Modern Japan," *Japan Weekly Mail,* V. 19 (May 27, 1893), pp. 625-628; (June 17, 1893), pp. 710-712, is detailed and authoritative. Masujima Rokuchirō's pet project of "The Anglo-American Law Institute" is described in the *American Bar Association Journal*, V. 12 (September 1926), pp. 639-641. Suenobu Sanji summarizes postwar interest in "Anglo-American Law" in the *Japan Science Review: Law and Politics*, no. 1 (1950), pp. 102-103.

American contributions to medical training, despite the predominantly German orientation of the profession, are discussed in Willis Norton Whitney, "Notes on the History of Medical Progress in Japan," *Transactions of the Asiatic Society of Japan*, V. 12 (1885), pp. 245-470. There are interesting biographies of two early missionary doctors: William Elliot Griffis, *Hepburn of Japan and His Wife and Helpmates* (Philadelphia: Westminster Press, 1913) and Katherine Fiske Berry, *A Pioneer Doctor in Old Japan: The Story of John C. Berry, M.D.* (New York: Revell, 1940). Two reports by American missions on postwar development in Japanese medical training are available in mimeographed form from the Unitarian Service Committee: "Report, Institutes of Medical Education, Japan, July 19-September 5, 1950," and "Report of the Unitarian Service Committee's 1951 Medical Mission to Japan." Chiwaki Morinosuke's paper on "Dentistry in Japan," in *Transactions of the Fourth International Dental Congress . . . 1904* (Philadelphia: Dental Cosmos, 1905), V. 3, pp. 425-441, shows how that profession developed from the beginning along American lines. The report of the postwar U.S. Dental Mission to Japan was printed in the *Journal of the American Dental Association*, V. 43 (November 1951), pp. 593-599.

The development of American-type athletic sports in Japan has been included somewhat arbitrarily in this chapter because in many cases the original stimulus came from teachers. For the history of Japanese baseball *Yakyū Taikan (Survey of Baseball)* (Tokyo: Ōbunsha, 1949) and Tobita Suishū's *Kyūdō Hanseiki (A Half Century of Baseball)* (Tokyo: Hakuyūsha, 1951) are both excellent. I. J. Fisher, "Popular Sports in Japan," *New Japan*, V. 1 (March 1928), pp. 11-13, is primarily concerned with basketball. *Swimming in Japan* (Tokyo: International Young Women and Children's Society, 1935) chronicles the remarkable progress Japanese have made in that sport. *A Reference Record of the Tenth Olympiad, 1932, and Japanese Participation in the World of Sport* (Tokyo: Japan Advertiser, 1932) includes considerable historical material, and there is a good chapter on sports in Shimizu and Unno's *Modern Japan.* The *Undō Nenkan (Sports Yearbook)* published by the Asahi Shimbunsha is a good source for recent events and records.

Chapter 6. Exchange of Students

Guy S. Métraux' *Exchange of Persons: The Evolution of Cross-Cultural Education* (New York: Social Science Research Council, 1952) is the best general historical introduction to the subject. A Commission on Survey of Foreign Students in the United States of America made an early study of *The Foreign Student in America* (New York: Association Press, 1925). Since 1928 the Committee on Friendly Relations among Foreign Students has published annually a pamphlet called *The Unofficial Ambassadors,* which includes a census of foreign students in America. The *Institute of International Education Bulletin* and various pamphlets issued by that organization have also been very useful. A mimeographed report of *Statistics Regarding Foreign Students in the Institutions of Higher Learning in the United States* (New York: Institute of International Education, 1925) gives unusually detailed figures about fields of study.

John W. Bennett, Herbert Passin, and others are now preparing a book on "The America-Educated Japanese" which will be the most thorough treatment of the subject. I have had the opportunity to read drafts of some of the chapters. The following articles cover only parts of the whole picture:

Griffis, William Elliot. "The Japanese Students in America," *Japanese Student,* V. 1 (October 1916), pp. 8-15.
Katō Katsuji. "Government Students from Japan," *Japanese Student,* V. 1 (December 1916), pp. 75-77.
Katō Katsuji. "The Japanese Students in the United States," *Student World,* V. 10 (April 1917), pp. 209-213.
Schwartz, William L. "Japanese Government Students in America," *School and Society,* V. 10 (August 16, 1919), pp. 202-204.

Thwing, Charles F. "Japanese and Chinese Students in America," *Scribner's Monthly,* V. 20 (July 1880), pp. 450-453.

Utsurikawa Nenozō. "The Status of Japanese Students in America Past and Present," *Education,* V. 33 (November 1912), pp. 144-149.

Ichihashi's *Japanese in the United States* contains information about the self-supporting "schoolboys." Koizumi Ikuko, "Major Problems in Women's Education in Japan," *Mid-Pacific Magazine,* V. 47 (July-September 1934) indicates the motives that have sent Japanese women to American colleges. Essays and poems by some of the earliest students are included in Charles Lanman, ed., *The Japanese in America* (New York: University Publishing Co., 1872). Similar material is found in the little magazines published by the Japanese Students' Christian Association in North America: *Japanese Student* (1916–1919), *Japan Review* (1919–1922), and *New Japan* (1927–1929). Special problems of the post-World War II exchanges are discussed in *Report of the Conference on Orientation of Japanese and Ryukyuan Students, Congress Hotel, Chicago, June 26 and 27, 1950* (New York: Institute of International Education, 1950) and in a mimeographed report entitled "Evaluation of Japanese Student Program" prepared by the Reorientation Branch, Office for Occupied Areas, Office of the Secretary of the Army. Emily C. Keeffe and Elizabeth Converse, *The Japanese Leaders Program of the Department of the Army: An Evaluative Report on the Program and Its Conduct by the Institute of International Education, 1950–1951* (New York: Institute of International Education, 1952) is a valuable report on short study tours by national leaders.

There are a few accounts of the Japanese who have studied in particular areas or institutions. Most of "The Japanese in New England" about whom K. K. Kawakami wrote in *New England Magazine,* New series, V. 35 (December 1906), pp. 440-444, were students. Martha Hale Shackford contributed a few notes on "Japanese Students at Wellesley College" to *New York Japan Review,* V. 2 (February 1914), pp. 65-66. William Elliot Griffis gathered material on *The Rutgers Graduates in Japan* (Rev. ed.; New Brunswick, N. J.: Rutgers College, 1916). For the Japanese cadets at Annapolis, see J. M. Ellicott, "Japanese Students at the United States Naval Academy," *United States Naval Institute Proceedings,* V. 73 (March 1947), pp. 302-307; Katō Katsuji, "Japanese Students at Annapolis," *Japanese Student,* V. 3 (November 1918), pp. 57-61; and Charles W. Stewart, "Rear-Admiral Uriu as an Annapolis Cadet," *World's Work,* V. 7 (April 1904), pp. 4654-4655. Some papers in the Foreign Office Microfilms (SP 206) and Edward Clarkson, "With the Class of '81 on a Cruise to Japan," *Japan,* August 1932 to December 1932, record the effect of these academy ties years later.

Biographies and autobiographies are the best material for getting a real insight into the experience of study abroad. Some of the items I have used are listed below:

The Autobiography of Baron Chōkichi Kikkawa. Edited by his sons. Tokyo: Privately published, 1917.

Danshaku Dan Takuma Den (Biography of Baron Dan Takuma). Tokyo: Ko Dan Danshaku Denki Hensan Iinkai, 1938. 2 v.

Danshaku Yamakawa Sensei Kinenkai. *Danshaku Yamakawa Sensei Den (Biography of Professor Yamakawa* [Kenjirō]). 2d ed. Tokyo: Iwanami Shoten, 1940.

Gobin, H. A. "Ambassador Sato was for Garfield," *Japanese Students,* V. 1 (February 1917), pp. 105-107.

Ishii Mitsuru. *Nitobe Inazō Den (Biography of Nitobe Inazō).* 6th ed. Tokyo: Sekitani Shoten, 1935.

Katayama Sen. *Jiden (Autobiography).* Tokyo: Kaizō-sha, 1931.

Kawai Michi. *My Lantern.* Tokyo: Kyōbunkan, 1939.

Kawai Michi. *Sliding Doors.* Tokyo: Keisen Jogakuen, 1950.

Maeda Tamon and Takagi Yasaka. *Nitobe Hakushi Tsuiokushū (Memories of Doctor Nitobe).* Tokyo: Ko Nitobe Hakushi Kinen Jigyō Jikkō Iin, 1936.

Matsuoka Yoko. *Daughter of the Pacific.* New York: Harper, 1952.

Minami Hiroshi. *Amerika no Shisō to Seikatsu (American Thought and Life).* Tokyo: Shinzenbi-sha, 1949.

Mishima, Sumie Seo. *My Narrow Isle: the Story of a Modern Woman in Japan.* New York: John Day, 1941.

Murata Gorō. *Beikoku no Gakusei Seikatsu (Student Life in America).* Tokyo: Jiji Tsūshinsha, 1950. (Intended as orientation for students going to the United States.)

Murray, David. "Hatakeyama Yoshinari of Japan," *Japanese Student,* V. 1 (February 1917), pp. 108-113.

Nishiyama, Robert Yukimasa. "What America Means to Me," *American Magazine,* V. 148 (November 1949), pp. 21, 129-132.

Noguchi, Yone. "Some Stories of My Western Life," *Fortnightly Review,* V. 101 (February 1914), pp. 263-276.

Northrop, B. G. "The Three First Japanese Girls Educated in America: Their Influence in Japan," *Independent,* V. 48 (January 30, 1896), pp. 139-140.

Shinobu Jumpei. *Komura Jutarō.* Tokyo: Shinchōsha, 1942.

Soma Hanji. *Hanreki Shōki (Autobiography Upon Reaching 61).* Tokyo: Author, 1929.

Tsuru Shigeto. *Amerika Yūgakki (Record of Studies in America).* Tokyo: Iwanami Shoten, 1950.

Uraguchi Bunji. "Three Stalwart Sons of Harvard," *Japan Times Weekly,* V. 6 (June 20, 1940), pp. 271-273, 286.

Yamakawa Stemats [Sutematsu]. "First Impressions of Japan after Eleven Years' Absence in America," *Independent,* V. 35 (March 8, 1883), pp. 290-291.

Many former students in America are among the holders of doctor's degrees whose biographies are recorded in K. R. Iseki, ed., *Who's Who in Hakushi in Great Japan* (5 v.; Tokyo: Hattensha, 1921–1930).

G. Carpenter Barker discusses "The America-Japan Student Conference: An Experiment in Understanding," in *School and Society,* V. 51 (June 1, 1940), pp. 707-710. There are some personal reminiscences of the conferences in Matsumoto Toru and Marion Olive Lerrigo, *A Brother is a Stranger* (New York: John Day, 1946). *An Experiment in Oriental-American Friendship: Handbook of the Institute of Oriental Students* (Chicago: Brent House, 1934) records a somewhat similar venture in the United States. For the postwar seminars conducted by the American Friends Service Committee, see Kenneth Strong, "International Student Seminars, 1952: An Impression by a Group of Students," *Japan Christian Quarterly,* V. 18 (Autumn 1952), pp. 332-337. The views of Japanese secondary-school students who made summer tours of America are collected in Nakamura Kaju, *Gakusei no mitaru Amerika (America as Seen by Students)* (5th ed.; Tokyo: Gakusei Kaigai Kengakudan, 1927). Rolph Malloch, *Peace Tour* (New York: Covici Friede, 1938) is a humorous reminder that such expeditions are sometimes not all sweetness and light.

The few Americans who have studied in Japan have written little in the way of reminiscences. *Foreign Students in Japan* (Mimeographed; Tokyo: Education Research Branch, CI & E, SCAP, 1948) gives a few facts and figures. A brochure on the *1932 Session, July 4 to 22, held at the Imperial Universities of Tokyo and Kyoto* provided an account of the work of the Oriental Culture Summer College of Tokyo.

Chapter 7. Exchange of Cultural Materials

The variety of activities discussed in this chapter are best followed in the newspapers and magazines. Maeda Tamon, *Amerika-jin no Nihon Haaku (The Americans' Understanding of Japan)* (Tokyo: Ikuseisha, 1940) and Takaki [Takagi] Yasaka, *Japanese Studies in the Universities and Colleges of the United States: Survey for 1934* (Honolulu: Institute of Pacific Relations, 1935) are both general in scope. C. Walter Young's essay on "Japan as Tutor to the West," in *Some Oriental Influences on Western Culture* (American Council, Institute of Pacific Relations, 1929) is also suggestive.

I have discovered Japanese translations of American books by searching the annual *Shuppan Nenkan (Publishers' Yearbook)* (Tokyo: Tōkyōdō, annual) and library catalogues. *Zen Nihon Shuppanbutsu Sōmokuroku (General Catalogue of Japanese Published Materials)* (Tokyo: Kokuritsu Kokkai Toshokan, annual) is now the standard national bibliography. Yanagida Izumi, *Meiji Shoki no Honyaku Bungaku (Translated Literature of the Early Meiji Period)* (Tokyo: Kanda Ryūichi, 1935) and Toyoda Minoru, *Nihon Eigaku Shi no Kenkyū (Essays on the History of English Studies in Japan)* (Tokyo: Iwanami Shoten, 1939) discuss translations of belles lettres. Jugaku Bunshō has compiled *A Bibliography of Ralph Waldo Emerson in Japan from 1878 to 1935* (Kyoto: Sunward Press, 1947). The July 1950 number of *Amerika Kenkyū* contains a number of articles on American studies in Japan. The best list of Japanese works translated into English is found in Glenn Shaw, *Living in Japan* (Tokyo:

Hokuseido Press, 1936), pp. 189-210. Much work needs to be done before the major collections of Japanese books in America will be fully catalogued and described. *Nichi-Bei Bunka Gakkai ni Go-kashi, Kizō no Tosho (Kaiga, Hyōhon sono ta no Bunka Shiryo o mo fukumu) Mokuroku (Catalogue of Works [including Paintings, Specimens, and other Cultural Materials] donated by the Imperial Household and others to the Nichi-Bei Bunka Gakkai)* (Tokyo: Nichi-Bei Bunka Gakkai, n.d.) describe the gifts which form the basis of the collection at Columbia University.

Yoshioka Chōsaburō, *Eiga (Motion Pictures)* (Tokyo: Daiyamondo-sha, 1938) and International Cinema Association of Japan, *Cinema Year Book of Japan, 1936–1937* (Tokyo: Sanseidō, 1937) are good surveys of distribution and production of films in prewar Japan. "The Cinema in Cinema-Minded Japan," *Asia*, V. 31 (December 1931), pp. 768-775, is by Siegfried F. Lindstrom, who was United Artists sales manager in Japan. Ueno Ichirō, "Motion Picture Industry," *Contemporary Japan*, V. 23 (1954), pp. 57-74, is a good account of the postwar film industry. Yamamura Eikichi, "Nihon ni okeru Amerika Eiga (American Movies in Japan)," *Gakusei Hyoron*, October 1950, includes some valuable statistics and is particularly interesting for its unfriendly leftist tone. John D. Montgomery, "Rashomon: Gateway to the New Japan," *Contemporary Japan*, V. 21 (1952), pp. 252-263, discusses the film that first made Americans aware of Japanese artistry on the screen.

Faubion Bowers, *Japanese Theater* (New York: Hermitage House, 1952) is an up-to-date summary that gives most attention to the Kabuki. Two articles give historical material on Western-style drama in Japan: Sano Saki, "The Tokyo Left Theatre and Its Relation to the Japanese Stage," *Theatre Arts Monthly*, V. 15 (October 1931), pp. 836-842; Sekiguchi Jirō, "The New Theatre Movement," *Contemporary Japan*, V. 7 (December 1938), pp. 478-487. The *Asaki Nenkan* (Tokyo: Asahi Shimbun-sha, annual) gives the best summaries of current performances. The 1939 visit of the Takarazuka Ballet Troupe to the United States is described in Shibusawa Hideo, *Amerika Ōrai (To and from America)* (Tokyo: Tōhō Shoten, 1948). Itō Michio, *Amerika* (Tokyo:

Hata Shoten, 1940) is a collection of essays by a Japanese dancer who spent many years in the United States.

For a general account of traditional Japanese music, I have used F. T. Piggott, *The Music and Musical Instruments of Japan* (London: B. T. Batsford, 1893) and Tanabe Hisao's essay on "Music in Japan" in Nitobe and others, *Western Influences in Modern Japan*, pp. 469-523. Miura Toshisaburō, *Hompō Yōgaku Hensen Shi (History of the Changes in Western Music in Japan)* (Tokyo: Nittō Shoin, 1931) contains a wealth of detail, while "Western Music in Japan," *Music Educators Journal*, January 1950, pp. 31-33, 37, 45-46, is a good brief summary of recent developments. S. Tsugawa has written about "The Christian Influence upon Music in Japan" in *Japan Mission Year Book, 1929*, pp. 225-232.

Howard Mansfield's essay on "American Appreciation of Japanese Art" in Lindsay Russell, ed., *America to Japan*, pp. 239-250, and Benjamin March's *China and Japan in our Museums* (New York: American Council, I.P.R., 1929) give an account of public collections of Japanese art in this country. Louis V. Ledoux wrote a charming little piece on *Japanese Prints in the Occident* (Tokyo: Kokusai Bunka Shinkōkai, 1941). Yashiro Yukio, *Sekai ni okeru Nihon Bijutsu no Ichi (The Position of Japanese Art in the World)* (Tokyo: Tōkyōdō, 1948) contains some interesting comments on art as a medium for cultural amity.

Ernest F. Fenollosa's key role in reawakening Japanese appreciation of their own traditional arts, also in introducing some fine examples to Americans, is best detailed in Odakane Tarō, "Ānesuto Efu Fuenorosa no Bijutsu Undō (Ernest F. Fenollosa's Activities in the Field of Art)," *Bijutsu Kenkyū,* nos. 110-112 (February, March, April 1941). S. Miyoshi's "Ernest Fenollosa," *Japan Magazine*, V. 11 (October 1920), pp. 281-285, contains little that is new, but it is the most complete biographical sketch in English. Kaneko Kentarō, "How Professor Fenollosa Came to Appreciate the Art of Japan," *Asian Review*, V. 2 (January 1921), pp. 139-142, adds some personal reminiscences. Sidelights on Fenollosa also occur in biographies of his artist associates: Umezawa Waken, *Hōgai to Gahō* (Tokyo: Junsei Bijutsu-sha, 1920), and

Kiyomi Rokurō, *Tenshin Okakura Kakuzō* (Tokyo: Chikuma Shobō, 1945).

I have examined the catalogues of the outstanding loan exhibitions of Japanese art in the United States. *Bosuton Nihon Kobijutsu Tenrankai Hōkokusho (Reports on the Exhibition of Japanese Ancient Art in Boston)* (Tokyo: Kokusai Bunka Shinkōkai, 1937) collects and translates press notices of the exhibition at the Museum of Fine Arts in 1936. Harada Jirō, "Exhibition of Japanese Art Treasures in San Francisco," *Contemporary Japan*, V. 20 (October-December 1951), pp. 509-523, and Kenneth Rexroth, "Peace with Japanese Art," *Art News*, V. 50 (October 1951), pp. 23-25, 58-60, describe the exhibition in conjunction with the signing of the peace treaty. Harada Jirō, "Japanese Art Exhibitions in U.S.A.," *Contemporary Japan*, V. 21 (1953), pp. 617-630, describes the arrangements for the circulating exhibition of national treasures in 1953.

Wallace S. Baldinger discusses recent tendencies in "Westernization and Tradition in Japanese Art Today." *College Art Journal*, V. 13 (Winter 1954), pp. 125-131. The interplay of traditions in architecture is described and illustrated in Hamaguchi Ryuichi, "Japanese Architecture and the West," *Architectural Forum*, January 1953, pp. 138-149. An earlier case of mutual influence is recorded in Frank Lloyd Wright, *An Autobiography* (New York: Duell, Sloan & Pearce, 1943).

Chapter 8. The Role of American Missionaries

The standard historical work, Otis Cary's *A History of Christianity in Japan* (2 v.; New York: Revell, 1909) is now far out of date. Henry G. Bovenkerk has made a brief survey of "A Century of Protestantism in Japan," *Far Eastern Survey*, V. 22 (December 1953), pp. 175-178. The centennial of Protestant missions in 1959 would be a logical occasion for publication of a new study. Two Japanese monographs were generally valuable: Hiyane Antei, *Shūkyō Shi (History of Religion)* (Tokyo: Tōyō Keizai Shimpō-sha, 1941) in the *Gendai Nihon Bummei Shi (Cultural History of Modern Japan)* series, and Matsumiya Kazuya, *Nihon Kirisutokyō Shakai Bunka Shi (History of Christian Society and Culture in Japan)* (Tokyo: Shin Kigen-sha, 1948). Edward Caldwell Moore, *West and East: The Expansion of Christendom and the Naturalization of Christianity in the Orient in the XIXth Century, being the Dale Lectures, Oxford, 1913* (New York: Scribner, 1920) is an extremely thoughtful interpretation of familiar material. Maurice T. Price writes from a broad sociological point of view in *Christian Missions and Oriental Civilizations: A Study in Culture Contact* (Shanghai: Privately published, 1924). Another excellent article of general scope is S. H. Wainright, "Western Influence and Missionary Opportunity in the Orient," *International Review of Missions*, V. 10 (April 1921), pp. 161-173.

The mission yearbook which began publication in 1903 as *The Christian Movement . . . in Japan* and continues today as the *Japan Christian Year Book* is a veritable mine of information. I have also examined files of the *Japan Evangelist* (1893–1925) and the *Japan Christian Quarterly* (1926–1941, 1951–current). *Proceedings of the General Conference of the Protestant Missionaries of Japan, held at Osaka, Japan, April, 1883* (Yokohama: R. Meiklejohn, 1883) and *Proceedings of the General Conference of Protestant Missionaries in Japan, held in Tokyo, October 24-31, 1900* (Tokyo: Methodist Publishing House, 1901) are good summaries for the early period. The *Fact-finders' Reports: Japan* and *Regional Reports of the Commission of Appraisal: Japan* (New York: Harper, 1933) also contain a wealth of data.

Saitō Sōichi's *A Study of the Influence of Christianity upon Japanese Culture* (Tokyo: Japan Council, I.P.R., 1931) was a suggestive attempt at evaluation of results. Charles M. Warren makes some good comments on "Some Results of Christian Work in Japan," in G. H. Blakeslee, ed., *Japan and Japanese-American Relations*, pp. 190-203. Harada Tasuku makes a penetrating study of "Japanese Character and Christianity: A Study of Japanese Ethical Ideas as compared with Teachings of Christianity," *Pacific Affairs*, V. 2 (November 1929), pp. 693-698. The general intellectual influence beyond the church membership is discussed in T. Kagawa and J. Merle Davis, "Christian Movements outside of the Christian Church," in *The Christian Movement in the Japanese Empire, 1919*, pp. 211-219, and in H. Van Straelem,

"Christian Influences on Japanese Non-Christians," *World-mission*, V. 3 (Autumn 1952), pp. 287-297. Nakazawa Koki, "The Mukyokai or Non-church Movement in Japan," *Occasional Bulletin of the Missionary Research Library*, V. 3, no. 1 (January 15, 1952) gives a good picture of that influential group of intellectuals under Christian influence. Milton Stauffer, ed., *Japan Speaks for Herself: Chapters by a Group of Nationals Interpreting the Christian Movement* (New York: Missionary Education Movement, 1927) contains some significant statements. William Axling's *Kagawa* (Rev. ed.; New York: Harper, 1946) is a vivid account of Japan's most famous native Christian leader, with translations from his "Meditations."

The long historical background of Roman Catholic missions in Japan is discussed in the first volume of Cary's *History*. Everett F. Briggs, *New Dawn in Japan* (New York: Longmans Green, 1948) and the Most Reverend Maximilian de Furstenberg, "The Church in the New Japan," *World-mission*, V. 3 (Winter 1952), pp. 442-450, describe postwar activities, in which Americans have played a more active part. Information on the orders and the location of their work comes from *U. S. Catholic Missionary Personnel Overseas in 1951* (Washington: Mission Secretariat, n.d.). Robert Considine, *The Maryknoll Story* (New York: Doubleday, 1950) has one chapter on Japan. Hugolin Noll, "Roman Catholic Literature in Japan," *Japan Christian Quarterly*, V. 7 (April 1932), pp. 150-155, is a guide for further research.

For the general history of Protestant missions the following items, most of them biographical, have been of particular value:

Davis, J. Merle. *Davis, Soldier Missionary: A Biography of Rev. Jerome D. Davis* . . . Boston: Pilgrim Press, 1916.

DeForest, Charlotte B. *The Evolution of a Missionary: A Biography of John Hyde DeForest, for Thirty-Seven Years Missionary of the American Board in Japan.* New York: Revell, 1914.

Dooman, Isaac. *A Missionary's Life in the Land of the Gods.* Boston: Richard G. Badger, 1914.

Gordon, M. L. *Thirty Eventful Years: The Story of the Amer-*

ican Board's Mission in Japan, 1869–1899. Boston: American Board of Commissioners for Foreign Missions, 1901.

Greene, Evarts Boutell. *A New-Englander in Japan: Daniel Crosby Greene.* Boston: Houghton Mifflin, 1927.

Hardy, Arthur Sherburne. *Life and Letters of Joseph Hardy Neesima.* Boston: Houghton Mifflin, 1891.

Kozaki Kirmichi [Hiromichi]. "The Kumamoto Band in Retrospect. A Chapter in the History of Christianity in Japan," *Missionary Review of the World,* V. 36 (September 1913), pp. 661-669.

Kozaki Hiromichi. *Reminiscences of Seventy Years. The Autobiography of a Japanese Pastor.* Tokyo: Christian Literature Society of Japan, 1933.

MacCauley, Clay. *Memories and Memorials: Gatherings from an Eventful Life.* Tokyo: Fukuin Printing Co., 1914.

Ōkubo Toshitake and others. *Nihon ni okeru Berī Ō (Dr. Berry in Japan).* Tokyo: Tōkyō Hogokai, 1929.

Uchimura Kanzō. *The Diary of a Japanese Convert.* New York: Revell, 1895.

Uchimura Kanzō Zenshū (Collected Works of Uchimura Kanzō). Tokyo: Iwanami Shoten, 1932–1933. 20 v.

The Unitarian Movement in Japan: Sketches of the Lives and Religious Work of Ten Representative Japanese Unitarians. Tokyo: Nihon Yuniterian Kyōkai, 1900.

Vories, William Merrell. *The Omi Brotherhood in Nippon . . .* Omi-Hachiman: Omi Brotherhood Book Department, 1934.

Wainright, S. H. "Christian Literature in Japan, 1888–1932," *Japan Christian Quarterly,* V. 7 (April 1932), pp. 110-121.

Work in the comparatively undeveloped rural field is discussed in Edward M. Clark, *The Other Half of Japan (A Rural Perspective)* (Harrisburg: Evangelical Press, 1934) and in Ralph A. Felton, *The Rural Church in the Far East* (New York: Dept. of Social and Industrial Research, International Missionary Council, 1938). Matsumoto Hiroshi's "The Rural Social Situation in Japan and Church Education," *Japan Christian Quarterly,* V. 19 (Autumn 1953), pp. 274-283, is a more recent estimate of possibilities. Matsumiya's *Nihon Kirisutokyō Shakai Bunka Shi* is good on all aspects of social work. Mildred Anne Paine wrote a short survey of "Social Movements and Christian Projects in Japan," for the *Japan Christian Year Book, 1938,* pp. 183-197. Yamamoto Kyohei, "Temperance Movement in Japan," *Japan Christian Intelli-*

gencer, V. 1 (April 5, 1926), pp. 62-70, and Hisata A. Santo, "Prohibition in Japan," *Japan Review,* V. 5 (April 1921), pp. 97-99, give the basic facts about that movement. Among the periodic reports on Christian leadership in the anti-vice crusade, E. C. Hennigar's "Licensed Prostitution and its Suppression," in *Japan Mission Year Book, 1930,* pp. 149-158, is most detailed and complete. John C. Berry compiled a pamphlet on *Medical Work in Japan* (Boston: Woman's Board of Missions, Congregational House, n.d.). James Thayer Addison, "Social Service in Japanese Buddhism," *International Review of Missions,* V. 15 (October 1926), pp. 704-713, relates how the Buddhists have been stimulated by the Christian example.

Christian Education in Japan (New York: International Missionary Council, 1932) was the report of a survey by a Commission on Christian Education in Japan. Charles Wheeler Iglehart's "The Educational Situation in Relation to the Christian Movement," *Japan Mission Year Book, 1929,* pp. 147-156, is an excellent article that both generalizes and criticizes. For the important role of Christian schools in education of women, I have found Margaret E. Burton, *The Education of Women in Japan* (New York: Revell, 1914) and Charlotte B. DeForest, "The Devolution of Mission Girls' Schools in Japan," *International Review of Missions,* V. 31 (October 1942), pp. 421-433, particularly helpful. Matsumoto Tōru, "The Meiji Gakuin Story," *Japan Christian Quarterly,* V. 19 (Winter 1953), pp. 22-34, reveals some of the problems that Christian schools have faced since the war. Press stories, leaflets issued by the Japan International Christian University Foundation, and Maurice E. Troyer's article on "Planning a New University," *Journal of Higher Education,* V. 21 (November 1950), pp. 419-422, have given me some idea of that promising venture.

The experience of Japanese Christians during eight years of war, 1937 to 1945, is summarized in Richard Terrill Baker, *Darkness of the Sun* (New York: Abingdon-Cokesbury Press, 1947). J. W. Decker's "The Sino-Japanese Conflict and the Christian Movement in Japan," *International Review of Missions,* V. 29 (1940), pp. 519-532, is an important article. Kakehi Mitsuaki, "Nine Years After," *Contem-*

porary Japan, V. 19 (July-September 1950), pp. 389-402, gives some interesting sidelights on efforts by Christians to avert war in 1941. *The Return to Japan: Report of the Christian Deputation to Japan, October-November, 1945* (New York: Friendship Press, n.d.) was the first attempt by American churchmen to assess the damages of war and defeat. Some of this material is expanded slightly in Walter W. Van Kirk, "Japan's Christians Stood Firm!" *Christian Century,* V. 62 (December 19, 1945), pp. 1409-1411. "The Japanese Church during the Pacific War," *Japan Christian Quarterly,* V. 20 (January 1954), pp. 51-55, translates the retrospective views of a number of Christian leaders.

The following four articles differ considerably in emphasis and selection of details. Taken together they give a fairly good picture of the current situation of Christian work in Japan:

Durgin, Russell L. "Christianity in Postwar Japan," *Far Eastern Survey,* V. 22 (January 28, 1953), pp. 13-18.

Iglehart, Charles. "The Christian Church in Japan," *International Review of Missions,* V. 41 (July 1952), pp. 273-287.

Jones, E. Stanley. "Evangelism in Japan after the Occupation," *World Dominion and the World Today,* V. 31 (September-October 1953), pp. 261-264.

Yashiro, Michael H. "Christianity in Japan since the War," *International Review of Missions,* V. 41 (July 1952), pp. 360-363.

Chapter 9. Coordination, Private and Public

Very little has been published on the work of the binational cultural organizations. I have had the opportunity, however, to use the archives of the Japan Society of New York, which contain many communications with other groups in this country and in Japan. Kaneko Kentarō has given an account of "The American Friends' Association," *Overland Monthly,* V. 55 (February 1910), pp. 159-161. Obata Kyūgorō, *An Interpretation of the Life of Viscount Shibusawa* (Tokyo: Shibusawa Seien Ō Kinenkai, 1937) discusses the work of the Japanese-American Relations Committees. From 1937 to 1941 there was a quarterly *America Japan Society Bulletin.*

The New York Society now publishes the *Japan Society Forum* at irregular intervals.

Ruth Emily McMurry and Muna Lee, *The Cultural Approach: Another Way in International Relations* (Chapel Hill: University of North Carolina Press, 1947) surveys the official cultural programs of several countries. America's first steps in this field are recalled in Ben M. Cherrington, "Ten Years After: Ten Years of International Cultural Relations," *Association of American Colleges Bulletin*, V. 34 (December 1948), pp. 500-522, and in *The Cultural-Cooperation Program, 1938–1943* (Department of State Publication 2137) (Washington: GPO, 1944). The most comprehensive surveys are Charles A. H. Thomson, *Overseas Information Service of the United States Government* (Washington: Brookings Institution, 1948), and Edward W. Barrett, *Truth is Our Weapon* (New York: Funk & Wagnalls, 1953). Much detailed information is included in *Overseas Information Programs of the United States: Hearings before a Subcommittee of the Committee on Foreign Relations*, U.S. Senate (3 pts.; Washington: GPO, 1953–1954). The new United States Information Agency has published its *First Review of Operations, August-December 1953* (Washington: GPO, 1954).

Almost nothing has been published specifically on the cultural program in Japan. Robert B. Textor's *Failure in Japan, with Keystones for a Positive Policy* (New York: John Day, 1951) is very critical of SCAP's slowness in action. One of the most ambitious projects is recorded in photographs in *Amerika Hakurankai* (The American Exposition) (Ōsaka: Asahi Shimbun-sha, 1950). The *Oriental Economist* for January 1954 included short articles on French, British, and American cultural programs in Japan.

INDEX